# GLOBALISM, REGIONALISM AND NATIONALISM

# GLOBALISM, REGIONALISM AND NATIONALISM

## ASIA IN SEARCH OF ITS ROLE IN THE TWENTY-FIRST CENTURY

### Yoshinobu Yamamoto

 BLACKWELL
*Publishers*

Copyright © The Japan Association of International Relations 1999

The right of The Japan Association of International Relations to be identified as author of this work has been asserted in accordance with the Copyright, Designs and Patents Act 1988.
ISBN: 0631 214003
ISBN: 9780631214007

First published 1999

Blackwell Publishers Ltd
108 Cowley Road
Oxford OX4 1JF, UK

Blackwell Publishers Inc
350 Main Street
Malden, Massachusetts 02148, USA

*British Library Cataloguing in Publication Data has been applied for*

*Library of Congress Cataloging in Publication Data has been applied for*

# CONTENTS

# LIST OF CONTRIBUTORS

*Tsuneo Akaha*
Professor, Graduate School of International Political Studies, Monterey Institute of International Studies, California, USA

*Davis B. Bobrow*
Professor, Graduate School of Public and International Affairs at the University of Pittsburgh, Pittsburgh, Pennsylvania, USA

*\*Prasert Chittiwatanapong*
Former Professor, Department of Political Science, Thamassat University, Bangkok, Thailand

*Shigeko N. Fukai*
Professor, Faculty of Law, Okayama University, Okayama, Japan

*Rodney Bruce Hall*
Professor, The Thomas J. Watson Jr Institute for International Studies at Brown University, Providence, Rhode Island, USA

*Ryuhei Hatsuse*
Professor, Faculty of Law, Kobe University, Kobe, Japan

*Kenichiro Hirano*
Professor, School of Political Science and Economics at Waseda University, Tokyo, Japan

*Glenn D. Hook*
Professor of Japanese Study, Centre for Japanese Studies, University of Sheffield, Sheffield, UK

*Takehiko Kamo*
Former Professor, Faculty of Law, University of Tokyo, Tokyo, Japan

*Satoko Kurata*
Gender Specialist, Tokyo, Japan

*Tatsumi Okabe*
Professor, School of Law, Senshu University, Tokyo, Japan

*Hideo Sato*
Senior Adviser to the Rector, The United Nations University, Tokyo, Japan

*Shigeaki Uno*
Professor Emeritus, Seikei University, Tokyo, Japan, and Member, Science Council of Japan

*Yoshinobu Yamamoto*
Professor, Department of Advanced Social and International Studies, Graduate School of Arts and Sciences, University of Tokyo, Tokyo, Japan

*Deceased

# FOREWORD

## *Hideo Sato*

This book has been compiled to commemorate an historic international convention in Makuhari, near Tokyo, in September 1996 which was jointly organized by the International Studies Association (ISA) and the Japan Association of International Relations (JAIR) under the co-sponsorship of the Science Council of Japan.

The central theme of the convention was 'Globalism, Regionalism and Nationalism: Asia in Search of its Role in the Twenty-first Century', and over a thousand people from 43 different countries (628 from within Japan) attended. In addition to the opening plenary session, which consisted of the opening ceremony and two keynote speeches, there were two plenary round tables, two symposia, three ISA–JAIR joint workshops, eight ISA–JAIR joint panels, and 110 regular panels and round tables. At the opening reception on 20 October, Prime Minister Ryutaro Hashimoto gave a foreign policy address. Attendance was generally high at most panels, even during the last day of the conference (22 October), when the 'Divine Wind', or Typhoon Violet, helped keep most of the conference participants inside the convention centre!

There seems to have been consensus among most participants who expressed their views during and after the convention that nationalism will continue to be important, even in an era of globalization, possibly coexisting with regionalism and globalism. Consequently, it is incumbent upon us to try to understand the complex and dynamic relations among these various currents and undercurrents in the post-Cold War international relations, instead of taking a simplistic view that the nation-state is obsolete in this day and age. This particular point was emphasized in the two keynote speeches in the opening plenary session, one by President Davis Bobrow of ISA and the other by President Takehiko Kamo of JAIR (read by Takahiko Tanaka of Hitotsubashi University because of Kamo's illness at the time).

Asia is a region of diversity, both in terms of levels of economic development and industrialization, language, religion and culture and in terms of political and economic systems. The region is much less integrated and less institutionalized than Europe or North America. On the surface, therefore, it seems much more unstable; and in fact, military expenditure in most Asian countries has been substantially increasing in the post-Cold War period. At the same time, however, the region (at

least until recently) has enjoyed dynamic economic growth, as seen in China, South
Korea, Taiwan and the ASEAN countries, and thus most countries in the region
have a keen interest in cooperative economic relations, even without creating strict
institutional arrangements such as the European Union (EU) or the North American
Free Trade Agreement (NAFTA). This is reflected in the basic attitude towards the
Asia–Pacific Economic Cooperation forum (APEC). In the security arena, too, most
Asian countries are interested in loose fora for discussion and dialogue, such as the
ASEAN Regional Forum (ARF), which are intended to foster confidence-building
among them. If an Asian region of such diversity could learn to foster interstate and
transnational cooperation, this could be an important model for other regions as well.

On the impact of globalization on Asia, Phan Doan Nam (Institute for International
Relations, Vietnam) said: 'No nations today enjoy complete national sovereignty as
they are unable to control transnational information flows.' 'The globalization trend
today', said Shinji Fukukawa (Dentsu Institute for Human Studies), 'tends to equalize
wealth and values among nations.' In the Round Table II discussion he emphasized the possibility of 'harmony among civilization', completely contrary to Samuel
Huntington's emphasis on a 'clash of civilizations', in the coming century. Nam
qualified this point by saying that nations' basic values would not easily change as
a result of globalization, though he and Teng Teng (Chinese Academy of Social
Sciences) agreed that interstate cooperation based on multicultural diversity would
be possible.

On possible role(s) of Asia in the twenty-first century, Kim Dalchoong (Yonsei
University, South Korea) pointed out the need on the part of Asian countries to
create a common desirable conception among themselves. Susan Strange referred to
the possibly positive role of the consensual style of decision-making common among
many Asian countries in resolving issues in a non-conflictual way. Tsutomu Kikuchi
(Nanzan University, now Aoyamagakuin University Japan) mentioned the need for
Asian (and Pacific) countries to strengthen multilateral consultative fora which do
not require any rigid form of institutionalization.

Should Japan or China exercise any leadership role in Asia? In a workshop on
'The Legacy of Modern History: Japan in Asia', Intaek Hyun (Korea University)
and other Asian participants emphasized that, while Japan is expected to exercise
some leadership in Asia, it has to win the trust of other Asian countries by doing
something tangible to counter the negative legacy of its modern history. Japan's
'lack of vision' was mentioned as another factor possibly preventing Japan from
exercising any effective leadership. Prasert Chittiwatanapong (Thammasat University) felt that Japan had been paying too much attention to its relations with the
United States and suggested that from now on it should work more closely with other
Asian countries in creating cooperative frameworks. Virginia Miralao (Philippine
Social Science Council) referred to the potentially positive roles of Japan's NGOs
and voluntary organizations in promoting cooperative ties between Japan and other
Asian countries.

There was consensus on various discussions on China that other Asian countries
(as well as the United States) should continue to involve China in expanding networks of economic interdependence and political dialogue, rather than isolating
China or treating it simply as a potential security threat. Zhang Yuling (Chinese
Academy of Social Sciences) confirmed that China could no longer ignore the im-

portance of close interdependence with the rest of the world. H. W. Maull argued that Japan, like Germany in Europe, should act more effectively as a civilian power, focusing largely on its non-military contributions but possibly playing a more responsible role in UN peacekeeping operations.

After the Makuhari convention, many scholars from different countries wrote in to say that the convention was 'a great success' and 'a memorable experience'. In any case, it is about time that Asia, and particularly Asian international studies scholars, started taking a much more active role in 'exporting' their ideas and research results to the rest of the world. In today's changing world we need more intellectual impact from all continents, not simply from North America and Europe. In short, we need more international interactions and interdependence among international studies scholars (as well as practitioners). I hope Makuhari has proved to be an important first step, if not a great leap forward, in the right direction.

This English-language publication is another of our attempts at internationalization, as well as a reflection of our strong interest in recording for posterity some of the best papers presented at the Makuhari convention. Two-thirds of the papers published here are by Japanese scholars. It is hoped that this commemorative volume will pave the way for an annual publication in English of JAIR's journal.

Finally, I would like to take this opportunity to express my sincere thanks and gratitude to all those people who helped edit this volume, particularly to Professor Yoshinobu Yamamoto, who has been acting as editor-in-chief and who has recently succeeded me as president of JAIR.

Hideo Sato
President, Japan Association of International Relations, 1996–8

In editing this volume, I owe a great deal to many people. Professor Osamu Ishii edited a special volume of Kokusai Seiji (the journal of the Japan Association of International Relations) for the Makuhari Conference and Professor Kenichiro Hirano has edited the Japanese version of the proceedings of the Makuhari Conference. This English version is based on their efforts and some of the articles included in this volume appeared in Japanese and in slightly different versions in either one of the two previous publications. I would like to thank those who were on the Committee for the English Publication of our Association when the publication of this volume was planned and when the basic framework was decided: Professors Tadashi Aruga, Shigeaki Uno, Osamu Ishii, Fumiko Nishizaki, Hideo Sato, Kenichiro Hirano and Ryo Ohshiba. Our Association would like to extend our great appreciation to Ms Claire Andrews who encouraged us to publish an English version of the proceedings through her publishing house and who did not hesitate to take whatever action was necessary: in this regard, I am much obliged to Mr Teruzo Kubota who assisted us back in Tokyo. Ms Sue Hughes must receive our gratitude for her excellent copy editing and Mr Stephen Raywood for the production of this volume. Finally, I would like to express my deepest regret that Professors Takehiko Kamo and Prasert Chittiwatanapong were not able to receive their copies of this volume when they were alive.

Yoshinobu Yamamoto

# INTRODUCTION

## Yoshinobu Yamamoto

This volume is a collection of selected papers originally presented at the ISA–JAIR Conference on 'Globalism, Regionalism and Nationalism: Asia in Search of its Role in the Twenty-first Century', held in Makuhari in 1996. Most of the papers have been revised since then. Although they were not written under a coherent direction or analytical framework, and although the twelve papers included herein will set out their own arguments as the reader goes through them, I cannot refrain from presenting my own impression and commenting on the entire volume and on some of the major points each of the papers raises.

The adoption of a theme such as 'globalism, regionalism and nationalism' in Asia must be regarded as a bold, and important, measure. In thinking about international relations in the post-Cold War era, one cannot avoid using such concepts as globalism/globalization, regionalism/regionalization and nationalism/nation-states in an attempt to explain current international relations, and to conjure up future developments of international relations by examining not only each of these concepts but also their interrelationships. The endeavour is bold in that each of the concepts is multifaceted, complex and controversial. In addition, Asia is not only very distant from North America or Europe, but also is so diversified within that it would require a skilful management of research and discussions to obtain meaningful results, even though we base our research efforts on such universal terms and languages as 'globalism, regionalism and nationalism'.

When we think about these three terms, particularly in the post-Cold War era and in Asia, each must bear differing components or aspects and include different issue areas. One aspect is institutional or organizational in nature. In the post-Cold War era, or during the period between the Cold War and the post-Cold War era, we have witnessed the resurgence or creation of such global institutions and organizations as the United Nations and the World Trade Organization. The United Nations is said to have been revitalized when it played a crucial role in the Gulf war/crisis in 1990/91 since its function of collective security did work, mainly owing to collaboration among the permanent five members, collaboration that had been stunted during the Cold War. The United Nations has also been playing an essential role in peacekeeping operations in many intrastate conflicts, including Cambodia. The ASEAN Regional Forum (ARF) was established in 1994 as a security dialogue framework in the Asia–Pacific region, and encompasses not only most of the countries in the Asia Pacific but also the EU and now India. In addition, the Korean Peninsula Energy Development Organization (KEDO) has been playing a crucial role in stabilizing the Korean peninsula, and the Four Party Talks among the United States, China and the two Koreas are expected to play an important role in achieving a new peace framework in the peninsula. In fact, the bilateral alliance system between the United States on the one hand and such countries as South Korea, Japan, the Philippines and Australia on the other has also been discharging essential security functions in the region.

As the Cold War has come to an end, the division between the market economies and socialist economies has been evaporating, even though in Asia there still remain political elements of socialism in China and Vietnam, and North Korea retains its own peculiar political and economic system. The World Trade Organization, which was created in 1995 as the offspring of the General Agreement on Tariffs and Trade, now includes more than 130 countries, most of them developing countries which were once strongly opposed to the GATT; many of the ex-communist countries are already its members, and China has been vying for membership for more than ten years.

In the Asia–Pacific region, Asia–Pacific Economic Cooperation (APEC) was created in 1989 to promote economic cooperation in the region and has been making efforts to liberalize economic interactions in trade and investment in the region. APEC is in contrast to, say, the EU in that it includes quite heterogeneous members, ranging from developed economies to ex-socialist countries, and is based on the principle of open regionalism without formal external discriminations. Compared with the EU or other regional economic integrations, APEC is not institutionalized. For example, in the process of economic liberalization, APEC gives a weighty consideration to the autonomy of the member-states and has coined the term 'concerted unilateralism' to denote one way of liberalization. This kind of informality can also be discerned in ARF. As APEC was forged, ASEAN (Association of South-east Asian Nations), which was established in 1967 and has been a regional political collaborative body, started the ASEAN Free Trade Area (AFTA) so that these countries could have a renewed political objective in the post-Cold War era and their economies could avoid being marginalized in an ever-competitive world economy. Furthermore, in 1989 the prime minister of Malaysia, Dr Mahathier, proposed what has come to be called the East Asian Economic Caucus (EAEC), which includes ASEAN countries and China, South Korea and Japan (ASEAN+3), to consolidate the Asian voice. While EAEC was not institutionalized, partly because of strong American opposition in the earlier stage, it lingers as an idea, and one may argue that it has partially materialized through the Asia Europe Meeting (ASEM) which started up in 1995, since the Asian participants in ASEM are also members of EAEC. Moreover, ASEAN+3 met in Hanoi in 1998 and such meetings will be institutionalized in future. The idea of EAEC has posed, among others, the issue of Asian solidarity or identity — or, what Asia is. A similar event re-emerged when Japan and other South-east Asian countries in 1997 aired the idea of creating what is called Asian IMF in order to cope with the recent Asian economic crisis.

As the concept of 'concerted unilateralism' indicates, Asia is still a state-centric world, even in the area of regional economic integrations. In this regard, I should note that Japan, South Korea and China are the only major economic powers that do not yet belong to any economic integration schemes with formal external discriminations — i.e., customs unions and free trade agreements. However, there are signs of change. In 1998 Japanese and South Korean government officials considered possibilities for the two governments to forge a free trade agreement. This move is part of the efforts of the two governments to promote bilateral cooperation in the backdrop of the Asian, particularly South Korean, economic crisis, and arises from the new, cooperative, policies of President Kim Dae-jung; some even argue that the move reflects a certain dissatisfaction about liberalization in the APEC process. However remote the possibilities are of realizing a free trade agreement between them, it is amazing that the two countries, which have been enmeshed in historical problems and in the consequent psychological animosities, have even begun to talk about such possibilities.

Furthermore, economic regionalization can be proceeded by linking some subnational parts of different nations; the Growth Triangle between Malaysia, Indonesia and Singapore and the Guangdong Economic Zone are two such examples. These economic integrations are called micro-regional or subregional economic zones, or natural economic zones. In these subregional economic zones, the division of labour is forged between the capital/technology-rich areas and labour-rich areas, and the economic activities are designed to develop in the labour-rich areas. As a matter of fact, global and regional economic integration schemes do interact with national institutions. And, while nations cooperate to develop global and regional economic institutions through their policies and by changing their own domestic institutions and systems, each nation strives to enhance its own economic welfare and competitiveness in the world market-places.

While Asia is still a world of strongly guarded nation-states, globalization and regionalization have evidently been occurring. Transnational flows of goods, money, information and people have been radically increasing, both regionally and globally. It is not uncommon in Asia that more than half of the national capital formation comes from foreign direct investments; and you will find foreign multinational companies, people, films and music on Asian soil. This phenomenon raises a series of psychological and cultural issues beyond political/security and economic expediencies; and such concepts as identity, culture and norms become essential when you try to understand how Asian nations relate themselves to other countries and to regional and global institutions, and how regional institutions are formed, maintained and deepened. Changes in identity, culture and norms are vehicles for changes in national and regional, as well as global, systems in the post-Cold War era. Identity, culture and norms play differing roles depending upon the country or region and upon different issue areas.

Let me give a few examples from some of the cases in this volume in which identity, culture and norms are differently treated. The first case is concerned with what is called the 'clash of civilizations' thesis, invented by Samuel Huntington. In essence, the thesis contends that conflicts in the post-Cold War era will be waged not between states or between ideologies but between 'civilizations'. While the thesis seems to assume sovereignty and equality among civilizations, it has been provocative to Asians not only because of the thesis's conflict-prone view based on cultures/ civilizations, but also because Asia comprises different 'civilizations' *à la* Huntington, both domestically and internationally. The thesis is touched upon by many papers in this volume, including Kamo, Hirano and Uno, suggesting a deep concern about the thesis among Asian and Japanese scholars. None of these authors is supportive of the thesis on either normative or empirical grounds. Rather, they tend to support mutual understanding between different cultures (and 'civilizations'). Some even argue that the existence of the thesis itself represents a threat. Even though many clashes of cultures occur in some of the Asian countries, such as between Christians and Islams in Indonesia and the Philippines, Asia is not (yet?) a zone of chaos resulting from a clash of civilizations.

The second view about identity and culture concerns the dominant influence of Western culture over Asian countries and the Asian resistance to such Western (American) influence. In the age of globalization, transnational information flow, including that from music and films, has become enormous and is usually one-sided. Asian countries try to resist the one-sided influence in order to maintain and protect their own cultures and identities by praising their own cultures, and sometimes by directly controlling the flow of information at national and even local levels. However, although some Asian leaders such as Lee Kuan Yew stress the superiority of Asian values, Asian countries are not fanatic and do not try to wage a *jihad* against the West. They tend to utilize the old principle of national sovereignty and non-interference and advocate cultural autonomy — they are basically very much on the defensive. One possible reason for this is that they see such inflow of information as part of globalization and they know that they have been beneficiaries of globalization, particularly in the economic area. Thus, the dominance–resistance thesis does not presuppose the inevitable clash of cultures and civilizations.

Japan is probably placed in a position different from that of other Asian countries in the debate about Asian values, owing to the 'long' position of its developed economy. (Japan joined the Organization of Economic Cooperation and Development (OECD) in 1964.) As stated above, Japanese scholars tend not to be supportive of the 'clash of civilizations' thesis but are inclined to support mutual understanding instead; and, except for a very small minority, it is difficult to find hard-nosed anti-Western arguments.

While the 'clash of civilizations' and the dominance–resistance theses assume that identity and culture (and 'civilization') are given, the third view may be termed the 'identity formation thesis'. Notwithstanding the argument of Asian values, Asian identity is very weak or non-existent, even though some (sub)regional identity, as seen in ASEAN, is in the process of being forged. Furthermore, most of the regional economic and security arrangements are, in effect, regionalization without regional identity or ideology, i.e. *regionalism*. Even though some talk about the possible formation of multiple identities in the region or within a certain country, this seems far from being realized. It is for these reasons, paradoxically, that the issue of identity formation becomes important in Asia or the Asia–Pacific region.

Identity formation can be approached from different perspectives. One is concerned with the relationship between identity formation and institutional formation. On the one hand, there are intentional and unintentional efforts to forge regional and subregional identities and to create regional institutions on the basis of such identities. But, as regional institutions have been forged and maintained for economic and/or political expediency without much identity, it is possible that these institutions could develop a sense of regional identity. The second perspective is concerned with whose identity we are talking about. Although we are discussing collective identity in general, we can imagine cases in which the national leaders (the elite) could well develop a (sub)regional identity while the masses hold only national or even local identities — or, instead, cases in which people in some local or provincial communities develop (sub)regional identities while the national leaders maintain the national identity.

As Hall argues in Chapter 3, the national collective identity comprises the basis of the current nation-state system. And Hall's thesis is ever more salient in Asia. Most Asian countries have experienced colonization and have tried to forge nationalism (collective national identity) even though it is based on an imagined community; and they have passed through the state of 'nationalization without nationalism'. Moreover, Hall seems to suggest that collective identity is one-dimensional, in the sense that collective identity is based on one factor, be it the nation or the territory. Thus, to infer from his argument, if regionalism comes to be the basis of the international system, collective identity must shift from the nation to the region. But other arguments can also be made. For instance, one may argue that collective identity can be multidimensional, and thus that collective multiple identity is possible. As we pursue the case of multiple identity, we should develop a theoretical framework of formation and maintenance of multiple identity and the identities' relations with, and impacts upon, regional institution-building.

Identity is geared not only towards space (territory) and/or a group of people (e.g. the nation), but is also attached to certain norms and principles. In fact, these three factors (space, group and norms) interact with each other differently depending upon the circumstances. A certain group of individuals shares historical experience and traditions which have formed their norms and lives in a certain space. This convergence of the three factors comprises an ideal type of the nation. However, a certain norm, not being constrained by space or by particular groups of individuals, could draw identity from all quarters of the world. Human rights and gender equality would be two such examples. These norms (values) are not shared by all the people from the beginning: an agent (harbinger) of transformation is needed. While such norms become established in certain countries and spread to other places through their acceptance by people in other places, the norms, which by themselves are not uncontested, raise an action–reaction process between the agent of transformation and the target people. Nevertheless, some norms do become accepted through learning and mutual understanding and become the basis of new national policies. If we can nurture such norms, which draw identities from every quarter (or most quarters) of the world, we could then begin talking about globalism on the basis of collective identity in addition to globalization without globalism.

Given the complexities of globalism, regionalism and nationalism, there are many different approaches that could be taken. Let me mention here only two of the basic components for different approaches. One is the level of analysis problem, and the other is the problem of the issue area. When considering globalism, regionalism and nationalism, we naturally have to decide on the level of analysis that should be adopted. There are several levels for analysis that could be chosen: global (or international), regional, national and subnational. We can also approach the subject from different issue area perspectives: we could adopt the politico-strategic perspective or the economic perspective or the culture/identity perspective. We can combine the problems of choosing a level of analysis and an issue area in many different ways. As the international system is still basically the nation-state system, and in Asia still more so than in other regions, we could focus on the Asian international system as the basis of interactions among the nation-states and analyse globalization and regionalization from the politico-strategic or economic or cultural perspectives. Or, we could look at a particular nation and analyse how the nation relates to global and regional systems as well as to other nations. Another effective way would be to examine the interactions between and among different levels of analysis. For example, we could look at the interaction between the global level on the one hand and the national and subnational levels on the other in order to clarify how globalization affects the national and subnational actors and how, in turn, the national and subnational actors shape globalization from economic or cultural perspectives.

The first two papers that follow were originally the keynote speeches of the Makuhari Conference. In the first chapter, contrasting Kenneth Waltz's neo-realism and Francis Fukuyama's 'end of history' thesis, Kamo argues that Waltz's theory assumes no basic changes in international politics even after the Cold War has ended, while Fukuyama saw the post-Cold War international political economy as a quite new international system with fundamental changes. But, regarding the latter, Kamo wonders whether nationalism can be superseded by economic and political liberalism and argues that, no matter how interesting Fukuyama's argument is about the 'common marketization' of world politics, we must try to test his hypothesis against the real dynamics. After having posed several fundamental questions to be addressed in the Makuhari Conference, such as how the nation-states in Asia are actually changing their thinking and behaviour in terms of nationalism, regionalism and globalism, Kamo moves on to discuss the structural characteristics of the Asia–Pacific region. He notes that the international political structure of the Asia–Pacific region demonstrates remarkable tendencies towards great power centrality. He asserts that the 'balance of power' policy has never guaranteed international peace for long, and that we have to adopt a strategy to institutionalize the system of multilateral cooperation, aiming at international confidence-building. Having criticized the recent Japanese move to legislate a scheme to cope with the critical security events surrounding Japan, Kamo argues that we should instead develop the means to prevent such crises through open discussions.

Bobrow, in Chapter 2, starts (and ends) with the proposition that the persistent tendency in Asia is to follow a strategy of 'avoiding choices and pursuing opportunities'; he states that different parties at any one time, and the same party at various times, will use different mixes of policies based on each of globalism, regionalism and nationalism to evade pressures to choose between the three. He asserts that international relations within Asia and between Asia and the rest of the world will take place in a context of beliefs, images and information gaps. For instance, he examines US interpretations and opinions about Japan. One of the things he points out is that Americans tend to assume that Japan's international decision-making is little motivated by the pursuit of domestic political ends and is shaped primarily by a few individuals in high positions and secondarily by foreign pressure and bureau-crats. Given this image, Bobrow contends that: '[I]f domestic factors are crucial in Japan . . . the possibilities of misinterpretation and confusion are substantial.' He also finds, by utilizing some of the public opinion surveys, that Asian opinion towards other Asians is quite diversified. For example, suspicions and resentments of the political and military past of Japan are very pronounced for Koreans and Chinese, while the South-east Asian populations are less concerned with historical grievances. He suggests that Asians will not favour any single Asian nation repres-enting their interests in relations with the USA or in international politics, and he concludes that Asian striving for betterment will continue, as will rejection of external attempts to lock Asians into their current position in world affairs by a wholesale replacement of their indigenous (and diverse) policy systems.

The next three chapters examine the cultural and identity issues from different perspectives. In Chapter 3, Hall tries to explain system change by setting up five variables: individual identity, collective identity, legitimating principle, institutional forms of collective action, and norms, rules and principles. He posits that three distinct systems have existed in history: Augusburg, Westphalia and the nation-state system. In the nation-state system, individual identity is as citizen or subject of the nation and collective identity is as a member of the national community by shared ancestry/culture/history or national citizen. The legitimating principle is national self-determination, and the institutional form of collective action is the nation-state. Socio-political norms, rules, principles of the nation-state system consist of allegiance to an imagined community of shared ancestry, culture or history. Furthermore, global division of labour, global capitalist economy and international economic interdepend-ence are socio-economic norms, rules and principles. Inter-societal norms, rules and principles consist of national self-determination and limited international law.

Hall points out two possible ways in which systems can change. One is that change in collective identity occurs first, then triggers changes in legitimating prin-ciples and finally in system change. The other is that changes in the system occur and then trigger a series of other changes, including changes in collective identity. In the latter case, traditional societies, for example, find themselves under siege by the agency of the system that is transforming society, irrespective of the form these traditions take. Hall considers that the current international system is based on nationalism and that, should the system change, collective identity must change. Whether the international system is moving towards globalism or regionalism, he argues, we would do well to recall the contribution of the emergence of nationalism to its present and ever changing structure.

Prasert Chittiwatanapong in Chapter 4 takes up the issue of globalization from the view of developing countries, particularly his own country, Thailand. Having defined globalization as the freer flows on a global scale of information, goods, services, capital, technology, values and cultures, he tries to scrutinize the responses to globalization by South-east Asia at three different levels: regional, national and communitarian. To him, ASEAN is a regional cooperative group formed to cope with globalization. He argues that, 'for smaller and weaker countries, there is only one effective approach to deal with stronger centres of globalization, regionalism'. The freer flow of information caused ASEAN member-countries to seek ways to deal with the use of cyberspace. Their main concern is about the possible domination of Western media in shaping world policies and values. Prasert analyses, in particular, how the developing nations are coping with the impact of Hollywood films and other information on national culture and identity and concludes that 'it is quite clear that globalization is now destabilizing the root of nationalism'. The human rights issue is more salient than other issues. While some criticize the Western approach, South-east Asian countries and ASEAN have shown how to deal with human rights issues more constructively; for example, regarding the Myanmar's human rights issue, ASEAN developed what is called *constructive engagement*. Prasert is not sure what will happen in the future. He concludes: '[I]t is not clear whether there will be more or less tensions in the society as we are moving away from dual structure based on modernity vs. tradition to dural structure based on globalization vs. marginalization. . . . One only hopes that the gap will be small.'

In Chapter 5, Hirano examines the cultural aspects of transnational relations, focusing particularly on transborder flows of people. Today's global migrant moves across national borders with return tickets in hand. Precisely because it has become easier for us to move across national borders, it is also easy to keep our ethnicity, he contends. In the post-Cold War era, international cultural contacts and cultural changes germinated by those contacts will be promulgated ever more frequently and will continue to acquire new characteristics. Those contacts will make it possible for people to identify themselves as living all together on this single planet, despite the 'clash of civilizations' thesis. Hirano argues that the current international society is no longer a society of separate states. We now have an international society with a multilayered structure, and an individual personality with multiple identities. Japanese international exchange has gone through several distinct stages since the end of World War II, and Japan is now in a new wave in the international exchange, engaged in what is called 'internal international exchange activities'. Grass-roots international exchange activities are popular and thriving. And, from NGOs and local governments, a new view of culture and cultural differences is emerging. Some grass-roots activists believe that international exchange is a way to change and remodel Japanese society peacefully. Hirano proposes the concept of '*kyosei*', which indicates that international exchange is a two-way process of mutual understanding which works to sensitize people towards cultural similarities and dissimilarities.

In the following two chapters, Hatsuse and Hook each examine regionalism and regionalization in Asia. According to Hatsuse, (Chapter 6), regionalism is defined as an ideology or slogan and regionalization is defined broadly to encompass spontaneous regional formation, regional cooperation and international regional integration, with or without the formation of a regional ideology. Throughout the paper, Hatsuse seems to suggest that the basic trend in East Asia and the Asia–Pacific is regionalization without regionalism. He examines four different types of 'region' that have been observed in Asia: mega-regions (APEC), macro-regions (East Asia), meso-regions (ASEAN/AFTA) and micro-regions. While the APEC countries are quite heterogeneous, economic expediencies bring them together. Hatsuse contends that a big gap among the member-states in economic strength might work forcefully against further integration. Even though East Asia has come to operate to some extent as an economic unit, the East Asian economies are still weak in fundamentals and economic regionalization is not so firmly achieved internally. Thus, Hatsuse seems to conclude that there is little probability for a macro-regional formation.

ASEAN is a kind of political caucus which shares a common will among its member-states, and in this respect is comparable with the EU. However, it is internally much weaker in economic terms and less cohesive in social terms. After having examined the data about micro-regionalism such as the South-east Asian Growth Triangle, Hatsuse finds that these micro-regionalisms are based on a vertical division of labour between capital-rich areas and labour/land-rich areas, and on the external market for export of the productions; he thus argues that these micro-regions will continue successfully so long as economic growth continues. Hatsuse suggests that Japan should get positively involved in micro-regionalism, be supportive of ASEAN in principle, adhere firmly to regionalization without regionalism at the macro level, and work as a coordinator between Western and Asian countries at the mega-regional level (i.e. APEC).

In Chapter 7, Hook analyses the creation of micro-regionalism from a constructivist viewpoint, looking at the Japan Sea Rim Zone Project which would cover the 'back of Japan', Korea, Russia and China. The end of the Cold War opened a new space for cooperation among these countries. From the Japanese viewpoint, the prefectures and cities located on the Japan Sea coastal side of the nation have tended to be left behind in the postwar scramble for growth centring on Tokyo and the Pacific seaboard. The construction of the Japan Sea Rim Zone is faced with the burden of history, as to the Koreans even the name 'Japan Sea' evokes memories of Japanese imperialism. However, the connotation will undoubtedly be overcome by the emergence of micro-regional interests, which with time may gradually come to link the Japan Sea coastal regions with other parts of East Asia. In the transformation of the regional order in post-Cold War East Asia, these new subnational linkages, which are creating gradually subjective as well as objective links between Japan and other parts of East Asia, can be expected to take on increasingly important meaning in the redefinition of Japan's regional role and identity.

Okabe and Uno, Japan's leading China specialists, deal with China from different perspectives in Chapters 8 and 9. Okabe argues that, as a subordinate member of the modern international system since the nineteenth century, China has not been in a condition to develop its own theory of international relations. Chinese leaders, both in power and in opposition, have tried to use the theory of international relations originating in the West to promote their perceived national interests. The foreign policy of the People's Republic of China (PRC) has been quite similar to that of other countries in corresponding situations and was nationalistic and classically power-political. Ideology played a role, but not as a factor apart from Chinese national interests as defined by the Chinese leaders. China's foreign policy is understandable largely from the point of view of classical power politics. From this logic, China thinks that, since both Taiwan and the Spratlys should be under its sovereignty, it can handle these internal affairs as it wishes. This idea of sovereignty is very old fashioned and anachronistic; however, the gap between classic aims and current reality does not seem to be recognized by the Chinese leaders. The main reason for this misperception, Okabe argues, must be the strong memory of humiliation suffered by China since the mid-nineteenth century.

Uno proposes two theories to explain and understand Asia, China and Japan in particular: the endogenous development theory, and the mutual contact stimulation theory. Both theories emphasize culture and traditions. The endogenous development theory, as first advocated in the middle of the 1970s in Japan, drew attention to communities and to small regions where people live in a traditional manner. Referring to their field research conducted in Chinese villages, Uno states that, while they witnessed foreign capital, equipment and so forth advancing deeper into China year by year, the traditional China is repeatedly being restructured. The concept of mutual contact stimulation is very similar to the concept of 'alternative development' in the West, which indicates a possibility of mutual stimulation between the West and East. After introducing some concepts and ideas about Japan's endogenous development, including Zen Buddhism, Uno turns to Japan's postwar diplomacy. He argues that, while the peace constitution has become firmly established within the spiritual life of the Japanese over the last fifty years, the initial establishment of the security framework with the United States was never properly debated among Japanese citizens as an issue concerning the people's internal value. Uno concludes that it will be possible for both West and East to continue to stimulate one another in a productive manner only if they independently recreate and redevelop their own values.

The last three chapters deal with Japan. In Chapter 10 Akaha takes a fairly standard framework to analyse Japanese security policies, and in Chapter 11 Fukai approaches Japan's adaptation process to globalization based on interview data, while in Chapter 12 Kurata sheds a new light on the process of Japan's acceptance of new international norms.

Akaha examines Japan's foreign and security policies after the Cold War, focusing particularly on its regional role, on participation in the United Nations peace activities and on US–Japan security relations. While Japan has chosen South-east Asia to exercise its diplomatic leadership, including security-building, with official development assistance (ODA) playing a central role in the process, Japan's options are severely limited in North-east Asia. The uneven equation of power foundations between Japan and Russia severely limits the countries' ability to establish a stable, interdependent relationship. While Japan's relations with China are more developed, the combination of economic growth and military modernization in China is a growing concern to the Japanese. And Tokyo's influence over developments in the Korean peninsula is similarly limited. While Japan has dispatched Self Defence Forces (SDF) personnel overseas on several occasions for participation in UN-sponsored peacekeeping operations, Akaha contends that a stable national consensus has not yet been produced on the general issue of Japanese participation in international peacekeeping. Although many countries support Japan's move to be given a permanent seat in the UN Security Council, some major countries, including China, remain cautious. The prevailing view in both Japan and the United States is that the two countries should keep their security ties intact. The single most crucial question that emerged from the bilateral summit in 1996 is how the bilateral security alliance will be developed and whether the review of the 1978 Guideline for Japan–US Defence Cooperation will envision the broadening of the geographical limits of Japanese–US defence cooperation. Akaha concludes that neither policy-makers nor their critics have yet developed a clear vision for a post-Cold War Asian–Pacific security system, and that the Japanese government and public must seriously debate what kind of a post-Cold War order they want to develop and what kind of a role they want to play in it.

Fukai presents a case study about the impacts of ongoing changes in the structure of the international political economy on the domestic politics and political economy of Japan. The study seeks to examine how business, bureaucratic and labour leaders in Japan see changes in Japan's ruling coalition, the dominant policy networks and Japan's neomercantilist policy line, based mainly on information and ideas collected through personal interviews with Japanese business, labour and bureaucratic leaders. Fukai finds that the Iron Triangle between business, bureaucracy and politics has been undergoing significant changes. The mercantilist consensus has been breaking down as Japan has caught up economically with the West and as the gaps in international competitiveness among and within industries have grown in the business sector. While little change has occurred in the bureaucracy-led policy-making process, many have observed that the globalization of the markets will greatly increase the need for political leadership to coordinate and mediate conflicting interests. However, the politicians' focus is on the domestic side, and little international thinking has played a role in many of the major decisions, while business (and labour) leaders were most eloquent about the impacts of global systemic changes and the crisis situation engulfing Japan. Since the beginning of the coalition era (1993), deregulation and administrative reform have become the priority goal for all the parties, but little has been achieved owing to the absence of political leadership and of a clear vision of reform.

Kurata examines how the principles (or norms) of Women in Development (WID) and Gender and Development (GAD) have been accepted and put into practice in Japanese official development assistance policies through external pressures, the occurrence of critical events, learning and institutionalization. She looks particularly at the two major official assistance agencies of Japan: the Overseas Economic Cooperation Fund (OECF), and Japan International Cooperation Agency (JICA). Women in Development was not known, or at least had not gained much attention, until the late 1980s, even though the Development Assistance Committee (DAC) of the Organization for Economic Cooperation and Development (OECD) had adopted WID Guiding Principles in 1983.

Japan started taking WID into their ODA policies in the late 1980s as a result of external pressures such as Japan's selection as bureau member of the DAC Expert Group on WID in 1989. The gap between Japanese understanding of WID and that of DAC then became apparent. While DAC meant that women's participation was critical, the Japanese understood that WID was mainly an issue of the inclusion of women among the beneficiaries. While OECF has been slow to regard WID as a social reform movement towards gender equality, JICA has been more progressive in internalizing the WID concept. JICA is in charge of technical cooperation through grant aid, which gives it more room for accepting the basic principles of WID and GAD, while OECF is responsible for large economic infrastructure projects in which the participatory approach of GAD is considered to be difficult. The Fourth World Conference on Women in Beijing in 1995 gave a momentum to legitimize the concept of GAD. Kurata argues that, if Japan's approach in gender and development is to acknowledge and understand the conflict between the local culture and pursuit of gender equality, it is important to conduct more research and analysis on Japan's experiences in these matters.

# 1

# GLOBALISM, REGIONALISM AND NATIONALISM

## ASIA IN SEARCH OF ITS ROLE IN THE TWENTY-FIRST CENTURY

### Takehiko Kamo

---

## 1

### Introduction: Why is Argument Necessary in the Post-Cold War Era?

No one today can deny the fact that the Cold War has ended. However, we cannot predict how history will change as world politics move towards the twenty-first century. It is true that we have witnessed a termination of East–West ideological tensions as well as an end to the bipolar system symbolized by Pax-Russo Americana. But the end of the Cold War has not meant the end of all international conflicts. In fact, both interstate and intrastate conflicts have increased in each international region since the demise of the Cold War. Therefore, it is not correct to talk of the post-Cold War era with any sense of euphoria, as if we have reached a new stage in world security. Precisely because of the instability and uncertainty, and also the ambiguity, in the regional and global order, it seems urgent now for scholars of international relations to ask many relevant questions about the essence of the profound international political economy changes that are under way. We should consider in depth what these new changes are, for instance in terms of the behaviours of subnational, national, and transnational actors with respect to the nature of competition and cooperation.

Quite as importantly, not only current theoretical frameworks but also perceptions and paradigms appear to be in serious conflict. The major theme of this conference urgently needs to be debated in this context, that is, bearing in mind such conflicting paradigms and perceptions with regard to changes in history in the post-Cold War era.

First, I will consider the two conflicting views about changes in world politics that have been discussed in academic journals since the end of the Cold War. One is that

---

I am grateful to Dr Silvia Casale and Dr Takahiko Tanaka for their very useful comments and suggestions on the earlier draft of this paper.

world politics is experiencing a cyclical change of power relations between nation-states, rather than a fundamental change in national foreign policy behaviour. The other view sees current international political economy changes as fundamental in terms of national behaviours and the nature of the international system.

Let me start by way of introduction to the first of these views, i.e. that of a cyclical change of world politics, with Professor Kenneth N. Waltz's recent argument which appeared in the journal *International Security*. Professor Waltz admits that the end of the Cold War has produced an important change in the international system through the ending of bipolarity. However, he argues that, while this can be called a structural change, it is a significant change at the unit level of the system. According to his view of cyclical change, what we are today observing is the Rise and Fall of the Great Powers; in other words, owing to the demise of the Cold War bipolar system, he assumes that, in addition to the United States, 'in the fairly near future, say ten to twenty years, three political units may rise to great-power rank: Germany or a West European state, Japan, and China' (Waltz 1993, p. 50). Professor Waltz's argument puts much emphasis on the role of nuclear weapons, particularly the role of nuclear deterrence, as though a nuclear balance of power between a certain number of countries were an ideal situation in the post-Cold War era. Aside from the argument of nuclear weapons, why is Waltz so wedded to the theme of cyclical, instead of fundamental, change in world politics illustrated by the repeated rise and fall of great powers? The answer seems to be very clear to me. It is because he maintains that the basic structure of international politics continues to be anarchic, without any fundamental transformation of the nature of the international system.

As a distinguished neo-realist, Waltz's view of change is often simple but stimulating in indicating that, in the anarchic structure of international relations, nation-states are always giving priority to their concern for relative gains rather than their concern for absolute gains. In this situation, he predicted that both Germany and Japan could become nuclear powers in the near future. In his view, 'the probability of both countries' becoming nuclear powers in due course is all the higher because they can so easily do so' (Waltz 1993, p. 67).

I am inclined to disagree with most of Professor Waltz's argument with regard to probable nuclear proliferation in post-Cold War Europe. Focusing on the matter of nuclear power for Japan, however, we should not dismiss Waltz's case for Japan becoming a nuclear power. In fact, a former prime minister told me at the beginning of the 1970s that Japan should be allowed to possess nuclear weapons in the future regardless of the US–Japan Security Treaty. My answer was categorically opposed to this idea.[1] I believe that in the post-Cold War era there is a minimal likelihood that Japan will decide to possess nuclear weapons in the near future, unless nuclear proliferation were to occur in the Korean peninsula without any effective arms control and disarmament framework for nuclear weapons in East Asia.

One of the major gaps in Waltz's argument is that he has insisted on a cyclical change in power relationships as we approach the twenty-first century, without any reference in his article to the issue of nationalism. In fact, I cannot find any word

---

[1] This information is based on my own interviews with Mr Nobusuke Kishi on 1 April 1974.

related to the concept of nationalism in his article. Professor Waltz is concerned only with theories of nuclear deterrence and the balance of power in the emerging multipolar international system. Therefore, it may be no accident that he has not analysed the change in the international system in terms of nationalism. Nor is it an accident that he has not discussed the complex nature of relationships between nationalism and regionalism, and between nationalism and globalism. His argument for the cyclical change, in terms of the rise and fall of great powers, seems to be concerned only with statism or state behaviour within a narrowly defined strategic framework. In this context, he is quite sceptical of the important theme, to which I will later refer, that democracies do not fight democracies. He is not interested in the changes in intranational regime whose issues are increasingly important to an analysis of national foreign policy behaviour.

Let me move on to the second view of change in world politics in the post-Cold War era. Here, I would like to take up Francis Fukuyama's argument, which appeared in the journal *The National Interest* in 1989. In contrast to Professor Waltz's argument, Mr Fukuyama sees the post-Cold War international political economy as quite new and fundamental. According to his view, 'what we may be witnessing is not just the end of the Cold War, or passing of a particular period of postwar history, but the end of history as such: that is, the end point of mankind's ideological evolution and the universalization of Western liberal democracy as the final form of human government' (Fukuyama 1989, p. 4). His argument is also quite simple but stimulating in indicating the direction of history in international relations. To him, the complete victory of economic and political liberalism meant the end of the Cold War. In his view, this victory of economic and political liberalism can be found in one form or another, if not entirely institutionalized, in the former Soviet Union and China. His argument is quite noteworthy, particularly in regard to the breakup of the Soviet Union: the magical incantations of Marxism–Leninism had become nonsense; hence the conservative opposition in the USSR was strong enough to oust Gorbachev from the political leadership. Mr Fukuyama's prediction turned out to be correct when Gorbachev was removed from power in 1991.

It is interesting to note that Fukuyama argued that there would be two potential ideological rivals to liberalism: religion and nationalism. Even if liberal democracy won, he asserted, ideological challengers such as religion and nationalism would occur. His argument seems to be realistic in this regard. However, we should also note that his analysis and prediction of nationalism has not been persuasive enough to make us believe that nationalism, however defined, could be superseded by economic and political liberalism in each international region, not to mention in developing countries. Is it correct to say that nationalism would be powerless and insignificant even for highly advanced countries in the next century?

It is particularly interesting to note Mr Fukuyama's argument in relation to post-war Europe: he says that, 'since the Second World War, European nationalism has been defanged and shorn of any real relevance to foreign policy, with the consequence that the nineteenth-century model of great power has become a serious anachronism (Fukiyama 1989, p. 16). In regard to the case of the European Community (EC), Fukuyama further argues that 'we are far more likely to see the "Common Marketization" of world politics than the disintegration of the EEC into nineteenth-century competitiveness'. Fukuyama's argument reminds us of Walter Hallstein's passionate statement about European integration in the 1960s. Mr Hallstein, who was first president of the EEC Commission, maintained in the preface of his book, *United Europe: Challenge and Opportunity*, that 'what the unity in Europe means, in fact, is not the magnification of nineteenth-century nationalism to a more than national scale, but a chance to transform the old order of international relations and, by building anew, to build better' (Hallstein 1962, pp. ix–x).

It is true that the European integration processes have worked to transform the nineteenth-century type of great-power politics into a much more multilayered, polycentric, interdependent, non-zero-sum type of international relations. However, it seems wrong to say that, as a consequence of the development of European integration, we are witnessing the disappearance of nationalism from the stage of the European Union.

I find from the history of European integration, particularly from post-Cold War European international relations, that both nationalism and transnationalism are competing fiercely with each other to defend their own interests and goals, hopefully to reach a political compromise within the framework of multilateral institutions. As a result of the increasing European integration demonstrated by the Single European Act (1986) and the Maastricht Treaty (1992), not only national but subnational forces, not to mention transnational forces, appear to persist and gain their own interests within the complex networks of political bargaining.

No matter how interesting Mr Fukuyama's argument about the 'Common Marketization' of world politics looks, we must attempt to test his hypothesis against the real dynamics of the current international political economy. With regard to the European Union, one can argue that the nation-state is no longer so central to national security and prosperity as it was for centuries. However, this may not signify that the nation-state and nationalism are quickly disappearing from the international stage. When we focus on the institutional aspect of European integration, I agree with Professor William Wallace's observation concerning this integration: '[it] represented a carefully constructed compromise between sovereignty and federation, in which the governments of participating states negotiated to gain as many of the benefits of integration as possible while yielding as little as they might of national autonomy' (Wallace 1994, p. 60). The real question is, therefore, not whether nationalism will vanish from highly advanced countries like most members of the EU, but how both nationalism and the nation-state are and will be transformed into a new type of international dynamics with new rules in developed countries.

Mr Fukuyama's argument concerning China is also quite interesting. According to his observation, 'Chinese competitiveness and expansionism on the world scene have virtually disappeared.' Hence, '[the] new China far more resembles Gaullist France than pre-World War I Germany'. Later, I will comment on China in the context of the Asia–Pacific region. But I am inclined to disagree with Mr Fukuyama's optimistic view of China today. An important question is obviously whether the current Chinese political leaders can continue the very delicate policy of balancing socialism (i.e. rule by the Chinese Communist Party) with a market economy (capitalism) as they move towards the twenty-first century, without causing serious intranational turmoil or conflicts arising from the expected increase in disparity in wealth among the population as well as from the probable growing tension between political and economic rules and norms in such a delicate balance of policy. Fukuyama does not explore such important aspects of intranational changes in arguing for the primacy of liberalism over nationalism.

## 2

### Seven Fundamental Questions: What Do We Argue in the Context of the Interrelationship between Nationalism, Regionalism and Globalism?

About forty years ago, Edward Hallett Carr wrote an important book entitled *Nationalism and After*. In this book Mr Carr indicated that, since the end of the Second World War, modern international relations had entered the fourth period of nationalism, 'whose character will probably shape the destinies of mankind for a century to come'. Carr suggested that 'nations and international relations are in the process of undergoing another subtle, not yet clearly definable, change'. In his view, 'the climate at the end of the second world war would be very different from that of 1919'. And yet, the nation-state must face two important challenges, both from within and from without — that is, from the standpoint of the moral credentials of nationalism, and from the standpoint of the power credentials of nationalism. Especially in the European theatre, one of Mr Carr's predictions was that a shattered Europe 'may be united by the same desire to find an answer based on principles which diverge from the Soviet ideology of state monopoly and from the American ideology of unrestricted competition'. A corollary to this prediction was that 'common economic planning, as well as joint military organization, will alone enable Western Europe to confront the future with united strength and confidence' (Carr 1945, pp. 34, 36, 38, 74).

Interestingly enough, some of Carr's predictions turned out to be correct, though not entirely. Why do we say this? The European nation-states are continuing to survive in a quite different international milieu, within which they are trying to create a nationally and transnationally mixed international community. At this conference it seems important, first of all, to raise the question of *how the nature of the nation-state system and the characteristics of nationalism have been transformed, and will be changed at global as well as at regional levels, as the new century approaches.*

In regard to this first question, let me begin with the analysis and prediction that Stanley Hoffmann attempted in his stimulating article, 'Obstinate or Obsolete? The Fate of the Nation-State and the Case of Western Europe'. Professor Hoffmann emphasized the consistency of the nation-state system as well as the powerfulness of nationalism, although postwar Europe witnessed the integrative processes observed in the evolution of the European Community. According to Hoffmann, three dimensions of nationalism can be distinguished: (1) national consciousness, (2) national situation and (3) 'nationalism' as a specific doctrine or ideology which gives to the nation in world affairs absolute values and top priority (Hoffmann 1966, pp. 867–9). Analysing the three features of nationalism against actual international relations in Europe, Professor Hoffmann did not agree with the neo-functionalist prediction of the nation-state and the nation-state system. He asserted that the nation-state was not yet obsolete; nor was it going to be 'beyond state' in the foreseeable future. Contrary to the neo-functionalist prediction, Hoffmann anticipated that both the nation-state and the nation-state system would continue to survive. To him, 'in the international arena the state is still the highest possessor of power'. Even if we see the decline of the state's capacity to defend its citizens in postwar Europe, it is 'neither total nor sufficient to force the nation-state itself into decline'. It seems noteworthy, however, that Professor Hoffmann wished to see some innovative change in the nation-state and its international system.

As one of his concluding remarks, he said that 'the nation-state today is a new wine in old bottles, or in bottles that are sometimes only a mediocre imitation of the old'. Hence, 'there are many ways of going "beyond the nation-state", and some modify the substance without altering the form or creating new forms' (Hoffmann 1966, pp. 227–30). I wonder how much truth there is in Hoffmann's very careful analysis of the postwar European nation-state system. The first question is also related to our analysis of the Asian nation-states. If the nation-state and its international system in Europe were totally different from those in Asia, what would be the real reason for this difference? Would it be related to the newness or oldness of the national states, or related to the difference in nationalism in terms of maturity, or related to the difference in the nature of the international system?

Our second question is very closely connected to the first one. Focusing on the case of Europe and on the case of advanced countries, the second question may be summarized as follows: *Can we argue that the nature of the nation-state and the nature of nationalism are obviously in the process of changes that are more or less found in the international relations among the highly advanced countries, for instance between the European Union members, the United States and Japan?*

Concerning this question, Susan Strange's argument seems particularly stimulating. In her recent article 'Defective State' in *Daedalus*, she argued that the nature of competition between states has fundamentally changed. In her view, 'in the past states competed for control over territory and the wealth-creating resources within territories, whether natural or man-created'. 'Now they are increasingly competing for market shares in the world economy.' Professor Strange does not argue, however, that nation-states are already obsolete. 'Collectively, they are still the most influential and therefore critical sources of authority in the world system.' 'But they are increasingly becoming hollow, or defective, institutions' (Strange 1995, pp. 55–7). Why is this so? According to Professor Strange, it is, first, because we have witnessed accelerating technological change with the rapid internationalization of production in the world market economy. As a consequence of this rapid 'globalization', these processes inevitably attenuate the authority of the state over the enterprises based on and directed from inside their territorial borders. Second, it is because the affluent states are aware that 'their affluence depends on a continued world market share rather than a command of territory or resources'. Accordingly, 'war could destroy that source of affluence, so they now show every sign of regarding a major war between themselves as unthinkable'. Third, it is because 'the authority has shifted from states as a collectivity of political authority both upward (i.e., to international organizations) and downward (i.e., local or regional authorities)' (Strange 1995, pp. 58–68).

Professor Strange's propositions are very plausible in the real world, particularly when we are concerned with international relations between advanced countries. Assuming that a major war would be quite unthinkable among advanced nation-states such as the member-countries of the EC (EU), the United States, Canada and

Japan, we should wonder if the proposition concerning the change in the nature of competition between highly developed countries could be equally applicable to the political economic relationships between the member-states of the EU and the United States, or between the United States and Japan.

The third question which we should explore is, therefore: *How similarly or differently would the change in the nature of competition between advanced countries actually function, for instance between the member-countries of the EU, and in the triangular relationship between the EU countries, the United States and Japan?* As William Wallace argues, the EU's institutional structure represents an intricate mixture of the federal, the functional and the intergovernmental (Wallace 1994, p. 3). The collective decision-making processes for the 'sharing of sovereignty' are not yet complete, though the member-countries of the EU are trying to pursue not only economic and monetary union, but also political union by the year 2000. However, unlike the case of the current US–Japanese relations, the member-countries of the EU have developed not only informal integration (e.g. patterns of integration that flow without further deliberate governmental decisions), but formal integration (e.g. common institutions, through which to develop rules and policies (Wallace 1994, pp. 5–6). There is neither formal nor informal integration between the United States and Japan. In fact, there is no such transnational regime or framework such as the EPC (European Political Cooperation) and the CFSP (Common Foreign and Security Policy) in the bilateral relationship between the United States and Japan.

The existence or absence of informal and formal integrative frameworks is important to the management of the competition between advanced countries. In regard to the bilateral relationship, neither the Americans nor the Japanese can escape from the new reality that the two nations have already reached the stage of natural alliance within which they are so interdependent, in strategic as well as economic terms, that their national lives cannot be separated from one another. However, we should note another reality: that the US–Japan relationship is undergoing a period of change. First, the bilateral relationship is no longer the patron–client relationship (or the leader–follower relationship) that it was during most of the Cold War. Second, as a result of the disintegration of the Soviet Union, the Soviet threats have virtually gone. Therefore, we need to define strategic interests in the new context which both the United States and Japan could share in maintaining the US–Japan Security Treaty framework. Third, a new nationalism is emerging in Japan which Americans may have to worry about. In this context, Joseph S. Nye's remark seems to be quite interesting. After the US Department of Defence published *United States Security Strategy for the East Asia Pacific Region* in 1995, he warned: 'Threatening to remove American security assurances might force Japan to make trade concessions in the short run. But not only would it fail to solve the problem, it would also encourage Japan to alter its long-term strategy so that it would be free of such pressures in the future.' Therefore, according to Professor Nye, 'We each need the other to protect our national interests and meet our security goals. Japan provides forward bases for the American presence and serves as the corner stone of security strategy for the entire region. Because of our long-term symmetrical interdependence, tactical efforts to leverage our security relationship would cost both countries greatly and jeopardize the broadly held long-term interests of the American people in a stable East Asia' (Nye 1995, p. 99).

Is it possible for the United States and Japan to institutionalize their long-term symmetrical interdependence without integrative, multilateral regimes and frameworks, whether informal or formal? The change in the nature of competition between advanced states may not become a guarantor for the institutionalization of symmetrical interdependence without mutually institutional efforts among the countries concerned.

Our fourth question is related to Professor Strange's proposition about the change in the nature of the competition between states. As a direct consequence of predominantly economic competition, nation-states are obliged to promote structural change to seek commercial allies rather than military ones. Because economic competition aims at the affluence of nation-states, war between states tends to be unthinkable. However, despite the proposition of the unthinkability of war between states, we must look further into the problem of the intranational political regime. *The fourth question is thus the problem of maintaining democratic peace.*

Bruce M. Russett and his colleagues have published an excellent book entitled *Grasping the Democratic Peace: Principles for a Post-Cold War World* (Russett *et al.* 1993). Professor Russett's view of change in world politics is quite different from Professor Waltz's view of cyclical change. First, Russett argues against the theme of the 'longest peace' achieved through nuclear weapons and the bipolarity of the international system during the Cold War period. Peace among democracies was not maintained simply by pressure from a common adversary in the Cold War, and it is outlasting that threat. According to Russett's propositions, 'the more democratic each state is, the more peaceful their relations are likely to be'. Russett and his colleagues found that democracies in the modern world would be unlikely to engage in militarized disputes with each other. They rarely fight each other even at low levels of violence, and almost never go to war against each other. Interestingly, they found that 'the phenomenon of democratic peace can be explained by the pervasiveness of normative restraints on conflict between democracies' (Russett *et al.* 1993, pp. 119–20).

Here, we must wonder if the theme of democratic peace would and could be extended beyond the relationships of industrial democracies towards other international relations, assuming that democracies would increase in number in each international region. We must also ask whether democracies would not use military force against undemocratic countries under certain conditions. Another interesting question is how much the behaviour of democracies is related to nationalism.

Concerning the proposition that democracies rarely fight each other, two points deserve to be mentioned: one is an objective analysis, and the other is a philosophical statement. Professor Russett's proposition of democratic peace seems to be supported by the objective analysis of 'democratization'. In this regard, Samuel P. Huntington's analysis of democratization is particularly noteworthy. In his well-known book, *The Third Wave: Democratization in the Late Twentieth Century*, Professor Huntington demonstrated that the third wave of democratization has been under way since 1974, and that, especially since 1989, the movement towards democracy has seemed to take on the character of an almost irresistible global tide moving on from one triumph to the next (Huntington 1991, pp. 21–6). He made a further important statement based on objective analysis: that the spread of democracy has implications for international relations. The significant implication is that 'the spread of democracy in the world means the expansion of a zone of peace in the world'. 'On the basis of past experience, an overwhelmingly democratic world is likely to be a world relatively free of international violence' (p. 29). Huntington's objective statement appears to support Russett's proposition of democratic peace.

A philosophical statement is Immanuel Kant's argument in his *Zum Ewigen Frieden* (1795). Kant's idea of a pacific union (*foedus pacificum, Friedensbund*) is quite significant in its support of the proposition of democratic peace. Why do we think so? Perpetual peace between nation-states requires the institutionalization of peace, which is not merely a termination of hostility, but the assurance of a non-war community among nations. To Kant, a peace treaty (*pactum pacis*) was not sufficient to establish international peace. Interestingly, his idea of a pacific union was based not on the idea of *Völkerstaat* (or *Weltrepublik*), but on that of *Völkerbund*. Kant's idea was not a supranational, but a transnational peace project (Kant 1914, ss. 38–43). This might mean that democratic peace could be institutionalized without the abolition of nationalism. His idea of a pacific union seems to fit in with post-Cold War world reality.

Our fifth question is: *Could nationalism be superseded or replaced by regionalism and/or globalism?* Regardless of the change in the nature of competition between nation-states, both the nation-state system and nationalism are likely to continue in international relations, although transformed in dynamics by a number of challenges to nation-states which are coming from economic interdependence, technological revolutions and heightened global concern for human rights, ecological environment and human security. A British sociologist, Anthony D. Smith, in his excellent book *Nations and Nationalism in a Global Era*, asserts that the nation and its nationalism are likely to remain the only realistic and widespread popular ideal of community. In discussing what is actually occurring in present-day Europe, Professor Smith argues that, no matter how much European integration develops towards super-nationalism, nationalism will not disappear from the scene. Instead, 'we can hardly imagine that a European economic and political union, or a European federation, will abolish or erode the deeply ingrained historic identities and cultures of the very diverse peoples of Europe'. He added that 'to pool sovereignties is not the same thing as fusing culture or amalgamating identities, and the creation of a European super-state [is not the same as forming a] super-nation [of Europe]' (Smith 1995, p. 125).

To Smith, a working definition of nationalism is 'an ideological movement for the attainment and maintenance of autonomy, unity and identity on behalf of a population deemed by some of its members to constitute a "nation"'. Thus, particular nations are characterized by their particular nationalism, with shared memories, common symbols and myths. Europe, whether integrated as a supernation or reorganized as a regional framework, cannot supersede nation-states in Europe. He asks: 'who will feel European in the depths of their being, and who will willingly sacrifice themselves for so abstract an ideal? . . . In short, who will die for Europe?' (Smith 1995, p. 125).

Professor Smith's argument seems persuasive in indicating the powerfulness of nationalism in terms of its identity, and its cultural or ideological elements. However, we should consider whether or not in the contemporary world nationalism would continue in its present form without any change. Particularly when we focus on a number of developments in regional and functional frameworks and organizations in postwar Europe, nationalism has been, and is, challenged in many ways to transform its meanings its identities, and its legitimacy. I do not intend to discuss here the cultural or ideological aspects of nationalism. However, what Benedict Anderson said in his famous book, *Imagined Communities*, seems to suggest that nationalism is not always the same and authentic in the contemporary world. According to him, nationalism itself is filled with paradoxes: first, there is the paradox in the relationship between the objective modernity of nations to the historian's eye and the subjective antiquity in the eyes of nationalists; second, there is the paradox in the relationship between the formal universality of nationality as a socio-cultural concept and the irremediable particularity of its concrete manifestations; and third, there is the paradox in the relationship between the political power of nationalism and its philosophical poverty and even incoherence (Anderson 1991, p. 5).

Historically, everything is changeable. Not even nationalism is an exception to this. A relevant question is how regionalism and/or globalism can change these paradoxes of nationalism, by what means and in which direction. With regard to regionalism, we need to make clear what we mean by that term. If it means only the formation of interstate associations or groupings on the basis of regions, and the advocacy of such formations, regionalism is less likely to transform the essence of nationalism, because regionalism and nationalism can co-exist without serious contradictions. However, if regionalism means more than the formation of interstate associations or groupings — if it means challenging the contemporary nation-system, as member-countries of the EU have attempted for almost four decades in Europe, and changing the rules of the game for national and transnational actors — then it surely competes with, and often contradicts, nationalism.

If we take into consideration regionalism in the latter sense, has it really contributed, as David Mitrany once said, to creating a web of interdependence that gradually makes state sovereignty irrelevant or at least diminishes its potential for conflict? (See Nye 1968, pp. vii–ix.) In discussing regionalism, we should be quite cautious about what type of regional organization we would select to compare with nationalism. Not only during the Cold War, but also in the post-Cold War era, we have seen the formation of a number of functionally different regional organizations and frameworks, from the ECSC, the EEC and NATO, through the LAFTA and the OAU to the OSCE, the APEC and the NAFTA. The EEC was, for instance, essentially different from NATO; while the former was basically a regional organization for economic integration, the latter is essentially a regional collective alliance for military purposes. And yet, during the Cold War period, many regional organizations and frameworks were closely associated with strategic aims, whether military or economic in their functions. What we are witnessing, in regard to the emergence of regionalism in the post-Cold War period, is quite different from what we saw during the Cold War period. We have to look at how non-governmental regional associations differ from intergovernmental regional organizations.

Concerning globalism, we should shed light on a number of important global associations and frameworks as well as on a variety of global movements and concerns in the field of human rights, democratization, economic assistance and ecological environment. At our Joint Convention here at Makuhari, the United

Nations should be widely discussed in terms of the coordination of nationalism and regionalism with globalism. Also, we should examine very closely the question of how the United Nations, for instance the Security Council, could be reformed to fit the reality of multilateralism and polycentrism in the post-Cold War era. Hans J. Morgenthau once called the UN Security Council 'a Holy Alliance within a Holy Alliance' (Morgenthau 1963, pp. 479–80).

Democratic principles should be applied to reform the Security Council. As a global organization, the United Nations should be further strengthened in terms of 'international [and transnational] security'. Here, 'international security' implies 'a common interest in security transcending the particular interests of sovereign states' (Howard 1993, p. 63). As we all know, by the early 1990s it seemed, that the United Nations, and particularly the Security Council, was beginning to function more or less as the UN's founders had expected. However, the credibility of the UN is now being tested because of unsuccessful operations, particularly the former Yugoslavia and Somalia. As Sir Brian Urquhart put it, 'if collective security, peace-keeping, and peace-enforcement are to function more effectively in future, a far more consistent pattern of activity needs to be established'. He goes on to say that one of the important questions is 'whether in the new international, post-Cold War climate, the countries of the world are capable of the effort, and expenditure, to create and maintain in the UN a system for international peace, security, and stability based on vigilance, consensus, common interest, generally accepted principles, collective action, and international law'. Therefore, unless the level of international security is greatly improved, 'it will be very difficult, if not impossible, to mobilize the necessary efforts and resources required to deal with the so-called global problems which will determine the general state, if not the fate, of the human race in the 21st century' (Urquhart 1993, pp. 94–5).

In fact, with regard to the peacekeeping operations by the UN, evidence in the 1990s has confirmed that respect for certain basic principles of peacekeeping are essential to its success — that is, consent of the parties, impartiality and the non-use of force except in self-defence. In this regard, the analysis in the *Supplement to An Agenda for Peace* (1995) is especially notable: 'it was also not possible for them [existing peacekeeping operations] to be executed without much stronger military capabilities than had been made available, as is the case in the former Yugoslavia'. 'In reality, nothing is more dangerous for a peace-keeping operation than to ask it to use force when its existing composition, armament, logistic support and deployment deny it the capacity to do so.'[2] The necessity for a much more credible and effective peacekeeping operation by the UN is in fact global, whether the operation takes place in the Middle East, in Africa or in Asia, in terms of international security. It seems imperative to think about the way in which preventive diplomacy, peacemaking and peacekeeping could be institutionalized in East Asia as the new century approaches, particularly when we assume that intranational as well as interstate conflicts will continue to occur because territorial and national unification issues remain unresolved. How could such diplomacy be established? This is exactly what we should be discussing at this convention.

---

[2] *Supplement to An Agenda for Peace*, A/50/60-S/1995/1, January 1995, pp. 14–15.

Our sixth question is related to the questions mentioned above: *Can nation-states overcome the dynamics of 'power politics' in the post-Cold War era?* By 'power politics' I mean 'an implicitly authorized international rule of conduct by which the threat or use of military force is legitimized as an effective diplomatic and strategic tool'. My proposition is that 'power politics' is still operating, regardless of the end of ideological and military strategic conflicts between the superpowers, regardless of the wave of irresistible democratization and of development in multilateralism, and so forth. It seems correct to say that the end of the Cold War has not meant the end of 'power politics' in international affairs. It is true, however, that in Europe 'power politics' is transformed into 'new politics' because of the introduction of 'a pluralistic security community', if we use Karl W. Deutsch's famous concept (Deutsch *et al.* 1957). It is also true that we cannot find any pluralistic security community among the nations of Asia. Why is there a difference in terms of the strength or weakness of 'power politics' between Europe and Asia in the 1990s? What can we say about the cases of North America and Latin America with respect to the continuity or discontinuity of 'power politics'? I shall try in the next section, very sketchily, to take up the Asian case for analysis and prediction.

Our seventh question, though this should not necessarily come last, is: *How are the nation-states in Asia actually changing their thinking and behaviour in terms of nationalism, regionalism and globalism?* Without considering this question in depth, we cannot discern the likely role that is to be played by Asia in the twenty-first century. Let me stress again a point that is related to the insufficiency or serious weakness in the realist paradigm of international relations. A distinguished book, *International Relations Theory and the End of the Cold War*, showed, in its sharp and extensive studies, that our analysis and prediction of changes in international relations tend to be quite inadequate and even wrong if we are concerned only with the nature of the postwar international system. The realist paradigm is based on the core assumption that anarchy is the defining characteristic of the international system. We need to analyse and predict the changes in world politics from trans-formations in the domestic political regime and political culture.[3]

Here, I shall refer to the case of Japan, especially in terms of internationalization or globalization. Can we say that Japan is now moving towards globalization or internationalization in order to play an active role and make a contribution to international affairs as 'an ordinary or normal nation-state'? The concept of inter-nationalization or globalization of the nation-state implies a global process whereby nation-states will or can make attempts to reconstruct the world system not only for national interests, but for transnational (common) interests in international society.[4]

There is no question that before World War II Japan had made serious efforts to catch up with the European nation-state model of modernization: that is, with the

---

[3] See Lebow and Risse-Kappen (1995, Introduction and Chapter 2). Particularly, in regard to criticism of American realism, see Sakamoto (1994, pp. 45–9).

[4] The definition of internationalization or globalization is different, for instance, from what Professor Robert W. Cox proposed in *Production, Power, and World Order* (1987, p. 253). To Professor Cox, the concept of internationalization or globalization means, *inter alia*, that there is a process of interstate consensus formation regarding the needs or requirements of the world economy within a common ideological framework (p. 254).

processes of westernization, industrialization and militarization. (The Japanese expression is *Fukoku–Kyohei*, a combination of military strength with economic prosperity.) Japan's *Fukoku–Kyohei* policy gave the country momentum to pursue centrality not only in world politics, but in Asia. Since the end of World War II, one may assume that, while *Fukoku-Kyohei* policy has changed, with more emphasis now placed on economic prosperity than on military strength, Japan has retained its own unique political culture. This political culture may, if I may be so bold as to hypothesize it, be characterized by a socially hierarchical regime with the emperor system at the apex, and a very homogeneous family type as a national race, distinguishing 'in' people from 'out' people. The emperor system has long been considered the most important symbol of integrity and continuity for the Japanese. Thus, the Japanese community has been identified as the "family nation" (*Kazoku-Kokka*). To be sure, the emperor system changed after World War II, to become a symbol of the integration of the Japanese people rather than a system whereby the emperor ruled the state. However, the emperor system still seems to be a powerful political cultural mechanism for maintaining the idea of the homogeneity of the Japanese community (see Maruyama 1961, pp. 37–52).

It is also true that Japan has not been allowed to become a military great power because of enforced self-restraint in national security policy. In other words, there has been no political room for Japan to become an imperialistic or hegemonic power. However, the question deserves to be raised whether Japan has essentially transformed the substance of the nation-state towards humility in external behaviour, and towards active creative policy in improving the international regional and global systems. One apprehension is that the gap in attitudes and policies between the internalization of Japanese political culture and externalization of global commitment may have widened, so that the issue of internationalizing or globalizing Japan continues to be full of contradiction and paradox.

## 3

### Structural Characteristics of the Asia–Pacific Region

I have so far discussed broad and fundamental issues related to the main theme of this conference. I would like now to move to another significant but more specific issue: the structural nature of international relations in the Asia–Pacific region after the end of the Cold War. The security problems of Japan will be discussed in the final section, in the broader context of the transformation in post-Cold War world politics and the Asia–Pacific political structure.

What we have to discuss here in the first place is whether or not the 'China-threat thesis' is relevant. The so-called 'Nye Initiative' recommends that the United States not adopt the 'containment policy', which had been the core of US foreign policy towards China from the end of the 1940s to the beginning of the 1970s. The Nye Initiative suggests, instead, that the United States should bring China into the existing international society, preventing the proliferation of weapons of mass destruction, and making Chinese military policy and activities more transparent. It must be right to suggest that the Clinton administration should not adopt the containment policy against China. In order to construct new international relations for the coming century, however, we have to make elaborate diplomatic efforts to prevent the 'China-threat thesis' from being realized. If Chinese foreign policy and external behaviour seem to be leading to the dangerous emergence of power politics in East Asia and the Asia–Pacific region, it is necessary for us to try to criticize these tendencies and persuade China to restrain itself in the most logical manner.

It is undeniable that, since the termination of the Cold War, the 'China-threat thesis' has been regarded by many as a growing reality, even though countries' specific attitudes towards the 'thesis' vary. At least two reasons for this should be mentioned. First, the Asian states, and the East Asian ones in particular, have come to perceive China as excessively powerful in terms of population, territory and national power.

In fact, in geopolitical terms, China occupies almost 68 per cent of the total territory, and 65 per cent of the total population, of East Asia. According to a calculation by the International Monetary Fund (IMF), the gross national product (GNP) of China, though still less than that of Japan, is now greater than the sum of the British and French GNPs. The IMF report even suggests that China might surpass the United States in economic size by 2020. In military aspects, moreover, China, as one of the nuclear powers, was in 1993 the fifth biggest exporter of arms (following the USA, Britain, Russia and France), and incontestably the first in Asia, nineteen times as large as the second, i.e. the Republic of Korea. In this sense, China is already — or soon will be — a 'quasi-superpower'.[5]

The second reason can be seen in China's negative external attitudes towards international efforts at multilateral rule-making or maintaining the existing frameworks and regimes of international security. China repeatedly launched missiles in the Taiwan Channel in order to exert some influence on the presidential election in Taiwan in spring 1996. This action was naturally interpreted by many of the neighbouring countries, including Taiwan, as a policy of military threats and clear proof of the violent power-political nature of Chinese behaviour to its neighbours.

We should not, however, overlook the fact that the Sino-Taiwan tensions were drastically attenuated after the Taiwanese presidential election, and that China itself has been making diplomatic efforts to prevent the 'China-threat thesis' from prevailing over Asia and other parts of the world. It has also been trying to become less isolated. The Chinese attempted to improve their relations with the Americans in the Sino–US meeting of foreign ministers held on 19 April 1996, in The Hague, and to strengthen their strategic ties with the Russians through the Russo-Chinese Summit on 26 April 1996. At the same time, Chairman Jiang Zemin of China sent a letter to President Kim Young Sam of Korea, saying that China would play a constructive role in the quadripartite conference for perpetual peace in the Korean peninsula proposed at the US–Korean Summit.

This being so, it is rather rash to judge China as a new and salient threat in East Asia and the Asia–Pacific region by employing Paul Dibb's contention that it is a 'revisionist state' (Dibb 1995). It is more significant for the states in those and other regions to avoid being hostile to China and to endeavour to establish rules of co-existence and interdependence by inducing China to enter into a multilateral

---

[5] Source: *Department of State Documents, 1995*; also cited in Dibb (1995, pp. 26–7).

**Table 1** Tendency of Multipolarization: the World

| Year | GNP | Military expenditure | Arms exports |
|---|---|---|---|
| 1983 | 0.319 | 0.406 | 0.466 |
| 1984 | 0.322 | 0.409 | 0.419 |
| 1985 | 0.321 | 0.413 | 0.437 |
| 1986 | 0.321 | 0.418 | 0.477 |
| 1987 | 0.320 | 0.421 | 0.465 |
| 1988 | 0.320 | 0.427 | 0.463 |
| 1989 | 0.321 | 0.417 | 0.487 |
| 1990 | 0.321 | 0.407 | 0.476 |
| 1991 | 0.321 | 0.391 | 0.461 |
| 1992 | 0.321 | 0.381 | 0.477 |
| 1993 | 0.324 | 0.388 | 0.529 |

**Table 2** Tendency of Multipolarization: the Asia–Pacific Region

| Year | GNP | Military expenditure | Arms exports |
|---|---|---|---|
| 1983 | 0.548 | 0.632 | 0.701 |
| 1984 | 0.546 | 0.631 | 0.682 |
| 1985 | 0.542 | 0.629 | 0.710 |
| 1986 | 0.537 | 0.626 | 0.738 |
| 1987 | 0.534 | 0.630 | 0.699 |
| 1988 | 0.530 | 0.628 | 0.688 |
| 1989 | 0.529 | 0.621 | 0.681 |
| 1990 | 0.528 | 0.610 | 0.686 |
| 1991 | 0.526 | 0.599 | 0.685 |
| 1992 | 0.560 | 0.608 | 0.794 |
| 1993 | 0.561 | 0.616 | 0.785 |

**Figure 1** Tendency of Multipolarization: the World

**Figure 2** Tendency of Multipolarization: the Asia–Pacific Region

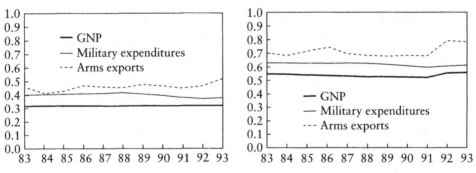

*Source: World Military Expenditures and Arms Transfers, 1993–1994*, Washington: US Arms Control and Disarmament Agency, 1995.

international order. Moreover, we should not overlook certain structural features in the Asia–Pacific region — the slower pace and lesser intensity of multipolarization and polycentricity even after the end of the Cold War, compared with other international regions.

The international political structure of the Asia–Pacific region still demonstrates remarkable tendencies towards great-power centricity. These tendencies are clearly indicated in Tables 1 and 2 and Figures 1 and 2, which describe the degree of multipolarization and its chronological development. In the tables I used GNP, military expenditures and arms exportation as the variables indicating the 'power resources' of states. I then calculated the *CONCENTRATION* indices and placed them chronologically. The indicators of 'power resources' cannot be limited to these three. GNP is, however, one of the most effective indicators of the productive and financial power of a nation-state, which constitutes the economic element of 'power resources'; military expenditure is another relevant indicator of the size of military power of a nation-state.

As for the CONCENTRATION index, which was developed by James Ray and David Singer (see Ray and Singer 1973), the more the distribution of power resources is concentrated in a small group of nations such as the USA and China — in other words, the more 'hegemonic' it is, the closer to 1.000 (a unity) the index becomes; the more dispersed or multipolar the distribution is, the closer to zero it becomes. I intend here to compare the time-series development of multipolarization at the global level and in the Asia–Pacific region during the ten-year period 1983–93.

What becomes clear from the comparison is that, for all three of the variables of 'power resources', the Asia–Pacific region irrevocably demonstrates more distinctive characteristics of the hegemonic system. Apart from that, the arms exportation column shows greater concentration than that of military expenditure, which is greater than that of GNP. Export of military weapons is concentrated in the USA, China and Russia, which incontestably constitute a hegemonic system. Thus, even after the end of the Cold War, the Asia–Pacific region still shows hegemonic power concentration, in contrast to the global trend of multipolarity. In other words the Asia–Pacific international political structure is great-power-centric.

In a region with this structural character, can the states effectively employ the classical policy of power politics, such as the 'balance of power' policy? If they can do so, should they? A long history of world politics clearly tells us that the 'balance of power' policy has evoked a series of raw struggles for power among great powers which could lead to the outbreak of war. The 'balance of power' policy has never guaranteed international peace for long. Instead, we have to adopt a strategy to institutionalize the system of multilateral cooperation by eroding and democratizing the great-power-centric structure in the Asia–Pacific region.

---

# 4

## Japan's Choice for the Future: the Creation of Peace

Finally, I should like to discuss the choices for the future open to Japan. It is obvious that Japan can escape neither from the ongoing transformation of world politics nor from the structural character of Asia–Pacific regional politics. What should Japan do at the end of the twentieth century and the beginning of the twenty-first to help create more peaceful international relations in the region and the world?

I would like to return to the 'China-threat thesis'. If we are to continue the US–Japanese Security system, it should not embrace a containment policy against China as a core element. A hostile containment policy towards China would never be a wise option. Instead, Japan should patiently try to persuade the Chinese to participate in the process of making an Asia–Pacific multilateral security organization aimed at international confidence-building. Although, as expected, the Chinese government has not attached any positive evaluation to the joint declaration on US–Japanese Mutual Security, it is interesting that their reaction to the declaration was unexpectedly reserved. In other words, China does not intend to intensify the tensions or crises with Japan and the United States by emphasizing the 'US–Japanese threat thesis'.

The *People's Daily* has paid special attention to the development of US–Japanese security relations. On 16 April 1996, it published the agenda and purposes of Clinton's visit to Japan. Two days later, it issued a statement referring to the contents of the US–Japanese joint declaration to the effect that the *Daily* would be interested to see whether the declaration would transform the 'emergency of Japan' into an 'emergency in the Far East'. The next day, the *Daily* did not hide its anxiety that the US–Japan security system could change its nature from defensive to offensive, and that the strategic role of Japan might evolve from that of the protected to that of a participant. However, the editorial did not show any strong reaction aimed at inflaming hostile sentiments against Japan which could lead to a more critical situation.

The US–Japanese security system seems to have intensified the degree of Asianization and strengthened the nature of the military alliance. Japan should *not* write a rather thoughtless 'crisis scenario' enflaming the feelings of a 'China-threat' to the changing US–Japanese security system. Even the US government has taken a very cautious diplomatic stance on the issue of anti-Chinese sanctions, after the settlement of the China–Taiwan crisis. In May, in fact, the Clinton administration decided to renew the Most Favoured Nation (MFN) status of China. If Japan were to respond in terms of the 'China crisis' on the strength of the transforming US–Japanese security system, it would be a reaction far removed from US strategic intention.

In the 1990s, the problem of how to adjust the US–Japanese security system to the changing realities of international political environments following the end of the Cold War emerged as one of the most crucial security issues in Japan. Mainly in relation to the political uncertainty in the northern part of the Korean peninsula, Japanese decision-makers and scholars of international relations have resumed a series of arguments about *yuji*. *Yuji* is a Japanese word expressing a certain sort of critical situation, but it is not easy to find a direct translation in the English language, because of its highly ambiguous and arbitrary nature. In the word *yuji*, *yu* means occurrence and *ji* means something crucial. It might be possible to define it very roughly as 'occurrence of something crucial or critical', which is still very vague. Although I shall come back to the meaning of this intractable word, I would like here to use *yuji* as it is without translating it into English.

Faced with the fluid, or rather floating, situations in the Far East in the 1990s, the Japanese have begun to talk about what to do if *yuji* occurred. The *yuji* arguments in Japan have quite naturally placed their focus upon some assumed critical situations which might possibly take place in the Far East and on how to reconstruct or amend the US–Japanese defence cooperation to cope with them (see Kamo 1996).

When Japanese and American decision-makers say that they are coordinating the crisis strategy scenario, and when they promote their military cooperation for dealing with 'Far Eastern *yuji*', they must have *yuji* in the Korean peninsula in mind. The Japanese government seems already to have begun examining the following three issues as a 'policy to cope with Far Eastern *yuji*': (1) temporary use of military facilities and areas by US forces; (2) logistic assistance to US forces (such as provision of services and supplies by the Defence Facilities Administration Agency on behalf of US forces, lease of goods including petroleum to the American forces by the Self Defence Forces (SDF) on the seas, transportation of US soldiers and equip-ment by the SDF's airplanes, search and rescue of missing soldiers, medical care for US soldiers and supply of information to US forces); (3) rescue of Japanese inhabit-ants overseas, coastguard anti-terrorist operations for protection of crucial facilities, and treatment of large numbers of refugees. On these assumptions of *yuji*, and of the necessity of US–Japanese defence cooperation, both governments agreed to start consultation to re-examine the Guidelines for US–Japan Defence Cooperation. Between the Self Defence Forces and the US military forces, the Acquisition and Cross Servicing Agreement (ACSA) has been concluded for peacetime. Through the process mentioned above, the issue of legislation for *yuji* has suddenly become the significant political question in Japan.

The topics of *yuji* and *yuji* legislation are no longer taboo in Japanese political circles, among Japanese intellectuals or in public. It is, however, very dangerous to treat those topics as if they were part of a new and urgent strategic game for Japan, even when the US–Japanese security system tends to become more Asianized and to strengthen its nature as a military alliance. Instead, what the 'Far Eastern *yuji*', in particular '*yuji* in the Korean peninsula', specifically means needs to be objectively and logically investigated and defined.

It might be possible to define *yuji* roughly as an international environment that is not at peace, or as an international environment not without violent conflicts. In other words, the word *yuji* means tense and hostile situations among nation-states which can take various forms covering a very wide range between 'crisis' and 'war'. Even so, it should be noted that neither 'crisis' nor 'war' has ever been firmly or decisively defined by international political theory. When does an interstate 'crisis' begin and when is it settled? Or, on what conditions does 'crisis' link with 'war' as explicit and open military collision? It is not easy to provide universally relevant answers to these questions. The standard of judgement with regard to the existence of crisis and war varies in each historical case.

In traditional international politics, a clear distinction was drawn between diplo-macy and domestic politics, in particular from the realist viewpoint. 'Crisis' and 'war' were apt to be respectively regarded as 'international crisis' and 'international war' among sovereign states. But this kind of view is no longer relevant when looking at the ongoing structural transformation of world politics in the 1990s. Diplomacy and domestic politics are getting more and more interwoven, both in the developed and the developing countries. In addition, 'crisis' takes place not only on interstate issues such as shifts in military balance and territorial boundaries, but also in the arena of international relations originating from a crisis at intrastate level — e.g. the crises in the former Yugoslavia.

This trend is one of the least negligible aspects of international political trans-formation after the end of the Cold War, and it has significant meaning for the diplomatic stance of Japan with regard to Far Eastern *yuji*, in particular *yuji* in the Korean peninsula, as presumed in the context of the US–Japanese security system by the decision-makers. It is not too much to say that the arguments over *yuji* and *yuji* legislation in Japan have been focusing too much upon how to cope with these 'crises' in the external arena of international politics, though the direct origins of those crises must be located mainly within a country. Those arguments also tend to treat the 'crises' as given. What is lacking in those arguments, and what needs to be thoroughly examined, is what the Japanese government and society can do to prevent those 'crises', by understanding correctly the changing aspect of world political structure and the transformation of 'crises'.

Second, arguments and policy considerations based on the *yuji* assumptions contain the danger of 'groupthink'. According to Irving Janis, the history of international politics tells us that, when a small group of decision-making elite holding strong enemy-images or prejudices leads the will of larger groups and collections of people, only rigid and critical policies can be produced (Janis 1972).

The *yuji* type of consideration is a relevant example of the danger of 'groupthink'. Because *yuji* arguments inevitably involve the problems of expertism and secrecy, the small circle of policy elite can easily manipulate ordinary citizens who have only a limited access to the relevant information and to the reality of the decision-making process. The danger contained in this *yuji* type of consideration should be definitely avoided. It would be deplorable if the arguments and the transformation of the US–Japanese security system were to develop within a closed circle of policy elite, ignoring Japanese public opinion.

Third, we should be very aware that the arguments over *yuji* and *yuji* legislation will have serious impacts and repercussions not only on US–Japanese relations, but also on the much wider foreign relations of Japan with both South and North Korea, China, Russia and South-east Asian countries. As mentioned above, the arguments lack the idea of crisis prevention and are too preoccupied with the bilateral framework of the US–Japanese security system. In other words, policy plans derived from those arguments exclusively focus upon forms of US–Japanese military cooperation. Broader and more constructive views or policy plans, such as the prevailing 'preventive diplomacy' of the United Nations throughout East Asia, can hardly be seen in those arguments.

Finally, we should clearly distinguish between what we can and cannot do within the framework of the Japanese Constitution. It is necessary to examine the *yuji* arguments from the viewpoint of their consistency with and contradiction to the constitutional framework. There is a strong opinion that the constitutional framework stands in the way of Japan's 'international contribution'. However, I believe that it is imperative for Japan to put forward to the world a policy formula for the 'pacification of crisis', staying within the constitutional framework. We should consider our future course in accordance with the existing policy principles of 'non-exercise of the right of collective self defense'. It is necessary for Japanese politicians and intellectuals to exchange views with people of other countries as to whether or not the existing rules and norms of Japan are really obsolete. Japan must make a constructive proposal for the 'creation of peace' in the Asia–Pacific region from the global point of view.

We are living in a transitional period of history after the ending of the Cold War. Japan should not therefore hesitate to continue to assert that Asian–Pacific international circumstances, still dominated by power politics, should be transformed into an interdependent regime of multilateral cooperation and competition created without the exercise of force, such as in Europe. This, I believe, is the best way for Japan to gain greater confidence and trust from the international community. Never have the Japanese needed to determine 'the way ahead' as seriously as today.

# References

Anderson, B. (1991), *Imagined Communities: Reflection on the Origin and Spread of Nationalism*, rev. edn, London/New York: Verso Press.

Carr, E. H. (1945), *Nationalism and After*, London: Macmillan.

Cox, R. W. (1987), *Production, Power, and World Order: Social Forces in the Making of History*, New York: Columbia University Press.

Deutsch, K. W. *et al.* (1957), *Political Community and the North Atlantic Area: International Organization in the Light of Historical Experience*, Princeton University Press.

Dibb, P. (1995), 'Towards a New Balance of Power in Asia', *ADELPHI Papers* no. 285, International Institute for Strategic Studies, London.

Fukuyama, F. (1989), 'The End of History?' *The National Interest*, Summer: 3–18.

Hallstein, W. (1962), *United Europe: Challenge and Opportunity*, Cambridge, Mass.: Harvard University Press.

Hoffmann, S. (1966), 'Obstinate or Obsolete? The Fate of the Nation-State and the Case of Western Europe', *Daedalus*, no. 95: 862–915.

Howard, M. (1993), 'The Historical Development of the UN's Role in International Security', in A. Roberts and B. Kingsbury (eds.), *United Nations: Divided World*, Oxford: Clarendon Press.

Huntington, S. P. (1991), *The Third Wave: Democratization in the Late Twentieth Century*, Norman: University of Oklahoma Press.

Janis, I. (1972), *Victims of Groupthink: A Psychological Study of Foreign-Policy Decisions and Fiascos*. Boston: Houghton Mifflin.

Kamo, T. (1996), 'Nichi-bei Anpo: "Yuji" no Shiso' (US–Japan security system: the idea of 'yuji'), *Asahi Shimbun*, 1 August.

Kant, I. (1914), *Zum Ewigen Frieden: Mit Ergänzungen aus Kants übrigen Schriften und einer ausführlichen Einleitung über die Entwicklung des Friedensgedankens*, ed. K. Vorländer, Leipzig: Felix Meiner (first published 1795).

Lebrow, R. N. and Risse-Kappen, T. (eds.) (1995), *International Relations Theory and the End of the Cold War*, New York: Columbia University Press.

Maruyama, M. (1961), *Nihon no Shiso* (The Japanese thought), Tokyo: Iwanami.

Morgenthau, H. J. (1963), *Politics among Nations: The Struggle for Power and Peace*, New York: Alfred A. Knopf.

Nye, J. S. Jr (ed.) (1968), *International Regionalism: Readings*, Boston: Little, Brown.

Nye, J. S. Jr (1995), 'The Case for Deep Engagement', *Foreign Affairs*, 74(4): 90–102.

Ray, J. and Singer, D. (1973), 'Measuring the Concentration of Power in the International System', *Sociological Methods and Research*, 1(4): 403–37.

Russett, B. M. *et al.* (1993), *Grasping the Democratic Peace: Principles for a Post-Cold War World*, Princeton: Princeton University Press.

Sakamoto, Y. (1994), 'A Perspective on the Changing World Order: A Conceptual Prelude', in Y. Sakamoto (ed.), *Global Transformation: Challenges to the State System*, Tokyo: United Nations University Press.

Smith, A. D. (1995), *Nations and Nationalism in a Global Era*, Cambridge: Polity Press.

Strange, S. (1995), 'The Defective State', *Daedalus*, Spring: 55–74.

Urquhart, B. (1993), 'The UN and International Security after the Cold War', in A. Roberts and B. Kingsbury (eds.), *United Nations: Divided World*, Oxford: Clarendon Press.

Wallace, W. (1994), *Regional Integration: The Western European Experience*, Washington, DC: Brookings Institution.

Waltz, K. N. (1993), 'The Emerging Structure of International Politics', *International Security*, 18(2): 44–79.

# 2

# AVOIDING CHOICES, PURSUING OPPORTUNITIES

## ASIA IN INTERNATIONAL AFFAIRS, 1996 AND 1998

### Davis B. Bobrow

## 1
### Introduction

In September 1996, when I had the honour of presenting an earlier version of this paper as a keynote address to the ISA–JAIR convention at Makuhari, I noted that the meetings were themselves a sign of internationalization of perspectives and an opportunity to further develop bridges between the international relations scholarly communities on both sides of the Pacific. Much has transpired in Asia and in governmental and non-governmental relations between North America and Asia since then which has demonstrated a certain lack of foresight on my part and that of others. Yet many of the fundamentals that seemed evident in 1996 seem to retain their importance.

The temptations to substitute rejection or dictation for trans-Pacific understanding have hardly been diminished. Popular books which advocate saying 'No' to each other (e.g. Ishihara 1991), or label some trans-Pacific other as the current or potential source of economic hard times and security threats (e.g. Bernstein and Munro 1997) retain an audience. It continues to be the case that, in many countries, ministries, political parties and firms, there is either support for saying 'no' across the Pacific or an equally unconstructive 'do it our way or else . . .' And some influentials continue to be quick to seize on such stances to urge a reciprocally negative response.

It seems to me even more clear now than it was several years ago that we can and should reject such simple if perhaps emotionally satisfying stances and instead follow a harder, more complicated, and less linear road. Accordingly, the factors affecting the destinations (note the plural and not singular) of Asia in the world in the twenty-first century remain matters of global importance, an importance only emphasized by the financial crises of 1997 and their continuing consequences and challenges.

## 2

### Starting Points

Much of academic international relations analysis in the last several decades, especially but not exclusively in North America, has had two preoccupations. The first has been the advocacy and defence of one versus some other unifying concept about how the world can and does work. The central issue is then formulated in exclusive 'or' terms rather than in inclusive 'and' terms. Examples include military *or* economic emphases, globalism *or* regionalism *or* nationalism, the 'developmental state' *or* free market capitalism. The second preoccupation has been with concentration and exercise of power in world affairs in the present and the future — for example with great powers, both current and emerging, and their relative gains.

Yet time and again, particularly with respect to developments involving Asia, these emphases have missed evolving realities. The lessons seem clear: expect a world in which multiple concepts are needed to capture the mixture of practices and motives at work; recognize the efforts of the small as well as the large to shape their respective futures; attend to the pursuit of plenty as well as power, and absolute as well as relative gains. Those lessons follow in large measure from the persistent tendency of many in Asia to follow an international affairs strategy of 'avoiding choices and pursuing opportunities'.

There are obvious reasons for being very modest about our ability to forecast international relations. One needs only to compare what we were writing and saying in 1986 with the world of 1996, or in 1996 compared with late 1998, to become duly modest about the fit between our current views and how the world will in fact be near the end of the first decade of the twenty-first century. I am neither courageous nor foolish enough to offer specific predictions about the what, the when or the how of even the near-term future course (five to ten years) of the many issues concerning Asia's role in the world which currently preoccupy us.

I will nevertheless take the risk of making three more general predictions. First, there will be a continuity of general style of approach to international affairs, that is, a style of avoiding choices and pursuing opportunities. Second, several factors underlying that style will intensify, as will some already visible macro features of Asia and relations between Asians and of Asians with others. Third, international relations within Asia and between Asia and the rest of the world will take place in a context of beliefs, images and information gaps which will impose heavy policy management burdens and substantial constraints on the practice of international affairs among Asians, and between Asians and others. Those burdens and constraints are perhaps subject to erosion by time and effort, but at any particular point in time the challenge is how to function most effectively, given their presence.

## 3

### Some Elements of the Big Picture

Many specific alternative futures are possible. Yet these differing particulars will resemble each other in terms of their being shaped by six general phenomena.

First, Asian economic and technological dynamism will insure that developments in Asia and with Asia will have strong impacts elsewhere. That is a reality on which balance-of-power, hegemonic, liberal institutionalist and domestic political culture perspectives can agree. That reality has not been eliminated by the recent difficulties. Indeed, the chill in markets elsewhere that followed the downturn of Asian economies was indicative of that importance. So too has been the demands from North America and Europe for Japan to stimulate its economy. There is little reason to believe that most Asian economies will not recover, that their attractiveness as markets and investment sites will in general fall to that of several decades ago, or that they will lose competitiveness in increasingly higher value added exports.

Second, Asian developments will continue to be marked by diversity rather than homogeneity. Apart from the limited world of maps and of racial categories in the US Census, there is no 'Asia', in the sense of a unitary actor in world affairs which can be usefully treated in isolation from others; nor is there likely to be one. The future of the entities we sometimes lump together as 'Asia' will be to an important extent the product of factors internal to each of them — the mix of material endowments, economic and technology achievements, historical experiences and cultural patterns — and their resulting political conventions, institutions, players and capabilities. This diversity has been well illustrated by the varying responses to the financial crises of 1997 — compare Malaysia with Korea or Thailand.

Third, proximate and distant states, firms and non-profit organizations will continue to permeate into affairs on the Asian side of the Pacific. As in the past, their penetration will play an important role not only with those with whom they deal directly, but also as an acknowledged intermediary or major structural element (albeit sometimes an implicit one) in the dealings between states, firms and social groupings in the geographical space we call Asia. Here too, responses to the financial crises bolster rather than erode the point, be it with regard to the involvement of international financial institutions (IFIs), opening measures for trade and investment or financial transparency conducive to the involvement of external economic actors.

Fourth, the permeation and striving for influence and absolute and relative gains will continue increasingly to go the other way as well. That is, governments, firms and social groupings based in the Asian region will intrude (often in benign and welcome ways) in processes internal to states, firms and social groupings based elsewhere. These activities will continue to be increasingly pro-active and future-oriented rather than just reactive to external developments. Asian dynamism and achievement will create in others substantial if sometimes wary appetites for such involvements. So will Asian difficulties. Here the lack of protectionist response to cheaper Asian exports after the crisis-induced wave of devaluations is instructive, as is the American concern with a possible wave of Japanese selling or at least a cutback in purchases in US financial markets.

Fifth, intellectual, policy and commercial elites in Asia will draw inferences for their own countries even more from an examination of the experience of others in and of Asia. This will follow in part from visible successes by many Asian actors, in part from 'missionary activity' by the proponents of approaches pursued by one or another Asian government or firm, and in part from visible failures. At the same time, a global scanning by Asians will continue to consider experiences, changes and policy strategies elsewhere. The resulting interpretations will differ within Asia, and they may well not resemble predominant Western interpretations. Examples include attention by non-democratic Asian regimes to the consequences of Helsinki-like human rights measures for encouraging domestic political opposition (Kurusu 1996), or the efficacy of policies by neutral states such as Finland to garner security indirectly rather than by joining military alliances (Miwa 1996). Of course, the financial crises have further increased Asian attention to the actual workings and consequences of 'reform' packages being urged by the West. Yet here, too, there is evidence that their consequences for nations in Asia loom large together with the actual Western experience associated with such measures.

Finally, the participation revolution in international affairs will continue to sweep across Asia. That is, flows across national juridical borders will continue their rapid growth in the sheer numbers of involved national ministries and parliamentarians, sub-national government organizations, firms and social groupings. That will be true, as it has already been true, with respect to military matters, economic development, human rights, the environment, labour, drugs and information. The image of Asia's world role as limited to a few foreign affairs specialist ministries, political party organs and major trading enterprises will become increasingly obsolete. Whatever else, that revolution carries with it a decline in the ability of central governments or even central sectoral peak economic organizations to decide what happens, to know what is happening and to determine what their citizens can know and tell about external matters. Since the Makuhari convention, the participation revolution has continued to advance in Asia, be it in an orderly fashion (Korea, Thailand) or a disorderly one (Indonesia).

The role of Asia in world affairs will be complex and diverse. Different parties at any one time, and the same party at various times, will use different mixes of policies based on each of globalism, regionalism and nationalism. The familiar (at least in Japan) debate about whether or not to be 'in Asia' or in a broader world will in practice concern how to be in both (Mendl 1995). The familiar (at least in Japan) debate about special relationships and their dilemmas will not be limited to either particular non-regional great powers or a particular functional aspect of relations across borders. The dilemmas associated with interdependence and engagement among Asians and between Asians and others will become compounded in ways that will defy decisive resolution. Those dilemmas include defining and achieving a tolerable balance of autonomy relative to dependence, and the problems of entrapment relative to abandonment, of prosperity versus military coverage, of reassurance relative to cautionary warning and of cultural emulation relative to 'spiritual pollution' (Tsuchiyama 1995).

Governments and firms whose leaderships exercise due diligence pay serious attention to those that can hurt them or help them. For Asian governments and firms, this will mean paying even greater attention to those dilemmas in relation to each other, without any slackening (and perhaps even an increase) of attention to non-Asian actors, including multilateral organizations and fora. The portents are more than clear: for example, multinational growth triangles; several step transfers of weapons technology; the emergence of the ASEAN Regional Forum and more embryonic efforts for North-east Asia; China's drive for membership in the World Trade Organization and its shift in strategic conception from a 'main enemy' to a 'total national power' (Abe 1996); and Japan's interest in shifting trade bargaining, at least for globalized industries, from bilateral (Japan–US) to multilateral settings (Yamakoshi 1996b; Pollack 1996).

Faced with so much complexity and diversity, two fundamental guidelines emerge both for Asians and for those engaged with them. One is to shun simple general choices — e.g. between globalism and regionalism, between economic and military priorities, between a strong state and a strong market — in favour of a diverse portfolio of strategies. The second is to seek, use and share information about oneself and significant others. Transparency does not guarantee consensus, but it does provide a conducive condition for policy management, serious bargaining and co-ordinated problem-solving. Realism in the fullest sense requires information, and the financial crises demonstrate the risks of opaqueness.

# 4

## Some Illustrations

As students of international affairs, one of our professional functions is to provide and interpret information. Let me now turn to several illustrative sets of information bearing on the difficulties facing Asia in the world now and into at least the early part of the twenty-first century. The examples I have chosen for the most part centre on Japan. To avoid misunderstanding, they are not introduced to recommend or condemn particular Japanese policies and practices in foreign affairs. Nor do I mean to imply that Japan is the key, and the only key, to future development in and with Asia. The examples focus on Japan for three reasons. First, Japan apparently is committed to the diversified portfolio conceptual approach to international affairs (see the 1996 White Paper on Trade from the Japanese Ministry of Trade and Industry, and the 1996 Diplomatic 'Bluebook' from the Japanese Ministry of Foreign Affairs). Second, Japan has made an unusually great effort to be well informed about significant others and to aid them in becoming better informed about itself. Third, Japan has had in recent years especially multifaceted and intricate relations with the major states of North America and Europe which others in Asia are only now beginning to approach.

The illustrations that follow do not involve the familiar and important domains of economic stocks, flows and trends, or the military. They involve instead images and beliefs among publics, and in mass media and academic literature. Those sorts of information are offered not as sufficient, but rather as windows into the context in which specific actions by governments and firms will be chosen and interpreted. Those sorts of information reflect factors that are relatively slow to change, absent extreme 'shocks', and thus are likely to have continuing relevance well into the twenty-first century.

## American Pictures

My first three sets of illustrations about the information base for Asia's role in future international affairs involve US interpretations and opinions about Japan. These examples have broader relevance in several ways. Relations with the United

States are and will be important for numerous Asian actors. They will then have to cope with any historical 'stickiness' in American thinking about them, or tendency to interpret Asian actions through the lenses of American experience and self-assessments.

Tadashi Aruga (1996) has observed that the period between World War I and the Pacific War was marked by inattention in both the United States and Japan to each other's domestic politics. He goes on to establish the very substantial research in recent years, perhaps in part for that reason, by Japanese on the internal workings of the USA (much of it by distinguished members of the JAIR). Yet we know that options in international affairs are constrained by what significant others know and believe, as well as by what we know and believe about them. What pictures are in Americans' minds?

One set of pictures is that presented by American scholars writing about Japanese international affairs decisions. Haas and Kuroda (1996) review writings about 425 such decision cases that occurred from 1980 to 1994. They code interpretations of each case for target (USA, other); goal (security, prosperity, prestige (international status) and domestic); and influence on the decision (emperor/prime minister/high cabinet minister, foreign pressure, bureaucrats, corporations, parliamentarians, public opinion).

The results appear in Table 1. The composite picture that emerges portrays Japan's international affairs decision-making as little motivated by the pursuit of domestic political ends, and as shaped primarily by a few individuals in high positions and secondarily by foreign pressure and bureaucrats — especially when the USA is the target. Japanese goals are portrayed as having shifted from an emphasis on security to one on prosperity, and on international status. Prosperity objectives have been most prevalent when the United States was the target, and international status objectives have been most prevalent when others were. The implied bottom line is that a small Japanese elite is neither very motivated by domestic goals nor constrained by domestic non-ministerial interests; in other words, they can do what they want to do, and what they do is focused on an external, self-serving purpose. As a corollary, if they refrain from taking actions sought by foreigners, it is less because of domestic goals and constraints than because of doubt about external payoffs.

Relative to many other Asian countries, there is a rather large number of US scholars researching Japan's conduct in international affairs, and information about Japanese domestic politics and public opinion is accessible. Thus, inattention to or downplaying of domestic considerations and influences in other Asian countries may be even more likely. If domestic factors are crucial in Japan or elsewhere in Asia, the possibilities of misinterpretation and confusion are substantial. Of course, individual Asian political personalities may welcome and use for external and internal bargaining the apparent importance given to them — as may bureaucrats. Whatever the other contributing factors, the initial responses by Western governments and the International Monetary Fund dominated by them have shown a lack of awareness of the domestic consequences of and responses to their prescriptions.

The second illustrative set of American pictures comes from a set of focus groups of Americans conducted to elicit images of Japan (Deutsch and Alexander 1996). The images draw on past historical experience, attach negative interpretations even to positive traits, project prevailing concerns about American society, and emphasize military zero-sum metaphors. In them, Japan is seen as having succeeded in

Table 1  US Scholars' Interpretations of Japanese Decisions

| Decision time period | 1980–4 (N = 143) % | 1985–9 (N = 124) % | 1990–4 (N = 162) % |
|---|---|---|---|
| Target | | | |
| USA | 32 | 43 | 18 |
| Other | 68 | 57 | 82 |
| Goal | | | |
| Security | 39 | 30 | 22 |
| Prosperity | 23 | 39 | 30 |
| Prestige | 37 | 29 | 44 |
| Domestic | 0 | 7 | 9 |
| Influence | | | |
| Emperor/prime minister/ high cabinet minister | 47 | 35 | 35 |
| Foreign pressure | 14 | 18 | 17 |
| Bureaucrats | 15 | 15 | 12 |
| Corporations | 6 | 14 | 4 |
| Parliamentarians | 2 | 3 | 7 |
| Public opinion | 1 | 2 | 3 |

| If target: | USA | Other |
|---|---|---|
| Goal | | |
| Security | 26 | 32 |
| Prosperity | 55 | 20 |
| Prestige | 22 | 45 |
| Domestic | 1 | 8 |
| Influence | | |
| Emperor/prime minister/ high cabinet minister | 34 | 43 |
| Foreign pressure | 28 | 11 |
| Bureaucrats | 20 | 12 |
| Corporations | 16 | 4 |
| Parliamentarians | 2 | 5 |
| Public opinion | 0 | 3 |

*Note:* Multiple coding was permitted.
*Source:* Haas and Kuroda (1996).

reopening World War II and conducting a successful economic offensive. Japanese have the characteristics of a strong military opponent — strategic calculation, effort and intense organized behaviour — and have replaced their failed soldiers with industrial might. They are tough; Americans are soft. They are determined to get even for military defeat, insatiable, and ungrateful for what the United States did for them. This imagery was fuelled by perceptions of American decline.

The third illustrative set (also from Deutsch and Alexander 1996) deals with the coverage of Japan in US national media. For this, it draws on nightly network TV news programmes over the past decade, and on headlines in the titles and subtitles of stories in three major weekly 'news' magazines (*Time, Newsweek, US News and World Report*). With regard to attention, coverage was greatest in 1985 (the fortieth anniversary of Hiroshima) and at the height of trade friction in 1989, only to decline in recent years to one-third of the 1989 level. The TV and news magazine treatments are similar and negative. Japan and the Japanese are characterized as having feelings of superiority, being fanatical in work and war, being sneaky and unfair, and focused on the pursuit of control and domination. (At least one study of other aspects of US media coverage (Budner and Krauss 1995) found less harsh imagery but also a fear of American decline.) The negative media themes are echoed in the results of a 1995 survey of US members of the US–Japan Business Council.

The focus group and media images may have broader implications in three respects. First, they suggest that how non-Asians view Asians will draw on historical residues and projections of how the non-Asians would feel if they had the Asians' history. Different Asian nations will carry different baggage or perhaps even a blank slate in that respect with Americans and other non-Asians. Second, they suggest that economically large and fast-track Asian countries will be viewed in terms of how non-Asians assess the performance of their own nation or its firms (relative performance). Given the competitive or antagonistic framing metaphors, Asian success can breed fear and resentment as well as respect and admiration. Asian difficulties can breed triumphalism and arrogance as well as resentment should Asians not accept a follower role. Third, at least for Japan, they suggest that foreign populations may react differently to policy initiatives than will foreign governments — notwithstanding head-of-state summit rhetoric. For example, it is not obvious that the US population and media would welcome Japan engaging in the military buildup and international activism being urged on it by Washington; nor is it obvious that Western populations will welcome an export-driven Asian recovery even if their elites see it as beneficial in the longer run. Knowledge of such divisions can strengthen Asian resistance to foreign pressures, and can even be used to justify resistance to the foreign government exerting the pressure.

Parenthetically, it is interesting to note that the focus groups and media analysis were funded by Japan's Ministry of Foreign Affairs, and published in English in Washington. Perhaps Asians find it useful to inform Western elites of the considerations that engender wariness about what policies Western populations will support and offer for exploitation by competitors in Western domestic politics.

## Asian Pictures

Two other sets of information deal with opinions in different Asian nations, one focused on Japan and the other on national publics' views of their quality of life and outlook for the future.

The first is based on a May 1995 report of public opinion survey results in *Yomiuri Shimbun*. The results report opinion in Japan, China, South Korea, Indonesia, Malaysia, Thailand and Vietnam. The questions deal with residual historical suspicions, views of participation by the Japanese military in peacekeeping operations, membership in the UN Security Council, military power including possession of nuclear weapons, and courses of action to improve relations with other Asians. They are summarized in Table 2.

A diversity of Asian opinion is evident. Suspicions and resentments of the political and military past are very pronounced for Koreans, followed by Chinese. Although by no means homogeneous, the South-east Asian populations interviewed voiced less concern with historical grievances and more support for international Japanese activism with respect to peacekeeping and membership in the Security Council. Yet even among South-east Asians, a substantial share of the respondents believe that Japan is or will be a military great and nuclear armed power.

In spite of these differences, few if any of the responding national samples viewed restraints on Japanese military power as a *sine qua non* for improved relations. Nor was there more than very modest support for Japan taking on a leadership role, either in representing Asia in opposition to the United States or in the broader field of international politics. What the other Asians wanted from Japan was economic: investment, import purchases, technology transfers and foreign aid, and access for their workers to jobs in Japan. Even in the economic sphere, however, emphases differed. The other widely shared view dealt with the importance of 'intangible' identity and status — appreciation from Japan of their cultures and history.

When Japanese opinions were provided, they resembled those of the South-east Asians in overall support for participation in peacekeeping (the status quo) and plurality support for a UN Security Council seat for Japan. In these respects, they differed from Chinese and Korean views. Where Japanese opinions were at marked odds with all the other Asian national samples was with regard to future military power and the possession of nuclear weapons. The resounding 'no' on both possibilities from the Japanese public stands alone in the set of Asian expectations.

At least for Japan, several policy management challenges are suggested by these results. First, the 'shadow of the past' lives on in relations with North-east Asia. Second, attempts to exercise greater political–military activism will be relatively well received by some and objected to by other Asians. One policy will not fit all. Third, improved relations with other Asians hinge on a further increase in two-way economic flows with Japan, flows that by their very nature will increase the national economic competitiveness of other Asian states and involve increased penetration by their goods and citizens into the domestic Japanese economy and society. Fourth, the preferences of other Asians are not the same as those of some American officials for treating Japan as the leading voice and power in Asia, or with Washington's urging on Japan more of a leadership role in international politics. Finally, in respect to military matters, other Asian views of future power clash with the suspicions some of them hold, and with the expectations (and, other data suggests, preferences) of most Japanese citizens.

That was a complicated setting for policy, but not one devoid of opportunities. There are obvious, and apparently continuing, opportunities for Japanese elites to use Asian views to counterbalance non-Asian pressures and vice versa, and obvious ones to use domestic preferences and expectations to resist foreign pressures from Asian and non-Asian quarters. These possibilities continue, as do the challenges underlying them. The 'shadow of the past' surely was present at the November 1998 China–Japan summit. The aftermath of the Asian financial crises has been rich

**Table 2**   Asian Images (%)

| | National sample[a] | | | | | | |
|---|---|---|---|---|---|---|---|
| | J | C | K | I | M | T | V |
| Q: Do you think that what the Japanese military did in your country is still an obstacle to the relationship between your country and Japan? | | | | | | | |
| Yes | | 49 | 71 | 12 | 25 | 36 | 16 |
| No | | 35 | 19 | 74 | 67 | 60 | 69 |
| Q: Japan sent members of the Self-Defence Forces to join the peacekeeping operation (PKO) in Cambodia. Do you support Japan's PKO participation in various places in the world? | | | | | | | |
| Yes | 66 | 27 | 42 | 67 | 74 | 74 | 62 |
| No | 25 | 45 | 40 | 8 | 13 | 21 | 13 |
| Q: Do you think that Japan should be named a permanent member of the United Nations' Security Council? | | | | | | | |
| Yes | 47 | 26 | 19 | 47 | 67 | 80 | 63 |
| No | 25 | 46 | 48 | 17 | 16 | 14 | 7 |
| Q: Do you think that Japan might become a great military power or that it already is one? | | | | | | | |
| May become | 19 | 35 | 56 | 23 | 40 | 33 | 33 |
| Won't become | 74 | 37 | 10 | 39 | 27 | 57 | 33 |
| Already is | 3 | 9 | 26 | 3 | 9 | 5 | 4 |
| Q: Do you think that Japan will possess nuclear weapons? | | | | | | | |
| Yes | 14 | 45 | 85 | 49 | 37 | 61 | 41 |
| No | 80 | 18 | 8 | 12 | 31 | 23 | 15 |
| Already has | – | 14 | – | 11 | 10 | 11 | 11 |
| Q: What should Japan do to further develop its relations with Asian countries? (multiple responses) | | | | | | | |
| Increase investments | | 42 | 17 | 33 | 49 | 43 | 67 |
| Curb investments | | 5 | 6 | 9 | 12 | 14 | 4 |
| Increase imports | | 39 | 27 | 28 | 49 | 52 | 24 |
| Promote economic cooperation and technological transfer | | 63 | 60 | 54 | 57 | 44 | 81 |
| Protect global environment | | 18 | 12 | 17 | 27 | 33 | 18 |
| Compensate for WWII damages | | 40 | 44 | 23 | 25 | 11 | 25 |
| Curb defence power | | 17 | 13 | 5 | 17 | 10 | 8 |
| Receive immigrant labourers | | 13 | 10 | 41 | 45 | 48 | 35 |
| Appreciate our culture/history | | 62 | 52 | 43 | 36 | 37 | 44 |
| Represent an Asian position against the USA | | 11 | 8 | 9 | 34 | 8 | 9 |
| Take leadership in international politics | | 18 | 13 | 14 | 25 | 22 | 14 |

[a] C = China; K = South Korea; I = Indonesia; M = Malaysia; T = Thailand; V = Vietnam.
*Source: Yomiuri Shimbun*, 23 May 1995; in Yamakoshi (1996a).

in demands from other Asians for action by Tokyo which would increase their international economic competitiveness (a strong yen), exports to Japan and direct financial help with their economic recoveries. And the other Asians have sought to press on the United States and Europe that their fate requires direct engagement with them, both bilaterally and in APEC and ASEM.

More speculatively, it may be the case that some of the features of opinion towards Japan may mark Asian opinions towards each other more generally. If that is true, we would expect that in their dealings with each other many Asians will emphasize the pursuit of dense economic relations and 'identity equality' (rather than submergence). Again by extrapolation, they will not favour any single Asian nation 'representing their interests' in relations with the United States or in international politics. Finally, they will be sceptical of assuming that other Asian nations have permanently turned away from the pursuit of military power. The implications for relations with China and the Chinese are the most obvious — a desire for supportive economic policies (e.g. opposition to yuan devaluation), suspicion about military intentions, and historically based hedging alignments against excessive future pressure (e.g. the bonding of Vietnam and Taiwan). Yet the implications are not limited to China and the Chinese, and clearly are cautionary for non-Asian governments who would try to deal with Asia now and in the future through a policy that emphasizes the priority of relations with one or two large states in the region, and expects the others to fall in line.

A final set of information consists of the opinions held by general populations in twenty-nine countries about their current quality of life and outlook for the future expressed in polls taken in May/June 1997 and a year later in mid-1998 (the Economist/Angus Reid World Poll, 1998: www.angusreid.com). The Asian nations sampled were China, Japan, Malaysia, South Korea, Taiwan and Thailand. Relevant data appear in Table 3.

The results suggest persistence in relative Asian dissatisfaction with current quality of life and, with the notable exception of Japan, positive hopes for the future

**Table 3**  Asian Appraisals

| | Satisfaction with quality of life (Hope Index score) | | | | | | | |
| | Today[a] | | | | Outlook for the future[a] | | | |
| | 1997 (N = 25) | | 1998 (N = 29) | | 1997 (N = 25) | | 1998 (N = 29) | |
| | Rank | (%) | Rank | (%) | Rank | (%) | Rank | (%) |
|---|---|---|---|---|---|---|---|---|
| China | 21 | (25) | 23 | (23) | 2 | (67) | 7 | (58) |
| Japan | 19 | (27) | 26 | (14) | 29 | (12) | 29 | (12) |
| Malaysia | 15 | (35) | 19 | (30) | 1 | (73) | 1 | (66) |
| South Korea | 23 | (24) | 25 | (19) | 3 | (64) | 4 | (62) |
| Taiwan | 21 | (25) | 24 | (22) | 11 | (38) | 8 | (50) |
| Thailand | 20 | (29) | 28 | (12) | 5 | (59) | 6 | (60) |

[a] Today = % choosing 6 or 7 on 7 point satisfaction scale; Outlook = composite score across 3 'future expectations' items.
*Source:* The Economist/Angus Reid World Poll, 1998.

compared with many of the other nations (largely, advanced industrialized countries) polled. Together, these citizen appraisals suggest that some of the driving forces of Asian dynamism have not been eliminated by the economic events that intervened between the 1997 and 1998 polls. Asian striving for betterment will then continue, as will a rejection of external attempts to lock Asians into their current position in world affairs, most obviously economic affairs, by a wholesale replacement of their indigenous (and diverse) policy systems.

The results also suggest both widespread discontent and pessimism in Japan, which can only impede attempts to strike out on bold, different policy lines, and carry greater burdens and initiative in international affairs. The policy challenges for Japanese elites have thus, if anything, become more rather than less difficult.

# 5

## Open Questions

Writing about US relations with East Asia, the distinguished American historian Ernest May (1996) summarized the past as marked by movement from exploitation to mutual exploitation (with intermittent conflict in each of those phases) and then to cooperation. In the mutual exploitation phase, the great power often gave more than it got (at least to ruling Asian elites). If the mutual exploitation stage was marked by the linked pursuit of different interests, that of cooperation has rested on perceived common interests, a narrowing gap in the confidence and capabilities of Asians and Americans and the growth of mutual understanding. In his view, these pillars of cooperation have laid the basis for future cooperation as opposed to separation or antagonism.

Perhaps the phases he suggests are equally applicable to relations between East Asians, and between them and the rest of the world. Surely there has been exploitation, mutual exploitation, intermittent conflict and even cooperation. Our question then becomes to what extent the pillars of cooperation are or will grow to be in place within East Asia and with neighbouring and distant states. These pillars — of self-confidence, perceived common interest and shared understanding — are far from uniformly strong at this time. They are unlikely to attain such a degree of robustness before we enter the twenty-first century. Until they do, we can expect to see the simultaneous pursuit of policies that evade pressures to choose between globalism, regionalism and nationalism. We will see policies that try to seize on situational opportunities embedded in each course without foreclosing on the others. Non-Asians who perceive or expect anything else open themselves to unwarranted extremes of optimism or pessimism about Asia's role in the world. If they fall into one or the other of these traps, the results are likely to be either unrealistically rapid timetables for cooperation and integration, or unrealistically magnified threat estimates.

## References

Abe, Jun-ichi (1996), 'Chinese National Security Perception after the Cold War and its Implications for East Asia: Independent Peace Diplomacy and "China Threat" Thesis', *International Relations* (Tokyo), 112 (May) pp. 63–83.

Aruga, Tadashi (1996), 'Japanese Scholarship in the History of US–East Asian Relations', in Warren I. Cohen (ed.), *Pacific Passage: The Study of American–East Asian Relations on the Eve of the Twenty-First Century*, Columbia University Press, pp. 36–87.

Bernstein, Richard and Munro, Ross (1997), *The Coming Conflict with China*, New York: Alfred Knopf.

Budner, Stanley and Krauss, Ellis (1995), 'Balance and Objectivity in Newspaper Coverage of US–Japan Frictions', *Asian Survey*, April, pp. 336–356.

Deutsch, Robert D. and Alexander, A. J. (1996), 'Americans' Images of Japan', *JEI Report*, no. 19A (17 May).

Haas, Michael and Yasumasa Kuroda (1996), 'How Does Japan Make Foreign Policy?' Paper presented at the Annual Meeting of the International Studies Association, San Diego, 16–20 April.

Ishihara, Shintaruo (1991), *The Japan that Can Say No*, New York: Simon & Schuster.

Kurusu, Kaoru (1996), 'The Human Dimension of the Conference on Security and Cooperation in Europe: A Case Study in Regime Theory', *International Relations* (Tokyo), vol. 112 (May) pp. 139–157.

May, Ernest R. (1996), 'Epilogue: American–East Asian Relations in the Twenty-first Century', in Warren I. Cohen (ed.), *Pacific Passage*, Columbia University Press, pp. 375–88.

Mendl, Wolf (1995), *Japan's Asia Policy*, New York: Routledge.

Miwa, Yoshiaki (1996), 'The EU Membership and Security Problem for Finland: The Formation of New Security Order in Europe and Neutral Countries', *International Relations* (Tokyo), vol. 112 (May) pp. 158–174.

Pollack, Andrew (1996), 'Japan's Tack on Trade: No More 1-on-1', *New York Times*, 30 July, C1 ff.

Tsuchiyama, Jitsuo (1995), 'The End of the Alliance? Dilemmas in US–Japanese Relations', in Peter Gourevitch, Takashi Inoguchi and Courtney Purrington (eds.), *United States–Japan Relations and International Institutions After the Cold War*, University of California Press, pp. 3–35.

Yamakoshi, Atsushi (1996a), 'Japan in Asia: Perceptions and Realities', *JEI Report*, no. 17A (3 May).

Yamakoshi, Atsushi (1996b), 'Taking the World Trade Organization to the Next Stage: Will Japan Move Multilateralism Forward?' *JEI Report*, no. 31A (16 August).

# 3

# COLLECTIVE IDENTITY AND EPOCHAL CHANGE IN THE INTERNATIONAL SYSTEM

*Rodney Bruce Hall*

## 1
### Introduction

Nationalist and ethnic conflict, not Cold War tensions or 'superpower balancing in the periphery', now largely consume the agendas of the United Nations and Nato as well as the foreign policy concerns of powers, great and small. Curiously, these events, and the attention that the great powers would lavish on them, were as unpredicted and unpredictable by our current repertoire of international relations theory as was the end of the Cold War. Yet little attention has been given to the issue of nationalism in recent literature in the discipline of international relations theory.

While it has been contended in international relations theory that the international behaviour of state actors has been uniform throughout history, I argue that the eighteenth-century system consisted of territorial–sovereign state actors whose regimes relied upon dynastic legitimating principles. By contrast, the late nineteenth and twentieth-century systems have consisted increasingly of national–sovereign actors whose regimes have relied upon the 'imagined community' of the nation as a legitimating principle (see Anderson 1983).

Currently dominant theories of international relations are strongly state-centric. They take the state as a fundamental unit of analysis that is unproblematically given, and fail to enquire into its origins or to delineate it from the nation. These theories relegate domestic–societal interaction, sources of conflict or societal cohesiveness (such as ethnic, religious and other domestic sources) to the status of

Portions of this argument appear in a different form in Rodney Bruce Hall, *National Collective Identity: Social Constructs and International Systems* (New York: Columbia University Press, 1999).

epiphenomena.[1] The current resurgence of nationalism, and the potential consequences of past and present national movements, are therefore opaque to our current repertoire of international relations theory, despite the fact that the relative novelty of national collective identity has significant implications for the current practice of modern international relations.

I argue below that societal collective identity is a collective manifestation of self-identification. Individuals identify with numerous social groupings on the basis of cognitive or emotive affiliations. Collective identities that can be readily seen to have significant consequences for the social action of societal groupings include identities based upon gender, regional factors, socio-economic class, religion, culture and ethnicity, to name but a few (see Smith 1991, pp. 3–8). This paper will focus on the elements and consequences of specifically national collective identity, which 'draws on elements of other kinds of collective identity [and thus] is fundamentally multidimensional; it can never be reduced to a single element' (Smith 1991, p. 14).

In providing a focus on collective identity and its role in transforming individual, societal and 'national' interests, I allow state and 'national' interest to vary depending upon the independent variable of societal collective identity. Such an analytic focus is necessary not only to provide us with a better understanding of the historical development of the international system, but also to advance beyond theories of international relations whose neglect of domestic social interaction has resulted in a failure to anticipate the end of the Cold War, and the proliferation of nationalisms that have followed its demise. Societies recently orphaned by the eclipse of proletarian internationalism have sought alternative legitimating principles upon which to found social order. While states have tended to arrive at this destination by different paths, national sovereignty, legitimated by shared ethnicity, shared culture and shared history, appears to be the favoured alternative of many. Developing a richer understanding and framework for the analysis of the past consequences of the creation of newly nationalized states may lead to a significant advancement of theory, from which we might derive not only testable hypotheses, but policy prescriptions for dealing with contemporary national newcomers.

An investigation of the systemic consequences of changes in collective identity, and its rigorous delineation from the consequences of earlier forms that supported a state system, will simultaneously help us to understand several important issues. These include the origins of the modern nation-state system, historical variations in the institutional forms of collective action, and the distinction between territorial sovereignty and national sovereignty. I seek to uncover the consequences of national collective identity and nation building (as opposed to state building) in the modern era within a framework that results in a useful correction to an existing body of theoretical literature.[2]

I will argue that we cannot explain nationalism or its causal significance for international politics within a theoretical framework that is committed to a conception of structure that is largely static, or in which structure merely constrains action.

---

[1] The archetypical example of this type of theorizing is found in Waltz (1979).

[2] For a description of the difficulties of dominant theories of international relations in contending with nationalist phenomenology see Lapid and Kratochwil (1994).

Crucial to my argument is the assertion that *changes in the collective identity of societal actors transform the interests of relevant collective actors that constitute the system*. Sovereign state actors may well have autonomous interests that help shape state policy, but the influences, beliefs and prejudices of individuals and sub-state groups within society help to determine how ostensibly objective state interests get translated into state policy.[3] The interests of societal groups are not immutable or objectively determined. Group interests are strongly conditioned by the self-identifications of members of these groups with respect to other groupings within society and with respect to the state.

Thus, to explain the differences in behaviour of the late nineteenth to mid-twentieth-century nation with that of the eighteenth-century dynastic state, we must assert that 'the "national interest" cannot be the object of a rational determination' (Aron 1966, p. 285). We cannot assume that the 'interests' of eighteenth-century states and twentieth-century states are equivalent and determinable *ex post facto* by the analyst with recourse to logical inference alone. It is often asserted by critics of theories of rational choice, specifically in structural theories and especially structural neorealism, that interests must not be given or assumed, and thus must be exogenized. In developing this argument, I will move beyond these criticisms and endeavour to explain why static 'as-if' theorization regarding the interests (and attendant motivations) of international actors obscures analysis of the behavioural variations of national *v.* state actors. I will develop the impact of the redefinition of group and individual interests as a consequence of changes in their self-identification and self-understanding as social actors within the state. This approach abandons the assumption of the state-as-unitary-actor and removes what may be a deterministic impediment to richer analysis of the causes of state action.

Nationalism brought with it the abstract notion of 'citizenship'. The nineteenth-century manifestations of this notion range from full enfranchisement and universal suffrage in the United States (among white males), to, at the least, national populism and suffrage, weighted by social class, in constitutional–monarchical Europe. In all but autocratic Russia, the 'revolution of 1848' had injected into European regimes constitutional checks on autocracy and a conception of the 'rule-of-law', both of which were also binding upon the monarch, and at least limited participatory, parliamentary institutions. Some conception of 'citizenship' was emerging nearly everywhere and was replacing the more traditional self-identification of being 'subject' to a prince or a state. The consequences of these events for the determination of 'state-interests' is captured in a trenchant passage in a recent work by Michael Mann:

> As classes and other actors attained civil and political citizenship, the state became 'their' nation-state, an 'imagined' community to which they developed loyalties. Its

---

[3] An important debate on the extent to which the state apparatus possesses, and is empowered to express, autonomous interests is ongoing in the comparative politics literature. For the strongest elaboration of the neo-statist view, see Skocpol (1979, 1985, pp. 3–37) and Krasner (1984, pp. 233–46). Critical reviews of the neo-statist perspective may be found in Almond (1988, pp. 853–74); Himmelstein and Kimmel (1981, pp. 1145–54); and Mitchell (1991, pp. 77–96).

power, honor, humiliations, and even material interests came to be sensed as their
own, and such feelings were mobilizable by the statesmen, pressure groups and militaries.
Nationalist parties and pressure groups pressed these feelings on statesmen . . . [a] . . .
populist, passionate, national tinge . . . [was given to diplomacy by the] . . . growth of
national identities. *But this lacked the precise rationality of interests pursued by classes
or particularistic pressure groups and the precise, normatively rooted understandings
of insulated old regime statesmen.* (Mann 1993, p. 74; emphasis added)

# 2

## The Will-to-Manifest Identity and International Systems

A developing body of theory that argues for recognition of the social construction
of political structure has called attention to the disparate motivational assumptions
underlying theories of rational choice, and hermeneutical or phenomenological theories of agents. Theories of rational choice assume that human beings are primarily
and causally motivated by an instrumental rationality. The latter variants argue that
they are motivated by complex belief systems, requiring analysts to 'empathize with
these beliefs before human actions can be comprehended and interpreted'.[4]

Alexander Wendt, drawing in part upon the structurationist sociology of Anthony
Giddens and the norms-based critical theory of Friedrich Kratochwil and Nicholas
Onuf, has proposed a 'constructivist' approach to resolve this impasse with the
assertion that 'social structures are only instantiated by the practices of agents'.
What interests us most from this discussion is Wendt's derivative insight that *social
structures are 'inseparable from the reasons and self-understandings that agents
bring to their actions'* (Wendt 1987, p. 359). This insight is essential in forging the
link between collective identities and the institutional forms of collective action
derived from these identities. These concepts will be the subject of much attention a
bit later in this paper.

Theories of rational choice attempt to avoid the problem of self-understandings of
national agents with the assumption that they are rational actors impelled to action
by instrumental rationality and systemic forces. As a matter of empirical fact, however,
most contemporary states view themselves as 'national' actors: as communities of
shared ethnicity, or language, or history, or belief, or heritage. They regard these linkages as transcending a purely political association that functions corporately — as
might the firm in the competitive market place — to maximize their gains from
interaction with other international political units. These self-understandings produce action that cannot be explained solely with recourse to the prescriptions of
rational instrumental action. Rational instrumentalism would, for example, argue
for the maintenance and strengthening of multi-ethnic federations in order to maintain economies of scale and to maximize bargaining leverage with respect to other
international actors. How can we explain the recently observed movement towards
political fragmentation solely with recourse to state-centric rational instrumentalism?
As I have repeatedly suggested, the logic of state-centrism alone will not do.

---

[4] Little cites this assertion by Nicholas Onuf in Buzan *et al.* (1993, p. 103).

Wendt has argued for the assignment of equal ontological[5] status to the state and to the system. His earlier work argues that one cannot develop a coherent theory of international relations unless both the state and system are problematized.[6] The theory must be capable of explaining the emergence of each and of capturing the 'generative moment' of the system. I will take this argument a bit further than Wendt does. I argue that the state is simply the rational, bureaucratic, institutional manifestation of the societal collective identity of the nation in the age of nationalism. The state is not coterminous with the nation. Historically the state has both preceded and followed the nation. Significantly, it is the legitimating principles of a given, historical social order that privilege this rational bureaucratic manifestation of those principles as an institutional artefact of the system.

As the state is privileged at the level of the 'system', communities of shared identity construct states to serve their needs as 'nations' in the course of systemic interaction. This was so in the past because the Westphalian system, organized under the legitimating principle of *raison d'état*, privileged the sovereign with rights and legitimacy. This is so in the newer era of national sovereignty, organized under the legitimating principle of national self-determination, because the state is still the privileged institutional form, with the provision that it must at least claim to serve as an institutional form of the collective action of a 'national' collective identity. Thus, I would extend Wendt's 1987 argument and ascribe equal ontological status to the nation (sovereign), as well as to the state (sovereign) and the system.

## 3

### Collective Identity and International Systems

Nations and the international national-state system are now a natural feature of the international political landscape, because they have a 'template' to work with.[7] Political entities have enormous incentives to mould themselves into this landscape owing to the privileging of the state in the rules, or incentive structure, of the contemporary international system. But this was not always so. We must examine how this 'template' was constructed if we are to clearly and conceptually delineate the nation from the state, and apprehend the nature and modes of differentiation of the primary units of a historically developing, rather than an ahistorically continuous, international system. The most central argument of this paper is that change in the international system occurs with changes in the collective identity of crucial social actors who collectively constitute the units from which the system is comprised.

---

[5] Ontologies are 'the substantive entities and configurations the theory postulates'. They provide the 'concrete referents of an explanatory discourse' and consist of 'the real-world structures (things, entities) and processes posited by the theory and invoked in the theory's explanations'; see Dessler (1989, pp. 444–5).

[6] Wendt's more recent work appears to veer away from this suggestion. He has recently asserted that 'a theory of the states system need no more explain the existence of states than one of society need explain that of people' (Wendt 1994, p. 385).

[7] This is Anderson's explanation for post-colonial nationalism in the Third World (Anderson 1983, pp. 139–40).

Figure 1 provides my view of how the system changes with changes in collective identity, in tabular form. The table describes the transformation of the European system from a post-Reformation system of largely independent dynasts, segmented by confessional distinctions, to a system of sovereign nation-states. The first column provides the relevant variables that are subject to change in the historical development of the international system. Changes in these variables are strongly interrelated.

In the discussion that follows, I will attempt to provide a causal linkage between the factors or variables presented in the first column of Figure 1. I argue that historical changes in societal collective identity have a causal significance for the principles by which domestic and international social orders are legitimated. Legitimate authority over domestic society, and the perception of the legitimacy of one's rule by other societies and their governments, is established by societal recognition that the exercise of this authority is consistent with principles[8] (beliefs about the nature of legitimate authority) that are generally accepted among members of domestic society and by, at least, the elites of other societies.

My argument, expressed succinctly, is that changes in co-constituted individual and collective identity result in changes in the legitimating principles of global and domestic social order, and in consequent changes in the institutional forms of collective action, through which that identity is expressed to other societies. The norms, rules and principles of social interaction within, and between, these new institutional forms of collective action are developed by social actors through practice in order to accommodate the new institutional structure. This new structure manifests the new societal identity and system change.

The institutional forms of collective action listed in Figure 1 are historically contingent modes of social organization. Historically, society has been organized into different institutional forms. Different forms serve the needs of society at different times. These forms strongly reflect prevailing concepts of the legitimate relationship of the individual members of society to the prevailing conception of legitimate authority. Lordship was a legitimate form of authority in feudal Europe; thus, the feud and fief were constructed to institutionalize the relationship between lord and vassal. Absolute monarchy, in which the king was thought to hold authority to rule directly from God, was a legitimate form of authority in eighteenth-century Europe; thus, the territorial–sovereign state was constructed to institutionalize his unmediated sovereignty over the peoples within the territory that he administered. More recently, national self-determination of a sovereign people united into a community of shared language, ethnicity, culture or history has become an accepted form of legitimate authority; thus, the national-state has been constructed to institutionalize these communal affiliations, and to serve them with an institutional form that can manifest to the world the social action that this form of collective identity seeks to express.

Therefore I am also arguing that what I refer to as the institutional forms of collective action change with prevailing, historically contingent conceptions of societal

---

[8] The definition of 'principles' employed in theories of international regimes is wholly applicable here. Stephen Krasner defines principles as 'beliefs of fact, causation and rectitude'. It is specifically beliefs about the 'rectitude' of authority that interests us in the present argument (see Krasner 1983, p. 2).

**Figure 1** International System Change with Changes in Collective Identity

|  | Dynastic–sovereign | Territorial–sovereign | National–sovereign |
|---|---|---|---|
| Individual identity | Subject of Protestant or Catholic prince | Subject of sovereign state | Citizen or subject of nation |
| Collective identity | 1. Reformed/ unreformed people of Christendom<br>2. Subjects of Prince 'X' | 1. Member of social class (aristocrat, *Bürger* or peasant)<br>2. Subject of crown and state 'Y' | 1. Member of national community by shared ancestry/ culture/history<br>2. National citizen of 'Z'-land |
| Legitimating principle | *Cuius regio eius religio*[a] (dynastic authority) | *Raison d'état*[b] (territorial authority) | National self-determination (popular or national authority) |
| Institutional forms of collective action | Kingdom and realm | Territorial-state | Nation-state |
| Norms, rules, principles<br>    Socio-political | Allegiance to prince and his creed; prince gives the domestic law | Allegiance to sovereign in service of his/her state; sovereign gives domestic law; emergence of civil society | Allegiance to imagined community of shared ancestry, culture or history; welfare state gives domestic law with counsel of enfranchised citizenry |
|     Socio-economic | Division of labour expands to encompass lay bureaucracy; limited international trade | Division of labour expands to encompass capitalist production relations; expansion of international trade | Global division of labour; global capitalist economy; international economic interdependence |
|     Inter-societal | Prince *de facto* emancipated from papacy; legal anarchy | State emancipated from all sacral legitimacy; inception of idea of international law | Nation self-determination; limited international law |
| Resulting system | Augsburg system[c] | Westphalian system[d] | Nation-state system |

[a] Translate loosely as 'whose the reign, his the religion'. In post-Reformation Europe, an individual was wise to practise the religion of his or her prince.
[b] From the French, 'reason of state'. The defence of the state and the advancement of its 'interests' were seen as adequate justification for international action. Significantly, however, the state was still often strongly identified with a monarch.
[c] Many monarchies, particularly in western Europe, were conducting their policy in a manner that was *de facto* emancipated from papal jurisdiction well before the legal ascription of this right in the Treaty of Westphalia in 1648. This intent is found in a legal context in the Peace of Augsburg (1555), more than a century before the Treaty of Westphalia.
[d] The Treaty of Westphalia formally emancipated the policy of the central European powers in 1648.

collective identity. *That which constitutes an appropriate institutional vehicle through which society may take social action is strongly conditioned by what form of polity the society considers itself to be.* A society that rejects lordship as an agency of legitimate authority cannot employ the institution of vassalage to take social action. A society that regards itself as an historically continuous nation, constituted by the ancient common bloodlines of the *Volk*, cannot take the social action it wishes to take, cannot express its self-understanding with social action consistent with this understanding, through the institution of a polyglot territorial–sovereign state.

Thus, it is no accident, for example, that, as German national collective identity developed in the nineteenth century, it turned to relatively ethnically homogeneous Hohenzollern Prussia, and Berlin, rather than the polyglot Hapsburg court in Vienna, for a vehicle by which German national collective identity might receive an institutional form. It is no accident that German national collective identity opted for a *kleindeutsche* boundary, incorporating only ethnic Germans as far as possible, rather than a *grossdeutsche* boundary, which would have incorporated the Slavic and Magyar peoples bound up in the Hapsburg empire.

I argue that the norms, rules and principles of interaction in domestic and international society then develop in practice. They derive from the principles that legitimate the domestic and international social orders. Their development is mediated by the institutions that enshrine and reproduce these principles. To illustrate this assertion, I argue that norms of political allegiance develop within domestic society which are consistent with the principles that legitimate the prevailing form of political authority in that domestic society. Domestic institutions reproduce these norms *of* behaviour until they become norms *for* behaviour, or rules. The individual's allegiance to the institutional manifestation of these principles of legitimate authority not only is expected by norms, but is commanded by the rules developed to regulate institutional society in accordance with prevailing (and historically contingent) legitimate notions of sovereignty. Societies with different conceptions of the nature of legitimate authority choose to endow different elements of society with this authority. It is important to note that the element(s) of society in which this sovereignty is lodged emerge as an artefact of societal collective identity. What or whom is regarded as sovereign is strongly conditioned by the self-understandings of members of domestic society with respect to legitimate authority. That which we call 'sovereign' says a lot about whom we believe ourselves to be as a polity, whether we are a passive polity (regarding ourselves as subjects of authority) or an active polity (regarding ourselves as sources of authority).

Thus, with reference to Figure 1, the subject of the dynastic–sovereign state gives his or her allegiance to the prince, who rules domestic society, and to his creed; the subject of the territorial–sovereign state gives his or her allegiance to the sovereign of that state; the citizen of the national–sovereign state gives his or her allegiance to the nation, to the imagined community of shared ancestry, culture or history to which he or she believes himself or herself to be a part. Domestic law is given to domestic society by the prevailing sovereign. The sovereign is that person, institution or community in which legitimate social authority is lodged in accordance with the legitimating principles of the social order.

The division of labour within and between societies also develops normatively, through practice and subsequent interaction. These arrangements are conditioned as well by the historically contingent, prevailing legitimating principles of social order. As Figure 1 suggests, the emergence of an educated, literate lay class permitted the development of the rational accounting principles and the technical requirements of finance necessary for the development of a significant intersocietal trade in the dynastic–sovereign era. Important as this division of labour became for the growth of the economy in the private sphere, it also permitted an expansion of the division of labour in the public sphere. Educated lay bureaucrats secularized the 'clerisy' of which Gellner has written, and was an enormously important feature in the penetration of the state into the private sphere.[9]

As sovereign identity became segmented more in terms of territorial than confessional or dynastic criteria, the wealth of the territorial–sovereign state became a paramount concern as a resource for use in the defence and expansion of the state. The private economy was encouraged. Surpluses of trade were sought and their proceeds skimmed off by the state to fill war chests for further expansion. Capitalist production relations ensued and the privatization of the extraction of surplus resources from society became a vehicle by which the state could harness private sphere activity in order to advance state capabilities. In the nationalist era, this division of labour expanded globally, as a byproduct of European economic *and* cultural imperialism. For the first time, however, the global social order witnessed the emergence of transnational economic interdependence. The colonial periphery became dependent upon western manufactures and cultural products, and the West was in turn dependent on access to raw materials in the periphery for the production of finished luxury goods, and for an outlet for western surplus labour.

Most significantly, the norms, rules and principles of intersocietal interaction (interstate and inter'national' relations) also developed in the practice of interaction. They are very much derived from the principles that legitimate the domestic and international social orders. Their development is mediated by the specific institutions that enshrine and reproduce these principles. In the text to follow, it will hopefully become clear that these institutions enshrine a particular form of sovereign-identity, derived from the principles of the prevailing social order that legitimate this form of sovereign identity. The behaviour of the institutional forms, which serve as an instrument by which societies may translate this identity into social action in the international system, is strongly conditioned by this identity.

Thus, when in 1555 the German princes are *de facto* emancipated from the heteronomous influence of the late medieval papacy, juridical anarchy ensues. Dynastic sovereign authority is legitimated no longer through the mediation, or the prop, of the legitimacy of a universal Church, but instead by the principle of the confessional and dynastic hegemony of the prince. The medieval feudal–theocratic order was transformed into a new system, which I call the dynastic–sovereign system, or *Augsburg system*. In 1648, when the conflictual results of the Augsburg system

---

[9] Gellner argues that an educated 'clerisy' provides a high culture through which legitimate social governance is effected, and through which the technical requirements of centralized social organization are derived. When the literacy and high culture of the clerisy is secularized and ultimately universally held, societal self-identification, in essence, derives from this culture which now pervades the entire society. 'That is the secret of nationalism' (Gellner 1983, p. 18).

were surveyed at the end of the Thirty Years War, confessional hegemony was abandoned as a legitimate organizing principle. Sovereign identity was enhanced by its further emancipation from all sacral notions of legitimacy. Dynastic legitimacy remained valid, but became circumscribed by the principle of territoriality. The emergence of territoriality as an innovative principle of social closure is of considerable interest. Problems of coordination of common objectives resulted in the development of games of coordination that blossomed into the foundations of an embryonic international law. This coordination process matured throughout the territorial–sovereign era.

The emergence of national collective identity transformed sovereign identity within the state. The notion that nations — national communities based upon common language, ethnicity, culture or shared history — are the legitimate wielders of the sword of state sovereignty has had causal significance for the norms, rules and principles of international as well as domestic society. The notion that the nation, however defined or segmented, is inherently sovereign and self-determining, transformed the legitimate purposes of state action. The conflict of competing national visions, many of which are housed in national-states bristling with arms, enhanced the urgency of coordination between national-states, providing impetus to the development of a more significant corpus of international law.

The discussion above provides a preliminary illustration of the manner in which historical transformations of societal collective identity ultimately result in the transformation of the international system. I have made a strong claim here. I have claimed that an essentially cognitive factor — the self-identification of social aggregates — has causal significance in effecting system change. I regard this to be so and state the case unambiguously. Let me say what I am *not* arguing. I do not argue that societal collective identity *determines*, of any necessity, the international system. Political structure exists. This structure constrains but does not determine the behaviour of social actors and aggregates. Material factors such as geography and technology also have systemic consequences. The present study recognizes these contributors to the constitution of historical international systems both implicitly and explicitly. The purpose of the present theoretical discussion is not to develop a monocausal theory of systems change by replacing material and structural variables with cognitive or ideational variables, but rather to illustrate that these cognitive factors have causal significance both for constituting the system and for explaining interaction within it. My purpose is to describe and explain a system that is dynamic rather than static. Change in the international system cannot be explained without recourse to the factors developed in these pages. If we do not consider the consequences of actor self-identification, we cannot apprehend either the nature or the consequences of national sovereignty or of the national state.

Having briefly elaborated these ideas connecting systemic change with changes in collective identity, the reader will now hope for a fuller elaboration of the interaction between these factors. I will therefore move to develop the concepts of individual and collective identity, legitimating principles, the institutional forms of collective action and the norms, rules and principles of interaction in an analysis intended to illuminate the manner in which changes in the former result in changes in the latter. In the terms of positivist discourse, I will 'causally link' these 'variables' to one another theoretically, then move on to a fuller empirical illustration of their operation in the generation and transformation of empirically observable international systems.

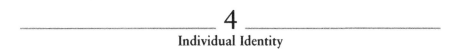

## 4
## Individual Identity

The self-identification of the individual (individual identity) is important in as much as it is in part defined in terms of the individual's participation in a collective identity. This collective identity is subject to change by forces and events that are both endogenous and exogenous to domestic society. I might, for example, develop German national collective identity merely because I feel a cultural and linguistic affiliation with my neighbours and subjects of other German-speaking states, in spite of the fact that my culture and language were transmitted to me by my experience of growing up in Prussia, whose borders I may never have left. This is an endogenous source of collective identity. I am a German-speaking Prussian. Conversely, I might develop German national collective identity because Napoleon's armies rolled over Saxony and the rest of German-speaking Europe, occupied my home town, raped my mother and shot my father, and it occurs to me to consider how this might have been prevented by the creation of a single political and military actor from all of the fragmented German-speaking states of early nineteenth-century Europe. The experience of suffering at the hands of those ethnically and linguistically different from me can affect how I view myself both as an individual, and as a member of a social collectivity. This is a societally exogenous source of collective identity. Thus, we can see that this collective identity locates the individual's identity both with respect to other actors, and with respect to the global order.

Collective and individual identity are co-constituted. My individual identity acquires social significance only with reference to the identities of others, within both domestic and international society. If for example I say that I am a German-speaking Prussian (in the nineteenth century), I am also saying that I am a subject of the Hohenzollern dynasty, and that I regard the crowned scion of that dynasty as sovereign (in possession of legitimate authority) and thus as a source of legitimate domestic law. When I say that I am a German-speaking Prussian, I am also saying that I am not a German-speaking Bavarian; I do not regard King Ludwig as a legitimate source of my domestic law; he does not exercise legitimate authority over myself or my people. On the other hand, if I were simply to say that I am a German, then I am saying something else entirely about whom I believe myself to be, and about what I regard to be a legitimate source of authority. If your language and ethnicity is Czech, for example, and not German, I am also saying something about you. I am saying that you are not part of 'us': you are 'other'.

Both Friedrich Kratochwil and William Bloom have helped to illuminate the relationship between individual identity and collective identity in their analyses of the sociology of Durkheim. Kratochwil stresses Durkheim's investigation of the emotive content of social life. In Kratochwil's analysis, which draws here upon Freud, identity is obtained with reference to the structure of relations of individual desires with respect to cherished persons and institutions ('love objects'), and conversely with respect to persons and institutions that become 'objects of aggression'

(Kratochwil 1989, p. 126). In other words, one identifies with those and with that which one loves and cherishes, which are familiar and comfortable; we do not develop strong feelings for individuals and things with which we are unfamiliar; that which threatens our objects of affection, or our relationship with them, becomes an object of our aggression.

Bloom links individual identity to collective identity by invoking Durkheim's notion of 'collective consciousness' which, in Durkheim's sociology, creates what he calls 'organic solidarity . . . [among] . . . dissimilar individuals' (Bloom 1940, pp. 14 ff.). The non-emotive link between personal identity and collective identity in Durkheim is, in other words, provided through the process of the socialization of the individual into the behavioural norms of her society. Aided by Erik Erikson's developmental psychology of identity formation, Bloom recognizes that Durkheim's linkage of personal identity to collective identity through the socialization process may have enormous emotive content as well. Nevertheless, he stresses socialization because '[t]heoretically . . . socialization is the precise point at which the individual meets society, at which psychology meets sociology' (Bloom 1940, p. 15).

Put differently, socialization is a process by which we become familiar with and habituated to people, places, environments and institutions, and the modes of operation and rules of the latter. Socialization is not, in this context, a remorseless selection mechanism through which successful societal socializers are selected for survival by imitating successful behaviour.[10]

This discussion of individual identity has, then, led us to three theoretically pertinent observations. (1) Socialization, in the context of identity formation, is a process by which the individual is habituated to her society, forms cognitive and emotive attachments to it, and incorporates its features and norms into her identity. (2) The individual's identity is not constituted independently of her membership in one or more social collectivities. (3) The individual forms and reforms identity commitments from experiences that result from forces both within and external to domestic society.

## 5
### Collective Identity

Through emotive identification (emotional attachment) and the forces of socialization, our individual identity — our ideas about whom we regard ourselves to be — are derived in a social context. Individual identity and collective identity are co-constituted. The individual possesses social agency. He is self-regarding, but is constrained by his nature as a social organism to self-identification with social collectivities. In the literature on developmental psychology, this self-identification with respect to others begins at the earliest stages of development of the human being and continues throughout much of his life (see e.g. Erikson 1968).

---

[10] This is Waltz's development of the term and of the concept of socialization in the context of international interaction. In this view, in the international arena, socialization functions only as a structural constraint on the behaviour of international actors (see Waltz 1979, pp. 74–7).

Durkheim's intuitive theoretical construct of the 'organic solidarity of dissimilar individuals' is given a fuller theoretical form, and receives empirical affirmation, in the literature on social psychology. This is particularly so in the literature on in-group bias.[11] These biases help centre the individual with respect to others in the world. They help the individual to order and organize his understanding of the world, and to enhance the individual's self-esteem by his identification with the group. But the question of how this group identification becomes an impetus to social action remains. We have explained why the individual forms identity commitments to social groupings and the processes involved. We have explored the nature of the collective identity that helps to constitute individual identity. We have not, however, addressed the issue of how these collective identities generate social action with respect to other groups, or with respect to members of another group.

Daniel Druckman addresses this issue in a recent analysis of the literature on in-group biases. He suggests:

Membership in a clan, religious group, or ethnic group becomes part of the individual's *self identity* and critical to a *sense of self-worth*. The self is threatened by information that calls into question the groups to which one belongs. People learn to react based on their loyalties; they defend those groups that are important to their definition of who they are. Moreover, these loyalties differentiate whom in their environment is appropriate to support and whom to avoid. And such loyalties can foster a *consensus among members* that becomes self-fulfilling and difficult to change. The stronger the loyalty, the more likely members of a group are to *hold similar views and endorse similar strategies. They approach the world in lockstep, perceiving and defining others in the world similarly. There is little, if any, chance for discrepant information to filter through or for reasons to change to be considered.* (Druckman 1994, pp. 49–50; emphasis added)

This passage nicely captures both the emotive and socialization mechanisms that Kratochwil and Bloom have identified in Durkheim. It also suggests that collective identity and individual identity are not merely co-constituted; they are mutually reinforcing and therefore likely to become institutionalized and to be reproduced. Collective identity carries with it the means by which it becomes institutionalized. This institutionalization mechanism is the will of the participants in a collective identity, that the identity be perpetuated. This *will-to-manifest-identity* is an artefact of the importance of the collective identity in the constitution of the individual identities of those who share it.

What is suggested by my assertion above is that, to the extent that collective identity has causal significance for the construction of social collectivities — which become actors in the international political arena — interest may be explained in terms of the aggregated *will-to-manifest-identity* as well as in terms of the will-to-power of the realist tradition. Individual identity is threatened by hazards to those collective identities that are constitutive of individual identity. Therefore the perception of the individual is that his or her interest lies squarely in the defence and promotion of this collective identity. The fundamental, even primordial, motive (or

[11] The most persuasive examples of this literature, to my reading, are Bion (1959); Volkan (1979, 1988); and the Group for the Advancement of Psychiatry (1987).

'interest') of self-preservation will then ensure that the individual will come fully to the defence of the collective identity that she sees as fundamentally constitutive of herself, when she feels that collective identity is threatened.

Significantly, however, it does not necessarily follow that the individual will invariably promote the aggrandizement of a collective identity that is constitutive of her individual identity under any and all circumstances. This is particularly so when the aggrandizement may threaten the collective identities of others, which the individual's reason suggests to her do not constitute a threat to her own (collective or individual) identity. The significance of this assertion is revealed by recourse to an analytic device that appears to be so essential to founding realist analysis of the interests of international actors. This is the domestic analogy. In this context, individuals in domestic society who will react, and often react violently, when threatened will nevertheless not necessarily exhibit reflexive belligerence to others in the absence of threat. Significantly, some individuals do reflexively behave aggressively, boastfully, deviously, wilfully or violently, even in the absence of threat. They must always be 'on top'. They must always have 'the last word'. Everyone must be made aware of their accomplishments, and of the insignificance of our own accomplishments in comparison. We regard them as obnoxious at best, socially psychopathic at worst, and we ostracize them from the company of polite society. Their personality disorders are seen as pathologies of inadequate socialization in the context of domestic society. In the international context, when social collectivities exhibit similar behaviour, they are 'cultural attributes'. In either the domestic or the international case, in the absence of threats to constitutive identity, the actor can either behave modestly and cooperatively, or immodestly or belligerently. There is a 'will-to-power' in some individuals in the domestic context, and not in others. So it is in the international context.

All social actors share the will-to-manifest-identity, however, in both international and domestic society. A physical threat of extermination is not required to threaten the will-to-manifest-identity in either domestic or international society. The will-to-manifest-identity may result in a new form of collectivity, a new form of sovereignty, legitimated in a new way. When this occurs, social transformation is in the wind. This can result in transformation of global social orders. When this occurs, the international system, while it may retain features of its previous manifestation, does not escape its own metamorphosis.

# 6

## Legitimating Principles

Collective identity is legitimated by the same principles that legitimate intrasocietal and intersocietal authority patterns. Collective identity is closely coupled to the legitimating principles within which it is constituted and interpreted. Social order is predicated on conceptions of legitimate authority, as it is too costly to maintain a social order on the basis of coercion alone. As Kratochwil has pointed out, the nature of legitimate authority cannot be understood with recourse to Hobbesian analysis and premises alone. The relationship between the 'sovereign' and the objects of authority is not one that leaves the sovereign in the state of nature with society. The disinterestedness of the authority cannot be assured under such circumstances, therefore 'no "contract", setting up a governmental authority would ever be possible' under these conditions (Kratochwil 1989, pp. 116–17).

Rather, as Habermas, Kratochwil and Weber all suggest in somewhat different contexts, the relationship between members of society and constituted public authority, is mediated by what Weber refers to as the concept of legitimate social order. It is this order to which members of society, the objects of authority, feel a sense of obligation or duty. As Weber intones,

> Action, especially social action which involves social relationships, may be oriented by the actors to a *belief* [*Vorstellung*] in the existence of a legitimate order. . . . orientation to the validity of an *order* [*Ordnung*] means more than the mere existence of a uniformity of social action determined by custom or self-interest. . . . such action in addition is determined by . . . [the individual's] . . . subjection to an order, [and] the rules which impose obligations on him, which he is usually careful to fulfill, partly because disobedience would carry disadvantageous consequences to him, but usually also in part because it would be abhorrent to the sense of duty, which, to a greater or lesser extent, is an absolute value to him. (Weber 1964, p. 124; emphasis in original)

Here Weber's analysis suggests unambiguously that, while there are good reasons from the perspective of instrumental rationality for the individual to comply with the injunctions that issue forth from legitimate authority, the act of compliance with these injunctions may not be said to have been explained without stricter analysis of motives for compliance. Certainly one good reason to comply with these injunctions is to avoid sanctions for non-compliance. A rational instrumental conception of interests can handily explain compliance with the directives even of illegitimate authority in this context. I must comply or I will be punished. The social actor acquires an interest in compliance with the injunctions and directives of legitimate authority because he values that authority. His own notions of a moral order in which his identity has meaning, and in which his compliance with the injunctions of the order takes on a moral character, are at issue when the question of compliance arises.

Similarly, Kratochwil's analysis uncovers Durkheim's distinction between material and moral authority in the context of the Durkheim analysis of 'social facts'. He discovers that moral authority (legitimacy) helps to establish the notion of obligations, and justifies the threat of physical sanctions for non-compliance.

> Durkheim maintains that certain social phenomena are best investigated by tracing their origin to a collective experience, and that there are significant analogies between the sacred and the moral. This last claim allows for a clearer conceptualization of obligation. Sanctions are then no longer simply the penalties attached to certain actions by the Hobbesian sovereign, who thereby changes the utility calculations of the individual. As Durkheim emphasizes again and again, the term 'moral authority' is 'opposed to material authority or physical supremacy. . . . moral facts expressed in rules of conduct are valid not because of threatened deprivations, but because of their duty-imposing character, which is in turn the precondition for the legitimacy of physical sanctions' (Kratochwil 1989, p. 124).

Thus, Kratochwil reminds us that physical (material) sanctions, and the material authority whose agency they manifest in a social context, are not legitimated solely by their role in mitigating anarchy by enforcing order. They are legitimated by the belief that compliance with them is a moral act, the fulfilment of an obligation to a moral (legitimate) social order. People comply because they wish to comply in order to fulfil an obligation to the order which they value as legitimate. The threat of physical sanctions is extended to the minority who have not apprehended this duty. No social order would be possible if the threat of physical sanctions alone stood in the way on non-compliance. It is not the existence of law, or of institutions dedicated to their enforcement, alone that ensures compliance with the strictures of the social order. As Helen Milner recently reminds us, regarding the questions of compliance with international law and the strictures of its institutions,

> It seems not to be their existence that matters, but their capacity for commanding obedience. This capacity depends much on their perceived legitimacy, as it does for domestic institutions. These institutions will have little influence internationally or domestically if they lack legitimacy . . . A sense of legitimacy is essential to the maintenance of any order. (Milner 1991, p. 74)

But notions of moral or legitimate social order are not static. They change over time. The analysis above helps us to understand how legitimate social order is upheld and reproduced, even in the absence of material or physical sanctions, or just the threat of them. It is not so helpful in explaining how notions of legitimate social order decay, become transformed and are replaced. We need a framework of analysis that addresses the dynamic nature of societal notions of the legitimacy of social ordering principles.[12] Why do notions of the legitimacy of the social order change? How do changes in collective identity transform the legitimating principles of social order, and thus generate a new order? I turn to the work of Habermas to establish further the link between specifically *collective* identity and the legitimating principles of social orders.

Significantly, Bloom observes that Habermas comes at the notion of identity from the epistemological perspective of philosophy rather than psychology (or sociology). For Habermas, the unravelling of the mysteries of identity and identification is a major task of philosophy. He argues that it is through the 'self-reflective symbolism of identity' that both the individual and society attempt meaningfully to locate themselves in their profane (material) and cosmic (transcendent) environments (Bloom 1990, p. 47). Habermas proposes that this is accomplished by the individual or collective social actor with recourse to an 'identity-securing interpretive system' (a system of beliefs about self-identity and social function in a legitimate social order). If this identity-securing interpretive system generally conforms to the experience of the social actor of the 'realities of social existence', the social order is legitimated. But

> if there is not an appropriate symbolic mediation . . . between the individual or the group and the social structure, the anxious need for a secure and meaningful identification will manifest itself in either the change of the interpretive system [a new ideology of legitimate social order] or a demand for change in the social structure. If the interests inherent in identification are not met, then the system is not legitimated. (Bloom 1990, pp. 47–8)

---

[12] These social ordering principles are not to be confused with Waltz's systemic 'ordering principle' of anarchy (Waltz 1979).

This is the 'legitimation crisis' upon which, in the view of Habermas, social orders rise and founder. Crucially important to my argument is Habermas's assertion that it is threats to social identity that bring about these legitimation crises. In my own view, these threats result in the transformation of the legitimating principles upon which social orders rest. As Habermas observes,

> Only when members of a society experience structural alterations as critical for continued existence and feel their social identity threatened can we speak of a crisis . . . Crisis states assume the form of a disintegration of social institutions.
>
> Social systems too have identities and can lose them; historians are capable of differentiating between revolutionary changes of a state or the downfall of an empire, and mere structural alterations. In doing so, they refer to the interpretations that members of a system use in identifying one another as belonging to the same group, and *through this group identity assert their own self-identity*. In historiography, *a rupture in tradition, through which the interpretive systems that guarantee identity lose their social integrative power, serves as an indicator of the collapse of social systems*. From this perspective *a social system has lost its identity as soon as later generations no longer recognize themselves within the once-constitutive tradition*. (Habermas 1975, pp. 3–4, quoted in Bloom 1990, p. 48; emphases added)

Hopefully it is not too ambitious a goal to propose that international relations theorists should be as capable as historians of differentiating between these different macro-level social phenomena. Habermas's discussion above provides a plausible linkage between the ideologies that legitimate a social belief system and the principles of social action by which members of a society are socialized into this belief system. The belief system, or 'interpretive system', links individual identity and a collective identity in a context in which meaning is granted to individual identity through its ideological subsumption in a collective. This provides the individual with a 'transcendent' identity in as much as the collective will transcend the individual. *The principles that legitimate the collective identity are the principles that legitimate the social order that provides a social meaning to collective identity*. These principles are institutionally reproduced and transmitted to the individual through his socialization into the society that is generated and regulated by this system of beliefs.

As Habermas observes, 'ruptures' in this institutionally transmitted tradition occur when the interpretive system (ideology of identity) that legitimates social order, and gives meaning to collective identity, is challenged. The challenge deprives the interpretive system of its utility in locating individual identity in the social milieu. It does so by challenging the validity or legitimacy of the collective identity that is constitutive of individual identity. This challenge can arise from sources that are either endogenous or exogenous to domestic society. It often involves the creation of what Kratochwil refers to as new 'institutional facts' (Kratochwil 1988, pp. 270–2).

It can also result from various discontinuities with tradition, specifically, discontinuities in 'community', in 'society' and in 'authority', particularly if these occur

---

[13] For the role of social change, especially rapid social change, in evoking mass societal transformation in conceptions of legitimate social order see Kornhauser (1959). For a related discussion in the context of developing societies, see Huntington (1968, esp. chs. 1–3).

rapidly so as to induce the discomfort of disorientation in the individual and in society.[13] Discontinuities in community, society and authority can involve urbanization and industrialization, war and/or economic deprivation, and collapse of political regime, respectively. All of these social discontinuities, however, can have sources that are exogenous to domestic society. All can result in transformation in the orientation of a polity with respect to international society.

Most important, however, is the observation that the social order's survival is crucially dependent upon the consent given to its legitimating principles by social actors. The social order must continue to provide an institutional framework for social action that is consistent with the dominant forms of societal collective identity. *Neither legitimating principles nor social orders can survive change in the other without being transformed.* Thus, the agency of collective actors is found in their tendency to express their collective identity through institutional forms that are consistent with that identity. These institutional forms must also be amenable to the social action that is characteristic of a particular form of collective identity. They enshrine the principles that legitimate these identities. Agents of the societies whose principles these institutional forms represent take social action that is impelled by 'interests' that are defined in terms of the *will-to-power* only to the extent that this social action promotes the *will-to-manifest-identity* that is enshrined in the legitimating principles and institutions of the new social order.

# 7
## Institutional Forms of Collective Action

The next variable in the first column of Figure 1, the institutional forms of collective action (kingdom/realm, state, nation, etc.), are the institutional artefacts of societal relations and authority patterns. I have suggested above that this authority is constructed from the prevailing collective self-identifications and self-understandings, and from the principles that legitimate them. Importantly, these institutional forms are constituted with, and by, prevailing conceptions of legitimate collective identity. *They are not fundamental. They are not theoretically or ontologically primitive. They are not enduring.* They change with the prevailing conceptions of legitimate social order and with the collective identities consistent with that order. This observation calls into serious question the utility of state-centric theories precisely because the state is merely one of many possible and historically observed institutional forms of collective action.

It is not by accident that social revolutions within domestic society result in immediate transformation of domestic political institutions that are deemed constitutive of the despised regime that has been supplanted. The destruction of the institutions of the *ancien régime* in this context is a wilful and public act of nullification of the principles that legitimated the social order that spawned these institutions. The first act of the French National Assembly, upon learning of the plans of Louis XVI to restore absolutist rule in France with the assistance of foreign armed force, was radically to assert the collective identity of the sovereign people of France by destroying the institution of the monarchy. In this case, this was most effectively accomplished by the physical destruction of the incarnation of that institution,

Louis. The American Revolution replaced a parliament with a congress, a king with a president, an aristocracy with a bureaucracy. The Bolshevik revolution similarly replaced a monarch with a politburo, a *duma* with soviets, the Okhrana with the Chekists (see e.g. Ulam 1965). When the Soviet Union gave up the ghost, the entire political structure studied by Western scholars and intelligence analysts, 'Kremlinologists', diplomats and journalists for decades came down with a thud in an instant, like a bulldozed segment of the Berlin wall.

The fact that these institutions have been variously replaced by institutions modelled on those of liberal Western states, or very often by nothing at all, reflects the ambiguity with which the successor states of the Soviet Union have addressed the task of defining and articulating the principles of the new social order, especially in Russia. But this does not attenuate the force of the reality of the destruction of the old institutions that had been identified with the old regime. Two of the most discredited of these institutions, the KGB and Red Army, have suffered the most. The former was almost entirely demolished, particularly with regard to its domestic surveillance function; the latter has been allowed to starve for lack of resources to the point of evident ineffectiveness (see e.g. Lambeth 1995). This outcome is as inexplicable within the confines of neo-realist analysis as was the collapse of the Soviet state and its Eastern European compatriots.[14] When we realize how closely these institutions of state security are associated with the *ancien régime* in Russia, the rationale behind their neglect and demise becomes not only clear but familiar, in spite of the loss of the security functions that they provided.

Significantly, Theda Skocpol, in her influential treatment of social revolution, *defines* social revolutions as 'rapid, basic transformations of a society's state [institutional] *and class* structures' (Skocpol 1985, p. 4; emphasis added). I will pause here to briefly analyse Skocpol's notion of social revolution in order to illuminate the distinction between this concept and transformation in a social order.

First, Skocpol analyses what is really a very much more circumscribed phenomenon than transformation of a global social order. She analyses social revolution in a domestic context while the social orders that interest us transcend state boundaries. Yet, importantly, she delineates between social revolutions and political revolutions in the domestic context, and we should do no less in a broader context. While political revolutions can simply result in a change of personnel within a constant institutional context, or can even go so far as a change in personnel and institutional transformation, social revolutions are accompanied by 'transformations of class relations' (Skocpol 1985, p. 5):

> In contrast, rebellions, even when successful, may involve the revolt of subordinate classes — but they do not eventuate in structural change. Political revolutions transform state structures but not social structures, and they are not necessarily accomplished through class conflict ... What is unique to social revolution is that basic changes in social structure and in political structure occur together in mutually reinforcing fashion. And these changes occur through intense sociopolitical conflicts in which class struggles play a key role. (Skocpol 1985, pp. 4–5)

---

[14] For novel attempts to explain these transformations with a theoretical framework outside the realist tradition, see Koslowski and Kratochwil (1994), and Kuran (1991).

Skocpol's structural Marxian heritage appears to constrain her to talk for ever about 'structures' and to muddle through the various determinisms that this mode of analysis throws in her path. Yet her distinction between social and political revolution in the domestic context is useful to the extent that it demonstrates that social transformations involving the ascendancy of one socio-economic class over and in place of another, in additional to transformations of political institutions, are more fundamental than mere institutional transformation. This distinction will be essential in understanding the radical distinction between the institutional forms of the territorial state and the nation-state. Not only was the territorial state constructed from institutions such as monarchy that the nation-state has dispensed with, it represented the interests of a fundamentally different class actor than does the contemporary nation-state. It is legitimated by different principles, and these principles articulate distinctly different class interests.

# 8

## Norms, Rules and Principles

The norms, rules and principles for intrasocietal and intersocietal relations are developed, in practice, by newly constituted social actors within and between societies, and always by interaction. These norms, rules and principles take forms that foster interaction among the prevailing institutional forms of collective action. They are distinct from, but derived from, the legitimating principles of these collective self-understandings. As they develop in practice, I will defer further discussion of them until later, when their development and causal significance for the patterns of politics between the 'units' of the three historical systems depicted in Figure 1 will be developed in the course of an empirical analysis of these systems.

In the preceding pages, I have outlined the principles by which the units are constituted and interact, and said that the result is a 'system'. This system is not static. Definition of its 'structure' alone does not serve to tell us how the units interact, nor does it say much about the probable outcomes of interaction.[15] The system may be transformed as well as reproduced. The system's 'structural form' is mediated as much by the interests of relevant social actors defined in terms of the will-to-manifest-identity as it is defined in terms of the will-to-power.

Figure 1 outlines the manner in which I regard changes in these variables in Western European history as having resulted in changes from the Augsburg system, which effectively sprang from the Reformation, and ended the medieval feudal–theocratic order, to the Westphalian system, which legally ended the wars that were one long-term result of the Reformation, to the present nation-state system, which followed the age of nationalism. Systems reproduce themselves so long as the institutional forms of collective action are capable of providing modalities of social action for the expression of societal collective identity. Systems are transformed

---

[15] This assertion stands in opposition to the assertions of Waltz (1979, p. 79) that an international system may be described fully by designating systemic structure, units, and interaction between these units.

when they begin to serve as structural impediments to the social action and as self-conceptions of both domestic and international social actors, and as the principles that legitimate these self-understandings. The norms, rules and principles by which the system functions are transformed, through subsequent practice, to regulate social action in accordance with the new legitimating principles of the new social order.

The above discussion has been intended to provide a causal linkage between the variables in Figure 1, which I argue change to produce change in the international system. Little space was devoted to the norms, rules and principles of interaction within these systems, in large measure because these develop in practice, through regularized interaction between social actors and institutions.

## 9

### Sequencing: Agents and Objects of Systemic Transformation

One topic of theoretical relevance that I have so far left untreated is the question of the sequencing of the changes in the factors of variables of systemic transformation that I have linked causally in the preceding discussion. Must collective identity change within a given society or within all societies before the system changes? Can the converse be true? Can the system change and thus force changes in societal collective identity upon some members of international society? Do changes in collective identity at the level of domestic society result in changes in the rules of the international system, or is the converse the case? The answer, I believe, is actor-specific. It depends upon whether a given international actor is an agent of systemic transformation or an object of systemic transformation, constrained to respond to the agency of others.

I believe that evidence may be presented that the causal sequencing of the variables I have sketched in Figure 1 may work both ways, under specific conditions. As I suggested earlier, it does not appear to be the case that changes in collective identity must precede changes in the legitimating principles of the social order within which the collective identities have meaning. It is not clearly necessary for collective identities and legitimating principles to change first in order to evoke changes in the institutional forms of collective action; it would seem that the reverse sequencing can easily occur, under certain conditions. It is important to stress, however, that a given form of societal collective identity, a given legitimating principle for a global social order and a given institutional form (which manifests that collective identity to other societies) must prevail and must be held in common by the recognized actors in the system for a system to be constituted, or to be transformed from a prior configuration of these variables. The legitimating principles of a social order privilege some institutional forms, and not others.

Once constituted, a given system can provide, as neo-realist scholarship suggests in more Darwinian terms (see Waltz 1979, pp. 74–7, 127–8), enormous incentives for a given society to reconstitute itself in conformity with the privileged institutional forms, and for its members to mould their identities and societal legitimating principles into collective identities and legitimating principles that are similarly privileged by these forms. Thus, in the age of nationalism, for example, societies organized along traditional, tribal or otherwise distinctly non-national forms, perhaps impelled by the norms, rules and principles of the national–sovereign state system not only to construct states to provide rational bureaucratic agencies of their collective identity as an actor in the system, but also to construct nationalist movements and myths to legitimate their participation (see Conner 1992). Thus, many societies that have suffered from the experience of European colonialism have set upon nation-building projects in order to construct national collective identities that will legitimate the institutional forms of collective action that they have acquired as a colonial legacy.[16] These projects have been taken on precisely because the self-identifications of former colonial peoples have been rather rudely transformed by the colonial experience. They have learned that colonial occupation and exploitation were the consequences of their failure to construct the rational bureaucratic organizational structures (states) that serve to manifest collective identity to other societies and ensure the maintenance of these identities (societal security). Having acquired states as institutional artefacts of the colonial experience, in the age of nationalism they have endeavoured to construct the collective identities that are required to legitimate, in both domestic and international society, the institutional forms of collective action that are privileged in the national–sovereign system. Those countries that have been successful have enjoyed relative societal cohesion and a more healthful atmosphere in which to focus societal energies on economic and technological development; those that have been less successful have seen their developmental aspirations thwarted by periodic outbreaks of conflict arising from ethnic, religious or linguistic divisions.

The above discussion emphasizes my assertion that *the development of national collective identity has both international and domestic (systemic and unit-level, in neo-realist parlance) sources*. National collective identity can develop from a very large number of domestic sources of that identity, and can then provide a new legitimating principle for a domestic social order. The new legitimating principles then require a new institutional form — leading to a new global social order and 'system' when aggregated with those of societies that have achieved a similar collective identity by their own path. Conversely, national collective identity can develop in response to what might amount to a structural condition. This condition entails the privileging of a specific institutional form of collective action, and therefore of specific legitimating principles of that institutional form. In shorthand,

$$\{\Delta \text{ collective identity} \rightarrow \Delta \text{ legitimating principles} \rightarrow \Delta \text{ institutions} \rightarrow \Delta \text{ domestic } \& \text{ international norms/rules/principles} \rightarrow \Delta \text{ system}\}$$

(Sequence 1)

or, conversely, under different conditions,

$$\{\Delta \text{ system} \rightarrow \Delta \text{ domestic } \& \text{ international norms/rules/principles} \rightarrow \Delta \text{ institutions} \rightarrow \Delta \text{ legitimating principles} \rightarrow \Delta \text{ collective identity}\}$$

(Sequence 2)

---

[16] Robert Jackson (1987) argues that post-colonial states in the Third World have retained state-structures and juridical sovereignty left them by departing Europeans for precisely this reason.

The sequencing of this transformational logic, for a given society that is *en route* to a change in collective identity, depends strongly upon (1) whether that society is experiencing transformations in domestic relations (irrespective of whether the source of this transformation is exogenous to that society) and (2) whether that society is in a position to make its agency felt throughout international society. The second of these criteria is, of course, fertile ground for bringing the structural variables of classical and neo-realism (such as the distribution of capabilities across the system) into the analysis, with the caveat that we must expand what counts as a capability to include, at a minimum, cultural resources.

In any event, societies that experience rapid and/or far-reaching transformations in domestic relations, and who are well positioned to exert influence on other societies, tend to follow sequence 1: they constitute *agents* of systemic transformation. Societies that are domestically socially conservative or stagnant tend to reproduce their social structure and institutions domestically and — to the extent that they are in a position to exert influence on other societies — to reproduce international systemic structure as well. If these domestically socially conservative societies are poorly positioned to exert influence on other societies, they tend to follow sequence 2: they become *objects* of systemic transformation. The agency of those who follow sequence 1 creates a systemic transformation, whose influential norms and rules the subject society cannot avoid.

To the extent that the norms and rules of the international system privilege an institutional form that is at variance with the institutional form of collective action of the target society, the latter experiences powerful incentives to replicate the privileged institutional forms, their legitimating principles and associated collective identities. These traditional societies find themselves under siege by the agency of the system-transforming societies, irrespective of the form these traditions take. This is so precisely because the legitimating principles of the traditional social orders are challenged when their institutional forms cannot replicate the success (the agency, felt throughout the system) of the system-transforming societies. In both of these sequences, societies encounter the transience of institutional facts. In the first sequence societies are impelled to create new institutions; in the second they are required to adapt to new institutional facts. The forms that these adaptations take encompass, but are not exhausted by, the structural neo-realist concept of socialization of these actors by the structure *qua* agency of the international system.[17]

# 10
## Conclusion

In this paper I have outlined a theoretical framework for the analysis of systemic transformation with changes in societal collective identity. I have provided an analysis of the causal linkages between the elements of this theoretical framework and have suggested the reasons why changes in these elements or variables result in a change in systems. In my doctoral dissertation (Hall 1996) and a forthcoming book derived from it (Hall 1999), I have proceeded from a similar point to operationalize these

---

[17] For a discussion of structure as a causal agency, see Waltz (1979, pp. 73–4).

variables with a discussion of collective identity and (1) early–modern dynastic sovereignty, (2) territorial sovereignty and (3) national sovereignty. I have applied this theoretical formulation to an extended analysis of the consequences of the change from territorial–sovereign legitimating principles to national–sovereign legitimating principles for the behaviour of state actors and for transformation of the international system. Societal self-identification is demonstrated to have had causal significance for the state identities and interests in the transition from what I call 'territorial–sovereign' identity, which arose at the Westphalian settlement of the Thirty Years War, to the 'national-sovereign' identity, which had manifested itself in Europe by the late nineteenth century. State interests and behaviour emerge from this analysis as variable products of the evolution of societal collective identity. The emergence of national–sovereign identity has brought significant changes in the behaviour of nineteenth and twentieth-century national–sovereign nation-states relative to the behaviour of the territorial–sovereign states of the eighteenth century. The behavioural differences are explained as manifestations of the transformation of the historically contingent notions of interest which derive from the distinct sovereign identities that emerge between the two periods. Whether the international system is moving towards globalism or regionalism, we would do well to recall the contribution of the emergence of nationalism to its present and very-changing structure.

## References

Almond, G. (1988), 'The Return to the State', *American Political Science Review*, 82(3): 853–74.

Anderson, B. (1983), *Imagined Communities: Reflections on the Origins and Spread of Nationalism*, London: Verso.

Aron, R. (1966), *Peace and War: A Theory of International Relations*, New York: Praeger.

Bion, W. R. (1959), *Experiences in Groups*, New York: Basic Books.

Bloom, W. (1990), *Personal Identity, National Identity and International Relations*, Cambridge: Cambridge University Press.

Buzan, B., Little, R. and Jones, C. (1993), *The Logic of Anarchy*, New York: Columbia University Press.

Conner, W. (1992), 'The Nation and its Myth', *International Journal of Comparative Sociology*, 33: 48–57.

Dessler, D. (1989), 'What is at Stake in the Agent-Structure Debate?' *International Organization*, 43 (Summer): 441–74.

Druckman, D. (1994), 'Nationalism, Patriotism and Group Loyalty: A Social Psychological Perspective', *Mershon International Studies Review*, supplement to *International Studies Quarterly*, 38, suppl. 1 (April): 43–66.

Erikson, E. H. (1968), *Identity: Youth and Crisis*, New York: W. W. Norton.

Gellner, E. (1983), *Nations and Nationalism*, Ithaca: Cornell University Press.

Group for the Advancement of Psychiatry (1987), *Us and Them: The Psychology of Ethnonationalism*, Report no. 123, New York: Brunner/Mazel.

Habermas, J. (1975), *Legitimation Crisis*, Boston: Beacon Press.

Hall, R. B. (1996), *Territorial and National Sovereigns: National Collective Identity and the Transformation of the International System*, PhD dissertation, University of Pennsylvania.

Hall, R. B. (1999), *National Collective Identity; Social Constructs and International Systems*, New York: Columbia University Press.

Himmelstein, J. L. and Kimmel, M. (1981), 'States and Social Revolutions: The Limits and Implications of Skocpol's Structural Mode', *American Journal of Sociology*, 86(5): 1145–54.

Huntington, S. (1968), *Political Order in Changing Societies*, New Haven: Yale University Press.

Jackson, R. (1987), 'Quasi-states, Dual Regimes, and Neoclassical Theory: International Jurisprudence and the Third World', *International Organization*, 41(4): 519–50.

Kornhauser, W. (1959), *The Politics of Mass Society*, New York: Free Press.

Koslowski, R. and Kratochwil, F. V. (1994), 'Understanding Change in International Politics: the Soviet Empire's Demise and the International System', *International Organization*, 48(2): 215–47.

Krasner, S. D. (1983), 'Structural Causes and Regime Consequences', in S. D. Krasner (ed.), *International Regimes*, Ithaca: Cornell University Press, pp. 1–21.

Krasner, S. D. (1984), 'Approaches to the State: Alternative Conceptions and Historical Dynamics', *Comparative Politics*, 19(2): 233–46.

Kratochwil, F. (1988), 'Regimes, Interpretation and the "Science" of Politics: A Reappraisal', *Millennium*, 17(2): 263–84.

Kratochwil, F. V. (1989), *Rules, Norms, and Decisions: On the Conditions of Practical and Legal Reasoning in International Relations and Domestic Affairs*, Cambridge: Cambridge University Press.

Kuran, T. (1991), 'Now Out of Never; The Element of Surprise in the Eastern European Revolution of 1989', *World Politics*, 44(1): 7–48.

Lambeth, B. S. (1995), 'Russia's Wounded Military', *Foreign Affairs*, 74(2): 86–98.

Lapid, Y. and Kratochwil, F. (1994), 'The Taming of the Shrew? Neorealist Appropriations and Theorizations of Nationalism', paper presented at the 35th ISA Annual Convention, Washington DC, March 1994; revised in Y. Lapid and F. Kratochwil, 'Revisiting the "National": Toward an Identity Agenda in Neorealism?' in Y. Lapid and F. Kratochwil (eds.), *The Return of Culture and Identity in IR Theory*, Boulder, Colo.: Lynne Rienner, 1995, pp. 105–26.

Mann, M. (1993), *The Sources of Social Power*, vol. 2, *The Rise of Classes and Nation-States, 1760–1914*, New York: Cambridge University Press.

Milner, H. (1991), 'The Assumption of Anarchy in International Relations Theory: A Critique', *Review of International Studies*, 17: 67–85.

Mitchell, T. (1991), 'The Limits of the State: Beyond Statist Approaches and their Critics', *American Political Science Review*, 85(1): 77–96.

Skocpol, T. (1979), *States and Social Revolutions*, New York: Cambridge University Press.

Skocpol, T. (1985), 'Bringing the State Back In: Strategies of Analysis in Current Research', in Evans, Rueschemeyer and T. Skocpol (eds.), *Bringing the State Back In*, New York: Cambridge University Press, pp. 3–37.

Smith, A. D. (1991), *National Identity*, Reno: University of Nevada Press.

Ulam, A. B. (1965), *The Intellectual, Personal and Political History of the Triumph of Communism in Russia*, New York: Collier Books.

Volkan, V. D. (1979), *Cyprus, War and Adaptation: A Psychoanalytic History of Two Ethnic Groups in Conflict*, Charlottesville: University Press of Virginia.

Volkan, V. D. (1988), *The Need to Have Enemies and Allies*, Northvale: Jason Aronsin.

Waltz, K. N. (1979), *Theory of International Relations*, New York: Random House.

Weber, M. (1964), *The Theory of Social and Economic Organization*, trans. A. M. Henderson and T. Parsons, ed. with an introduction by T. Parsons, London: Free Press of Glencoe/Collier-Macmillan.

Wendt, A. (1987), 'The Agent-Structure Problem in International Relations Theory', *International Organization*, 41(3): 335–70.

Wendt, A. (1994), 'Collective Identity and the International State', *American Political Science Review*, 88(2): 384–96.

# 4

# CHALLENGES OF AND RESPONSES TO GLOBALIZATION

## THE CASE OF SOUTH-EAST ASIA

### Prasert Chittiwatanapong

## 1
### Introduction

Like the challenge of modernization a century ago, the globalization challenge has been transforming societies in the developing world into something more closely resembling those of the West. And, like the modernization challenge, the future of these societies will be shaped largely by the way they respond to this challenge. Unlike the era of modernization, however, military force is not being used. Without the need for military force, less developed societies have been opened up to freer flows of information, goods and services, including values and cultures, from the centres of the globalization process. South-east Asia is worth our attention because this region is under the influence of multiple centres of globalization, or globalizers, namely, the West (particularly the United States), Japan and China. Countries in this region have faced such challenges by strengthening their regional organization, ASEAN, which was created during the height of great-power rivalry over influence in the area in 1967.

Calls for a greater awareness of globalization have been made by many scholars of international communication and management. The names of Alvin Toffler, John Naisbitt, Michael Hammer, Peter Drucker, Bill Gates and Omae Kenichi are known worldwide. Many of their works have been translated into various languages. Their writings have contributed to a number of popular terms such as the Third Wave, the Borderless World, the Computer Age, the Telecommunication Age, the Information Superhighway and Post-modernism. These ideologues have led us to believe that globalization is creating a great turning point in the history of mankind; and that, with the arrival of space communication, the world will be borderless.

However, none of these writers paid enough attention to the responses to globalization from the weaker societies. None of them brought up the viewpoints made by critics of globalization, or suggested how weaker societies might cope with the increasing influence from the centres of globalization.

## Definition

Globalization is defined here as the freer flows at global level of information, goods, services, capital, technology, values and cultures, including social problems like pollution and AIDS.[1] Of these, information flows much more freely, more quickly and in much greater quantity than the others. This is due to great scientific progress made in the field of information technology (IT). Goods and services also flow more freely and in greater quantity than before, thanks to the progress made in international trade negotiations. Entertainment goods such as movies, songs and fashion flow more freely and in greater quantity as well, owing to the IT revolution and success in market-opening negotiations. Values and cultures also flow more freely and in a similar way, though they are less tangible and complex. Some of these values take the form of human rights and democracy, while some take the form of oriental values depending on where the sources are.

The word 'globalization' carries a specific emphasis on the nature of the dismantling of barriers to the flows of information, goods, services, capital, technology, values and cultures. The emergence of a 'borderless world' has become possible because of scientific revolutions in the fields of information and telecommunications. Globalization is thus different from internationalization, because the latter term carries no emphasis on the disappearance of national barriers.

Globalization is comparable to modernization in the sense that it poses challenges to weaker societies. These nations are compelled not only to open their markets, but also to adjust their societies accordingly. The resulting social transformation in these societies is indeed exiting to see and to compare with the process of social transformation in the era of modernization.[2]

## Objective of the Paper

Globalization is a complex process of societal transformation. As such, it is one of the most difficult subjects to analyse. This paper has the modest objective of diagnosing globalization and discussing responses to the challenges, taking South-east Asia as a case study. It should be pointed out that it was only in the early 1990s that globalization trends began to take shape as a result of several emerging favourable conditions. It is thus a bit early to discuss and analyse this complex subject. I shall start off by making a general diagnosis about globalization.

---

[1] One recently published book defined globalization as 'the spread of capital at a global scale'. Another defined it as 'the linkage of trade, investment, finance and services at a global scale'. See these two contrasting definitions of globalization in two best-seller books (in Thai): Thongchai Wongchaisuwan (1994, p. 6) and Somchai Phakaphasvivat (1995, p. 24). Because of their differences in definition, the two works present different analyses of the problems Thailand was facing and different suggestions of how to deal with globalization.

[2] One leading scholar in South-east Asia, Chai-anan Samudavanija, pointed out that the crucial difference of modernization, internationalization and globalization is the differing contexts under which the three processes emerged. Modernization occurred under colonialism, while internationalization occurred under the Cold War. In the globalization era, however, there was no threat to use military forces, nor any ideological domination. See Chai-anan Samudavanija (1996).

## 2

### A General Diagnosis

### *Factors of Globalization*

Factors contributing to the expansion of globalization include the revolution in information technology, and success in trade liberalization talks at the GATT Uruguay Round and the end of the Cold War. In the early 1990s, these three factors greatly contributed to freer flows in the quantity of information, goods, services, capital, technology, values and cultures. Other contributing factors may have included progress made in transportation technology, printing technology and materials technology. Of all these factors, the most important is definitely the IT revolution. Computers, facsimile (fax) machines, mobile telephones, satellite communications, the Internet and the Worldwide Web are just some of the products of this great revolution. The Gulf War, which broke out in January 1991, demonstrated vividly the effect of globalization in terms of information flows and the value implications as to who is the good guy and who is the bad guy.

These four objects that flow more freely on a global scale are making our world increasingly borderless. Global problems like environmental pollution and AIDS have also contributed to increasing awareness of the arrival of the 'global village'. To solve problems of pollution, AIDS and other global issues, such as drug trafficking, terrorism, prostitution and refugees, requires enormous cooperative efforts among individual countries and international organizations.

### *Historical Perspective*

In this study, globalization is seen as an extension of modernization. Less developed societies have for centuries experienced flows on a global scale of information, goods, services, capital, technology, labour forces, values and cultures, all introduced to them, or forced upon them, by colonial and imperial powers. Countries that managed to escape colonization, such as Japan, Thailand and Turkey, made more conscious efforts to modernize. They decided to abolish and reform their traditional institutions and values in order to be accepted by Western powers.

Globalization differs from modernization in the sense that military force is not used in its promulgation; more importantly, there are multiple centres of globalization, rather than just that of the West. For South-east Asian countries, new globalization centres include Japan, China and, to some extent, the newly industrialized economies.

### *Centres of Globalization*

Weak societies cannot be sources of global-scale flows of information, goods, services capital, technology, values and cultures to stronger societies. The West, especially the United States, continues to be the most important source of globalization, but there are others as well. This complex and hierarchical nature is an important characteristic of globalization. Societies in South-east Asia thus face multiple flows of information, goods, services, capital, technology, values and cultures, from both West and East.

The United States is the most influential source of globalization. It has the most advanced information technology; more than half of the foreign news we consume flows from US media. The strongest competing centre is Japan. With its enormous economic power, Japan is the largest source of the flows of goods, services, capital and technology in the region, and is also becoming a strong source of entertainment goods, including comic books, films and computer games. China (including Hong Kong and Taiwan) is another rising centre. Apart from being a major source of goods, services, capital and technology, it is also a very influential source of entertainment goods; Chinese films find their largest market in South-east Asia, mainly comprising the sizeable audience of Chinese origin in Thailand and elsewhere. Nowadays Chinese-language education is being revived as China attracts an increasing number of visitors from South-east Asia. Chinese values and culture also flow into the region more freely. They take the form of traditional values and philosophy, rather than human rights and democracy. Korea is becoming a new centre, but its overall influence is still limited. It is however already a leading source of the flows of goods, services, capital and technology to Vietnam.

## Local Impact of Globalization

The freer flows of information, goods, services and other objects, including values and cultures, have enormous impact on local societies in South-east Asia. Generally speaking, the freer flows of information, etc., enrich the lives of people in these societies. Consumers of globalized information, goods and services generally believe they benefit from such globalization, because through it they have more choices.

One of the far-reaching impacts of globalization on local societies in South-east Asia is the expansion of Western values and cultures. In most countries now the teaching of English starts in the lower grades, and efforts at training English teachers are being intensified.[3] The popularization of English is accompanied by greater influence of Western higher education. An international study programme has become an increasingly popular undertaking at many universities in the region. This usually involves using English as a means of instruction, with Western academic practice as a standard.[4] Many programmes are jointly operated with universities in

---

[3] In Thailand, for example, the teaching of English at the primary education level now begins in first grade, rather than in fifth or sixth grades as previously.

[4] There are more than 100 international study programmes in Thailand starting from the level of BA to MA and Ph.D. and using English as a means of instruction. At Thammasat University there are six programmes, and at Chulalongkorn University there are five. This is part of the national government's fifteen-year plan of internationalizing higher education in Thailand. See *The Thai Manager*, Bangkok, 6 September 1976, p. 10 (in Thai).

the United States, Europe, Canada or Australia.[5] We can probably say that, in the field of education, globalization virtually means computerization plus Westernization.

The cultural influence of the United States has often been overlooked. Globalization has turned the American way of life into a more and more global one. Some people are conscious of its penetration into their societies, but most are not, assuming that it is not American but rather transnational.[6] The French are more sensitive than the Asians to the rapid influx of the American way of life. They are concerned about Hollywood films and the rapid spread of American fast food restaurant chains such as McDonald's, Mister Donut, Kentucky Fried Chicken.[6] The European aircraft industry finds it difficult to compete with Boeing, Lockheed, McDonnell Douglas, General Dynamics and others; but it is the American cultural impact that makes French people view globalization (Mondialization) with most suspicion.

Another impact of globalization on societies in South-east Asia is the dilution of nationalism. This works in the following ways. First, economic nationalism loses its rationale, the anti-Japan movement in Thailand criticizing 'Japan's economic domination', for example, has lost ground.[7] Second, the national identity campaign aimed at ethnic minorities is becoming more difficult to pursue. The identity with the globalization centres and with globalization itself tend to work against such campaigns. More and more, minority peoples are less willing to accept such an imposed 'national identity', and are coming to criticize past national identity campaigns, which humiliated their minority's identity and their individual dignity.[8] Finally, the role of the state in the overall national economic management has begun to decline. It is the multinational corporation, especially in the field of telecommunications and information technology, that wields global influence.

The final impact of globalization is the erosion of local identity and the plight of the rural population. Slowly, some villagers have begun to shed their local and even national identity and to assume a global identity instead. Information technology has linked villages more closely to the outside world. In a matter of seconds, they can get information about what is going on in New York, London, Paris, Frankfurt, Wimbledon and Tokyo. Globalization has also brought more investors, traders, machinery and capital into the villages. More importantly, it has provided a legitimacy

---

[5] For example, the MBA programme in English of the Sasin Graduate Institute of Business Administration at Chulalongkorn University is a joint academic endeavour with two academic institutions in the USA, the J. L. Kellogg Graduate School of Management of Northwestern University, and the Wharton School of the University of Pennsylvania.

[6] One noted scholar of American cultural diplomacy echoed this point very well when she wrote: 'Rock music, for example, is no longer "American" but also Japanese and Chinese; indeed it is a transcultural musical form'. See Rosenberg (1994, p. 19).

[7] There were five protests against 'Japan's economic domination', led by students in Thailand in 1972, 1983, 1984 and 1985. The trade deficit with Japan had been widely seen as the symbol of Japan's economic domination. There is no sign of protest or demonstration as the Thai trade deficit with Japan changes from worse to worst, from 94 per cent of total Thai trade deficit in 1993 to a predicted high of 142 per cent in 2000.

[8] Through globalized consumerism, the national identity imposed on the minority groups by national governments has increasingly lost its relevance. In the past, such imposition was easily carried out, but now the minority is 'liberated'; see Chaiwat Satha Anand (1996, pp. 83–127) (in Thai).

to both villagers and visitors to trade whatever they have. This local-level impact of globalization has been viewed with alarm by critiques of globalization. Not only the urban elite, but now even the rural masses are subjected to the penetration of globalization into their localities.[9]

# 3

## Responses to Globalization: Regionalism

It is difficult to answer the question of how South-east Asian countries deal with the challenges of globalization. The difficulty lies in the fact that the challenge is not simply a challenge from the West. As indicated earlier, there are multiple centres of globalization. There is also a variety of ways in which each country copes with the arrival of globalization. However, we have observed that there are three levels of response: regional, national and communitarian. In the ASEAN perspective, region-alism means joint efforts in dealing with centres of globalization and regional prob-lems, rather than efforts to create an ASEAN identity. One could say that, in the case of Europe, the identity of the EU has never been the focus of debate; or, if discussed at all, it is likely that it will be 'unity in diversity', not much different from the case of ASEAN.[10]

South-east Asian countries have resorted to ASEAN, a regional cooperation body that they created, to deal with the globalization challenge. This approach has proved to be very effective, since ASEAN is a widely recognized regional body. For smaller and weaker countries, there is only one effective approach to deal with stronger centres of globalization, and that is regionalism.[11] The end of the Cold War has provided a favourable environment for regionalism and ASEAN has made full use of it.

## *Membership Expansion*

ASEAN quickly moved to strengthen its organization by expanding its number of member-states. Vietnam became the seventh member at the ASEAN annual meeting in Brunei in 1995. With its inclusion under the ASEAN umbrella, conditions for stronger countries' power rivalry and hegemonic ambition in the region have been sharply reduced.

At its annual meeting in Indonesia in July 1996, ASEAN decided to invite Myanmar (formerly Burma) to participate in the ASEAN ministerial meeting (AMM) as an

---

[9] A professor of anthropology concluded from years of field research that, so long as decentral-ization of power, especially the power to manage local natural resources, is not actually carried out, there will be no solution to the increasing number of local problems brought about by globalization. See Ananda Kanjanaphun (1995, pp. 151–92).

[10] Interview with Dr Sukhum Rasmidatta, Director-General of the ASEAN Affairs Department, Ministry of Foreign Affairs of Thailand, at his office on 28 August 1996. From his experience as former Thai ambassador to Greece, he said he would disagree with any assertions implying that Greek civilization serves as a cultural basis for EU identity.

[11] Ibid.

observer. Myanmar has also become a member of the ASEAN Regional Forum (ARF), along with India. ASEAN wanted to grant Myanmar full membership status in 1997, despite continued criticism and calls for condemnation of the country from the European Union and some American congressmen because of the massive abuse of human rights of the SLORC (the State Law and Order Restoration Council, reorganized as the State Peace and Development Council (SPDC) in November 1997). Laos and Cambodia began receiving assistance from Thailand and other ASEAN member-states to become better prepared to join ASEAN; in September 1996, government officials from these two countries were invited to Bangkok to receive training about ASEAN technical matters, language (English) and various ASEAN procedures.[12] ASEAN celebrated its thirtieth anniversary in 1997 and it granted full membership to Laos and Myanmar in July 1997. Because of the forceful capture of political power by the second prime minister, Hun Sen, in the same month, ASEAN was unable to give full membership to Cambodia. However, in April 1999 Cambodia was granted full membership and the SEA-10, envisaged by the founding fathers of ASEAN in 1967, was ultimately realized. ASEAN is now a larger regional body than the EU and NAFTA with a population of 480 million.

## Establishment of AFTA

In order to strengthen their economic cooperation and make full use of economies of scale, ASEAN decided, at the ASEAN summit in Singapore in 1992, to create the ASEAN Free Trade Area (AFTA), to stimulate intraregional trade by lowering the tariff rate to not more than 5 per cent within fifteen years from January 1994. At the ASEAN Economic Ministerial Meeting (AEM) in Chiangmai in 1993, it was decided that the above target should be achieved within ten years, i.e. by 2003. (This target date was later brought forward.)

Regionalism has also been adopted as an approach to deal with globalization by certain centres of globalization. NAFTA and the EU are two such examples, but Japan, a very strong centre without any membership in regional bodies except for a loosely structured APEC, naturally feels alarmed. Japan feels increasingly concerned as the trends become more obvious when NAFTA and the EU, as well as ASEAN, keep expanding their membership and strengthening their integration. Policy-makers in Japan consistently call for 'open regionalism', 'constructive regionalism' and 'positive regionalism' lest non-member-states be discriminated against. Japan's economic policy-makers call for the principle of free trade and investment world-wide, while security policy-makers reject any idea of forming an Asia-only regional organization. This logic is easily understood when one considers Japan's position as a very strong centre of globalization.[13]

---

[12] Ibid.

[13] See the Policy Recommendations on 'The Future of Regionalism and Japan', drafted by Minoru Kobayashi, Jin Nakamura, Motoshige Ito and Kazuo Watanabe, and signed by Hisao Kanamori, Seizaburo Sato and 75 other members of the Policy Council of the Japan Forum on International Relations, Tokyo, June 1994, pp. 6–10.

## Initiating a Regional Security Dialogue Forum

ASEAN convened a regional security dialogue meeting called the ASEAN Regional Forum (ARF) at its annual meeting in Thailand in 1994. In addition to ASEAN member-states, China and Russia (now dialogue partners) joined to discuss security issues of common concern. At the ARF meeting in Jakarta in July 1996, India and Myanmar became new members, making ARF a forum of twenty-one countries. In ARF, all the great powers are represented and all regional security issues are discussed; for example, at the Jakarta meeting, the Korean peninsula problem was discussed at great length. ARF has become an ASEAN-led forum covering the entire Asia–Pacific region, not just South-east Asia alone. If North Korea and Mongolia are admitted, ARF will be a forum for both friends and enemies and for both superpowers and small states, which not many people realize. Britain and France have expressed their wishes to join as individual members in the ARF, even though they are already represented by the EU.

The main objective of ARF is 'mutual assurance' on security matters. As it has evolved during the past few years, there are now three working groups: on Confidence-Building Measures, Preventive Diplomacy, and Elaboration of Approaches to Conflict.[14] ARF allows input from academics and other non-government organizations, the so-called 'second track' consisting of security think-tanks in the Asia–Pacific region.[15] It remains to be seen if ARF can really play any role in conflict prevention, as there are regional flashpoints in the Korean peninsula and the South China Sea. There are also 'domestic issues' of international concern in Myanmar and China, including the issues of Tibet and Taiwan. At any rate, a forum for security dialogue has been initiated by ASEAN and some concrete achievements have been made. One of them is the publication for the first time of a defence White Paper in some countries such as Thailand, Indonesia and China. The real significance of ARF, however, is the efforts made to persuade conflict partners to commit to dialogue and, hopefully, self-restraint, rather than resorting to arms to settle their disputes.

ASEAN's dialogue partners automatically participate in the ARF. At the Jakarta meeting, ASEAN has expanded its dialogue partners from seven to ten. Three big countries were admitted: India, China and Russia. India's status was raised from sectoral partner to dialogue partner in ASEAN, and China and Russia's were raised from consultative partners to dialogue partners. ASEAN-PMC is thus another useful mechanism through which seven South-east Asian nations can develop various

---

[14] One very important working group is that on confidence-building measures. Japan and Indonesia, the two countries playing active roles in regional conflict solutions, served as chairmen until the ARF meeting in Jakarta in 1996, when their chairmanships were taken up by China and the Philippines.

[15] ASEAN security think-tank experts have played increasingly important roles as ARF has expanded its scope from South-east Asia to the Asia–Pacific. Their views seem to be a few steps more forward-looking and radical than those of the officials of foreign ministries in ASEAN countries; see some of their recently published articles in *Harvard International Review*, 16(2) (Spring 1994).

cooperation programmes. True, this 10 + 10 meeting is mostly a speech-reading forum, but at the official level there are numerous cooperative works to implement.[16]

## Asia–Europe Meeting

The most recent effort by ASEAN to expand its role was a meeting with the European Union, the Asia–Europe Meeting. ASEAN approached other states in East Asia, Japan, China and Korea to join in discussing economic cooperation between Asia and the fifteen-member European Union. The first meeting, held in Bangkok in March 1996, was a gathering of the heads of ten Asian countries and fifteen EU member-states.

This forum could be seen as ASEAN's effort to deal with and make full use of globalization. ASEAN countries have now been freed from the Cold War structure that put them under the hegemony of the USA and USSR, neither of which was part of the Summit.[17] Asia now stands on an equal footing with Europe. According to the Declaration, both sides agreed to form the Asia–Europe Partnership for Greater Growth, aimed at strengthening links to contribute to peace, global stability and prosperity. The second meeting was held in Britain in 1998 and the following one is scheduled to convene in South Korea in 2000.

In the future, ASEAN will be able to learn more from the European experience on how to strengthen the spirit and promote programmes of cooperation. In the past little effort was made owing to ASEAN's basic policy of not wishing to create a supranational organization. Probably inspired by the EU-only lane, an ASEAN-only lane system at international airports of ASEAN member countries was recently opened.[18]

As early as the late 1980s, some ASEAN leaders made the suggestion that ASEAN should cooperate more with other regional groupings in the economic field. Prime Minister Mahathir Bin Mohamad of Malaysia, in a speech given in Singapore in December 1988, suggested a link-up of ASEAN with other regional groupings:

> But ASEAN is not the only regional grouping in the developing world. In South Asia, Africa and Latin America, there are also regional organizations which for the moment are still political in character. A link-up of these groupings in the economic field would make the South more capable of playing a role in the world's economy and even in the inevitable economic wrangles between the emergent kingdoms of the North. (Mahathir 1988, p. 602)

---

[16] Conversation with Ms Kusuma Tharasook, First Secretary, Department of ASEAN Affairs, Ministry of Foreign Affairs of Thailand, 19 August 1996.

[17] In terms of security, however, both the EU and ASEAN, including Japan and Korea, welcome the US security role and want to engage the United States in the region. In June 1996, a Thai government delegation led by the Permanent Secretary of the Ministry of Foreign Affairs Thep Devakula visited Washington DC. According to Dr Sarasin Viraphol, Deputy Permanent Secretary, Thailand's stance is to seek a more pro-active role from Washington; see 'Thailand to Seek Greater US Role', *The Nation*, Bangkok, 29 June 1996, p. 3.

[18] In July 1996, an ASEAN-only lane was opened at Bangkok International Airport to facilitate residents of ASEAN member-nations arriving at and departing from Thailand; see *Bangkok Post*, 2 July 1996, p. 3.

There is a good possibility that ASEAN will develop interregional cooperation mechanisms with other regional bodies. A discussion has been going on since 1996 to establish ASEAN–MERCOSUR cooperation. MERCOSUR is a regional body established in 1994 and encompassing four countries in South America: Brazil, Argentina, Uruguay and Paraguay. Its population is 200 million. Chile joined in October 1996, but not as a full member. The ASEAN–MERCOSUR cooperation will bring Asia and South America closer, even though geographical distance is a barrier.[19]

## Other Initiatives

Apart from the above-mentioned role expansion, ASEAN has made a number of other specific initiatives. In July 1992, the ASEAN ministerial meeting adopted an ASEAN Declaration on the South China Sea calling for a peaceful solution to the Spratly Islands issue. This is one of the three major documents indicating ASEAN stance on regional disputes; the other two are the Treaty of Amity and Cooperation (1976) and the Treaty on a South-east Asia Nuclear Weapons Free Zone. When China expressed its wish to have its status upgraded from consultative partner to dialogue partner in ASEAN, recommendations were made by ASEAN security think-tanks that, in order to become dialogue partner, China must endorse all three of these documents.[20] ASEAN may put more effort into calling for all players in South-east Asia to subscribe to the three documents; and in the future, it may start pressuring all nuclear powers to respect the Treaty on the Nuclear Weapons Free Zone in South-east Asia, after the ASEAN governments themselves all ratify the treaty.[21]

At the ASEAN Summit in Bangkok in December 1996, ASEAN leaders agreed to enhance cooperation in the field of social development to the same level as economic and political cooperation. Social development policy refers to the following three programmes: (1) human resource development; (2) technology development; and (3) social cohesiveness.[22] At the ASEAN Standing Committee Meeting in Yogyakarta, Indonesia, on 31 May–1 June 1996, a theme for ASEAN's sectoral cooperation was adopted: 'Shared prosperity through human development, technological competitiveness and social cohesiveness'.[23]

---

[19] Information provided by the International Studies Centre, Ministry of Foreign Affairs of Thailand.

[20] 'Hesitant ASEAN Gets Ready to Embrace China', The Nation, Bangkok, 10 June 1996, p. 2.

[21] At the ASEAN ministerial meeting in Indonesia in July 1996, ASEAN foreign ministers urged all ASEAN countries to speed up the ratification of the Treaty of South-east Asia Nuclear Weapons Free Zone by the time of the informal ASEAN summit scheduled for December 1996 in Indonesia; see ASEAN News (published by the ASEAN Affairs Department, Ministry of Foreign Affairs, Bangkok), no. 7, July 1996, p. 1.

[22] Press Release, Department of Information, Ministry of Foreign Affairs (of Thailand), Bangkok, no. 427/2539, pp. 1–2 (in Thai).

[23] ASEAN News, ASEAN Affairs Department, Ministry of Foreign Affairs of Thailand, Bangkok, no. 6, June 1996, p. 2 (in Thai).

In the field of culture and information, some cooperative efforts have been made. At the 31st Meeting of ASEAN Committee on Culture and Information in Bali on 1– 5 July 1996, four projects were adopted as ASEAN priority projects: (1) ASEANWEB, including homepage, on culture and information; (2) ASEAN Satellite Channel; (3) ASEAN Arts Festival, to be held every two years; and (4) ASEAN Youth Friendship Programme. The meeting also adopted a plan to have ASEAN stamps and other plans to commemorate ASEAN's thirtieth anniversary.[24]

The freer flow of information induced ASEAN member-countries' information officials to gather in Singapore in September 1996 to seek ways to deal with the use of cyberspace. During the three-day meeting, they discussed for the first time the challenges posed by the explosion of the global computer network. Their main concern is not only pornography but also the possible domination of Western media in shaping world policies and values.[25] A statement issued at the close of the Internet forum said that the meeting 'affirmed the importance of having safeguards against easy access to sites which run counter to our cherished values, traditions and culture. ASEAN would encourage other nations, especially the West, to understand its concern.[26] The statement, however, fell short of specifying a uniform ASEAN approach to the issue, leaving each country to regulate the Internet in its own way. Earlier in 1996, ASEAN information ministers met in Singapore to discuss the negative side of the IT revolution and agreed to set up a regulatory body to oversee the Internet invasion.[27]

It is clear that Singapore has played a leading role in policing the Internet. Singapore has a policy of strict control by licensing only three Internet service providers, who have to screen all material accessed by clients. The Philippines, Thailand and Malaysia are more relaxed, while Vietnam and Brunei are unconcerned since they have very few Internet surfers. In the years to come, it is possible that ASEAN will try to adopt a common stance as the menace of the Internet becomes more clearly felt.

## 4

### Responses to Globalization: Nationalism

Apart from the regional approach, each individual country in South-east Asia has its own policy and programmes in dealing with the freer flows of (1) information, (2) goods, services, capital and technology; (3) entertainment goods, and (4) values and cultures. Each government manages these four differently. Some keep the gate wide open to goods–services–capital–technology but closed to the kind of values and cultures they deem incompatible with their societies, such as human rights, freedom and democracy. Some are sensitive to films and music from Hollywood, some are not; Chinese films are welcomed in Thailand, but not in Malaysia; Japanese

---

[24] *ASEAN News*, ASEAN Affairs Department, Ministry of Foreign Affairs of Thailand, Bangkok, no. 7, July 1996, p. 4 (in Thai).
[25] 'ASEAN Grapples with Regional Internet Rules', *The Nation*, Bangkok, 3 September 1996, p. 7.
[26] 'Consensus on the Need to Police the Net', *Bangkok Post*, Bangkok, 5 September 1996, p. 6.
[27] Ibid.

cultural performances not allowed in Korea [this has been changing recently—Ed.], but are welcomed in all South-east Asian countries.

The cultural aspect of globalization, i.e. entertainment goods and values–cultures, is controversial. Except perhaps in Singapore, there have been numerous policies and programmes to revitalize national cultures and identities to deal with globalization. As the younger generation turns its attention to things global, government leaders and agencies responsible for national cultural administration have begun to view globalization with concern. There have been conscious efforts to strengthen national symbols and identity — Islam, Buddhism and Confucian values, the flag, the monarchy, armed forces, socialist ideology, meritocracy and long-serving government leaders.

Cultural nationalists have strongly reacted to globalization in several parts of the world. In Russia, the broadcasting of Western-style movies and shows and commercial programming on television have been criticized as the country has begun to be inundated by some of the worst of Western popular culture. They were seen by Russian composers, musicians and writers as 'entrepreneurship's filth', not freedom. The free flow of this kind of entertainment goods and services has aroused anti-Western movements and campaigns led by some populist leaders.[28]

The world of American pop music was represented overseas by a pop music star, Michael Jackson. His concert was not allowed in Malaysia, nor in many other South-east Asian countries. When it was shown in Bangkok in 1993, Thai cultural nationalists criticized it as destroying Thai culture to the point where it would take years to repair. They were also unhappy to find that teenagers were willing to pay so much money to see the show. In September 1996, Michael Jackson was on his East European tour beginning from Prague. His show on 15 September in Romania, a country unused to pop hysteria, attracted as many as 70,000 fans.[29]

The influence of American films has met some resistance from Western Europe as well. In February 1996, the European Parliament voted 292–195 to require television stations in the fifteen-nation EU to devote at least half their air time to homemade shows, an apparent move to reduce Hollywood's role on its air waves. Supporters of the measure said the legislation was needed to protect European culture from domination by US companies selling shows at rates up to ten times cheaper than European production costs.[30]

Reaction to globalized Chinese television shows occurred in Malaysia. A Taiwanese-made drama based on a legendary Chinese magistrate, 'Justice Bao', popular in Thailand and Singapore, was banned by government authorities in October 1996. The Information Ministry cited as the reason the Ministry's guidelines prohibiting 'costume dramas'. To this, the Chinese community protested that such television programmes have already been serving viewers.[31] The case of Malaysia demonstrated

[28] See 'Russia Gets the Worst of a Bad Bargain', *Bangkok Post*, Bangkok, 2 September 1996, p. 2.

[29] *Bangkok Post*, Bangkok, 16 September 1996, p. 9.

[30] See 'European Parliament to Limit US TV Programmes', *Japan Times*, Tokyo, 16 February 1996, p. 5.

[31] See 'Malaysian Ban on Taiwanese Show Sparks Row', *Bangkok Post*, Bangkok, 9 October 1996.

well the tension between globalization and the concern that national culture and identity might be destabilized and blurred.

In Thailand, a great number of such conscious efforts have been seen. Thailand has clearer national symbols and a more cohesive identity than many of its neighbours owing to its success in escaping colonialism. But since it is an extremely open society, some have argued that national identity campaigns are needed.

A series of national identity campaigns has been launched in Thailand during the last decade. The most outstanding one is the Thai Culture Campaign year, a campaign in 1994 with the slogan 'We Take Pride in Thai Culture'. The campaign was launched nationwide using schools, cultural facilities, television and other media to arouse public awareness in Thai art and culture, Buddhism, history, the monarchy and the Thai way of life. The campaign was extended until 1997 with a new name, 'The Programme to Continue Thai Culture'. The Office of the National Culture Commission under the Ministry of Education is the government agency supervising the campaign. Another responsible government agency is the Office of National Identity Commission under the Prime Minister's Office; this agency is in charge of defining what Thai national identity is.[32]

The year 1996 was made the year of the Golden Jubilee to commemorate the fiftieth anniversary of King Bhumiphol's reign. Earlier, there were great celebrations when the King became the longest ruling monarch in Thai history in 1988 and when he turned 60 in 1987. Before that, the bicentennial to commemorate the 200-year rule of the Chakri Dynasty, established by King Rama I in 1782, was launched in 1982. Along with Buddhism, the monarchy serves as the core value of Thai culture and identity. The present monarch, commonly called King Rama IX, has served as the symbol of Thai culture and identity both during the era of modernization in the postwar years and during the era of globalization in the late 1980s and 1990s.

## Representative Ideologue

There are several ideologues of the nationalist approach to globalization. Among them is Thanat Khoman, a senior citizen who long served as minister of foreign affairs of Thailand during the Cold War in the 1960s and 1970s. He is greatly credited as the founder of ASEAN in 1967. In his old age, he continues to be active commenting on international issues.

Dr Thanat Khoman expressed his concern that most people in Thailand do not understand globalization, and simply they think that it is smart, chic, elegant and fashionable to identify themselves with it. He feels that globalization is in fact a new form of hegemony, launched by the great powers, especially the United States; the Internet and worldwide web are their means; we cannot stop them; information control is more effective than military means; coupled with military means, it will be very difficult to guard against.[33] Deep in Dr Thanat Khoman's concern is the

---

[32] It was decided that 1995 will be the year of culture and development, 1996 the year of culture and tourism, and 1977 the year of culture and mass media; see *The Manager*, Bangkok, 19 April 1996, p. 10 (in Thai).

[33] Interview with Dr Thanat Khoman at his residence in Bangkok, August 1996.

possibility that the freer flow of information could be used by the globalization centres for their own purposes whenever they wish. He sees this new form of control as less costly since no military force has yet been used but as equally or even more effective than military force.

Dr Thanat Khoman is also concerned that Thai national cultural identity may be confused and destabilized by globalization. He criticized Western rock music and dance as lacking artistic values. When Michael Jackson staged a show in Bangkok in 1993, he came to reap a lot of money from the pockets of young boys and girls. Dr Thanat Khoman asked whether such people, who enjoy eating hamburgers and hot dogs, really know what their ingredients are (from Thanat Khoman 1996).

Nationalism has had firm foundations throughout modern history, but it is quite clear that globalization is now destabilizing the roots of nationalism. As indicated earlier, globalization has led to the dilution of national identity, which 'the majority' defined and imposed over the minority groups. It is much easier to mobilize popular support in the area of culture than in the area of economics, even though both are equally at the mercy of globalization. It is therefore possible to see more expressions of critical views against globalization in South-east Asia. What makes things difficult, however, is the absence of a single clear target for attack. There are multiple centres and complex modes of globalization. Organized protest is not therefore likely to happen.

# 5

## Responses to Globalization: Communitarianism

Globalization has been viewed with alarm by a great number of scholars and activists who are concerned about the future of the rural population. They suspect that globalization is merely a new form of development strategy which will put the communities and villages in the disadvantageous position.

It is difficult to identify a concrete response to globalization from the villagers and rural population. They expressed their plight in relation to a host of issues, not only globalization. It is, however, possible to introduce the views of those who are concerned about the future of the villages. Let us call them 'communitarians'. A representative communitarian who has written extensively critical works about globalization is Chatthip Narthsupha.

### Representative Ideologue

Dr Chatthip Narthsupha is a distinguished professor of economic history at Chulalongkorn University in Bangkok. His concern is not about weaker nations falling victim to globalization, but about the future of community and village as globalization transforms the planet to a borderless world, or 'global village'. He believes that local identity and uniqueness are too valuable to allow to be destroyed.

In an article he co-authored with Pornpilai Lervicha, 'Thai Village Culture and Globalization', Dr Chatthip Narthsupha viewed globalization as the extension of capitalism. The IT revolution, especially digital technology, only popularized and strengthened capitalism, consumerism and private-sector ideology. Digital technology will help to further compress the world through a common information network. Dr Chatthip sees that this common information network is making people believe that education systems, knowledge systems, production patterns, consumption patterns and mankind's living patterns should become similar, or even ultimately be the same, the world over (Chatthip and Pornpilai 1996).

As an implication for Thailand, Dr Chatthip Narthsupha called for more learning and awareness of the potentialities of communities that together form the nation. Local interest should be given priority and local resources should be used efficiently. He criticized monopolistic investment, which exploited resources and labour.

> The ability of Thai villages in maintaining their self-identity under the capitalism system in the last century has become a positive condition to serve as an important base to shape the direction of Thailand amidst globalization. At the same time, villages' weaknesses that have led to their destruction deserve our attention as to what we can do to correct them. (Chatthip and Pornpilai 1996, p. 14)

While Dr Thanat Khoman's views are widely shared among both economic and cultural nationalists, Dr Chatthip Narthsupha's views are widely shared among historians, NGO leaders, environmentalists and economic planners (see also Chatthip 1991). Some are concerned about village identity, and some are concerned that the urban–rural gap is being widened by the effect of globalization. The New National Economic and Social Development Plan of the Thai government (1998–2002), for example, has as its central concept the need to deal with the arrival of globalization. In the Philippines, where the income gap is very wide, globalization has been widely viewed with alarm. Numerous critical works along Dr Chatthip's line of argument have been published in that country (see Berneo and Korff 1994).

Another intellectual, Dr Thianchai Wongchaisuwan, defined globalization as the free flow of capital on the global scale, not unlike Charthip Narthsupha's definition. But Thianchai has focused much of his analysis on the role of Hollywood in influencing the younger generation. He sees that whoever controls the entertainment world controls the spiritual world, which is capable of creating dreams and values for men and society (Thianchai 1994). In this process, he is concerned that truth will not have a place in society. He writes:[34]

> Hollywood is dominating the world. Hollywood is creating a new culture for the young people all over the world. Not only in eating, dressing and living, but Hollywood is turning the world of illusion to the world of truth.

> Indeed in most societies in South-east Asia, a debate between the globalization school and the community school has been going on for years. It seems that the two schools of thought will continue to debate and it is unlikely that they will soften their stands. The communitarian school has attracted a large number of subscribers among historians, NGO leaders, activists and social workers. The globalization school on the other hand has attracted a large number of subscribers among businessmen, professional groups, youth and the middle class in general. Most analysts tend to forget that the third party, the nationalist school, is an important pillar standing in the middle of the two. (Thianchai 1994, p. 183)

---

[34] See Kasian Tejapira (1996); Chaiwat Satha-Anand (1993).

# 6

## Responses to Globalized Human Rights Values

No aspect of the local impact of globalization is as controversial as the increasingly globalized promotion of democratic and human rights values, which has resulted in aggravating debates and conflicts in the non-Western world. These values, flowing from the Western centre of globalization, when coupled with the local sources, have been one of the most dominant causes of social transformation in South-east Asia and elsewhere. The theme became even more prominent when local activists began to call for democratic reforms and human rights legislation, approaching the West as their ally, while their governments responded with brutal suppression and demanded that the West stop 'interfering in their domestic affairs'. The situation has become even more complicated as some Western countries started to apply political and economic sanctions. The final result is thus increased aggravation, tension and confrontation at two levels: that of the West–non-West, and of the state and society in the non-Western world. The West views human rights as universal, whereas most non-Western countries do not. In most Asian countries, the governments reject such 'interference in domestic affairs', while the champions of democracy and human rights support the condemnation of the West and sanction their governments.

In South-east Asia, this two-dimensional conflict has been highlighted by some massive abuses of human rights. In Thailand, in February 1991 the military staged a *coup d'état* overthrowing the elected civilian government, and in May 1992 the military opened fire at the pro-democracy demonstrators. In Indonesia, in late 1991 the Indonesian armed forces brutally killed hundreds of unarmed citizens in East Timor. In Myanmar, there are no hopes of improvement in the human rights situation; the massive abuses of human rights by the ruling SLORC included the suppression of democracy demonstrators in 1988, the house arrest of the democratic leader Aung San Suu Kyi in 1989, the failure to accept the result of the general election held in 1990, and the continued arrest and torture of members of the National League for Democracy.

## ASEAN and Human Rights Issues

There are signs that ASEAN is going to respond to human rights issues in a more positive way. In 1993 at the ASEAN Ministerial Meeting (AMM), there were talks about establishing a working group on human rights, but the idea was not pursued. A week before the Jakarta meeting in 1996, an adviser to the Committee on Justice and Human Rights of the House of Representatives of Thailand had a meeting with the Thai deputy minister of foreign affairs, asking him to push for the establishment of an agency on human rights within ASEAN. It was reported that Thailand, the Philippines and Indonesia were in support of the idea.[35]

---

[35] See *Siam Post*, Bangkok, 16 July 1996, p. 6 (in Thai).

Calls for ASEAN to be more open to people-to-people contacts were expressed twice by Thai foreign ministers: at the ASEAN ministerial meeting in Brunei in 1995 and in Indonesia in 1996. At the Brunei AMM, Foreign Minister Kasem S. Kasemsri suggested that ASEAN open discussions on the establishment of a 'regional parliament'. He warned his ASEAN counterparts that 'ASEAN's success depends on the expanding popular support and participation to involve the widest and broadest range of the public . . .' He talked at great length on the importance of 'support from and participation of the people'. He clarified his ideas with the following words:

> In this regard, I believe a separate, independent body could be established to guide our undertaking. The body I propose for our consideration would take the form of a regional parliament or council, comprising representatives elected to the body from each member country. These delegates would be drawn from political parties, parliamentary groups such as the AIPO, media, business, grass-roots movements and other popular political organizations to ensure the broadest representation. Their role would be to discuss matters that fall within the purview of ASEAN — be they political, economic, social — and recommend courses of action where appropriate. The idea is to provide guidance to our deliberations and make ASEAN truly responsive to the hopes and dreams of the common man. (Kasem S. Kasemsri 1995, p. 12)

At the AMM in Indonesia, Foreign Minister Amnuay Viravan repeated the call of his predecessor a year earlier. He said ASEAN must strive to become 'a people-based organization'. Thailand's proposal this time was taken up. The Thai proposal was discussed at the working dinner and was passed on to the official level for further deliberation. Amnuary made clear his proposal towards the end of his speech:

> Given the importance of our people in the scheme of things, we should encourage them to play a greater role in the development of the region and of ASEAN. The people must have a greater say in how their countries and region are run. Sooner or later, ASEAN must become a people-based organization to remain effective. (Amnuay 1996, p. 9)

The proposals made by Thai foreign ministers only reflected current feelings that the future of South-east Asia cannot be left to the government and the private sector without active participation from the people. In August 1996 a group of sixteen officials, academics and journalists who called themselves 'Citizens of South-east Asia' met in the Philippines and proposed a new vision of the region called 'Towards a South-east Asian Community: A Human Agenda'. According to the vision, the South-east Asian community must value human endeavour sustained by moral principles. The vision called for a human face and a moral purpose (see Kavi 1996, p. 4). This is the kind of vision by men of letters that Foreign Minister Kasem S. Kasemsri wants ASEAN to listen to. His idea is for a 'regional parliament or council' to act as an organ to incorporate suggestions like this.

### Myanmar's Human Rights Issue

The SLORC government was seriously condemned by the West in June 1996 when James Leander Nichols, who served until 1978 as honorary consul for Denmark, Norway, Finland, Sweden and Switzerland, died in prison in Myanmar. European nations expressed outrage at the death in prison of a man known to suffer from heart disease and diabetes. Myanmar's authorities claimed that Mr Nichols was jailed for illegal possession of two fax machines and a telephone switchboard, but it was widely believed that he was punished for his links to Aung San Suu Kyi. Denmark put economic sanctions against Myanmar on the agenda of a forthcoming EU meeting. The EU finally sanctioned Myanmar after the UK agreed at the last minute.

In a similar way, the US legislature and US public opinion have compelled the Clinton administration to mount pressure on the ruling SLORC. One bill, introduced by Senator Mitch McConnell, called for stiff trade, travel and economic sanctions, although the Clinton administration has pushed for a weaker version of the bill. Aung San Suu Kyi made full use of international pressures by calling for conditional sanctions to 'balance against the extreme measures'. This led to countermeasures from the ruling SLORC. An increasing number of her supporters were arrested and sentenced to long prison terms. The tension has escalated, and there are no prospects of any improvements at the moment.

The ASEAN governments' approach to this problem, the so-called 'constructive engagement', has not worked either. ASEAN continued to engage Myanmar. At the Jakarta meeting in 1996 Myanmar was invited to join the AMM as observer and to join the ARF as a full member. ASEAN's constructive engagement policy was generally criticized by the West, but ASEAN is confident that this approach serves many good purposes in the long run. In ASEAN's view, it is not desirable to see Myanmar move closer to China. During his visit to China in January 1996, Senior General Than Shwe, chairman of the ruling SLORC, witnessed the signing of three bilateral agreements with China which included a framework accord for low-interest Chinese loans.[36] In August 1976, SLORC's minister of planning and economic development visited southern China. When asked how Myanmar would fare if the United States imposed a full-scale economic embargo and the EU removed special trade privileges because of human rights violation issues, he replied: 'Myanmar can survive on its own. We cut ourselves off from the world for 26 years . . . We can divert our markets to other places. I don't think it will affect us'.[37]

Criticism of the Western approach to the problem of human rights in Myanmar was made by Lee Kuan Yew of Singapore, an advocate of stable and strong government and a staunch critic of liberalism. Claiming that he knew the country, the political situation and the military leaders, Lee expressed his views that Aung San Suu Kyi could not rule the country and that she should remain simply a political symbol. He said if he were Aung San Suu Kyi, 'I think I'd rather be behind a fence and be a symbol [than be] found impotent' to lead the country.[38] He also believed

---

[36] It was reported that the SLORC chairman was praised by Chinese President Jiang Zemin for stabilizing his country's political situation, realizing national reconciliation and upholding traditional culture. Jiang told General Than Shwe that 'China would like to enhance discussions with the Myanmarese government on international and regional affairs in order to safeguard the peace and stability in the region and the interests and rights of developing countries' (see *Daily Yomiuri*, Tokyo, 9 January 1996, p. 4).

[37] 'On the Road to Hell in Dealing with Burma', editorial, *The Nation*, Bangkok, 8 September 1996, p. A4.

[38] 'S'pore's Lee: Suu Kyi Can't Rule Burma', *Bangkok Post*, Bangkok, 9 June 1996, p. 5.

the country could collapse 'like Bosnia' into various constituent parts under outside pressure. 'I have visited the place and I know that there is only one instrument of government, and that is the arms.'[39]

## Linking Social Issues to Trade

ASEAN governments reject the idea, proposed by the EU and the USA, to link social causes to trade at the WTO meeting in December 1996 in Singapore. Social causes such as human rights, labour standards, the environment and corruption are generally seen by ASEAN countries as a new form of protectionism. The EU has been trying to propose that the WTO consider social causes such as labour standards and human rights conditions, while the United States has proposed that the WTO adopt rules to create transparency in the government procurement procedures to reduce corruption in trade. ASEAN trade ministers, except for Singapore on certain issues, have rejected the proposals, preferring the 120 WTO members to discuss only the obligations of the fifteen issues that were agreed to at the Uruguay Round of GATT multilateral trade talks. ASEAN believes that some countries have not yet opened up their markets to farm products even though they had committed to do so under the WTO; others have opened their markets on a discriminatory basis by setting restrictive rules.[40] ASEAN Secretary-General Data Ajit Singh expressed the following views on behalf of ASEAN:

> ASEAN has always taken a strong position on the issues. We think it is a form of protectionism. We don't like social issues to be linked to trade. It's a pressure on ASEAN and an obstacle to our development. (*Bangkok Post*, 26 April 1993, p. 3)

## Using Airwaves to Globalize Democracy

The globalization of information linked to human rights became an issue when the United States announced plans to broadcast a short-wave radio service, Radio Free Asia (RFA), to promote democracy and human rights in communist countries by providing news and information to the people of China as well as Tibet, North Korea, Vietnam, Laos, Cambodia and Myanmar. It was suspected that the United States would use RFA, later renamed the Asia–Pacific Network (APN), to destabilize and topple communist regimes in the same manner as Radio Free Europe/Radio Liberty contributed to the demise of the former Soviet Union and Eastern European bloc.[41] In August 1996, the Thai government decided to reject repeated US requests to use its territory and radio transmitter facilities to broadcast or relay the short-wave service. China and Vietnam praised its decision and expressed their gratitude for the

---

[39] Ibid.

[40] See 'WTO Ministers Unlikely to Discuss Labour at December Meet', *The Nation*, Bangkok, 3 September 1996, p. B3.

[41] See 'US Plea on Radio Free Asia Rejected', *The Nation*, Bangkok, 2 September 1996, p. 1; see also earlier reports in *Bangkok Post*, 15 August 1996, p. 4, and 16 August 1996, p. 10.

Thai government's tough stance against US pressures.[42] The use of information as a tool in international relations has revived ASEAN scepticism about the meaning of globalization. For the United States the Cold War does not yet seem to have ended, but for ASEAN, communist regimes that pursue economic reform policy and do not 'interfere in domestic affairs' of others are perfectly acceptable. Not only is peaceful coexistence possible, but economic cooperation also works out fairly well. The Thai decision is a good illustration of the region's awareness of the use of information by the most influential centre of globalization, the United States.

## Social Order and Democracy

The application of pressures and sanctions on human rights violations happened to occur at a time when the West was experiencing an economic recession; on the contrary, countries in South-east Asia, including China, were enjoying rapid economic development. But what is more important is the decline in social order that is occurring in the United States and in EU member-states. Excessive freedom has been seen by some leaders in South-east Asia as a source of this social disorder.

No one points out the disparity between needed social order and excessive freedom in the West as forcefully as Lee Kuan Yew. In Lee's view, Western society has lost its appeal as a model of nation-building for countries in the non-Western world. He finds American society on the decline owing to the collapse of its moral base. He writes:

> As an East Asian looking at America, I find attractive and unattractive features. I like, for example, the free, easy and open relations between people regardless of social status, ethnicity or religion . . .
> But as a total system, I find part of it totally unacceptable: guns, drugs, violent crime, vagrancy, unbecoming behavior in public — in sum, the breakdown of civil society. The expansion of the right of the individual to behave or misbehave as he pleases has come at the expense of orderly society. In the East the main object is to have a well-ordered society so that everybody can have maximum enjoyment of his freedoms. This freedom can only exist in an ordered state and not in a natural state of contention and anarchy. (Zakaria 1994, p. 111)

Asked whether he admired the America of twenty-five years ago and what had gone wrong, Lee replied:

> Yes, things have changed. I would hazard a guess that it has a lot to do with the erosion of the moral underpinnings of a society and the diminution of personal relationship. The liberal, intellectual tradition that developed after World War II claimed that human beings had arrived at this perfect state where everybody would be better off if they were allowed to do their own thing and flourish. It has not worked out, and I doubt if it will. Certain basics about human nature do not change. Man needs a certain moral sense of

---

[42] The Chinese ambassador to Bangkok called on the Foreign Ministry on 1 August 1996 to express his country's gratitude to Thailand. About the same time, Vietnamese officials in Hanoi sent a similar message to the Thai government.

right and wrong. There is such a thing as evil, and it is not the result of being a victim of society. You are just an evil man, prone to do evil things, and you have to be stopped from doing them. Westerners have abandoned an ethical basis for society, believing that all problems are solvable by a good government, which we in the East never believed possible. (Zakaria 1994, p. 112)

Asked what would he do to address America's problems, Lee had a clear answer:

What would I do if I were an American? First, you must have order in a society. Guns, drugs and violent crime all go together, threatening social order. Then the schools: when you have violence in schools, you are not going to have education, so you've got to put that right. Then you have to educate rigorously and train a whole generation of skilled, intelligent, knowledgeable people who can be productive. I would start off with basics, working on the individual, looking at him within the context of his family, his friends, his society. But the Westerner says, I'll fix things at the top. One magic formula, one grand plan. I will wave a wand and everything will work out. It's an interesting theory but not a proven method. (Zakaria 1994, p. 114)

# 7
## Conclusion

Different countries cope with globalization differently. There are also different views between governments and peoples, and among various groups in society. The challenge of globalization, not unlike that of modernization, thus brings about debates and conflicts in local societies. If the impact wrought by modernization has lasted for more than a century, that arising from globalization is going to last even longer.

The impact of globalization is indeed far-reaching. In economic terms, a national economy can be in trouble within days if its credibility rating by internationally recognized rating agencies plummets. The flight of capital can leave a country's economy in turmoil, as we have seen in the case of Mexico. In Thailand, in September 1996, Moody's Investor Services lowered the credibility status of Thailand's short-term sovereign ceiling rate from prime-1 to prime-2. This caused a particularly serious blow to the Banharn government, since the prime minister was facing a vote of confidence in parliament on 18 September. The timing resulted in a 'double punch' for the government.

Democracy and human rights issues will continue to divide most South-east Asian nations. One recurring issue is the freedom of the press. This means an independent media not subject to state control, and the professional dignity of reporters, editors and others in the field of journalism. If the globalization of information is not accompanied by this principle, there will be a serious problem. The IT revolution will be meaningless if the state continues its previous policy of media control as during the Cold War. We witness this problem in most South-east Asian countries including Indonesia, Singapore, Malaysia, Brunei, Thailand and to a lesser extent the Philippines.

In Thailand, a protest against the state's media control was made by the Confederation of Thai Journalists (CTJ), an umbrella organization of all Thai journalists, on 14 September 1996. CTJ issued a statement at the end of a meeting of representatives of ten press associations condemning attempts by people in the government to intimidate, interfere and harm reporters physically. The statement called for the insertion into the constitution of a clear principle of freedom of expression. It concluded by asking the Banharn government to treat the press 'in accordance with democratic principle of the civilized international community based on the United Nations Declaration on Human Rights'.

In some countries the media is so tightly controlled that there have been no voices of protest from the journalist community. Singapore is a perfect case: its government leaders are most concerned about the Internet and are trying to curb the flows of 'undesirable news and information'. In the former planned economies such as Vietnam, Laos and Cambodia, this problem will be a recurring one for decades to come.

It is not clear whether there will be more or less tension in societies as we move away from a dual modernity–tradition structure to a dual globalization–marginalization structure. It is the marginalized people and societies that will be our burden. We can only hope that the gap will be small. The Economic Declaration of the G-7 held in Lyon in June 1996 spelled out this problem most succinctly:

> Globalization provides great opportunities for the future, not only for our countries, but for all others too.
>
> Globalization also poses challenges to societies and economies. Its benefits will not materialize unless countries adjust to increased competition. In the poorer countries, it may accentuate inequality and certain parts of the world could become marginalized. . . . Globalization of the financial markets can generate new risks of instability, which requires all countries to pursue sound economic policies and structural reform. ('Making a Success of Globalization for the Benefit of All', G-7 Summit Economic Communiqué, Lyon, 28 June 1996, paras. 2 and 3)

## References

Amnuay Viravan (1996), Opening Statement at the 29th ASEAN ministerial meeting, Jakarta, 20 July, mimeo.

Ananda Kanjanaphum (1995), 'Social Change and Thai Community's Potentials', in *Criticizing Thai Society*, Bangkok: Social Science Association of Thailand, pp. 151–92.

Berneo, E. and Korff, R. (1994), 'Globalization and Local Resistance: The Creation of Localities in Manila and Bangkok', South-east Asia Programme Working Paper no. 205, Bielefeld.

Chai-anan Samudavanija (1996), 'The World in the Twenty-first Century', paper presented at the Thailand Research Fund conference on 'Re-engineering Thailand: Imagination towards the Year 2000', Bangkok, 26–28 September.

Chaiwat Satha Anand (1993), 'Society in Parenthesis: Globalization and Battle of Ideas in Thai Society', unpublished research paper, Thailand Development Research Institute, January.

Chaiwat Satha Anand (ed.) (1996), *Imagination towards the Year 2000: Paradigm Innovation in Thai Studies*, Bangkok: Thailand Research Fund, pp. 83–127 (in Thai).

Chatthip Narthsupha (1991), 'The Community Culture School of Thought', in Manas Chitkasem and Andrew Turton (eds.), *Thai Constructions of Knowledge*, University of London School of Oriental and African Studies, pp. 118–41.

Chatthip Narthsupha and Pornpilai Lertvicha (1966), 'Thai Village Culture and Globalization', *Social Science Review*, July–December: 5–14 (in Thai).

Kasem S. Kasemsri (1995), Opening Statement at the 28th ASEAN Ministerial Meeting, Bandar Seri Begawan, Brunei Darussalam, 29 July, mimeo.

Kasian Tejapira (1993), 'Globalizers vs. Communitarians: Post-May 1992 Debates among Thai Public Intellectuals', paper presented at the AAS Conference, Honolulu, April.

Kavi Chongkittavorn (1996), 'SEA Community's Human Face', *The Nation* (Bangkok), 30 August.

Mahathir Bin Mohamad (1988), 'Regionalism, Globalism and Spheres of Influence: ASEAN and the Challenge of Change into the 21st Century', Singapore Lecture 1988, 14 December.

Rosenberg, E. S. (1994), 'Spreading the American Dream to Asia', paper presented at a symposium on 'American Studies in the Asia–Pacific Region: American Values in US Diplomacy towards Asia', organized by the International House of Japan/Japanese Association for American Studies, Tokyo, 31 October.

Somchai Phakaphasvivat (1995), *Vision Thailand 2000*, Bangkok: Mathichon Newspapers.

Thanat Khoman (1996), Keynote Speech at a seminar on 'Women and Thai Culture', Thammasat University, Bangkok, 28 August.

Tianchai Wongchaisuwan (1994), *Globalization 2000*, Bangkok: Ionic Intertrade Resources.

Zakaria, F. (1994), 'Culture is Destiny: A Conversation with Lee Kuan Yew', *Foreign Affairs*, 73(2): 109–26.

# 5

# TRANSNATIONAL FLOWS OF PEOPLE AND INTERNATIONAL EXCHANGES

## PHENOMENA AND ACTIVITIES

### *Kenichiro Hirano*

In the last decade of the twentieth century, we are witnessing huge surges of transnational flows of people, goods, money and information all over the world. The Asia–Pacific region is not only no exception but is leading the trend, which seems certain to continue into the twenty-first century with an ever accelerating speed. There is a dilemma of how to conduct international exchange activities in the midst of this trend. It is a dilemma between phenomena and activities. In order to understand, if not to solve, the dilemma, we should perhaps try first to understand the nature of the phenomenon.

## 1

### Going Into and Out of Japan: Transnational Flows of People, Goods, Money and Information

First let us look at the recent transnational flows of people, goods, money and information into and out of Japan. As you can see from Figure 1, in the twenty years from 1968 to 1988, the annual flows of money into and out of Japan rose from a base of 100 to nearly 9,000. Likewise, the annual flows of telecommunications messages jumped from 100 in 1968 to 4,500 in 1988. The annual flows of goods expressed by values of export and import increased by almost twenty times in twenty years, and the combined annual number of Japanese people going abroad and foreign visitors coming to Japan increased by fourteen times in the same twenty years. More recently, it was reported that more than 15 million Japanese tourists were expected to go abroad in 1997 (*Nikkei* Newspaper, 30 August 1996).

A slightly different version of this paper was included in my privately published booklet, 'Reflections on International Cultural Relations in East Asia', 1998.

**Figure 1**   Changes in the volume of Japan's international exchanges, 1968–1988 (1968 = 100)

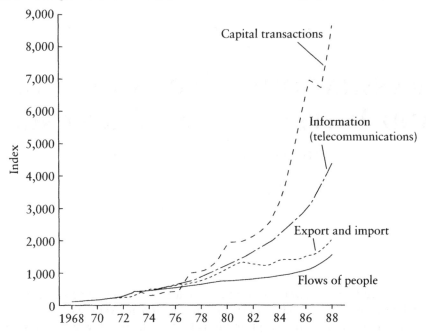

Some Japanese opinion leaders have been advocating that Japan should try to be a sender of cultural messages abroad. They say this because they think that Japan has long been a receiver of cultural elements and messages from abroad, especially from the West, ever since the era of the Meiji restoration, and is still a recipient of foreign cultures. Actually, Japan is now a big sender. The horizontal line in the centre of Figure 2 is a balance line indicating that the incoming volume is equal to the outgoing volume of any item. Above the centre line, the volume going out from Japan exceeds the volume coming in to Japan. As you can see from this graph, Japan has constantly been a net sender of money, goods and people and a net receiver only slightly of telecommunications information. It is likely, however, that the senders of these telecommunications messages coming into Japan are mostly overseas Japanese themselves.

Needless to say, cultural elements and messages are not carried overseas in the form of international telecommunications messages alone: goods are a potent means of sending and receiving cultural elements and messages internationally, as well as travelling people and money flows. Transnational flows of goods, people, money and information can all involve international movements of cultural elements and messages. Unintentionally, Japan has been a big mover of cultural elements and messages. As we saw above, it is now an established fact that far more Japanese visit other countries than foreigners visit Japan. Yet, it is doubtful if the Japanese overseas tourists come back home, having learnt sufficiently enough from other peoples. Herein lies one of the tasks for international exchange activities, which can be defined as conscious and conscientious activities to make up for gaps caused by transnational phenomena.

**Figure 2** Japan's international exchanges: the balance between outgoing and incoming exchanges, 1968–1988

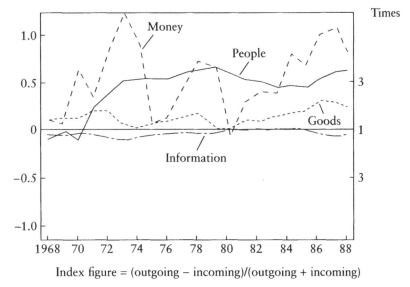

Index figure = (outgoing − incoming)/(outgoing + incoming)

## 2
## Moving with Return Tickets: Global Migration in the Asia–Pacific

Another more important factor we must bear in mind in considering the prospect of international exchanges is the characteristic changes of transnational flows of people. In the first place, why do so many people move across borders in recent years? The major backdrop for people's transborder movements is of course the economic development, or rather economic inequality, created by differing economic developments, and the development of international transportation technologies. Figure 3 lists some of the immediate impetuses for the rapid increase in the numbers of Japanese going abroad. For the Japanese, international travel had been restricted until 1964. In that year the Tokyo Olympic Games was held and international travel was liberalized. The number of outgoing Japanese gradually increased, surpassing that of incoming foreign visitors in 1970–1. In 1970, the jumbo jet was put into commercial service.

According to an estimate by the International Organization for Migration (IOM), 80 million people resided outside their countries of birth and citizenship in 1990. This figure is about equal to the population of the united Germany, and suggests that about 1.7 per cent of the world's population lives abroad. The Asia–Pacific region has been leading the trend; for instance, 3.5 million people moved from India and South-east Asia to the Middle East to be temporary workers in a peak year before the Gulf War (Abella 1993, p. 9). In the 1970s and 1980s, the biggest group of emigrants to the United States was from Asia (Morita 1987, Appendix, p. 9). Finally, people have started moving across national borders within Asia. Since 1983, Japan has been receiving fairly large numbers of workers from Asian countries such

**Figure 3**  Japanese outgoing and foreigners' incoming exchanges, 1952–1988

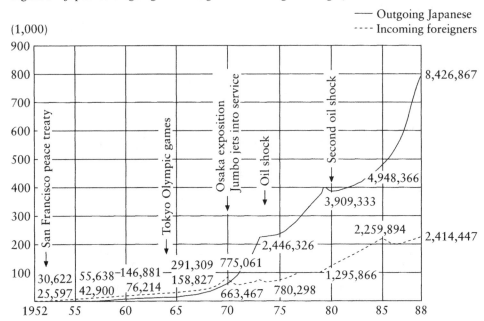

as Pakistan, Bangladesh, Thailand, the Philippines and Korea. Inside the ASEAN region, according to a report to a United Nations University conference, it is estimated that approximately 800,000 foreign workers coming from other ASEAN member-states are employed in one of the ASEAN countries (Abella 1993, p. 14). The same country both sends and receives those workers.

The figure of 80 million people residing abroad is huge. However, as Stephen Castles and Mark Miller suggest, quantitatively it may not be so significant, because 1.7 per cent of the world's population being migrants means that the vast majority of people are still residing in their own countries. More significant are qualitative characteristics of recent transborder movements of population.

Castles and Miller call today 'the age of migration', and they describe the general tendencies of migration movements as follows: (1) the globalization of migration, (2) the acceleration of migration, (3) the differentiation of migration, and (4) the feminization of migration. By the 'globalization' of migration, they mean the tendency for more and more countries to be affected by migratory movements at the same time, as well as by an increase in the diversity of the areas of origin. 'Acceleration' refers to the tendency for migrations to grow in volume in all major regions. 'Differentiation' points to the fact that most countries have a whole range of types of immigration at once. And finally, since the 1960s women have been playing an increasing role in all regions and all types of migration (Castles and Miller 1993, p. 8).

Why do we see the phenomenon of global migration as having these characteristics today? The usual economic explanation seeks the cause in economic gaps, which bring about all sorts of 'push' factors on the side of the sending countries and 'pull' factors on the side of the receiving countries. This push–pull mode of explanation

**Figure 4** Numbers of Japanese going to countries of major destination

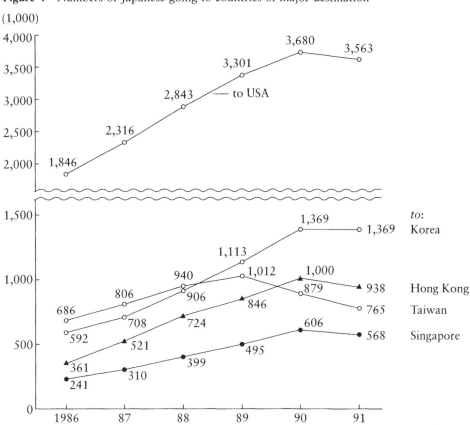

(1,000)

has a difficulty, however, in explaining why the same countries are both sending and receiving migrants at the same time; why many, if not all, foreign workers move back and forth so frequently; and why an increasing number of them do not permanently reside in the labour receiving countries. In order to answer these question, we should take into consideration a third factor, namely, the state of world transportation and communications today. After all, such transportation and communication factors, existing between the push factors and the pull factors, determine the actual patterns of people's transborder movements.

Figuratively speaking, today's global migrant moves across national borders with return tickets in hand. This is of course made possible by advances in means of transportation. Earlier, people could not move back and forth across the ocean and betweeen continents so easily. They ventured abroad with a one-way ticket only, and most of them could not go home for a lifetime. Migrants became immigrants almost inevitably. Today, migrants travel on jumbo jets for far less money. Even if they go abroad with just one-way tickets, they can fairly easily earn the money to return.

Because it was so difficult for earlier immigrants to go back home once they emigrated, it was inevitable that they did their best to become assimilated in the receiving countries. If that was not possible for the first-generation immigrants, then the second generations would achieve the necessary assimilation. Those days, assimilation was the concern of both the immigrants themselves and the receiving societies. Today, we see far less pressure to assimilate. Foreign workers are required only to gain the limited language ability necessary on work sites, and they can escape into their ethnic enclaves whenever they wish. Thanks to advanced international telecommunications technology, they can make international calls at relatively small cost. While living abroad for longer or shorter periods, they retain their ethnic ties.[1]

In short, it is now possible for us to keep our ethnic ties while we move globally, retaining our national identities as we carry our national passports. Precisely because it is easier for us to move across national borders, it is also easy to keep our ethnicity. People move globally, carrying their ethnicities along with them. We can even say that transnational movements increase our ethnic consciousness. Historically speaking, in the modern age, which was an age of sedentariness, of our national enclosure, we used to divide ourselves according to our nationalities alone; now, in the age of global migration, we can divide ourselves along our ethnicities too, but not only along those ethnicities.

Today, international society is no longer a society of states alone. Actors existing on all different levels — local, national, regional and global — come together to mingle and produce international and transnational relations. By shifting our perspective, we see that today's international society has a multilayered structure with a number of concentric circles forming something like complex nested boxes. Mark Hoffman, in his phrase 'overlapping or interlocking communities which embrace varying degrees of commitment as the basis for developing a just world order' (Hoffman 1994, p. 36), and Fred Halliday, in his phrase 'multiple dimensions of international society' (Halliday 1994, p. 123), are each trying to express ideas similar to the one employed in this paper. We now have an international society with a multilayered structure, and an individual's personality with multiple identities. This is the most important factor we must bear in mind when considering the prospect of international exchanges today and tomorrow.

# 3

## Culture and Identity in Increasing International Contacts

Our basic premiss should be that international exchanges of any sort, be they transnational flows of people or goods or money or information, and regardless of whether such exchanges are carried out intentionally or unintentionally, will result in cultural contacts because they carry elements of the culture of their origin. Even money, although it is theoretically void of cultural difference, realistically is a culture carrier, in that very often particular money buys particular goods and informations.

---

[1] Anthony H. Richmond (1984) says, '[t]he very nature of postindustrialism, with its technological advances in communication networks, facilitates the maintenance of language and cultural differences, even in remotely scattered populations' (1994 edn, p. 297).

Cultural contacts often bring changes to the culture, especially that on the receiving side. Asian cultures, for instance, since their first contacts with the Western civilization or cultures, have all gone through tremendous cultural changes. Cultural changes are often resisted by people who do not want their accustomed ways of living to be forcefully changed. The resistance to forced cultural changes is natural and the resistance sometimes becomes quite heightened, whether the cultural contacts that lead to cultural changes are made intentionally or unintentionally.

During the nation-state period, the nation-state almost monopolized international cultural contacts as much as it did international relations in general. During this period, which I would maintain entered its final phase around the 1970s, a typical nation-state would undertake international cultural exchanges in order to strengthen itself. A less developed nation would try to import selected cultural elements from a more developed nation, while a more developed nation would export its cultural values to other nations in order to increase its prestige or its sphere of influence. Thus, the dominant type of international cultural exchange during this period took the form of a one-way flow, with nations either sending or receiving cultural elements. In such a situation, the less developed nation was obliged to guard itself against international cultural exchanges, lest over-importation of foreign cultural elements should have destroyed its own culture or tradition. In Asia, since the latter half of the nineteenth century, we have witnessed long series of cultural conflicts of this sort.

Now, in the new post-Cold War era, which seems to be the initial stage of what may be called a post-nation-state period, some people say that the 'clash of civilizations' will be the theme. I am opposed to this view and would argue that the unit of international relations of this sort is not a civilization but has been and will continue to be cultural entities. Therefore, the issue should not be the clash of civilizations but the almost innumerable contacts and conflicts between cultural entities. I would rather agree with Fred Halliday, who sees 'culture as an important constituent of the modernity that all societies are forced to move towards' and says that[2]

> any approach based on the 'homogeneity' concept invites an alternative history of both international relations and the development of individual societies. For the latter, the shift is evident: what may previously have been seen as discrete, isolated, national histories, now appear much more clearly as the result of international processes, of imitation, competition, defensive modernization and influence. (Halliday 1994, p. 120)

International cultural contacts and cultural changes germinated by those contacts will go on ever more frequently, and will continue to acquire new characteristics.

We now have a well developed state of the mutilayered structure of international society and the multiple identities of individual persons. The rapid increase in people's transnational mobility and a multitude of existing global problems, such as the global environmental crisis, will further develop our multiple identities. In his article 'The Clash of Civilizations?' Samuel Huntington quoted Donald Horowitz, saying,

---

[2] In relation to his 'homogeneity' concept, Halliday (1994) sees 'culture as an important constituent of the modernity that all societies are forced to move towards' (p. 118). Although I find this view too narrowly centred on the modernity and perhaps on the modern West, I also agree with his sentences quoted in the main body of this paper.

'An Ibo may be . . . an Owerri Ibo or an Onitsha Ibo in what was the eastern region of Nigeria. In Lagos, he is simply an Ibo. In London, he is a Nigerian. In New York, he is an African' (Huntington 1993, p. 26). Should we suppose, as Huntington seems to suggest, that in New York this African has stopped being an Owerri Ibo or an Onitsha Ibo, an Ibo and a Nigerian, only to be an African belonging to the African civilization? Certainly not. To a passer-by he may simply look like an African, but within himself he is simultaneously all of these. He must surely have multiple identities which are achieved exactly because he has moved vertically from one level to another by having moved intranationally and transnationally. And people's transnational mobility makes it possible for this African in New York to have serious interactions with Asians, Arabs, Latin Americans and others, who all have their respective multiple identities. With the global problems hanging over them, their meetings will make it possible for them to identify themselves as all living together on this single planet.[3]

# 4
## Japanese Approaches to International Exchanges

Because this is a time of transition in a big way, there exist gaps between transnational phenomena and international activities. It is the task of international exchange activities to mend the gaps as much as possible, and in order to carry out this task we need new concepts and approaches for international exchanges. What kind of concepts and approaches are needed will better be discussed separately with regard to official international exchange activities and private and informal activities. Besides these two types of international exchange that are carried out more or less intentionally, there are international cultural exchanges resulting from unintentional cultural contacts which are typically transnational phenomena. Some of the new concepts and approaches particularly required of private and informal international exchange activities can also be applied in understanding the transnational phenomena of international cultural exchanges resulting from unintentional cultural contacts.

Generally speaking, a culture is a complex system composed of innumerable numbers of cultural elements. Within a culture, human rights, for example, is a part of the whole system and contains an amount of related cultural elements interlocking with each other. Of those cultural elements comprising the human rights portion of culture, some are unique to the culture and others have things in common with other cultures. And through international processes of cultural contacts, some elements may become common, while others may become more distinct. In other words, it is not that human rights *in toto* are either particular or universal, but that they are partly unique and partly common. This mode of thinking must be the basis for constructing new concepts and approaches for international exchanges.

In more concrete terms, in everyday international contacts we must be sensitive to similarities and dissimilarities between cultures as much as we can. Furthermore, as people's transnational movements keep enlarging, along with the transnational

---

[3] For my critical review of the Huntington thesis, see Hirano (1994).

movements of goods, services and information, conflicting values and cultural elements continue to arise. The individual and the group will both experience internal conflicts of cultural elements. In order to manage these internal cultural conflicts skilfully, so as not to become schizophrenic and instead to bring about an orderly, peaceful new world order, it is required of us to carry on productive cultural exchanges, consciously accumulating universal elements and preserving valuable distinct cultural elements simultaneously. Put another way, since international contacts inevitably involve cultural contacts and often invite cultural changes that are sometimes hard to swallow, we ought to be most attentive to which cultural elements may be changed and which must not be changed through international cultural exchange.

Let us now turn to the requirements of more intentional international exchange activities, focusing first on private and informal ones and then on public and formal ones. Conventionally, it was understood that international exchange activities were to promote international friendship among different nations. For decades after World War II, only a limited section of Japanese society was enthusiastic about twin-city relations with foreign countries. It was believed that such exchanges would promote international friendship. However, with ordinary citizens uninterested and not at all motivated, only city mayors exchanged courtesy calls. This type of movement and enthusiasm soon died down.

The second peak of international exchange activities in Japan came in the 1970s. The motto during this period was to promote mutual understanding. The phenomenon was related to the Japanese economic growth in the 1960s and resulting economic advances overseas in the 1960s and 1970s. It was in 1977 that former prime minister of Japan, the late Mr Takeo Fukuda, announced, in what came to be known as his 'Manila Doctrine', that mutual understanding should be the basic principle of Japan's approach to South-east Asia. Five years earlier, the Japan Foundation was established on the same principle of mutual understanding. But the Foundation was charged not with the introduction of other people's cultures to the Japanese people, but only with sending out Japanese culture to other peoples in order to increase their one-sided understanding of Japanese culture. It is often said that, to sensitize ourselves to cultural similarities and dissimilarities, mutual understanding is necessary and essential. But the mutual understanding that Mr Fukuda proposed and that the Japanese believed in those days was quite self-centred and apologetic of Japanese economic advances towards other Asian countries.

We are now in the third wave of interest in international exchanges in Japan. With non-Japanese people living in local communities such as foreign workers, who are often staying illegally, non-Japanese wives married to Japanese farmers, returned Japanese who were left in China as war orphans, children of Japanese *nisei* coming from Brazil as temporary workers and so forth, international and intercultural contacts are everyday matters. We must now live together with people of different nationalities, ethnicities and cultures within the same community. Japanese leaders of international exchange activities, who used to be rather narrowly outward-looking, in the sense that they understood the international exchange to be something like going abroad to visit a twin city and receiving foreign guests of the middle class or higher to 'international parties', are now engaged in what is called 'internal international exchange activities'. And, from among those leaders of international exchange activities, a new thinking about culture and cultural difference is now emerging.

New forces of international exchange in Japan today are concerned with youth, NGOs and local government. They join with veteran activists. The Japanese young today seem to feel more comfortable with other peoples and cultures than their seniors used to do. This is partly thanks to world music, pop Asian music, Asian art, Asian dramas, Asian films, ethnic food and so forth. A better understanding of other peoples and cultures is made possible partly by better communication. The development of international communication has been increasing the sense of international and interregional cultural communities. Furthermore, the way in which an individual places himself or herself in his or her social environment or in the world, namely his or her multiple identities, has something to do with the increase of the sense of transnational cultural community.

NGOs have been active in international development cooperation for quite some time in Japan, too. Some of them are fairly large and rather well established. In the field of international exchange activities, on the other hand, NGOs are still of rather small scale and on a more voluntary basis. For example, groups of housewives help foreign students and non-Japanese wives study Japanese; other groups encourage schoolchildren to exchange paintings; and groups of college students assist non-Japanese-speaking children of foreign workers in homework and in keeping up their native languages. Many of those local groups are nascent, relatively powerless and not well funded. However, I think they are important emerging new sectors in Japanese international exchange activities, because now ordinary Japanese are engaged in dialogues across cultures. All together, their number is by no means small.

It has been some time since Japanese local governments became active in international exchanges with local governments of other countries. Now, all the prefectural governments in Japan have created special international exchange sectors. They take charge not only of old twin-city relations but also of new international activities involving their citizens and even international development cooperation programmes.

As pointed out, the Japan Foundation is basically charged only with the task of increasing other people's understanding of Japan. Its Asian Centre, formerly the ASEAN Culture Centre, however, is the first public organization in Japan charged with introducing the cultures of other countries to the Japanese. Specifically, there is one type of exchange programme undertaken by the Asian Centre that is potentially very important. The Centre plans and sponsors joint productions of dramas, musical events, films and so forth by teams of multinational and multicultural artists from many Asian countries including Japan. Some other Japanese government agencies such as the Ministry of Education and the Ministry of International Trade and Industries are also engaged in official international exchanges, but no attempt is made here to explicate their activities.[4]

On the whole, today in Japan, grass-roots international exchange activities are popular and thriving. Perhaps for the first time in Japanese history, grass-roots activities are internationally minded and highly motivated. Some grass-roots activists,

---

[4] I have been proposing to build a new type of international network of universities; see Hirano (1996, pp. 88–97).

who are by no means revolutionary, believe that international exchange is a way to change and remodel Japanese society peacefully. Rather than aiming at the central power, they approach local governments about carrying out local initiatives together. The purpose of international cultural exchange, they say, is not for the state to propagate its foreign policies or to increase its power and reputation, but for ordinary people to exchange good ideas and to learn to live together.

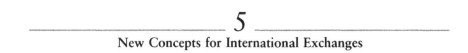

# 5

## New Concepts for International Exchanges

Summing up what has been said above, we can now enumerate some of the characteristics of the cultural situation of today's world that have a bearing on international exchanges. First, people's transnational movements continue to increase, thereby increasing international contacts, both intentionally and unintentionally, which will lead to cultural changes. Second, spurred in part by people's transnational movements, the multilayered structure of international society and the multiple identities of the individual person are more apparent. Third, people move around while retaining their ethnicities and tend to hold on to them even while residing or staying in other societies. Fourth, we will be more concerned with the universality and distinctiveness of cultural elements, while trying to accumulate universal elements and preserve valuable distinct cultural elements simultaneously. Fifth, therefore, we should be more attentive to cultural similarities and dissimilarities and sensitive enough to tell exactly which cultural elements can be changed and which cannot.

Thus, we are now in need of new concepts for international exchange. In particular, a new concept of mutual understanding is needed. Clearly, it is not one-way but a two-way mutual understanding. It works to sensitize people more towards cultural similarities and dissimilarities among them. And it is intended both to increase the universal and to increase the unique. Only by truly mutual understanding of each other's culture can we be most attentive to which cultural elements that other people have may be changed and which must not be changed, as well as learning from others those cultural elements that will enrich our lives.

Finally, a new concept is taking shape among Japanese activists in international exchanges. It is called *kyosei*. *Kyosei*, rather a new addition to the Japanese vocabulary, is translated in English as conviviality, or more plainly, living together. Newly found and advocated out of a necessity to cope with a situation in which people with different cultures must live together in the same community peacefully, mutually respecting cultural differences with tolerance, *kyosei* will be the guiding principle of international exchange for quite some time to come. To repeat, *kyosei* means peoples of different cultures living together peacefully and fruitfully. Thus, it can be expanded to mean that peoples of different cultures work together for a common purpose. Some people lament that official and formal international exchange activities are drowned in the big ocean of transnational phenomena of grass-roots exchanges and unintended cultural changes. But, as exemplified by the Japan Foundation's Asian Centre's experiments in multinational and multicultural joint productions of performing arts, the official and formal sector can take the lead in further advancing international exchange activities towards the stage on which peoples of different cultures work together for common goals.

Living together and working together requires a finer sensitivity to cultural differences. Those friends of mine in the field of international exchange are very keen to promote cultural differences, but they also say that, the longer they keep friends with other people, the more commonalities they find between peoples. By promoting living together and working together, international exchange activities help people develop the common sense of regional and global community, a *sine qua non* for peaceful international society.

## References

Abella, M. I. (1993), 'Manpower Movements in Asia and the Pacific', in *International Labour Migration in East Asia*, Tokyo: United Nations University Press.

Castles, S. and Miller, M. J. (1993), *The Age of Migration: International Population Movements in the Modern World*, London: Macmillan.

Halliday, F. (1994), *Rethinking International Relations*, London: Macmillan.

Hirano, K. (1994), 'Bunmei no shoutotsu ka bunka no masatsu ka? Hanchinton ronbun hihan' ('The clash of civilizations' or conflicts of cultures? A critique of Samuel Huntington's thesis), *Hikaku Bunmei* (Comparative civilizations), 10 (November): 21–37.

Hirano, K. (1996), 'Japan's Cultural Exchange Approaches in the Asia Pacific', in P. King and Y. Kibata (eds.), *Peace Building in the Asia Pacific Region: Perspectives from Japan and Australia*, Sydney: Allen & Unwin.

Hoffman, M. (1994), 'Normative International Theory: Approaches and Issues', in A. J. R. Groom and M. Light (eds.), *Contemporary International Relations: A Guide to Theory*, London: Pinter.

Huntington, S. P. (1993), 'The Clash of Civilizations?' *Foreign Affairs*, 72(1) Summer.

Morita, K. (ed.) (1987), *Kokusai rodo ido* (International labour migration), Tokyo: University of Tokyo Press.

Richmond, A. H. (1984), 'Ethnic Nationalism and Post-Industrialism', *Ethnic and Racial Studies*, 7(1); reprinted in J. Hutchinson and A. D. Smith (eds.), *Nationalism*, Oxford University Press, 1994.

# 6

# REGIONALISMS IN EAST ASIA AND THE ASIA–PACIFIC

*Ryuhei Hatsuse*

Regional integration would appear to be something to which we all aspire, because it implies harmony, prosperity and even peace. Upon further consideration, however, we can immediately perceive two other implications. First, this bright picture of the future often proves to be illusory, when viewed from the perspective of the oppressed, the weak or the worse-off, because it tends to sacrifice their interests to those of the strong and the better-off. A good example is that of empires — e.g. Chinese, Islamic, British, Japanese. Second, intensive integration often leads to international conflicts, because it is inwardly oriented, hence exclusive to others. Here a good example is the German reaction to the bloc economies (the pound sterling, dollar, gold, yen blocs) between the two world wars, which is generally considered as a fundamental cause of World War II. Human history through to the present has been witness to endless tides of political or economic integration and fragmentation.

We now seem to be living in a time of international integration, mostly of an economic nature, notwithstanding that nationalism, especially ethnic drives towards internal fragmentation, have regained enormous energy in the post-Cold War world. In the European context, the European Community (EC) was promoted to the European Union (EU) in 1993, which has implicitly become a contemporary model for regional integration throughout the world. In the American context, the Canada–USA Trade Agreement was enlarged to form the North American Free Trade Area (NAFTA) in 1993. In the Asian context, the intergovernmental conference of the Asia–Pacific Economic Cooperation (APEC) countries has been held every year since 1989. In addition, spontaneous but well-knit economic zones or trading blocs have come into being in East Asia, in accordance with the rapid industrializing of the Asian NIEs (Korea, Taiwan, Hong Kong, Singapore) in the late 1970s and 1980s and of Malaysia, Thailand and China in the late 1980s.

Although Asian economies are now experiencing an economic depression, they grew smoothly and in tandem until 1996. In the process of growth, regional schemes were attempted in economic activities or plans: the Asia–Pacific Economic Cooperation (APEC); the South China Economic Zone (Kwangtung, Fukien, Hong Kong, Taiwan); the South-east Asian Growth Triangle (Singapore, Johore–Malaysia,

Riau–Indonesia); the Baht Economic Zone (Thailand, Vietnam, Cambodia, Laos); the Yellow Sea Economic Ring (Korea and North China); the Asian Free Trade Agreement (AFTA, adopted in 1992 by the ASEAN countries and effective in part from 1993); the initiative of the East Asian Economic Caucus (EAEC) by Malaysian Prime Minister Dr Mahathir; development projects of the Tumen River Area (administered under UNDP auspices) of North Korea, South Korea, Japan, China, Russia, Mongolia, and voices for the 'Japan Sea (the East Sea)' Ring (Japanese prefectures on the Japan Sea, North-east China, Russia's Sikhote Alin Range and North Korea). Besides them, the Association of South-east Asian Nations (ASEAN) has been working as a political caucus, and we also see formation of the ASEAN Regional Forum as a security scheme (for consultation on security issues, with participation by ASEAN members, Japan, South Korea, China, Laos, Russia, the USA, Canada, New Zealand, Australia, Papua New Guinea and the EU). All of these are part of the global trend towards regionalism or regionalization.

The present paper focuses on four types of regionalism (mega, macro, meso and micro), utilizing them as an analytic framework for the consideration of the prospect of regionalisms in East Asia and the Asia–Pacific. It consists of six parts. The first section sheds light on the difference between two regional concepts, East Asia and the Asia–Pacific. The second deals with definition of regionalism and a typology of regionalisms in those areas. The third addresses the question of homogeneity and heterogeneity of nations situated in East Asia in order to examine the possibility for an EU-type of regional integration. The fourth section probes micro-regionalism and meso-regionalism in East Asia. Section 5 looks into the prospects for APEC fulfilling a mega-regional role in the Asia–Pacific, and also indicates some problems associated with this so-called 'open' regionalism. The sixth section investigates Japan's role in the four types of regionalism in East Asia and the Asia–Pacific. The paper concludes with a summary of these discussions.

# 1

## Defining East Asia and the Asia–Pacific

We understand that East Asia is a historical as well as a geographical concept, while the Asia–Pacific is an economic concept lacking historical depth and geographical legitimacy.

'East Asia' has a single meaning in Japanese usage, referring to Japan, Korea, China, Taiwan and (implicitly) Hong Kong. In terms of regional integration, we may be able to accept Mongolia as part of East Asia; perhaps we can also consider Russian Siberia as a part of this region. On the other hand, 'East Asia' has two meanings in English usage. One is a narrow concept identical with the Japanese usage, and the other is a broad concept, covering the South-east Asian countries (the Philippines, Singapore, Malaysia, Indonesia, Brunei, Vietnam, Cambodia, Laos, Thailand and sometimes even Myanmar) as well. In both senses of East Asia, however, we do not include the South Asian countries (Bangladesh, India, Sri Lanka, Pakistan and the Maldives). In the following discussion, East Asia is defined as consisting of both East Asia (in the narrow sense) and South-east Asia.

Recently another concept of Asia has increasingly gained popularity. This is 'the Asia–Pacific', a region defined as greater East Asia plus Canada, the United States, Mexico, Chile, Australia, New Zealand (the Pacific Rim), and Papua New Guinea (PNG) and other Pacific island countries (the Pacific Basin). This is reflective of the momentum that has led to the formation of APEC. In this regard, however, we pay little attention to Pacific island states such as Fiji or Vanuatu. In general discussions about APEC, the Asia–Pacific is understood to mean East Asia plus the countries of the Pacific Rim and Papua New Guinea minus the centre of the Pacific (the ocean islands and peoples). This is reflective of the standpoint adopted in those discussions, which is concerned less with the welfare of the small or weak peoples, simply trying to promote the Western type of economic development as a national panacea. Strictly speaking, the Asia–Pacific is no geographical concept in discussions about APEC.

Historically speaking, East Asia consisted of 'one and a half worlds'. It was autarkic in economic terms, and closed in cultural as well as political terms. Its centre was a Chinese empire that had more interest in inland than seaborne trade. Surrounding it however were peripheries, many of which had more interest in seaborne than inland trade owing to their small land area and hence limited domestic markets. They were looked down on as 'half a world' by Chinese political and intellectual elites. As is widely known, a reversal of these former positions has been in progress almost to the present in the modern history of East Asia. First Japan in the 1860s and then Korea in the 1970s came out against the former hegemony of China.

In contrast to East Asia, the Asia–Pacific has been attributed almost no historical significance, lacking regional identity and networks, until very recently. Even today it is very doubtful whether this area has gained a regional identity, although it is recognized as a regional entity in the economic sphere. Thus, the concept is unlikely to be anything more than a 'political' slogan, focusing on the economic aspects of the term, in the foreseeable future.

While East Asia is an old concept rooted in history, the Asia–Pacific is a new concept centring mostly on economic activities. This difference is important in discussing Asian regionalisms.

## 2

### Key Concepts

Andrew Hurrell singles out five elements of regionalism: (1) regionalization, (2) regional awareness and identity, (3) regional interstate cooperation, (4) state-promoted regional integration and (5) regional cohesion (see Fawcett and Hurrell 1995, pp. 39–45). If we accept this fundamental argument, we understand that regionalism is a mental and/or physical orientation towards forming a regional identity, predicated on the assumption that such an identity would lead to further regionalization (creation of a regional entity, closer cooperation and/or integration), which in turn would promote the peace and welfare for the people living in the region. Thus, the concept of regionalism is two-fold: regionalism defined in the strict sense, as an ideology or slogan, and regionalization defined in a broad sense, relating to spontaneous regional formation, regional cooperation, intentional regional integration and the formation of a regional ideology. In discussions about regionalism, we should make a clear distinction between these two levels.

*Regionalization* is a concept for analysis, or a word for description, centring on regional formation in some spheres, with or without ideological conformity. Historically, regional orientation has taken a variety of forms — empires, economic unions, common markets, free trade areas, custom unions, economic zones, trading blocs, preferential trade agreements, common security schemes, solidarity and military support between nearby revolutionaries, human networks for specific purposes and so on. On the other hand, *regionalism* in essence refers to a vision of regional solidarity, which also has historical examples, although they may not in practice have been supported by all people in the region. This includes ideas for European integration, ASEAN, the Greater Asian Co-prosperity Sphere and other 'regions' associated with regional ideologies or slogans. Such intensive regionalization or integration as empires and economic unions needs to be reinforced by some kind of regionalism in ideology.

Whenever 'regionalism' appears in real politics or economics, it is by definition proposed with reference to a specific region. Thus, to some extent, it is the size of the 'region' that determines the direction and content of the regionalism. The size of potential 'regions' varies tremendously in the East Asian or Asian–Pacific context. For example, the Asia–Pacific in its entirety is considered as a *mega-region*.[1] East Asia is understood as a *macro-region* or a 'standard' size of region similar to the EU. The South China Economic Zone, the South-east Asian Growth Triangle and the Baht Economic Zone are *micro-regions*. And ASEAN, the AFTA and the EAEC are considered as *meso-regions*, signifying something between a macro- and a micro-region. Corresponding to the size of the region in question, we can determine four types of regionalism: mega-regionalism, macro-regionalism, meso-regionalism and micro-regionalism. Here it should be noted that in general we consider the EU to be a model of regional integration, and we understand that this 'model' in practice corresponds to what has been called macro-regionalism. In addition, *sub-regionalism* is a term commonly used to designate both micro-regionalism and meso-regionalism.

The four types of regionalism are based on eight factors: (1) the number of actors, (2) leadership, (3) the stage of economic development, (4) production relationships, (5) cultural identity, (6) the level of regionalization and/or integration, (7) institutional formality and (8) ideology or slogan.

The characteristics of each type of regionalism correspond to these eight factors in the following way (see Table 1). As deduced from various micro-regional attempts in East Asia, *micro-regionalism* comprises: (1) regional cooperation among a few adjacent member-states or (domestic) regions; (2) one or two more advanced countries or regions as a nucleus in the scheme; (3) heterogeneity in terms of the actual level of economic development achieved by each member of the region, but rapidly growing economy shared by all; (4) a vertical exchange of production elements (capital/technology versus labour/land); (5) homogeneity in terms of culture, supportive of the scheme; (6) cooperation in specified spheres (e.g. trade, investment, development projects); (7) a more informal than formal institutional format; and (8) no ideology needed but a slogan preferably proposed.

---

[1] The concept of mega-regionalism originates in Yamamoto (1994).

**Table 1** Types of Regionalism

| Factor | Micro-regionalism | Meso-regionalism (ASEAN model) | Macro-regionalism (EU model) | Mega-regionalism (APEC model) |
|---|---|---|---|---|
| Actor | A few members (adjacent) | Several states | A number of states | A great number of states |
| Leadership by | One/two advanced countries/ regions | Shared equally by all | Some countries | Centre countries |
| Level of economic development | Heterogeneous but rapidly growing | More or less homogeneous | Homogeneous | Heterogeneous |
| Production relationships | Vertical | Outward: vertical | Horizontal | Horizontal/ vertical |
| Cultural identity | Homogeneous | More or less heterogeneous | Homogeneous | Heterogeneous |
| Regionalization/ integration | In specified spheres | Political caucus economic orientation | In a number of spheres | Open and flexible |
| Institutional formality | More informal | Less institutionalized | More formal | Various types |
| Regional slogan/idea/ ideology | Slogan accepted | Regional idea short of ideology | Ideology needed | Slogan without political implications |

Considering the ASEAN and its affiliates as a model, *meso-regionalism* is defined in terms of: (1) several member-states; (2) leadership equally shared by them; (3) differences in economic development among semi-centres, semi-peripheries and peripheries, but all identical in that they have adopted a development strategy essentially led by capital and technology from without; (4) production relationships determined mainly by the region's relations with the rest of the world (an autonomy of an intraregional division of labour has not yet been achieved); (5) diverse cultures, languages and religions existing alongside cross-border networks based on a shared Chinese culture; (6) political caucusing in action, and other schemes of cooperation in the making; (7) less institutionalized format; and (8) the idea of ASEAN falling short of an ideology.

Extrapolating from the history of the EU, *macro-regionalism* consists of: (1) aspiration to regional integration shared by a number of states; (2) leadership assumed by some countries; (3) homogeneity in terms of economic development, and economic growth resulting from the scheme; (4) a horizontal division of labour; (5) homogeneity in terms of culture, supportive of the scheme; (6) advancement in cooperation in a number of spheres (e.g. trade, investment, development projects, migration, information flows, cultural exchange); (7) having a more formal institutional format; and (8) some regional ideology. No regional attempt exists in Asia that can be now classified as macro-regionalism.

Adopting APEC as a model, *mega-regionalism* is composed of: (1) aspiration to create an economic zone shared by a great number of the member-states; (2) advanced countries as the nuclei to promote the scheme; (3) heterogeneity in terms of economic development, economic size, political system or civic culture, as a potential negative factor in the scheme; (4) a mixture of a horizontal and a vertical division of labour, implying an unequal distribution of economic achievement; (5) heterogeneity in terms of culture; (6) openness, or a flexible inward/outward cooperation scheme; (7) possessing a potential for a wide range of institutional styles, for example custom unions, free trade agreements, informal economic cooperation; and (8) a slogan accepted only if without any political implications.

Note that there is neither priority nor temporal sequence in these four types. In the Asia–Pacific context they proceed simultaneously, and sometimes overlap or skip an intervening level.

Finally, we must understand that economic regional integration generally follows five steps: (1) formation of a preferential trade agreement; (2) creation of a free trade zone; (3) formation of a customs union; (4) formation of a common market (commodity, services, capital, labour); and (5) creation of an economic union (adopting a uniform currency, building a central bank). But integrative activities with political implications can come at the early or final stages of integration. The former example is the European Coal and Steel Community, which was formed in 1952 to prevent Germany from military resurgence, or ASEAN (formed in 1967), which became effective in 1976 to establish a defence against Vietnam. The latter example occurs when political integration is achieved after the last stage of economic integration in the EU.

The next three sections will elaborate on these regionalisms in the East Asian and Asia–Pacific contexts.

# 3

## Prospects for Macro-regionalism in East Asia

In this section we will measure the potential for an EU-type of regional integration in East Asia by focusing on some social and economic indicators of East Asian countries and comparing them with those of the EU countries.

Applying the criteria of macro-regionalism to contemporary East Asia, we see economic advancement in the region, but no aspiration to macro-regional integration, leadership, horizontal division of labour, institutional framework or regional ideology. The question of homogeneity *v.* heterogeneity will be elaborated on later in this section. First, we find out some evidence of regionalization but little of regionalism.

Asian economies are currently in an economic depression. In Thailand the bubble economy collapsed at the end of 1996 and the depreciation of the *baht* started in July 1997. Since then, the currency crisis has rapidly spread to Indonesia, Malaysia, the Philippines, Singapore and Korea. The exchange rate of each currency to the US dollar fell dramatically between the end of June 1997 and the end of April

1998: by 33 per cent for the Thai *baht*, 70 per cent for the Indonesian *rupiah*, 32 per cent for the Malaysian *ringgit*, 34 per cent for the Filipino *peso*, 10 per cent for the Singapore dollar and 34 per cent for the Korean *won*. In the late 1990s, the Japanese economy is also in agony after the breakdown of the bubble economy, and the yen depreciated by 14 per cent against the US dollar during the above period (Sakura-sougou-kenkyuusho Kantaiheiyou-kenkyuu-sentaa 1998, p. 65).

However, growth of the East Asian economy seems, remarkably, to have gathered a momentum of its own by 1997. East Asia's share formed about a quarter of the total world GDP in 1995 (Japan: 16 per cent, and others countries: 8 per cent). This is comparable to the EU and the USA as the share of both was respectively 26 per cent. And East Asia's share almost doubled between 1965 and 1995, up from 13 per cent (1965). In terms of exports in 1995, East Asia's share was more than a quarter of the world total (Japan: 9 per cent and others countries: 12 per cent). In the same year, the EU accounted for 35 per cent and the USA for 27 per cent. Referring to the intraregional trade, its ratio to the total volume of trade of East Asia (excluding Japan) rose from 28 per cent in 1985 to 38 per cent in 1996. In terms of direct investment too, the recent achievements of the Asian NIES are outstanding. While Japan's share of direct investment in this region dropped from 32 per cent in 1987 to 21 per cent in 1996, the NIESs' share increased from 27 per cent in 1987 to 42 per cent in 1994. Meanwhile, the share of the USA remained more or less the same — 15 per cent in 1985 and 11 per cent in 1996 — as did that of the EU — 15 per cent in 1985 and 12 per cent in 1996. It should also be noted that, after Japan, most of the Asian investment came from Chinese in Hong Kong (70 per cent), Taiwan (15 per cent) and Singapore (10 per cent), and 60 per cent of it was directed towards the PRC in 1994 (Tsuushou-sangyoushou 1996, p. 10; Mitusi-bussan Boeki-keizai-kenkyuusho 1996, pp. 91, 336–7; Sakura-sougou-kenkyuusho, Kan-taiheiyou-kenkyuu-sentaa 1996, p. 207).

Although East Asia is understood to be one of the world economic centres, comparable with the USA and the EU, we must also bear in mind that all the above data indicate not absolute but relative values, e.g. percentages. While the EU and the US are in relative decline, in absolute terms they have played a greater role in trade and investment within this region than in the preceding decades. More-over, we cannot simply take the data on international trade as fully reflecting the situation of the East Asian nations, because the figures include multinationals owned by American and European capital, the advance of which has been extremely marked there in recent years. Hence East Asian economic growth does not preclude the West from exerting its influence over the economy in this region.

Turning to homogeneity–heterogeneity, East Asia is internally disparate in both cultural and economic terms, therefore heterogeneous, which is in contrast to the fact that the EU is very homogeneous in some important aspects. Although we under-stand that homogeneity and heterogeneity are not decisive factors for integration or fragmentation, we also admit that, generally speaking, homogeneity promotes integration and heterogeneity hinders it.

The countries of East Asia vary greatly in terms of income while those of the EU do not, and East Asia's economic structure has four layers: Japan as the centre, the NIEs as semi-centres, Thailand, Malaysia and China's coastal provinces as

**Table 2**  Classification by GDP per capita, 1995

| Income group | East Asia and Asia–Pacific | EU |
|---|---|---|
| Low income | Myanmar | |
| | Vietnam | |
| | Cambodia | |
| | Mongolia | |
| | Lao PDR | |
| | China | |
| Middle income (lower) | Korea, DR | |
| | Indonesia | |
| | Philippines | |
| | *Papua New Guinea | |
| | Thailand | |
| Middle income (upper) | *Mexico | Greece |
| | Malaysia | |
| | *Chile | |
| High income | Taiwan | Portugal |
| | Brunei | Spain |
| | Korea, R | Ireland |
| | *New Zealand | UK |
| | *Australia | Italy |
| | *Canada | Finland |
| | Hong Kong | Sweden |
| | Singapore | Netherlands |
| | *USA | Belgium |
| | Japan | France |
| | | Austria |
| | | Germany |
| | | Denmark |
| | | Luxembourg |

* Denotes APEC members apart from East Asia.
*Data source*: World Bank, *World Development Report 1997*; UNDP, *Human Development Report 1997*.

semi-peripheries, and the others as peripheries (see Table 2).[2] In terms of population size, the variation is more significant in East Asia than in the EU. Obviously, China itself is much bigger than all the EU countries combined. In terms of life expectancy and general education, while the EU countries seem to have reached the highest level of development, the East Asian countries have been doing their best to catch up with them, coming close in recent years (see Table 3).

However, if we turn to economic growth and life expectancy, the differences among the East Asian countries become somewhat smaller, as economic growth

---

[2] In terms of the world system in general, the world is composed of three layers: the centre, the semi-periphery and the periphery. However, in the contemporary Asian context, we should be able to introduce a new category (the semi-centre) as more suitable for the Asian NIEs.

**Table 3**  Homogeneity and Heterogeneity within Asia–Pacific and EU[a]

| | Population (million) 1994 | Real GDP per capita (ppp$) 1994 | Life expectancy at birth (years) 1994 | Adult literacy rate (%) 1994 |
|---|---|---|---|---|
| Brunei | 0.3 | 30.447 | 74.9 | 87.9 |
| Hong Kong | 6.2 | 22.310 | 79.0 | 92.3 |
| Japan | 125.2 | 21.581 | 79.8 | 99.0 |
| Singapore | 3.0 | 20.987 | 77.1 | 91.0 |
| Korea, R | 44.9 | 10.656 | 71.5 | 97.9 |
| Malaysia | 20.1 | 8.865 | 71.2 | 83.0 |
| Thailand | 58.2 | 7.104 | 69.5 | 93.5 |
| Korea, DR | 23.9 | 3.965 | 71.4 | 95.0 |
| Mongolia | 2.5 | 3.766 | 64.4 | 82.2 |
| Indonesia | 193.3 | 3.740 | 63.5 | 83.2 |
| Philippines | 68.6 | 2.681 | 67.0 | 94.4 |
| China | 1200.2 | 2.604 | 68.9 | 80.9 |
| Lao PDR | 4.9 | 2.484 | 51.7 | 55.8 |
| Vietnam | 73.5 | 1.208 | 66.0 | 93.0 |
| Cambodia | 10.0 | 1.084 | 52.4 | 35.0 |
| Myanmar | 45.1 | 1.051 | 58.4 | 82.7 |
| USA | 263.1 | 26.397 | 76.2 | 99.0 |
| Canada | 29.6 | 21.459 | 79.0 | 99.0 |
| Australia | 18.1 | 19.285 | 78.1 | 99.0 |
| New Zealand | 3.6 | 16.851 | 76.4 | 99.0 |
| Chile | 14.2 | 9.129 | 75.1 | 95.0 |
| Mexico | 91.8 | 7.384 | 72.0 | 89.2 |
| PNG | 4.3 | 2.821 | 56.4 | 71.2 |
| Luxembourg | 0.4 | 34.155 | 75.9 | 99.0 |
| Denmark | 5.2 | 21.341 | 75.2 | 99.0 |
| Belgium | 10.1 | 20.985 | 76.8 | 99.0 |
| Austria | 8.1 | 20.667 | 76.6 | 99.0 |
| France | 58.1 | 20.510 | 78.7 | 99.0 |
| Germany | 81.9 | 19.675 | 76.3 | 99.0 |
| Italy | 57.2 | 19.363 | 77.8 | 98.1 |
| Netherlands | 15.5 | 19.238 | 77.3 | 99.0 |
| UK | 58.5 | 18.620 | 76.7 | 99.0 |
| Sweden | 8.8 | 18.540 | 78.3 | 99.0 |
| Finland | 5.1 | 17.417 | 76.3 | 99.0 |
| Ireland | 3.6 | 16.061 | 76.3 | 99.0 |
| Spain | 39.2 | 14.324 | 77.6 | 97.1 |
| Portugal | 9.9 | 12.326 | 74.6 | 89.6 |
| Greece | 10.5 | 11.265 | 77.8 | 96.7 |

[a] ppp$ = purchasing power parity developed by the UN International Comparison Project; adult literacy = % of persons aged 15 and over who can, with understanding, both read and write a short simple statement on their everyday life. No data available for Taiwan. *Data source*: UNDP, *Human Development Report 1997*; World Bank, *World Development Report 1997*.

**Table 4** Homogeneity and Heterogeneity within Asia–Pacific and EU[a]

| | GNP per capita Average annual growth (%) 1985–95 | Increase in life expectancy at birth (years) 1960–92 | Adult literacy (%) 1994 | |
| --- | --- | --- | --- | --- |
| | | | Women | Men |
| Brunei | – | 11.7 | – | – |
| Hong Kong | 4.8 | 11.2 | 89.1 | 96.0 |
| Japan | 2.9 | 10.7 | 99.0 | 99.0 |
| Singapore | 6.2 | 9.7 | 87.2 | 95.6 |
| Korea, R | 7.7 | 16.5 | 96.8 | 99.0 |
| Malaysia | 5.7 | 16.5 | 77.5 | 88.2 |
| Thailand | 8.4 | 16.4 | 90.7 | 95.6 |
| Korea, DR | – | 16.8 | – | – |
| Mongolia | –3.8 | 16.3 | 75.8 | 87.9 |
| Indonesia | 6.0 | 20.8 | 77.1 | 89.4 |
| Philippines | 1.5 | 11.8 | 93.9 | 94.8 |
| China | 8.3 | 23.4 | 70.9 | 89.6 |
| Lao PDR | 2.7 | 9.9 | 42.7 | 68.6 |
| Vietnam | – | 19.2 | 89.9 | 95.7 |
| Cambodia | – | 8.0 | – | – |
| Myanmar | – | 13.1 | 76.8 | 88.6 |
| USA | 1.3 | 5.7 | 99.0 | 99.0 |
| Canada | 0.4 | 6.2 | 99.0 | 99.0 |
| Australia | 1.4 | 6.0 | 99.0 | 99.0 |
| New Zealand | 0.8 | 4.4 | 99.0 | 99.0 |
| Chile | 6.1 | 14.8 | 95.0 | 95.4 |
| Mexico | 0.1 | 12.8 | 86.7 | 91.5 |
| PNG | 2.3 | 14.6 | 60.7 | 79.8 |
| Luxembourg | 0.9 | 7.0 | 99.0 | 99.0 |
| Denmark | 1.5 | 3.2 | 99.0 | 99.0 |
| Belgium | 2.2 | 5.4 | 99.0 | 99.0 |
| Austria | 1.9 | 7.0 | 99.0 | 99.0 |
| France | 1.5 | 6.3 | 99.0 | 99.0 |
| Germany | – | – | 99.0 | 99.0 |
| Italy | 1.8 | 7.7 | 98.1 | 98.1 |
| Netherlands | 1.9 | 4.0 | 99.0 | 99.0 |
| UK | 1.4 | 5.2 | 99.0 | 99.0 |
| Sweden | –0.1 | 4.6 | 99.0 | 99.0 |
| Finland | –0.2 | 6.9 | 99.0 | 99.0 |
| Ireland | 5.2 | 5.4 | 99.0 | 99.0 |
| Spain | 2.6 | 8.4 | 97.1 | 97.1 |
| Portugal | 3.6 | 11.1 | 89.6 | 89.6 |
| Greece | 1.3 | 8.6 | 96.7 | 96.7 |

[a] Adult literacy = % of persons aged 15 and over who can, with understanding, both read and write a short simple statement on their everyday life. No data available for Taiwan. *Data source*: UNDP, *Human Development Report 1995, 1997*; World Bank, *World Development Report 1983, 1995, 1997*.

and extension in life expectancy have been very remarkable in these Asian countries in recent years (see Table 4). We interpret these shared phenomena of East Asia as an aspect of the increasing homogeneity of the region. Although the East Asian countries are heterogeneous in many aspects at present, they are homogeneous at least in that they all are striving for economic and social maturity.

We should, however, hasten to look at another part of Table 4: the aspect of gender discrimination as indicated by the comparison of adult literacy of women with that of men. There is some variation among the East Asian countries and less among those of the EU, but the important difference is that between the two regions. This traditional social psychology can unfortunately work as a social barrier against equal, open and mutually beneficial cooperation or integration in East Asia. Combined with obsessive developmentalism, it has tended to deprive the people of human rights in most East Asian countries (formerly South Korea, Taiwan; nowadays China, Singapore, Malaysia, Thailand, Indonesia, the Philippines and North Korea). For example, in Singapore, China and North Korea, human rights NGOs are forbidden (Jones 1993, p. 23). This problem of human rights relating to APEC as an aspect of mega-regionalism will be elaborated upon in Section 5.

East Asia has to some extent worked as an economic unit, by making the most of the division of labour, and by circulating money, goods and services within the whole. This is indicative of regionalization rather than regionalism. In addition, there are a few more homogeneous elements: the rapid economic development and accompanying social changes in recent years, and the tendency for traditional culture to be negative towards Western ideas of human rights. These cannot, however, be a driving force for an EU-type of regional integration, because East Asia is internally more heterogeneous than homogeneous in economic and cultural terms. In economic terms, the vertical division of labour still exists, as does a great gap in incomes. Religion rarely provides strong motivation for integration among Asian peoples, for there is no universally accepted religion in this region. No scenario has been designed for political integration, or for any common security system. Thus, we may conclude that there is little probability of a macro-regional formation, but that economic regionalization without regionalism proceeded smoothly until 1997.

However, the fragility of these economies became a serious problem after the economic crisis started at the end of 1996. As P. Krugman pointed out, the economic growth of the NIES was not a result of an increase in production efficiency derived from technological innovation, but rather was based on the export of labour-intensive products supported by increases in capital investment (foreign and domestic) and more inputs of domestic cheap labour (Krugman 1996, p. 175; see also Hara 1996, pp. 79–80). In terms of technology trade, while Japan showed a deficit (for the 1994 fiscal year) with both the USA (Japan's exports totalled 139.3 billion yen; imports were 261.9 billion) and Europe (Japan's exports equalled 81.0 billion yen; imports were 107.7 billion), it showed a great surplus with Asia, exporting 214 billion yen to the Asian countries, and importing only 1.1 billion yen from all the countries of Asia, Latin America and Africa. This implies that little innovation in technology comes from other Asian countries (Kagaku-gijutsucho 1996, pp. 420–1). Besides, as most of Asian economies have relied heavily on forms of money borrowed from other countries, in times of depression they have no choice but to suffer from serious currency crisis caused by the withdrawal of short-term investment. That can be predicted from the high ratio of the foreign debt to GNP in those economies (at the end of 1996, 59.7 per cent in Indonesia, 50.3 per cent in Thailand, 47.3 per cent in the Philippines and 42.1 per cent in Malaysia) and also from the high ratio of short-term to total debt (at end-1996, 41.4 per cent in Thailand, 27.8 per cent in Malaysia, 25.0 per cent in Indonesia and 19.3 per cent in the Philippines) (Sakura-sougou-kenkyuusho 1998, p. 87). We recognize that those economies are still weak in fundamentals, which implies that the economic regionalization is not so firmly achieved internally in this region as it may appear.

# 4

## Prospects for Micro- and Meso-regionalism in East Asia

In this section we will focus on regional cooperation schemes or activities at the micro level and regionalism or regional integration at the meso level.

Starting with micro-regionalism, some remarkable examples have arisen in recent years, namely, the South China Economic Zone and the South-east Asian Growth Triangle. As for the former, in terms of GDP per capita (1993), Kwangtung (US$610) and Fukien ($387) are far behind Hong Kong ($19,926) and Taiwan ($10,221). However, in terms of the annual rate of GDP growth (1982–93), Kwangtung (18 per cent) and Fukien (17 per cent) are clearly ahead of Taiwan (6 per cent) and Hong Kong (4 per cent). Obviously, the economic development of the Zone was based on a vertical exchange of technology and capital from Hong Kong and Taiwan with labour and land from Kwangtung and Fukien. As for the latter, in terms of GDP per capita (1991), Singapore (US$12,940) ranks ahead of Johore ($3,595) and far ahead of Riau ($500 in 1988). In terms of the annual rate of growth (1988–90), Singapore (10 per cent) and Johore (8 per cent) are very similar, but data are not available for Riau (Kakazu 1995, pp. 33, 35). Here too, a vertical exchange of production elements works between the industrial centres (Singapore and Johore) and the supplier of oil and natural gas (Riau).

In addition to the above examples, East Asia has seen the following sub-regional attempts at cooperation: (1) trading zones in action: the 'Yellow Sea Ring'; the Baht Zone; the AFTA; (2) trading zones in formation: the 'Japan Sea (the East Sea) Ring'; the EAEC initiative; (3) development projects: Tumen River Area and (4) a security scheme: the ASEAN Regional Forum (for consultation on security issues, with participation by ASEAN members, Japan, South Korea, China, Laos, Russia, the USA, Canada, New Zealand, Australia, Papua New Guinea and the EU) (Yamakage 1991; Aoki 1994; Nishihara 1994).

Turning to meso-regionalism, we focus on ASEAN and the AFTA. Although the ASEAN Regional Forum is more extensive in membership, its nucleus is ASEAN and in this sense it can be considered to be meso-regional.

Here we shall consider whether there are potentials for further success in micro or meso-regional cooperation schemes in this area.

Taken as a whole, Asia is rich in both natural and human resources, and had a more or less self-sufficient economy before Western industrialization began. However, from the sixteenth century onwards, the Western powers started to take resources from their colonies, using them for their own benefit and robbing this area of self-sufficiency. Before the Europeans came, trading blocs, centring on Malacca, the Spice Islands, Ryukyu, Gujarat and others, had been quite common, and were widely supported by the ongoing economic activities within this area (Abu-Lughod 1989; Takakura 1993; Pearson 1984). East and South Asia also enjoyed some advanced technology; for example, technology for the manufacture of Indian cotton and Chinese silk and pottery was more advanced there than in the West until the late eighteenth century. In fact, England had no choice but to prohibit the import and even the use of Indian cotton so as to protect its home textile industry in the first half of the eighteenth century (Kawakatsu 1993, pp. 48–9, 55). Asia has economic potential, although it has been blocked by Western and Japanese colonialism before 1945, American hegemony since 1945, and Japanese hegemony since the 1960s. It is time that East Asia (other than Japan) exerts its potential power.

Besides, the recent economic activities are very dynamic in the East Asian countries, and their pattern of development varies greatly. Any pattern might be possible in this region in the future, and at least some will be part of various attempts at micro- or meso-regionalism. The Asian NIEs (Korea, Taiwan, Hong Kong, Singapore) adopted the strategy of export-oriented industrialization, and they are succeeding in it. Moreover, the Korean and Taiwanese strategies were not identical. While Korea started with heavy industries under the strong leadership of the government, Taiwan started with light industries on the initiative of the people. The recent example of development in Thailand is also very interesting, because it is based on a strategy of export-oriented industrialization of agriculture, fisheries, poultry and jewellery (Suehiro 1993; Hara 1996, p. 12). The latest development of the Chinese coastal provinces is even more remarkable, in the sense that it is based on the socialist–market economy strategy, a concept that in itself appears contradictory. The success of this strategy is proof against Mao Tse-tung's Self-Reliance Strategy and the orthodox Marxist theory of imperialism. It is foreign capital, especially that introduced by Chinese outside the People's Republic of China (primarily from Taiwan and Hong Kong), that made this seemingly contradictory policy possible. Moreover, in South-east Asia recent approaches to development have come more or less from the idea of creating a free economy. This has led to strong inducements for less governmental engagement, a policy quite distinct from the development strategy adopted by the Asian NIEs.

It is trans-border local initiatives that have started micro-regional attempts in East Asia, reinforced by their relations beyond the micro-region itself. They are important to the extent that a few developing countries or regions provide joint enterprises or projects with their local labour and land, and an advanced country or region provides the capital and technology needed for these enterprises or projects. However, cases where capital technology, resources, labour and the market are fully arranged *within* the region are very rare. As their strategy is in general export-oriented, their relationship with the world economy is also important. Only if both global and national economies grow will micro-regionalism continue to be strong in East Asia.

In this context, it is the American market that has supported the recent development in East Asia. While East Asia has the potential to be self-reliant, in reality it has not been so. The economic prosperity of this region is possible only through a delicate balance of internal autonomy and external interdependence. Although the balance has recently shifted somewhat towards the inner autonomy, a good balance with the external elements will still continue to be maintained. In addition, the recent economic crisis has again invited American influences over this area through the tightening of each domestic policy under the control by the IMF. This does not tend to strike a good balance, but creates more dependency.

A specific factor of this region is the Chinese, those living both in China and overseas, who are very skilled at establishing excellent human networks, utilizing both money and ethnicity. Money refers to capital which flows into China, the homeland of overseas Chinese. This 'Bamboo Network', which 'bends but never breaks', covers the whole area of East Asia, and will continue to make a tremendous contribution to the Chinese economy, and hence to the micro- and meso-regionalisms surrounding the People's Republic of China (PRC) (Weidebaum and Hughes 1996, p. 3).

The major uncertainty of this micro-regionalism is what effect the vertical exchange of production elements will exert on the social atmosphere of the nations involved. Although it contains the seeds of conflict in the distribution of economic benefits, it will not be an issue as long as the economy of the micro- and meso-region as a whole keeps growing. However, if it does become a political issue, any micro-regional attempt that aims at coordination in functional economic terms alone is destined to failure.

As for meso-regionalism in East Asia, ASEAN is a kind of political caucus, whose member-countries share a common purpose, and in this respect it is comparable with the EU. This is also true of the AFTA and the ASEAN Regional Forum, both born of ASEAN. ASEAN is, however, internally much weaker in economic terms and less cohesive in social terms. Facing the recent economic crisis, it has been unable to take a joint action against the turmoil. It cannot be denied that each member-country has become more subservient to major economic powers through international financial assistance. This might be a temporary phenomenon, but the current economic crisis is sure to cloud the prospect of sub-regionalism, whether micro or meso, to some extent. An exception can be a version of micro-regionalism, which completely relies on the power of exports, which is strengthened by the lower prices caused by depreciation of currency of the countries concerned.

# 5

## Prospects for Mega-regionalism in the Asia–Pacific

In this section we will discuss mega-regionalism in East Asia, focusing on APEC and its problems. The APEC countries are agreed that the developed countries in the scheme will liberalize investment and trade fully by 2010, and that the developing countries will follow suit by 2020.

The APEC countries are much more heterogeneous than the East Asian countries in terms of population, economic size and capability, political system, religion and cultural values (see Tables 2–4). The existence of such a big gap in economic strength might work forcefully against further integration. The data on regionalization are misleading to a certain extent. Although APEC's share of world trade rose to 34 per cent in 1994, it was actually a combination of figures for East Asia and those for the USA, which also has strong economic ties with Europe. Viewed from the US standpoint, 28 per cent of its exports went to East Asia, and 20 per cent to the EU in 1994, while 41 per cent of its imports came from East Asia, and 17 per cent from the EU in the same year. Thus, although the United States was tilted towards East Asia in terms of imports, it is not necessarily biased towards East Asia in terms of trade as a whole, or in terms of its total economic activities. It enjoys strong economic partnership with Europe and the Americas as well as with East Asia (Mitusi-bussan Boeki-keizai-kenkyuusho 1996, p. 337).

Regionalization within APEC is still considered more as a goal than as a firmly established reality. In the context of APEC, political leaders make frequent use of this regional slogan, but it is not possible to persuade the entirety of the enormous population living in this huge area, as the slogan is not reinforced by a common culture or memory, or by a shared historical identity. So it is an irony of politics that we often call on 'APECism', without incurring any political conflicts. This is because APEC is merely an attempt to achieve 'economic regionalization lacking regionalism in mind'.

It is each nation's strength in the world economy that determines the size and content of the benefit that it receives through its participation in mega-regionalism. Developing countries try to overcome marginalization by participating in mega-regionalism. Potential benefits include gaining an inflow of more foreign capital, having easier access to overseas markets and receiving better technical assistance (Fawcett and Hurrell 1995, p. 22). In this sense they participate in mega-regionalism in a reactive way. On the other hand, developed countries are more active, endeavouring to exert hegemony by utilizing trade, investment and technology opportunities in the mega-regional scheme for their own benefit. Probably there are a few places where both can enjoy benefits from the scheme. Thus, at best, the future of APEC will be a loose type of free trading zone. As long as economic growth continues, APEC will advance the division of labour, both vertical and horizontal, to a higher level. Without economic growth, however, the potential conflicts among the member-states will assuredly turn into arguments or attempts to abandon the scheme.

As benefits to be derived from APEC are expected to be uneven, actions and reactions of the member-states with regard to the scheme differ. For example, there have been two voices with regard to the institutionalization of APEC. One is from the United States, which has pushed for forming an institution to manage free trade. The other is from Malaysia, on behalf of the developing countries, and calls for a loose type of economic cooperation. The developing countries are most concerned about being marginalized within the world economy, and support for APEC comes from the expectation that through this support they can evade the worst scenario. Japan is situated in between these positions, but tends to lean towards the American initiatives.

Turning to the environments of APEC, this mega-regionalism is closely related to various micro- or meso-regional attempts in the region. Mega-regionalism, meso-regionalism and micro-regionalism can go hand in hand as both the APEC pie and its slices are getting bigger and bigger. For that purpose, we need a more sophisticated advancement of the vertical division of labour. And, as the APEC pie becomes bigger, more weak nations will ask for membership, because they have no choice but to join it in order to avoid marginalization. India, Pakistan, Peru, Argentina, Ecuador and Russia are all now eager to join this mega-regional attempt.

NAFTA is another example of meso-regionalism which may have substantial impacts on the future of APEC. In that APEC is 'searching for economic regionalization without regionalism', it can coexist with sub-regional attempts in East Asia which amount to 'economic regionalization without regionalism', but it is probably incompatible with NAFTA in the following respects. NAFTA is comprised of three countries, one of which is the United States, a country comparable in economic power to the EU. Moreover, in view of the size of the area that is covered by the three countries, NAFTA can be classified as being macro-regional rather than meso-regional. In addition, NAFTA claims to be a free trade zone, but in fact is very restrictive in local content regulations. In contrast, micro- and meso-regionalisms in East Asia have expressed no will to be so exclusive in formulation. Thus, macro-regional NAFTA is a more or less divisive factor to APEC in that it is more closed within itself. The conflict between the two will become clearer if both become more firmly established as regional schemes (see Hosono 1995).

Mega-regionalism itself is also part of the process of globalization of the world economy, which promotes global increases in capital, goods, services and information flows. For this reason, the future of mega-regionalism will to a great extent be determined by the ebb and flow of the world economy, and by the process of globalization. If globalization spreads smoothly, then so will mega-regionalization, but if the pace of globalization drops, then mega-regionalism will lose momentum. If there is to be a crisis of APEC, it will come along with a crisis in the world economy. Thus, globalization is another factor in determining the future of APEC.

Factors other than economic ones will also exert influence on the future of APEC. For example, China is an unpredictable factor in Asia–Pacific economics, politics and security. A weak China implies instability, but so does a strong one. A huge state, China can work both positively and negatively for peace and stability in the region. China, as a continent in itself, is bigger than Europe as a whole. In that sense, regional integration similar in degree to that in the EU has existed in East Asia for a long time — since it was realized in ancient times. However, modern China has not yet become fully developed in economic terms, nor has it regained the former position of cultural leadership. Moreover, China is not very advanced in promoting human rights, which indicates the country's limited legitimacy in diplomacy. Thus, the revival of the former 'one-and-a-half' worlds is unthinkable in economic or political terms in the near future.

It is the well-knit network of Chinese people all over the world that is remarkable as an economic source to support a resurgent China. The active engagement of this network would allow China to activate its latent potentials in the PRC, Taiwan, Hong Kong, East Asia, Oceania and the rest of the world. But nobody can predict the ways in which this transnational network will shape the future of APEC.

Finally, let us probe the meaning of 'open' regionalism, a concept that some define as being the essence of APEC (e.g. No Teh-wu 1991; Bergstein 1994). Immediately the question arises as to whether APEC, so defined, is still a regional attempt at integration. In the literal sense, this definition is a contradiction, because an important element of regionalism is its inward orientation, or in essence its 'closedness' to non-members. Thus, the 'openness' or 'softness' cannot be the essence of regionalism. In discussions about APEC, however, this idea of 'openness' is useful in that it implies a negative end, to be avoided. More importantly, this has two messages to guide us in understanding regionalism. The first is that regionalism must be a balance of inward and outward forces. Thus, a crucial question about regional integration is how openly it should/could involve non-members. At least until now, the slogan of 'open regionalism' has been warmly accepted, in part because there exists no possibility of using APEC as a tight scheme of regional integration. The second implication is that APEC should be open to the people of the region; otherwise, it will not promote their welfare and peace in a real sense. For example, regionalism administered only by the government quite often insists on development policy at the sacrifice of the environment, hence threatening local welfare and peace. Those who support the idea of 'open' regionalism in APEC generally overlook this second implication.

In the APEC context, the goal of regionalism is judged to be economic growth promoted by the belief in growth or the ideology of developmentalism. At the time of the Osaka APEC Conference in November 1995, NGOs convened an 'NGO Forum on APEC' in Kyoto (since Osaka was closed to all foreigners other than the official APEC participants during the conference). In the NGO Recommendations towards the Osaka APEC Summit, they raised the voice of 'the worse-off and the socially disadvantaged', and rejected some governments' assertions that human rights must be applied according to each state's cultural background or developmental stage. They accused some governments of violating the right to the development 'of individuals' under the pretext of protecting the right to the development 'of the states' (NGO Forum on APEC 1995). It is likely that developmentalism is quite often given precedence over environmental protection or human rights promotion.

In general understanding, open regionalism means that participation in the regional scheme should be open to non-member countries; but we understand that it means being open to the people of the member-countries as well. If APEC continues to be kept closed to the people, there will be little advantage for them in the long run. Thus, the people's participation is an absolute necessity for the success of APEC as a promoter of peace and welfare in this region.

In sum, the future of APEC as a mega-regionalism will be in the form of a large-scale, loose trading bloc involving voluminous investment flows, the content and meaning of which will be determined by regional economic and non-economic factors, relations with various forms of regionalism, both inside and outside the region, and the advance of globalization in the world economy. At the same time, regional or national economies are also important as a factor for promoting the mega-regional attempt. In the context of the current economic crisis, while Asian countries might lose some interest in APEC, the USA and the EU could take this opportunity to exert more influence on the economies of the ASEAN countries and Korea. Although Japan should help other Asian economies more, it cannot afford to do so at present because it too is in serious depression.

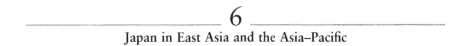

# 6
## Japan in East Asia and the Asia–Pacific

In this section we will focus on Japan's location and role in the four types of regionalism in East Asia and the Asia–Pacific. The recent economic depression has deprived Japan of the extra power it could afford to exert in the mid-1990s. It is a necessity that Japan help other Asian economies in serious crisis, but its ability is at present much limited owing to its own fragility.

In the previous analysis, we reached the conclusion that macro-regionalism is a very remote possibility in this area, but we must hasten to add that economic 'regionalization' in substance has already been achieved without regionalist ideology or slogans in the region of East Asia. The distinction between regionalization and regionalism is nowhere more important than in this area. Since the mid-nineteenth century, the strongest voice for regionalism came from Japan. The examples are Pan-Asianism, proposed by Japan in the late nineteenth and early twentieth centuries, and the idea of the 'Greater Asian Co-prosperity Sphere', advocated as a slogan to unite East Asian peoples during World War II. Neither of these schemes was widely accepted outside Japan. Since the end of the war, Japan has generally refrained from repeating the same mistake. Since the 1960s it has concentrated on economic regionalization, becoming an economic centre in this area in the 1970s. A slogan for regionalism is now emanating from the ASEAN countries rather than Japan, in the form of the idea of ASEAN or 'New Asianism'. Regionalization without regionalism at the macro level means maintenance of the *status quo* for Japan, which is currently situated at the centre and will continue to be there for the foreseeable future.

Japan is related to micro-regionalism in two ways: involvement and response. Micro-regional attempts involving Japan would not present any serious problems to Japanese leadership, because Japanese capital and technology are an absolute necessity for them. It is only Japan's backing that is required in this situation. However, micro-regionalism excluding Japan would probably raise more serious problems for the Japanese economy, if these schemes were closed to Japanese capital, goods and services in the future. This has not happened as yet, but is likely to occur if micro-regionalism proliferates more widely in this region. Japanese response will then be more difficult in this context.

Japan's relations with meso-regionalism are more indirect, because it cannot be a full member in any political scheme of ASEAN even though it has enjoyed an intensive relationship with each member-state, and because it is more directly involved in each national economy than with the whole ASEAN scheme.

With regard to APEC, Japan will have to make a choice between two alternatives: (1) being a transmitter of Western culture and economy, and (2) being a coordinator between Western and Asian cultures and economies. Until recently, Japan chose the first. It seems, however, that it may be time for it to switch to the second, in keeping with the expectation of other Asian countries. Japan is now expected to promote socio-economic development for the people, to render support for human rights activities, and to take the leadership for disarmament in the Asia–Pacific. This is in sharp contrast to its former policy of promoting development and security at home and abroad with the economic and military help of the United States under the government's leadership.

Underlying the above discussions, however, is a hidden assumption that Japan will be able to retain its position of economic power. This assumption is flawed. Japanese economic power has been derived from export capabilities and the offshore production of a certain type of manufactured good. For example, in 1995 75 per cent of Japan's exports was machinery, 26 per cent were electric goods and 12 per cent, cars. With regard to domestic watch production, 88 per cent was for export. Similarly, 87 per cent of cameras, 78 per cent of motorcycles, 77 per cent of VCRs, 43 per cent of automobiles and 40 per cent of TV sets produced in Japan were exported in 1994. The percentage of offshore production was 78 per cent for colour TVs, 69 per cent for stereo sets, 53 per cent for VTRs, 48 per cent for audio-visual sets and 31 per cent for cars in 1994 (Tsuushou-sangyoushou, 1996, pp. 188, 212 in *General Analysis*, pp. 773, 775 in *Sectional Analysis*). These are mass-produced goods for mass consumption, and they are not durable, although they are called 'durable' consumper goods. They sell well, and repeatedly, because they eventually break down or become obsolete. However, it has been getting more difficult for Japan to maintain this happy position, because the Asian NIEs have almost caught up with Japan in the production of these products.

Japan has not reached the highest stage of development in other types of technology. The United States is still far ahead of Japan in the production of computers, computer software, aircraft, chemicals, pharmaceuticals and in petroleum extraction. For Japan, it would seem to be time to switch to those kinds of more sophisticated products, and to invisible financial earnings such as insurance, royalty or patents. Up to now, Japan has always had a deficit in the international trade of anything other than commodities as well as in its trade of technology with the USA and European countries. As is well known, the UK has managed to maintain its external economy essentially with the help of invisible earnings from insurance, shipping, trade business and so on, successfully overcoming the persisting deficit of its commodity trade balance ever since the late nineteenth century. Now it seems that the time has come for Japan to follow the UK in this regard. What is urgent for Japan is to advance to a higher stage of economic capability, using more sophisticated technology and developing more competitive capabilities in all sorts of trade, rather than limiting itself to the export of the so-called durable goods.[3] If Japan should fail to do this, it will be nonsense to talk about its leadership in the context of regionalism any longer. In that case, the problem of marginalization would surely cast Japan into economic decline. It would also lose its cultural leadership in this area which it has enjoyed since the 1970s. Although Japan has not established full hegemony in Gramsci's sense, Japanese TV dramas, comic books and pop music have become very popular among East Asian peoples, with the exception of Korea (where Japanese culture has been prohibited as a reminder of the former colonial rule until October 1998). Cultural decline would necessarily ensue from economic decline.

---

[3] For information, the proportion of offshore sales to whole sales is high in machine and gadget industries (e.g. 79 per cent for Canon Cameras, 77 for Minolta Cameras, 75 for Citizen Watches) but low in chemical industries (e.g. 1 per cent for Sekisui Chemicals, 8 for Asahi Chemicals, 8 for Sankyo Pharmacy, 10 for Takeda Pharmacy, and around 40 for automobile manufactures) (calculated from Nihonkeizai-shimbunsha 1996). The competitiveness in the world is expressed using a combination of this number and the capability of offshore production. On the other hand, the USA is nothing but monopolistic in the Japanese market regarding some of the most sophisticated products (e.g. commercial aircraft — mostly Boeing, to a lesser degree MD and Lockheed; computers: CPU — pentium, language — Windows; Mac.). For the international balance sheet of the UK, see Miyazaki *et al.* (1981, p. 80).

# 7

## Concluding Remarks

In East Asia and the Asia–Pacific, we have four types of regionalism to consider in theory, although we miss out the third type (macro-regionalism) in practice. There have been various active and dynamic attempts at micro-regionalism and, meso-regionalism typical of ASEAN. Mega-regionalism, as represented by APEC, is also more or less a reality. (In this region an EU-type of macro-regionalism is, however, less probable.) But regionalism is one thing and regionalization is another. Actual regionalization without regionalism has been more in progress in the macro-region of East Asia. It is also in progress in APEC, but to a lesser extent.

So long as micro- or meso-regional endeavours and the mega-regional APEC take the form of a free trade area, both can coexist, perhaps reinforcing one another. However, NAFTA, as a closed macro-regionalism, might incur conflicts within the framework of APEC in the future. Moreover, micro-regionalism is based on a vertical exchange of production elements, and mega-regionalism is supported by a mixture of a vertical and a horizontal division of labour, where a vertical structure of the economy implies uneven distribution of income. Herein lie the seeds of conflict.

Thus, a decisive factor for the success of regional attempts is whether those nations can proceed to a higher level of division of labour, even if it remains vertical. A prerequisite for this is that the world economy or national economies keep growing in the years to come. Another important factor for mega-regionalism in the Asia–Pacific is a balance of autonomy of East Asia and a dependence on the United States in the economic sphere, which is a problem characteristic of this region, in contrast to the horizontal division of labour and intra-regional autonomy within the EU itself. In the recent economic crisis, internal autonomy has lost forcefulness, making national economies more subservient to the power of the USA or the EU.

It matters very much how regionalism works to better the lives of the people in the region. But behind all regionalisms lies the idea of developmentalism, which often promotes development policy and projects at the sacrifice of the environment and people's lives, and often is directed by repressive governments. In these instances, APEC would bring grief and suffering to the weak, the worse-off and the indigenous people. Proclaiming 'open' regionalism, APEC is expected to be open to the people of the region. Thus, the formation of a regional system for promoting human rights and efforts to disarm, as well as the creation of a regional security system, are badly needed in East Asia as a deterrent against obsessive developmentalism.

Relating to Asian regionalisms, Japan's task is: (1) either to get positively involved in, or respond with flexibility to, micro-regionalism; (2) to be supportive of the ASEAN in principle; (3) to adhere firmly to regionalization 'without regionalism' at the macro level; and (4) to work as a coordinator between Western and Asian countries at the mega level. But we should note that Japan is located in a delicate position with regard to Asian regionalism. While economic roles are relatively easy to play, cultural or political burdens are somewhat harder to share. Even when the Japanese economy itself is in a serious economic recession, the country is expected to contribute as much help as possible for other Asian economies. For example, foundation of the Asian Monetary Fund will be an agenda for the future which the United States has rejected.

# References

Abu-Lughod, J. L. (1989), *Before European Hegemony*, Oxford University Press.
Aoki, K. (1994), 'Economic Integration in the Asia–Pacific: The Implications of the AFR', *Kokusai Mondai* (in Japanese), October.
Bergstein, C. F. (1994), 'APEC and World Trade', *Foreign Affairs*, May/June.
Fawcett, L. and Hurrell, A. (1995), *Regionalism in World Politics*, Oxford University Press.
Hara, Y. (1996), *The Asian Dynamism* (in Japanese), Tokyo: NTT Shuppan.
Hosono, A. (1995), *APEC and NAFTA* (in Japanese), Tokyo: Yuuhikaku.
Jones, S. (1993), 'The Organic Growth: Asian NGOs Have Come Into their Own', *Far Eastern Economic Review*, 17 June, p. 23.
Kagaku-gijutsucho, (ed.) (1996) *White Paper on Science and Technology* (in Japanese), Tokyo: Okurasho-Insatsukyoku.
Kakazu, H. (1995), *Growth Triangles in a Borderless Asia* (in Japanese), Tokyo: Tokyo keizai shimpousha.
Kawakatsu, H. (1993), *Japanese Civilization and Modern Europe* (in Japanese), Tokyo: Nihon housou shuppan kyoukai.
Krugman, P. (1996), *Pop Internationalism*, Cambridge, Mass.: MIT Press.
Mitusi-bussan Boeki-keizai-kenkyuusho (ed.) (1996), *International Trade in Data* (in Japanese), Tokyo: Tokyo keizai johou shuppan.
Miyazaki, S., Okubayashi, S. and Morita, K. (eds.) (1981), *Indicators of the Modern World Economy* (in Japanese), Tokyo: Tokyo daigaku shuppankai.
NGO (1995), 'NGO Recommendations Toward the Osaka APEC Summit' (draft), NGO Forum on APEC, Japan, 13–14 November.
Nihonkeizai-shimbunsha (1996), *Annual Yearbook of Major Japanese Companies* (in Japanese).
Nishihara, T. (1994), 'A Scheme of Multilateral Security Cooperation in the Asia–Pacific: The ASEAN Regional Forum', *Kokusai Mondai* (in Japanese), October.
No Teh-wu (1991), 'The Model of Open Regionalism', Seoul.
Pearson, M. N. (1984), *Merchants and Rulers in Gujarat*, trans. into Japanese by Shigeru Ikuta, Tokyo: Iwanami shoten.
Sakura-sougou-kenkyuusho Kan-taiheihou kenkyuu-sentaa (1996), *The Asian Economy in Figures* (in Japanese), Tokyo: Purejidentosha.
Sakura-sougou-kenkyuusho Kantaiheiyou-kenkyuu-sentaa (1998), *A Quick Survey of the Asian Economy* (in Japanese), Tokyo: PHP Kenkyuusho.
Suehiro, Akira (1993), *Thailand Development and Democracy* (in Japanese), Tokyo: Iwanami shoten.
Takakura, K. (1993), *The Ryukyu Kingdom* (in Japanese), Tokyo: Iwanami shoten.
Tsuushou-sangyoushou (ed.) (1996), *White Paper on Trade* (in Japanese), Tokyo: Okurasho-Insatsukyoku.
Weidebaum, M. and Hughes, S. (1996), *The Bamboo Network*, New York: Free Press.
Yamakage, S. (1991), *ASEAN* (in Japanese), Tokyo: Tokyo-daigaku-shuppankai.
Yamamoto, Y. (1994), 'Regionalism in the Contemporary International Relations', in *Regionalism in the Asia–Pacific and Japanese Diplomacy* (in Japanese), Tokyo: Nihon Kokusai Mondai Kenkyuusho.

# 7

# JAPAN AND MICRO-REGIONALISM

## CONSTRUCTING THE JAPAN SEA RIM ZONE

### Glenn D. Hook

## 1

### Introduction

The ending of the Cold War has stimulated scholarly interest in the transition from ideology to space as a concept around which states and nations are organizing. As in the process of building a sense of the nation-state, the nation or the state, a sense of region emerges only out of contested socio-political processes, which transform relations in space and time into conceptual structures of understanding and identity. The process of producing and reproducing space as region implies a contest over demarcation: as a socio-political construct, certain aspects of a region are highlighted, shaded or obfuscated in the process of imputing meaning to economic, political, security and cultural relations in different time and space, thereby demarcating the boundaries to a region. The question of inclusion and exclusion is integral to this process, with the boundaries being subject to contestation as insiders, peripherals and outsiders produce, reproduce and shape space as region. The 'imagined region' (see Anderson 1991 on 'imagined communities') to emerge from this process is a composite of the objective relations imputed with meaning and their subjective representation by the social forces and actors at the heart of building a regional, sub-regional or micro-regional identity.

The region-building process at state level involves new institutional frameworks, as with the gradual institutionalization of the Asia–Pacific Economic Cooperation APEC; concepts and proposals for competing frameworks of economic coopera-tion, as with the sub-regional initiative to establish the East Asian Economic Caucus (EAEC) (see Hook, 1999, for details); and, as part of this process, actors seeking to demarcate the regional boundaries of 'Asia–Pacific' and the sub-regional boundaries

This is a revised version of an article which first appeared in *Kokusai Seiji*, vol. 114 (1997), pp. 49–62. For support in carrying out this work, I would like to thank the Leverhulme Trust for the award of a Research Fellowship for 1997–9.

of 'East Asia'. It is clear from the burgeoning activities of East Asian states and subnational actors in the post-Cold War era that, irrespective of the political shade of government in power in Japan, the Japanese state and subnational actors are set to play an increasingly important role in shaping the subjective representation of such regional and sub-regional identities as well as the objective economic and other links at the heart of these regionalization processes. Interest in Japan as a regional and sub-regional player, as well as in regional issues more generally, is a hallmark of the post-Cold War era. True, scholarship analysing regional-level economic cooperation abounds, but much of this work is by economists with little interest in the complex socio-political processes at the heart of region-building (e.g. Garnaut and Drysdale 1994). Other work has gone beyond the focus on regions as emerging economic regions, which may perhaps turn into 'economic blocs', by addressing region-building in Asia as a contested socio-political process generating competitive attempts to construct regional and sub-regional identities as 'Asia–Pacific' and 'East Asia' (e.g. Higgott and Stubbs 1995; Hook 1996a,b; Korhonen 1994). Still other work has examined the regional political economy (e.g. Hatch and Yamamura 1996), regional 'networks' (Katzenstein and Shiraishi 1997), regional culture (Shiraishi 1997) and so on. Nevertheless, the extant literature on micro-regionalism in the field of international relations (IR) remains rather limited (see Taga 1992; Hokuriku Kokusai Mondai Gakkai 1993), reflecting the way the boundaries of political science have tended to treat the 'local', the 'national' and the 'international' as different arenas for the study of human activity. Work in English by Rozman (1997, 1998a,b) and Postel-Vinay (1996) is helpful, but further research still needs to be conducted on cross-border micro-regionalism in East Asia. As will be discussed below, the Japan Sea Rim Zone provides a recent example of the way local, subnational actors are playing an international role in the region-building process in post-Cold War East Asia. In essence, therefore, this chapter seeks to demonstrate how, in promoting a transborder micro-regional zone centring on the Japan Sea, subnational as well as national actors are playing an important role in Japan's international affairs, as suggested by the pioneering work of Alger in the case of the United States (Alger 1990).

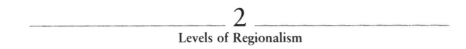

# 2
## Levels of Regionalism

The term 'micro-regionalism' has been adopted here in order to distinguish this level of regionalism from the 'higher' level of Asia–Pacific regionalism promoted by the developed great powers and the 'lower'-level sub-regional response to APEC regionalism initialized by a developing small power like Malaysia. This triumvirate is used in order to draw attention to the way regionalism is being promoted on different spatial levels. In essence, micro-regionalism, sub-regionalism and regionalism are metaphors alerting us to the complexity of regional cooperation, which involves a variety of actors, both state and non-state, and a variety of forms of power, both soft and hard, as well as these different spatial levels. Of course, as this reference to 'higher' and 'lower' levels of regionalism is metaphorical, with the metaphors serving to create a socio-spatial structure and understanding, 'region', 'sub-region' and 'micro-region' remain contested, with the 'micro-regional' level as contested as the 'regional' or 'sub-regional'.

To clarify, before going on to examine the Japan Sea Rim Zone, let us first briefly touch on a number of examples of regionalism, sub-regionalism and micro-regionalism in different parts of the world. As the lowest level of regionalism, metaphorically speaking, *micro-regionalism* focuses on transborder, subnational levels of cooperation, as with the so-called 'Growth Triangle' linking the national economy of Singapore with the subnational economies of Johor in Malaysia and Riau in Indonesia (for details, see Thant *et al.* 1994). In this way, micro-regionalism refers to a project seeking to build links across national boundaries, but without necessarily involving the total sovereign territory of the states involved. Examples of micro-regionalism exist in different parts of the world, but they are particularly conspicuous in East Asia, as in the cases of the Yellow Sea Economic Zone, which seeks to link subnational parts of different states centring on the Yellow Sea (for details, see Katsuhara 1997), and the Japan Sea Rim Zone, discussed below. In both cases, the micro-regionalist project is being pushed forward especially by subnational actors, such as prefectural and city governments, as part of an emerging and growing role for non-state actors in international affairs.

As far as *sub-regionalism* is concerned, we are here referring to a spatial level below the regional level but above the micro-regional level. Examples of sub-regionalist projects can be found in different parts of the world, both in the periphery of the core regions and in the periphery of the globe. Thus, whether in the wider Europe, as in the case of the Black Sea Economic Cooperation Scheme (BSEC), in the Americas, as in the case of the Association of Caribbean States (ACS), or in Asia, as in the case the Association of South-east Asian Nations (ASEAN), sub-regionalist projects are being pursued by a phalanx of policy-makers. They can also be found in the global periphery, such as Africa, as in the case of the Economic Community of West African States (ECOWAS).

Illustrative of a sub-regionalist project that appeared in the aftermath of the Cold War's ending is the Central European Free Trade Agreement (CEFTA). This emerged as part of the longer-term process of defining 'central Europe', suggesting how the subjective representation of the sub-region is an integral part of the sub-regionalist project. It also can be seen, in part, as a reaction to the difficulty that central European states have experienced in entering the European Union (EU). In this sense, the project can be viewed as a way for the weaker states in the international system to promote cooperation among themselves, with actors other than the state also being involved in promoting the sub-region. (For details on these cases, see Hook and Kearns, 1999.)

Finally, at the highest *regional* level, the actors seeking actively to promote the regionalist project are the strong states, with support from other actors such as businesses, interest groups and so on. Representative examples include both the APEC and the EU. (For a fuller discussion of regionalism, see Gamble and Payne 1996.) The case of regionalism in Europe serves to highlight the complexity of regionalism on these three different levels, as a comparison between the present EU and the earlier European Community (EC) demonstrates how the boundaries of the regionalist project have changed beyond recognition with the end of the Cold War.

For the EU has sought to not only deepen, but also to widen. It now embraces central European states like Austria, Scandinavian states such as Finland and Sweden; and, as we move towards the future, it can be expected to embrace those states of central and eastern Europe clearly outside of the 'European home' during the Cold War era, such as Poland and the Czech Republic.

These examples of sub-regionalism and regionalism from Europe are instructive, as they clearly show that different levels of regionalism are indeed contested, and that regionalism and sub-regionalism are both 'contested concepts' (Connolly 1974). For the process of inclusion and exclusion within these two overlapping levels of regionalism is a highly political process. Thus, the theoretical and empirical difficulty of coming to grips with regions, sub-regions and even micro-regions is that changes in the international system, as well as questions of the level of analysis, power, actors and so on, influence our understanding of regional boundaries. Now, looking back from the perspective of the post-Cold War era and the expansion of the European Community to the East, the EC appears as a sub-regionalist rather than a regionalist project. As, during the Cold War, space as a source of identity was suffocated beneath the weight of the bilateralism that was at the heart of the ideological confrontation between the East and the West, the Cold War's ending can be said to have led to a proliferation of regional initiatives on different spatial levels and in different parts of the globe. This can be seen in the case of the Japan Sea Rim Zone, which has been promoted by a variety of actors in the wake of the Cold War's ending and the 'thawing' of the Japan Sea.

# 3

## Background to the Japan Sea Rim Zone

Despite the economic downturn in Japan and the ongoing Asian financial crisis, the importance of Japan as a locomotive for the economic development of both the 'Asia–Pacific' and 'East Asia' remains widely acknowledged, whether within the framework of Japan as the lead goose in the 'flying geese model' of economic growth (Yamazawa 1990; for a critique, see Korhonen 1994, pp. 49–63), as part of the reorganized mode of production within the sub-regional political economy (Bernard and Ravenhill 1995), or as part of a still-to-be defined micro-regional relationship. Nevertheless, the role of subnational regions within Japan in promoting relations with subnational regions across the sea in other parts of East Asia deserves closer attention, for the micro-regional level is the least understood and least studied of the three levels of regionalism outlined above. Following on from our discussion so far, the Japan Sea Rim Zone is addressed here in terms of constructing a micro-region, both objectively and subjectively, through a multifaceted range of economic and other transborder relations. In other words, we are interested in the promotion of the subjective representation as well as the objective relations at the heart of this zone.

The surge of interest at the subnational level in developing links across the sea to other parts of East Asia has arisen at a specific historical juncture, where longer-term and shorter-term processes have brought the idea of promoting a micro-regionalism project to the fore. During the half-century since the failure of the Japanese empire's attempt to build the Greater East Asia Co-prosperity Sphere, Japan has been transformed into an economic superpower, with Tokyo now an 'overdeveloped global city' at the heart of the Japanese political economy. Even in today's economic climate, the nation clearly remains an economic top dog, but the worst recession for many years, the need to respond to fluctuations in the value of the yen, the maturing of the economy and the calls for decentralization are forcing profound changes in the structure of Japanese business and economy. One well known consequence of this is the non-stop movement of Japanese capital and manufacturing industry to other parts of East Asia, first primarily to the newly industrializing economies (NIEs) of Hong Kong, Singapore, South Korea and Taiwan; then to members of ASEAN, especially Indonesia, Malaysia and Thailand; and now increasingly to China and to a lesser extent Vietnam. Although the Asian financial crisis is in some cases leading to a short-term decline in foreign direct investment (FDI) in other parts of East Asia by Japanese manufacturers, especially in the automotive industry, over the longer term the sub-region, especially China, remains central to the future strategy of the giant manufacturers (Tejima 1998).

Less well known, however, is the profound effect that this overseas movement of Japanese manufacturers has been exerting on the domestic economy, especially on the less developed parts of the 'back of Japan' (*ura Nihon*); that is, the prefectures and cities located on the Japan Sea coastal side of the nation, which have tended to be left behind in the postwar scramble for growth centring on Tokyo and the Pacific seaboard. Indeed, '*ura Nihon*' connotes the pejorative 'backward', once used in English to refer to the economically developing countries of the world. For when looked at internally, Japan's postwar growth has been disparate growth, with the Pacific coastal region, rather than the Japan Sea coastal region, having become the home of many of the nation's strategic manufacturing industries. In a real sense, Japan's post-1945 economic development has been Pacific seaboard development, not Japan Sea seaboard development. The burgeoning attempts to promote decentralization away from Tokyo and to stimulate growth in *ura Nihon* are taking place at precisely the time that the ending of the Cold War has opened new horizons, with opportunities now seen to lie in developing stronger economic and other links not with only the Pacific, but also with Asia.

This lopsided economic development of Japan is rooted in the Meiji period, but more recently in the postwar settlement, which sought to integrate Japan into the Western camp in the bipolar Cold War confrontation between East and West. The ending of the Cold War has thawed what was largely a frozen sea, in so far as political, economic and cultural exchange across the Japan Sea is concerned. Now, instead of the sea being viewed as a frozen, Cold War sea — that is, as a barrier, a front line, or a possible battle site in a military confrontation between East and West — the post-Cold War Japan Sea appears as a pacific lake linking the Japan Sea coastal prefectures to different subnational regions in other parts of East Asia and the Russian Far East. In place of a conception of the Japan Sea as a central element in a security discourse, therefore, the same natural barrier now appears as a seaway for crossing national boundaries, with new potential markets, resources, business opportunities and cultural contacts just a short distance away from the Japan Sea seaboard. The seaboard prefectures and cities now increasingly view the sea as a lake linking the underdeveloped, less developed or 'hollowed-out' parts of the Japanese political economy to those parts of Asia once frozen inside the Cold War political and security structures, such as the Russian Far East; to other parts of Asia seen as belonging in some way to an emerging micro or sub-region, such as parts of China and Mongolia, which are on their way to embracing more fully the market economy; and to one of the showcases of NIEs economic development, South Korea. The breakdown, if not complete disappearance, of the Cold War ideological divide between East and West has given rise to a reconceptualization of Japan's spatial location in the region, with the Japan Sea coastal side of the nation now exerting a powerful pull away from the subjective representation of Japan as a 'Pacific power'. This contested process has gained momentum in the wake of the ending of the Cold War, with subnational actors in the prefectures and cities on the Japan Sea seaboard reconceptualizing their location as the 'core' of the newly emerging sub-region of 'East Asia', rather than as the 'periphery' of the Pacific-oriented post-1945 development of Japan as part of the 'Asia–Pacific'. In other words, the subjective construction of the micro-region is part of the larger contestation over Japan's identity as an 'Asian' or 'Pacific' power, as seen in the struggle over the APEC and EAEC (see Hook, 1999).

The meaning of the Cold War's ending for the development of the micro-region has been magnified by the passage of a half-century since the end of the Japanese empire's attempt to restructure the region through violence. Without doubt, the legacy of imperialism remains an issue of contention between Japan and the victims of its aggression. Nationally, this has led to the periodic souring of relations on the political level, resulting from the whitewashing of the war in school textbooks approved by the Ministry of Education, comments by leading politicians and ministers approving of the war and the 'benefits' of Japanese colonization, and the reluctance of the government to accept responsibility for wartime evils, as in the recent case of the women who served the empire's soldiers as 'sex slaves' (on the so-called 'comfort women', see Yoshimi 1995; Nishino 1995).

Despite the continuing effect of this legacy, the celebration of the fiftieth anniversary of the war's ending in 1995, which took place within the overall context of the Cold War's ending, has created a more positive environment for the development of relations between Japan and East Asia. The greater willingness to accept 'war responsibility' on the part of the recent political leaders who have headed the government after the end of thirty-eight years of Liberal–Democratic Party (LDP) rule has been significant in this regard. Prime Minister Hosokawa Morihiro, for instance, apologized to the Korean people for Japanese actions during colonial days. Similarly, Socialist Prime Minister Murayama Tomiichi went so far as to express 'heartfelt apologies' for Japanese actions, which was welcomed by Asian leaders (*Far Eastern Economic Review*, 24 August 1995, p. 18). As seen in the most recent apology to President Kim of South Korea (*Japan Times*, 6 October 1998), the return to power of the LDP has not meant an end to expressing apologies. This warming of relations facilitates the efforts being made by political, bureaucratic, economic and intellectual elites to promote links at the micro-regional level between the Japan Sea coastal prefectures and cities, on the one hand, and (especially) parts of the Korean peninsula, on the other.

# 4

## Naming and Subjective Representation

The Japan Sea Rim Zone (Kan Nihon Kai Ken) transborder project seeks to link together subnational parts of East Asia, as represented by the Japan Sea coastal region of Japan, particularly Niigata city and prefecture, and particularly the Russian Far East and South Korea (see map in Postel-Vinay 1996, p. 491). Although the concept goes back to the 1960s, the ending of the Cold War has stirred renewed interest in its realization. In seeking to regionalize the concept, however, the name of the sea at the heart of the zone, the 'Japan Sea', has evoked controversy between Japan and the victims of Japanese imperialist aggression, especially South Korea. The central concern is with employing the name 'Japan Sea' in order to designate the sea stretching between Japan and the Korean peninsula. For historically the name is implicated deeply in the expansion of the Japanese empire into other parts of Asia, with the sea being referred to as the 'Japan Sea' in the wake of the colonization of the Korean peninsula in 1910 (Hook 1996a, pp. 22–3; see also *Asahi Shinbun*, 30 November 1991).

The legacy of Japanese imperial expansion into East Asia during the late nineteenth and early twentieth centuries still precludes a consensus on a name for a micro-region that embraces subnational parts of modern-day Japan and the victims of old-style Japanese aggression. Because a name functions as a key form of symbolic representation which serves to link together the objective and the subjective into a regional meaning for the included, excluded and peripherals, this controversy over naming highlights indirectly the significance of the emerging links between the Japan Sea coastal side of the nation and the Korean peninsula. It contrasts markedly with the use of a colour as in naming the 'Yellow Sea Rim Zone', which has facilitated developing a consensus on promoting 'East Asian' micro-regional links among the putative members of this zone, such as China and South Korea.

### Subjective Representation

Despite the difficulty over naming, subnational efforts to promote micro-regionalism are emerging saliently on the Japan Sea coastal side of Japan. In many ways, as micro-regionalism is just emerging, rather than being well established in an institutional form, the actors at the heart of the process are at the early stages of region-building in a dual sense: first, in terms of promoting the economic, political and cultural relations between Japan and neighbouring East Asia, thereby giving the micro-region objective meaning, and, second, in terms of the representation of these links as *regional* links, thereby imputing subjective meaning to space as region. The institutionalization of the micro-region involves both processes, and the routinization of micro-regional symbols, as through the use of the name of the micro-region by prefectural and city politicians and officials, business groups, interest groups, the media and so on, serves to constitute the region in symbolic space. In seeking to demarcate the boundaries as well as the core of the region, actors with vested interests in constructing or undermining the 'Japan Sea' micro-region, generating centripetal forces towards integration and union or centrifugal forces towards dis-integration and fragmentation, are embroiled in a struggle over symbolic space and legitimacy. History and geography are crucial to this process.

This is to suggest that the social construction of the micro-region in the Japanese information environment (subjective representation) is as much a part of region-building as is the development of the objective political, economic, cultural and other links giving meaning to the micro-region as region. It is a process of appealing to the legacies of history and geography, space and time, within a certain framework of reference and identity. For Japan naturally has a deep relationship historically and geographically with other parts of East Asia. But, as is well known, this relation-ship in the prewar period was based on imperial aggrandizement, with the Korean peninsula and other parts of the putative micro-region exploited by Japan as part of the Greater East Asia Co-prosperity Sphere. This is hardly conducive to the imputation of space with regional meaning as part of the process of developing pacific, economic and other forms of cooperation between Japan and its former colony.

The answer, as can be seen in the case of officials in Niigata (interview, 20 November 1997), has been to focus more upon the positive links between the prefecture and the peninsula. Thus, instead of referring to the colonial period to demonstrate the strong links between Niigata and the Korean peninsula (when Niigata port acted as a gateway for imperial expansion, a negative symbol of aggression), the postwar role of the port as a positive symbol in repatriating Korean residents to the motherland, or as the gateway port for developing links with North Korea, are being highlighted. What is interesting about the use of the port in this way is how the history of imperial expansion and geographic reconfiguration at the heart of the Greater East Asia Co-prosperity Sphere is downplayed in favour of postwar history. This is not to deny the genuine regret that many if not all Niigata officials and citizens express about the role the port played in imperial aggression: rather, it is to suggest that the symbol of cooperation represented by the port's role in the postwar era serves better the interests of those seeking to promote the micro-region. For the port can then appeal to space and time in reconfiguring Japan–East Asian relations within a shared framework of identity, blotting out the image of aggression at the very core of Japanese imperial expansion into the Korean peninsula.

This selective use of history serves as a tool in developing a micro-regional iden-tity embracing the prefecture, city or subnational parts of the prefecture within a micro-region of East Asia made up of former victims of Japanese imperialism. It also serves to enhance the legitimacy of Niigata's claim to be the Japanese core of the micro-region, in contrast to other prefectures along the Japan Sea coastal region of Japan, which can enhance their own interests by eroding the image of Niigata as the emerging hub of the micro-region.

## 5
### Promoting Objective Links: the Actors

Along with imputing space with subjective meaning as the 'Japan Sea Rim Zone', a variety of national and subnational actors naturally are engaged in creating the objective links between the Japan Sea coastal region of Japan and other subnational parts of East Asia. As most work to date has concentrated on the economic links at the heart of micro-regionalism (see the output of the Kan Nihonkai Keizai Kenkyujo, e.g. 1996), this brief overview will focus on national and subnational governments as well as on business, academic and other interest groups. This approach should demonstrate how, in the post-Cold War era, these actors are playing a crucial role in pushing forward a project seeking to create a micro-regional zone of cooperation in East Asia.

## National and Subnational Governments

The national government in Tokyo has offered support to the emergent drive among the prefectures, cities and businesses along the Japan Sea seaboard in developing micro-regional links with the subnational parts of East Asia at the other side of the Japan Sea. The promotion of political links, transportation links, and technical links are at the heart of the central government's efforts. A number of examples should suffice to illustrate how the central government, often in cooperation with subnational governments (prefectural, city, town and so on) as well as businesses, has become engaged in promoting micro-regional activities. In other words, the state, as the sovereign actor in international affairs, is strengthening links in the micro-region at the same time as it is empowering subnational governments to develop transborder, international relations in the Japan Sea micro-region.

On the political level, the central government in Tokyo established a consular office in Khabarovsk in 1993, and granted permission for Russia to set up a consulate in Niigata. These consular offices on the Japan Sea coastal side of Japan and in the Russian Far East are playing a crucial role in facilitating the development of political and especially commercial and other economic links in the micro-region. In this way, the regional presence within Japan of the Russian consular and the regional presence within Russia of the Japanese consular serve not only the national interests of the Japanese and Russian states, but also the micro-regional interests of subnational actors.

This can be illustrated by reference to transportation links across the Japan Sea, which are essential to the region-building process, whether in terms of politics, economics or culture. Here national governments in the region are active in authorizing air links and sea links as well as in providing funds and expertise to facilitate communication. Given the Pacific-oriented economic development of Japan on the one hand, and the Cold War legacy on the other, improving transportation and communication links between the Japan Sea coastal region of Japan and other parts of East Asia is crucial for the development of a zone of cooperation centring on the Japan Sea.

The case of the Russian Far East during the Cold War era can serve as an illustration of the way transportation routes in the micro-region were circumscribed by the East–West confrontation. With the Soviet Union as part of the 'East' and Japan as part of the 'West', transportation links were limited between the Japan Sea seaboard and the Russian Far East, with only one direct flight inaugurated in 1973, when for the first time the two governments approved an air route between Niigata, the largest of the Japan Sea seaboard cities, and Khabarovsk, the administrative centre of the Soviet Far East (for details, see Taga 1995). This enabled Niigata to act as a bridge between East and West in promoting links with the Soviet Far East, as this air route proved the most convenient for other East Asian as well as Japanese passengers. For instance, as a result of the establishment of direct air links between Niigata and South Korea in 1979, the Seoul–Niigata–Khabarovsk air route could be used by South Koreans to reach a destination in the Russian Far East. The government later also approved an air route between Niigata and Vladivostok. In a similar way to the emergence of 'world cities' as hubs (Knox and Taylor 1995), therefore, the ending of the Cold War has presented Niigata with the opportunity to develop as a 'micro-regional hub' at the heart of the emerging Japan Sea Rim Zone. In this endeavour, the city and prefecture of Niigata are acting internationally in seeking to use the subnational contacts and micro-regional networks they have developed in order to promote their interests as a micro-regional transportation hub for air transportation (interview, 20 November 1997). In short, subnational governments are acting internationally in order to realize local interests in promoting a micro-regional project linking subnational parts of the region together by air transportation routes.

As far as shipping is concerned, the government is cooperating in the development of Foreign Access Zones (FAZs), as in the case of the ports of Maizu in Kyoto prefecture and Sakai in Tottori prefecture. The FAZ is based on legislation passed in 1992 in order to promote Japanese imports and domestic investment, with the Ministry of International Trade and Industry, the Ministry of Transport, the Ministry of Agriculture and Fisheries and the Ministry of Home Affairs working together with the private sector in carrying out FAZ projects. This 'third sector' development of Maizu and Sakai seeks to contribute to the future realization of the economic potential of the Japan Sea Rim Zone. As in the case of the Sakai Port Trade Centre, storage facilities, exhibition space, information on trade promotion and so on are provided as a way to develop the port as a gateway to East Asia (*Nihon Keizai Shimbun*, 15 September 1995). In this endeavour, the two ports are in competition, as they are with Niigata, in seeking to carve out a role as the shipping hub of the micro-region.

In this context, Niigata prefecture is seeking to establish Niigata port as a gateway to North-east Asia, especially to Changchun in China. Even today, approximately 90 per cent of shipments from the prefecture are still directed through the main Pacific ports, such as Yokohama and Kobe (*Nihon Keizai Shimbun*, 15 September 1995). The prefecture is attempting to promote the use of Niigata port by businesses in the prefecture and other Japan Sea coastal prefectures and to increase the number of services to the port. In contrast to, say, Yokohama, where the Southeast Asian service calls two or three times a week on the Yokohama–Hong Kong–Taiwan–Singapore route, this takes place only (on average) three times a month in the case of Niigata. On top of that, with more port calls on the Niigata route than on the Yokohama route, it takes more than twice as long to reach Singapore.

Not only Japanese ports but also other ports of use in developing micro-regional transportation links are being developed, as in the case of the Russo-Japanese agreement of 1995 to move towards work on a port in the coastal region of the Russian Far East. The national and the prefectural governments of Niigata and Yamagata have been active in conducting feasibility studies and providing information and intellectual support in order to develop the port (*Nihon Keizai Shimbun*, 13 September 1995). In this case, the governor of Niigata prefecture sees the port's development as 'a major contribution to the promotion of exchange in the Japan Sea Rim Economic Zone, which Niigata prefecture has been promoting' (*Nihon Keizai Shimbun*, 4 October 1995). Herewith, subnational actors are playing an international role in developing a port in the Russian Far East — 'Official Development Assistance' in all but name.

At the same time, Niigata prefecture has played an international role in providing technical training in the form of bookkeeping and accountancy at the Japan Centre in one of Russia's business schools, which forms part of the assistance provided by the Japanese Ministry of Foreign Affairs in order to promote economic reform in Russia (*Nihon Keizai Shimbun*, 4 September 1995). This is a different form of aid from the humanitarian aid offered as a sister city, as with Niigata's provision of buses to its sister city, Khabarovsk, after a fire destroyed the city's bus depot in 1992. It further suggests the empowerment of the subnational level in carrying out overseas activities normally associated with the national government.

Along with Khabarovsk, Niigata has established sister-city agreements with Vladivostok (1991) and Harbin (1979) in China. Other cities and prefectures also have sought to promote links in this way. In 1992, for instance, both Toyama prefecture and Osaka metropolitan government signed friendship agreements with subnational governments in the Russian Far East. Niigata has played a central role in developing subnational political links between the cities on the Japan Sea seaboard and other parts of East Asia, as with the inauguration of a meeting of seaboard mayors in 1970. Similarly, political links have been promoted by the institutionalization of meetings between the mayors and governors of Japan and the Russian Far East. At the third meeting in 1995 the participants discussed cultural and technical exchange and other issues related to promoting links between the Japan Sea seaboard prefectures and the Russian Far East.

Finally, Japanese subnational governments have played a role in setting up think-tanks in order to conduct research on economic links and on the promotion of micro-regional zones of cooperation. This is the case with the Kan Nihon Kai Keizai Kenkyujo (a direct translation would be 'Japan Sea Rim Economic Research Institute', but, given the sensitivity over the use of 'Japan Sea', touched on above, it is known in English as the Economic Research Institute for North-east Asia), which is sponsored by Niigata prefecture. Prefectures like Tottori, Aomori, Akita and others also have set up think-tanks. With the coastal prefectures in competition with one another to establish their own prefecture as the 'hub' or 'gateway' to the Japan Sea, however, collaboration between these different think-tanks remains weak.

## *Interest Groups*

The construction of a micro-regional identity is facilitated by the activities of business, academic and other interest groups as well as by political and bureaucratic leaders. In particular, academic groups have played an important role in imputing the micro-region with subjective meaning through their involvement in a variety of seminars and symposia which have been held over the past few years. Theoretically, such academic groups can be understood variously as playing a role in a 'policy network', 'policy community' or 'epistemic community' (for a discussion, see Higgott 1994, pp. 373–4) seeking to promote the Japan Sea Rim Zone. Suffice it to say that, irrespective of theoretical distinctions, these groups serve to promote the institutionalization of the micro-regional project by the creation of a discourse imputing space with a micro-regional identity as the 'Japan Sea Rim Zone'.

A sample of events from the 1990s illustrates how academic and various other interest groups are developing vested interests in micro-regionalism on the one hand, and how micro-regional membership is perceived on the other. In 1992 the Japan Sea Information and Communication Symposium was held for the first time with participants from Russia, China, South Korea and Japan. In the same year, the Osaka Chamber of Commerce sponsored a symposium on 'The Concept of the Japan Sea Rim Economic Zone and Japan's Role'. In 1993 the first international symposium on medical exchange in Japan, Russia and North-east Asia was held in Niigata, with medics from Russia, Mongolia, South Korea, China and the United States participating. In 1994 the Japan Sea Rim Learned Society was inaugurated with several hundred members. In this way, certain groups are aiming to promote a narrower conception of the zone, as with the Osaka Chamber of Commerce's focus on the economic aspects of the zone; whereas others are contesting the membership of the zone, as with the inclusion of participants from the United States as part of a regional Asia–Pacific identity, as with the meeting of medics.

The Japan Sea Rim Academic Forum, which was set up in 1995 with a membership of over 250, is illustrative of the contested nature of the putative zone. This is a network of members from the world of policy-making, business and academia which seeks to establish an economic zone in the future through the promotion of academic and cultural exchange as well as research. The forum is similar to the Pacific Economic Cooperation Council (PECC) (for a discussion, see Korhonen 1994), which also draws members from these groups. The main point of difference is the level of participation from government and bureaucracy, with the forum's membership being drawn largely from twenty-two prefectures, rather than from national government. In this way, the identity of the micro-region remains in flux, with participants drawn from a variety of nations and with a variety of motivations for seeking to institutionalize the zone as an economic or more widely based zone of cooperation in a narrow or very broad concept of the region.

# 6
## Motivations for Promoting the Zone

The motivations within Japan for promoting the Japan Sea Rim Zone or the Japan Sea Rim Economic Zone, at both the national and subnational level, differ according to the actors involved, but crucially important is the promotion of economic links across the Sea of Japan. At the national level, the central government is seeking to revitalize the economies of the Japan Sea region, with 'Japan Sea Rim' functioning as a new identity in the inter- and intra-bureaucratic rivalry over budgetary resources. With the bursting of the Japanese economic 'bubble', the relentless consolidation of economic, political and cultural power in an over-centralized Tokyo has slowed somewhat, with calls for 'decentralization' now being heard more loudly, especially in the peripheral regions of the nation. As one commentator put it: 'the end of over-concentration in Tokyo as a result of the bursting of the bubble is a plus for Kyushu. In China the regional development of the North East is expected from now on. If exchange deepens in the Yellow Sea Rim Economic Zone, the possibility for the development of these two regions can be expected to heighten' (*Asahi Shinbun*, 15 December 1994, *Seibu* edition). Similar sentiments are part of the motivation for promoting the Japan Sea Rim Zone.

At the subnational level, moreover, competition among the coastal prefectures and cities of the Japan Sea is part and parcel of building a micro-regional identity. In the case of the Japan Sea coastal ports, for instance, a 'port war' has broken out between prefectures seeking to establish their own ports as the trade gateway or hub to East Asia (*Nihon Keizai Shimbun*, 26 September 1994). This suggests that, in pushing ahead with transborder micro-regionalism, the prefectures and cities are seeking to develop links with other parts of the region as a way to revitalize their own prefectural economies, whereas the central government is concerned more generally with promoting micro-regional links as a way to revive the national economy. Needless to say, the prefectures seek to lobby the central government to promote their own position as the 'gateway' to East Asia, acting internationally in order to gain support from other subnational parts of the micro-region as a way to consolidate their position in the national competition with other prefectures.

On another level, the prefectures and cities on the Japan Sea seaboard are seeking to promote cross-cultural relations, regional peace and global peace, as well as the overall prosperity of the micro-region. Whereas the Cold War hindered the development of relations between the Japan Sea seaboard region and especially the Soviet Far East, the post-Cold War environment has created new opportunities for cross-cultural contact. In the case of Niigata and Khabarovsk, for instance, the sister-city relationship established in 1965 has been strengthened in the post-Cold War era, building on the earlier cultural and educational interaction which took place, such as the exchange of students, dance groups, films and so on. The relationship has built up a high degree of awareness and understanding between the two cities, with enough Russian speakers in Niigata now to enable the city to host product exhibitions and to promote Russo-Japanese relations in a wide variety of areas.

## 7
### Conclusion

As we have seen, the construction of the Japan Sea Rim Zone is faced with the burden of history, as even the name 'Japan Sea' evokes memories of Japanese imperialism, especially on the Korean peninsula. The attempts now being made to create a new micro-regional identity centring on the subnational coastal parts of Japan and subnational parts at the other side of the Japan Sea are integral to the ongoing process whereby the Japanese nation redefines its relations with Asia. In this process, the problem of naming will undoubtedly be replaced by the emergence of micro-regional interests which, with time, may gradually come to link the Japan

Sea coastal regions with other parts of East Asia. As a result, a new name and identity, or the use of different names in different languages, as with the Economic Research Institute for Northeast Asia, can be expected to take hold. The burgeoning power of the Asia–Pacific Economic Cooperation forum in comparison with the East Asian Economic Caucus suggests that, whereas on the national level the Japanese government will continue to prioritize APEC over EAEC, a whole variety of new and overlapping relations with East Asia will undoubtedly creep ahead at the subnational level. In the transformation of the regional order in post-Cold War East Asia, these new subnational linkages, which are creating gradually subjective as well as objective links between Japan and other parts of East Asia, can be expected to take on increasingly important meaning in the redefinition of Japan's regional role and identity. The imputing of the Japan Sea Rim Zone with a micro-regional identity is part of this wider process of reorienting the nation in the post-Cold War era.

It is important to recall that micro-regionalism is moving forward at a time when both the national and prefectural governments are seeking to stimulate the economy along the Japan Sea coastal region of Japan, and this is occurring in the context of restructuring the regional order after the end of the Cold War on the one hand, and the Japanese government's more proactive attempts to address the question of war responsibility and a new regional role on the other. The changing political economy of Japan suggests that, with the move towards greater decentralization, efforts to promote micro-regionalism will grow, even if not branded as such. The nature of this form of regionalism nevertheless remains contested. It is unclear which city along the Japan Sea coast will become the micro-regional hub linking Japan to continental East Asia in the twenty-first century. In seeking to promote their own interests, the prefectural governments are competing with each other for national resources, as in the attempt to locate FAZs in their own prefectures. This competition is likely to intensify, although the prefectures may be able to cooperate in areas of shared interests.

The competition to establish transportation links as the micro-regional hub has grown sharper with the ending of the Cold War. In the case of Tottori prefecture, for instance, success in moving forward with the development of the port of Sakai as the gateway port for East Asia, with the start of a container service between Pusan and Sakai in August 1995, on top of the already existing links between Sakai and China, Hong Kong, Taiwan and ports in South Korea, is a challenge to Niigata prefecture's attempt to establish the gateway port in Niigata. Similar competition has opened up in terms of air links, with Shimane prefecture also seeking to establish the local airport as the East Asian hub. As the spate of developments in both sea and air links in the post-Cold War era testifies, the Pacific-oriented transportation system, centring on the air hubs of Tokyo and Osaka and the sea hubs of Kobe and Yokohama, remains the core of the regional transportation system, with the new micro-regional links emerging gradually as an essential element in the construction of the Japan Sea Rim Zone. The further development of transportation links remains a key issue facing the Japan Sea coastal prefectures, whether in competition with the Pacific ports or with each other.

It is too early to suggest the implications of these emerging links for the restructuring of the regional order. What is clear, however, is the increasingly important role being played by subnational actors in international affairs. This is illustrated by the way in which the prefectural and city governments of the Japan Sea coastal region are becoming central to the promotion of transborder links. It involves promoting political, economic and cultural relations among the cities and prefectures of the coastal region and the Russian Far East, South Korea and so on. In this process, subnational governments are being empowered by the national government in Tokyo, as in the case of Niigata acting on behalf of the Ministry of Foreign Affairs in promoting Russia's economic reforms. More significantly, this level of government is also acting in its own right, as with Niigata's survey of ports in the Russian Far East, and the prefecture's proposed involvement in the port's development. In other words, these subnational governments are taking on some of the functions of a national government, with a 'foreign policy' of their own. This is not to suggest that this level of government will in any sense replace the national government, but rather that, in the emerging regional order, the pluralization of international actors is occurring, and that these actors are complementing, not replacing, the role of the national government. In this process, micro-regional identities and interests are starting to consolidate, as, over time, are competencies and perhaps authority. In other words, a transformation in the sites of governance seems to be taking place in disparate regional settings (for a discussion, see Payne 1998). The role of political, bureaucratic, economic and academic elites is crucial here. For these emerging identities and interests will be shaped by not only time and space, but by a multitude of actors. Which actors are involved, and which new ones come to play a role in the future, will no doubt exert a profound influence in determining the sites of governance in the East Asian regional order and the meaning of micro-regionalism for regional peace and security in the twenty-first century.

# References

Alger, C. (1990), 'The World Relations of Cities: Closing the Gap between Social Science Paradigms and Everyday Human Experience', *International Studies Quarterly*, 34: 493–518.

Anderson, B. (1991), *Imagined Communities*, London: Verso.

Bernard, M. and Ravenhill, J. (1995), 'Beyond Product Cycles and Flying Geese: Regionalization, Hierarchy, and the Industrialization of East Asia', *World Politics*, 47 (January): 171–209.

Connolly, W. E. (1974), *The Terms of Political Discourse*, Oxford: Martin Robertson.

Gamble, A. and Payne, A. (eds.) (1996), *Regionalism and World Order*, London: Macmillan.

Garnaut, R. and Drysdale, P. (1994), *Asia Pacific Regionalism: Readings in International Economic Relations*, London: HarperEducational.

Hatch, W. and Yamamura, K. (1996), *Asia in Japan's Embrace: Building a Regional Production Alliance*, Cambridge: Cambridge University Press.

Higgott, R. (1994), 'Ideas, Identity and Policy Coordination in the Asia–Pacific', *Pacific Review*, 7(4): 367–79.

Higgott, R. and Stubbs, R. (1995), 'Competing Concepts of Economic Regionalism: APEC versus EAEC in the Asia–Pacific', *Review of International Political Economy*, 2(3): 549–68.

Hokuriku Kokusai Mondai Gakkai (ed.) (1993), *Nihonkai: Taigan o nao Hedateru Mono wa Nanika*, Toyama: Kei Shobo.

Hook, G. D. (1996a), 'Contested Regionalism', in I. Cook, M. Doel and R. Li (eds.), *Fragmented Asia: Regional Integration and National Disintegration in Pacific Asia*, Aldershot: Avebury, pp. 12–28.

Hook, G. D. (1996b), 'Japan and the Reconstruction of Asia–Pacific', in A. Gamble and A. Payne (eds.), *Regionalism and World Order*, London: Macmillan, pp. 169–206.

Hook, G. D. (1999), 'The East Asian Economic Caucus: A Case of Reactive Subregionalism?' in G. D. Hook and I. Kearns (eds.), *Subregionalism and World Order*, London: Macmillan, pp. 223–45.

Hook, G. D. and Kearns, I. (eds.) (1999), *Subregionalism and World Order*, London: Macmillan.

Kan Nihonkai Keizai Kenkyujo (1996), *Tohoku Ajia: 21 seiki no furonteia*, Tokyo: Mainichi Shinbunsha.

Katsuhara, T. (1997), 'Towards Economic Cooperation in the Pan-Yellow Sea Economic Region', *East Asian Economic Perspectives*, 8 (March): 108–20.

Katzenstein, P. and Shiraishi, T. (eds.) (1997), *Network Power: Japan and Asia*, Ithaca: Cornell University Press.

Knox, P. L. and Taylor, P. J. (1995), *World Cities in a World-System*, Cambridge: Cambridge University Press.

Korhonen, P. (1994), *Japan and the Pacific Free Trade Area*, London: Routledge.

Nishino, Ryumiko (1995), *Nihongun 'Ianfu' o Otte*, Tokyo: Masukomi Joho Senta.

Payne, A. (1998), 'Rethinking United States–Caribbean Relations: Towards a New Mode of Transnational Governance', paper presented at the September meeting of the Third Pan-European International Relations conference, Vienna.

Postel-Vinay, K. (1996), 'Local Actors and International Regionalism: The Case of the Sea of Japan Zone', *Pacific Review*, 9(4): 489–503.

Rozman, G. (1997), 'Cross-national Integration in Northeast Asia: Geopolitical and Economic Goals in Conflict', *East Asia International Quarterly*, 16: 6–43.

Rozman, G. (1998a), 'Northeast Asia: Regionalism, Clash of Civilizations, or Strategic Quadrangle?' *Asia–Pacific Review*, 5(1): 105–26.

Rozman, G. (1998b), 'Flawed Regionalism: Reconceptualizing Northeast Asia in the 1990s', *Pacific Review*, 11(1): 1–27.

Shiraishi, S. (1997), 'Japan's Soft Power: Doraemon Goes Overseas', in P. Katzenstein and T. Shiraishi (eds.), *Network Power: Japan and Asia*, Ithaca: Cornell University Press, pp. 234–74.

Taga, H. (1992), *Kokkyo o Koeru Jikken: Kan Nihonkai no Koso*, Tokyo: Yushindo.

Taga, H. (1995), 'Niigata–Khabarovsk MIC', paper presented at the international symposium, on 'Japan, Asia Pacific, and Regionalism: Global and Regional Dynamics into the 21st Century', University of Sheffield, 13–15 September.

Tejima, S. (1998), 'The Effects of the Asian Crisis on Japan's Manufacturing FDI', unpublished paper, 28 September.

Thant, M., Tang, M. and Kakazu, H. (eds.) (1994), *Growth Triangles in Asia: A New Approach to Regional Economic Development*, New York: Oxford University Press.

Yamazawa, I. (1990), *International Trade and Economic Development*, Honolulu: University of Hawaii Press.

Yoshimi, Y. (1995), *Jugun Ianfu*, Tokyo: Iwanami Shoten.

# 8

# INTERNATIONAL RELATIONS THEORY AND CHINESE FOREIGN POLICY

*Tatsumi Okabe*

## 1

### The Chinese Contribution to the Study of International Relations

Since the Euro-American-centric civilization seems to have arrived at a stalemate, moves have been made to find an alternative type of civilization for Asia. Many different kinds of 'Asianism' have accelerated this quest. 'Asia' is often represented by China. It is true that China was a great civilization. The so-called 'four greatest inventions' — gun powder, the compass, paper and printing — are said to have originated there. In the mid-fifteenth century, Zheng He navigated repeatedly from China to South-east and South Asia, and even as far as Africa, well before Columbus's 'discovery' of the New World. Some of the ships Zheng used, according to documentary and archaeological studies, were as large as 8,000 tons, while Columbus's ships were around 150 tons (Terada 1981, p. 73; Levathes 1996, p. 11). It is assumed, therefore, that in the field of the social sciences, too, China must have contributed to humanity.

As far as international relations are concerned, there are several important classical writings, comparable to, but much earlier than, those of Thucydides and Machiavelli, which are not well known in the West.[1] In more recent times, however, the Chinese have made few contributions to the theory of international relations. Under the current open-door policy, the study of international relations has begun in China; but the Chinese, in essence, are merely learning from the West, even about Marxism–Leninism.[2] There are two reasons for this. First, in a society where freedom of

---

[1] *Sun Zi* is famous, but there are classics like *Hanfei Zi, Zhanguoce, Shiji, Dongzhou Lieguozhi, Zizhitongjian* and many others.

[2] Recently, in addition to ideas of 'classic realism', ideas such as hegemonic cycles, international regimes and the 'clash of civilizations' have been introduced (see Wang 1995; also see articles in *Zhanglue yu Guangli*, an active bimonthly social science journal).

speech is constrained, the social sciences have faced difficulties in developing independent research projects. They often merely serve the Chinese leadership with policy recommendations; or, at least, they remain compatible with the official policy line.[3] Second, the study of international relations deals mainly with the more or less anarchical sovereign nation-state system, with wide variations. This system was born in the West and spread throughout the world because the constituent unit of the system — the nation-state, which was connected closely with the industrial capitalist system[4] — was much stronger than any other power in the world and much more competitive. China, which was the centre of the East Asian world system, was not strong enough or competitive enough to cope with the Western nation-states and was integrated into their nation-state system in the mid-nineteenth century as a subordinate member of the system. A similar integration occurred in all non-Western areas of the world, although some survived as independent 'associate' nation-states in subordinate positions; while others became colonies of nation-states, becoming 'nation-states' in their own right only after World War II. The processes of integration into the system have been completed only recently.

The rules of the Chinese world system before the West came to East Asia were very different from those of the nation-state system (see Hamashita 1990, 1997). As a subordinate member of the modern international system since the nineteenth century, China has not been in a position to develop its own theory of international relations. The only exception to this generalization is that China may be providing a different viewpoint of the world: a view from below, or from the perspective of a former colony or subordinated country within the framework of the same logic.[5] In the long history of China, however, there have been mini-state systems, such as those during the Spring and Autumn Period and the Warring States Period. These can be compared to the Greek city-state system of classical times and to the northern Italian mini-state system of the Renaissance, and it explains how the Chinese came to produce the classics of international relations theory in ancient times.

# 2

## The World View of Chinese Leaders

As stated above, China's encounter with the modern international system occurred in the mid-nineteenth century. This encounter was a tragic one. China's great

---

[3] In one standard textbook published by China People's University Press, 'characteristics of Chinese studies in the theory of international relations' are: 'five principles of peaceful coexistence; strategic division of the world into three; peace and development being the two most important tasks; international new order' (Feng and Song 1992, pp. 36–7). Another standard text by Beijing University says that the Chinese characteristics are expressed in traditional Chinese in terms such as: 'esteem independence and oppose aggression; be devoted to peace; have contempt for offensive wars; advocate moderation; dislike extremes; pursue a harmonious world; advocate mutual respect and mutual help; pursue non-discrimination, non-exploitation, non-war, non-violence' (Liang and Hong 1994, pp. 39–40).

[4] Industrialization promoted not only military and transportation capabilities, but also the organization of society.

[5] More concretely, Mao Zedong may have contributed to tactics of guerrilla warfare in developing countries.

civilization was in a period of decay and was unable to oppose the power of nation-states that were deeply connected with the development of competitive, market-oriented capitalism. As a result, China was forcefully absorbed into the nation-state system. In order to survive in the system, to cope with the advanced nation-states and to catch up with them, China had both to learn the rules and logic of the nation-state system and to acquire the capabilities to cope with the other superior members of the system.

Japan faced a similar situation at the same time. Fortunately, it was able to rapidly escape the subordinate status and soon became itself one of the 'powers' in the international system (see Kuwabara *et al.* 1984, esp. p. 129). China tried to learn from Japan and solicited its help during the pre-modern period. Japan, how-ever, did not respond to the Chinese request,[6] although some Japanese did try to help Sun Yat-sen's revolutionary activities. (This was the beginning of the unhappy relationship between China and Japan in the modern period.)

Faced with such harsh international relations, Chinese leaders, both in power and in opposition, tried to use the rules of the classic nation-state system — notably sovereignty, non-intervention in internal affairs, and ostensible equality of nations — to China's advantage. Chinese modern history can be said to consist of continual efforts to realize these rules. The acquisition of 'equal status' became the cherished desire of all politically conscious Chinese. This makes the Chinese leaders' view of world politics classically 'realistic' and nationalistic (see Okabe 1996).

The Chinese Communist Party (CCP), established in 1921, was not international-ist in the manner of Marx, Engels or even Lenin. Propagating nationalism (*aiguozhuyi*) to replace the declining ideology as a base for legitimacy, an official document of the early 1980s pointed out that the founders of the Party had been nationalists before they found communism as the way to save their country (Propaganda Department 1983). One of the earliest Marxists, Li Dazhao, contended that 'pro-letarian nations' had to overthrow the rule of 'bourgeois nations' (Li 1959, p. 299). This idea transformed the Marxist theory of 'class struggle' into an international relations theory.

Mao Zedong was a nationalist from the start. It was widely believed that the Chinese were constitutionally weak, perhaps because of bad habits such as opium smoking, intermarriage (which resulted from the socio-economic fragmentation of pre-modern China in standard market towns: Okabe 1986, pp. 169, 173–4; see also Skinner 1964/5) and traditional rule by the literati. It is interesting that Mao, before he became a Marxist, wrote a paper entitled 'A Study of Gymnastics' (Mao 1972). This suggests that physical training was the young Mao's first idea for making China strong. Nationalistic Mao was also anti-Comintern during the revolutionary struggles and tried to be as independent as possible from Moscow, even when he felt it necessary to align China with the Soviet Union. After he came to power, he opposed the Soviet domination of the rules within the 'socialist camp' (see e.g. PRC 1956), and ultimately was responsible for starting the Sino-Soviet conflict.

---

[6] Sun Yat-sen, in his famous speech on 28 November 1924, in Kobe, Japan, on 'The Greater Asianism', called for Japan to take a benign policy (*wangdao*) to China rather than a high-handed policy (*badao*).

As a nationalist who had tried to make China strong and independent in the existing international system, Mao now tried to make China modernize rapidly through socialism. Unfortunately, he came into sharp conflict with the world's strongest country, the United States; and his modernization plan became distorted when he put China on a war footing against possible invasion. His guerrilla warfare — based on a style of dispersed fighting with little communication, but with a unified perception and close collaboration — served to preserve the traditional social structure (socio-economic fragmentation via standard market towns) and dictatorship.[7] The Great Leap Forward, the People's Commune and the Cultural Revolution all hindered the modernization of the country, contrary to Mao's personal intentions.[8]

The foreign policy of the People's Republic of China has been comparable to that of other countries in similar situations. It was nationalistic and classically power-political. Ideology played a role, but not as a factor apart from Chinese 'national interests' as defined by the Chinese leaders. Chinese ideological rhetoric, like its counterpart in the Soviet Union, served mainly as a guise for Chinese 'national interests', although it has functioned to legitimize the regime as the authentic bastion of Marx's idealistic vision.

This function was especially important in China's conflict with the Soviet Union. In the early 1950s, both the legitimacy of the Communist regime in China and its reputation as a model for the newly independent states rested heavily on the prestige of Stalin and on Soviet achievements under Stalin's leadership. Khrushchev's legitimacy, however, rested on his departure from Stalin's tyranny. Differences between the two governments became known in 1956 when Khrushchev made serious accusations against Stalin in a secret session, which later was made public. Those communist countries that relied on Stalin's prestige reacted strongly. In both Hungary and Poland, mass riots occurred. China escaped the crisis by building up the reputation of Mao Zedong and initiating what was to be a long-standing controversy with the Soviet Union, the touchstone of which was ideological legitimacy, even though the actual source of legitimacy was located in the interests of leaders of the two countries.

China's foreign policy, therefore, is understandable largely from the point of view of classical power politics. The famous Five Principles of Peaceful Coexistence — mutual respect for territorial integrity and sovereignty, mutual non-aggression, non-interference in each other's internal affairs, equality and mutual benefit, and peaceful coexistence — are no more than a summary of classic rules of international society in nineteenth-century Western Europe. What is new is the fact that these principles were advocated by newly independent countries, demanding actual equality.

Deng Xiaoping's China changed the course of the modernization strategy to a more familiar strategy. Under his reform and open-door policy, China's foreign policy changed, too, in style if not in essence. Reflecting the changed situation with the United States and Japan and the changed condition of Chinese legitimacy,[9]

---

[7] Refer to Durkheim's theory of the division of labour and 'mechanic solidarity'.

[8] Mao's original development plan was very gradualist: see his 'On New Democracy' (Mao 1972).

[9] By this time, the Chinese regime established its own legitimacy through Sino-Soviet conflicts, but the socialist way of economic management of society reached a stalemate everywhere.

China adopted an omnidirectional diplomacy in the early 1980s. Some, scholars, both in and out of China, argued that China finally gave up ideology and began sticking to 'national interests'. Those who argued in this way, however, did not understand the role of ideology in communist countries. When socialism, and therefore ideology, was combined with a nation-state in 1925 ('socialism in one country'), it departed from the Marxism that had aimed to realize world socialism after overcoming the capitalism connected with nation-states. Proletarian internationalism was replaced by 'unconditional support to the Soviet Union', and after World War II a new internationalism appeared among socialist nation-states under Soviet domination, lacking independence. This, according to China, was no more than Soviet chauvinism. China adopted the rules of nineteenth-century international society, and left the socialist camp as a genuine sovereign state.

## 3

### Anachronism and the Theory

The reality of the international relations has changed drastically in the postwar period, especially after the end of the Cold War era. Classic 'realism', with the nineteenth-century Western Europe as its main referent system, is anachronistic in this age.

A typical example of outdated Chinese behaviour occurred in March 1996, when Taiwan's presidential election was held. In order to intimidate the electorate into not voting for Li Denghui and Peng Mingmin (an advocate of independence), China conducted massive manoeuvres, including missile launchings in the Taiwan Strait. Nevertheless, Li Denghui was elected president with a solid majority of 54 per cent. The total combined votes for Li and Peng reached 75 per cent. This meant that, at the very least, the Taiwanese people do not want an early unification with the Mainland. China, in this kind of sabre-rattling, not only failed to hinder the election of Li Denhui, but also increased the perception of threat from China among its neighbouring countries. The Americans became more pro-Taiwan during the process. China's big failure in this case must have been brought about by its misjudging of the role of public opinion today. No one welcomes sabre-rattling, which is only marginally better than the actual use of force.

China's other activities in neighbouring areas such as the Spratly Islands are similar in nature. From the Chinese logic, since both Taiwan and the Spratlys should be under its sovereignty, these are internal affairs that China can handle as it wishes. The idea of sovereignty that China relies on is very old-fashioned (see e.g. Liu 1996). Besides, the claim itself belongs to a kind of irredentism that has been a cause of war throughout the history of international relations; so China's every action has been closely watched by all the people concerned. Here, China made a big mistake believing that its action would be an effective warning to those who tried to do anything China did not want.

In today's international relations, such anachronistic activities have rapidly become the focus of close attention. Owing to the rapidly changing nature of world society, classic 'realism' is most unrealistic today, especially for such a great power as China; yet China continues to follow the line of the 'classic' powers. Industrialization, once a symbol of strong nation-states, is no longer necessarily so. In the first place, most of the Asian developing countries are now industrialized, and some factories have been transferred from countries such as Japan to less developed areas for economic reasons. Besides, the old-style industrialization now faces problems of resources and environmental pollution, which will be the biggest obstacles in the way of further industrialization in China. Second, most countries can now produce conventional weapons — even nuclear weapons, in China's case. Higher-grade weapons may be imported from more developed countries, but it is difficult to import the most advanced technology related to electronics. Therefore, it is the development of such technologies that will become the core of the national power in future. The situation will be very different from that time in history when China was humiliated. Third, the effectiveness of the armed forces in dispute settlement has become very low, especially among industrialized countries, mainly because of their mutual vulnerability. Sabre-rattling, as China did in the Taiwan Strait, no longer works; rather, it increases fear and unsympathetic feelings among neighbours. Fourth, organizational power, which industrialization brought with it in the past, now prevails throughout Asia. Asians have imported administrative and business management skills, and have modified them through their own experiences of industrialization and administration. In the above sense, industrialization, especially in the sphere of heavy industry, does not increase the 'national power' much. It may however be able to improve the life of the people by raising their standard of living, if environmental conditions are protected.

The nature of nation-states has also changed dramatically. Very few nation-states today enjoy homogeneity and easy governance. With much closer communication among peoples, small differences between and among them have become sources of conflict. As a result, old nations are disintegrating into ethnic groups and often cease to be the loci for self-determination. Separatist movements have become popular, even in countries regarded as established nation-states. Many economic transactions are now transnational. These changes make the separation of domestic and international politics and economies almost meaningless. However, this does not mean the decline of nation-states as such. Even if they are unable to preserve traditional territories, nation-states will remain as suitable governing units for quite a long time to come.

As the largest country in the world, China will find it very difficult to act like an old-fashioned nation-state and retain its traditional patterns of societal fragmentation. The Soviet Union, which was nominally a federation, tried to create a 'Soviet citizen' through the integrating power of socialism and the Russian language. It failed, and the USSR has disintegrated into the Commonwealth of Independent States, even though similarities among these peoples are clear to outside observers, and despite the fact that the independent states are by no means sufficiently homogeneous to form unified nations.

The Chinese Communists, who once advocated making the new China a federation,[10] established a multi-ethnic unified state in 1949. The reasons for this change

---

[10] The Federation formula was officially included in the 'Outline Constitution of the Soviet Republic of China' in 1931 and continued at least until Mao's famous speech, 'On Coalition Government' at the 7th Congress of the CCP in 1945.

in the form of the state were natural resources and security of the border areas. Nation-building in China, however, has not been very successful in this centrifugal age. Not only minorities, but also Han Chinese groups like the Taiwanese and, more significantly, those in the south, have shown centrifugal tendencies. Central–local conflicts now occurring in China may promote such centrifugal tendencies.

These gaps between classic aims and current reality do not seem to be recognized by Chinese leaders. The main reason for this misperception must be the strong perception of Chinese humiliation since the mid-nineteenth century. The Spring and Autumn Period and the Warring States Period are still the most relevant models in Chinese history. Also, 'realist' thinking among leaders of the West continues to influence the Chinese through memoirs and other writings (Wang 1994, pp. 497–8). The general trend is unlikely to change in the near future.

But what does the 'future' hold for China? It will be a time when the Chinese leaders feel that China has been compensated enough for its humiliation since the nineteenth century and when it occupies a proper place in the world as a great power. A problem remains, however, because it is difficult to say how satisfactory that possible future situation will be to the Chinese leaders and the masses. Many developing countries will follow the Chinese lead in sticking to the older rules. Japan, as an insular country without much of an international sense among its people, may stick to older courses of action (even if not so old as those of China). In that sense, Asian prosperity will become an obstacle to China's flexibility to adapt to global trends. China will be the first to resist changes in international rules and/or structures. Its greatest influence to the international relations theory will be this conservative bias; any drastic departure from the 'classic' model may become impossible owing to China's objection.

An example may explain this possibility better. In a trilateral conference among Japan, the United States and China, a Chinese delegate asked Americans, in connection with the 'independence' of Taiwan, 'What would you do if Hawaii declared independence?' An American scholar said the United States would let Hawaii become independent. Another American scholar added that even Long Island (in New York State) could get independence if it wanted to. The Chinese delegate was appalled.

In recent years, Chinese disagreement with the developed West (often including Japan), is expressed by Chinese scholars as a conflict between 'Asian values' and European individualistic 'universalism'. Asian values are diverse. A Chinese scholar wrote that the essence of these values is 'collectivism' or the 'community-centred' way (*jitizhuyi*) (see Yan and Li 1995, p. 5). Do Asian values propose something new to international relations theory? The Japanese are often seen by others as very collective, but this has not influenced international relations theory in the past, although it may have influenced the study of management and the role of government in economic activities. The same is true with China.

The idea of 'Asian values' is problematical, but European 'universalism' is also a questionable concept. First of all, what is 'Asia'? It is a term adopted by Europeans to designate the areas east of present-day Turkey (often called Asia Minor). It includes vast and diverse areas and countries and has no specific meaning. The motivation behind use of the term 'Asian values' is usually as opposition to Euro-American-centric ideas. Sometimes the Euro-American-centric idea is the issue of human rights, which unfortunately is then selectively applied as a standard against some countries deemed undesirable from the viewpoint of, for example, the United States.

At other times the term 'Asian values' is used to explain East Asian economic development. Confucian influence on the cultures of some Asian countries is one such common explanation. This argument has been popular among some business-men, but to my mind the influence of Confucianism is different from country to country. In China, Confucianism has been criticized until recently as a cause of the country's underdevelopment. After the Tiananmen Incident, in order to prevent the influence of Western ideas, the glories of Chinese tradition have been emphasized; and Confucianism, one of China's greatest cultural heritages, has been revived con-veniently as a positive tradition. Koreans tend to view China, the motherland of Confucianism, as inadequately implementing the teaching of Confucius, and Japan too as insufficiently Confucian. Singapore, to the best of my knowledge the originator of the term 'Asian values', tried to inculcate Confucianism to improve labour ethics, but the effort failed, at least in schools, and been suspended (Tanaka 1990). 'Asian values' have not overcome the stalemate of Euro-American civilization. They cannot influence international relations theory in any positive way, as an analysis of major international relations textbooks in China clearly shows.[11]

In this perspective, China's major 'contribution' to the international relations theory as stated above will be its persistent use, as a non-Western and formerly subordinate state, of some of the 'classic' ideas of the nation-state system which originated in nineteenth-century Western Europe. The idea that state sovereignty is absolute is the best case in point; and China's desire to build a homogeneous nation is another good example. This approach suggests that China wants to recover its sovereignty and independence, once usurped by Western powers and Japan, by resorting to the principles of the 'usurpers'. There will be no worldwide decline of the nation-state as long as China sticks to these principles. The recent idea of a 'new medieval age' is attractive, but it seems to me that the exchanges of three different spheres (the new medieval age, modernity and confusion) are not taken into account (see e.g. Tanaka 1996). The medieval age sphere must take similar action when dealing with 'modern' countries. There are many countries similar to China among former colonies or subordinated countries in Asia and elsewhere, mostly in develop-ing areas. If they are in Asia, 'Asian values' becomes a convenient rallying point for them. The China–ASEAN connection against American 'human rights diplomacy' after the Tiananmen Incident is a typical example.

It goes without saying that changes are possible in China, or elsewhere in Asia. However, change is likely to occur very slowly in China. Unless China recovers sovereignty over Taiwan (several different types of unification are imaginable), and stabilizes Tibet and Xinjiang as integrated parts of a unified country, and unless Chinese leaders feel equal in power to Western leaders ('comprehensive power', to use recent Chinese terminology, which is very similar to Morgenthau's concept of 'national power'), they will modify their modernization policy. The criterion of equality will be the biggest problem, not only for the Chinese leaders themselves but

---

[11] See fn. 3.

also for people outside China. However, a new point of view is emerging in China, among the younger generation. When these people come to power, China may start changing.

With regard to homogenizing the nation, I would like to reflect on the Chinese idea of 'nation' and 'ethnic group'. The motive force of the Xinhai Revolution in 1911 was ethnic or even purely racial. The main slogan of the revolution was 'Overthrow the Manchus [the Qing dynasty, an ethnic Manchu group], and Make the Hans [the Han people, China's primary ethnic group] Flourish.' In fact, immediately after the success of the revolution, the revolutionary leader Sun Yat-sen reported to the grave of the first Emperor of Ming, a dynasty of the Han people which preceded the Qing, that the Han people had recovered power from the barbarians. Soon after that, in order to form a nation-state in the remaining Qing territory, Sun and others felt the need to make a single country out of the multiethnic situation. 'Coordination of Five Races' replaced the old slogan of Han chauvinism. Nevertheless, since the percentage of Han people in the total population of China today is 92 per cent (it was 94 per cent in 1949), Han chauvinism has not disappeared. This is reflected in difficulties in teaching Chinese history. In the past, Wen Tianxiang was viewed as an admirable patriot for resisting the Mongol invasion of China and devoting his life to maintaining the Song dynasty. But both the Han people of the Song dynasty and the Mongol people of the Yuan dynasty are regarded as Chinese nationals now. Under these circumstances, there is no official place for the traditional patriot. Official and private understanding of history have to split here. Furthermore, there are big differences among the Han people themselves (see Gladney 1995). They would constitute different nations, if the spoken language were the criterion for differentiating nations, as it is in Europe. There are however some characteristics unifying China, such as Chinese characters and the traditional idea of *dayitong* (meaning 'cherishing unification'), which appeared after the unification of the country by Qinshihuang in 221 BC.

Another problem today is that ethnic groups are not necessarily based on lineage. Most of the Taiwanese people are racial Han by origin, but they believe that they constitute a different ethnic group now (Okabe 1988), and even a different nation, as the 'independence' movement suggests. Not only are these contradictory ideas about the nation, ethnic group and lineage confusing, but they also make China's nation-building efforts more difficult.

Regarding another new idea in international relations, that of non-governmental organizations (NGOs), it should be noted that there are no NGOs in China in a real sense of the term. No really non-governmental exchanges will be possible for quite some time. Democratization of the country is a necessary precondition for realizing such exchanges, and this will be a very long and slow process (see Okabe 1998).

# 4

## The Foreign Policy of China in the Twenty-first Century

It is widely argued that Chinese foreign policy has become more and more assertive. Some say that China is or will be a 'threat' to the peace and stability of East Asia and even of the whole world. Usually, it is the potential impact of 1.2 billion people that is the core of this concern. From a systemic viewpoint, rapid change is a destabilizing factor, and in that sense China may well become a kind of 'threat'. Some smaller countries in South-east Asia may feel that China's existing capabilities are much stronger than their own and may perceive a direct military threat. China's activities in the Taiwan Strait and the Spratlys accelerate such a perception.

To be objective, one can note that China does not consider itself a 'threat' to any neighbouring country. As seen from China, both Taiwan and the Spratlys are lost territories; regaining sovereignty over these areas is regarded as a natural and legitimate right and as a domestic matter. Chinese leaders feel that they are showing generosity in proposing 'One state, two systems' in the case of Taiwan and 'Shelve the conflicts; develop jointly' in the case of the Spratlys. Besides, they think, China's weaponry is so old-fashioned that it could never be threatening to others. These perception gaps arise from China's classic image of international relations and from its own self-image of a humiliated country. China's leaders feel that their country is only potentially strong, even though it is already important as a permanent member of the UN Security Council. The potential of China's economic future is a very big attraction for other countries, so China cannot be ignored or insulted as before. China's leaders still feel that their country is far from attaining an ideal status which a great country like China deserves.

Regarding international law, there are some problems in Chinese claims to Taiwan and the Spratlys. Japan, in the Peace Treaty at San Francisco, renounced sovereign claims to both Taiwan and the Spratlys; however, owing to the international situation at that time, it did not make clear to whom the sovereignty was returned. The People's Republic of China, which was not represented in the peace conference, has declared that it is not bound by the Treaty. As a matter of fact, Taiwan was effectively occupied in 1945 by the Republic of China, at that time the legitimate government of China. This government continues to exist in Taiwan after having been defeated by the communists on the mainland. At the time of normalization between China and Japan, the joint statement said that Japan 'understands and respects' China's claim to Taiwan. The modest wording was to conform with the Peace Treaty, but Japan indirectly recognized China's claim by saying in the Joint Statement that it would 'stick to article 8 of the Potsdam Declaration'. This article stated that the Cairo Declaration, which supported the return of Taiwan and its related islands to China, should be implemented. It is clear enough from a legal point of view. China's concern arises from a lack of self-confidence originating from its humiliation in historical times. It has become more serious as the problem of self-determination of the native 'Taiwanese' has recently come to the fore. Legally speaking, however, China has nothing to worry about.

As for the Spratlys, here the legal problem is more complicated. After the renunciation of territorial claims by Japan, China (the Republic of China, then the legitimate government of the country) occupied the only inhabitable island in the Spratlys — an understandable action at that time, since uninhabitable shoals and reefs were of no use. Only in the late 1960s and early 1970s did these reefs become important because of the UN Law of the Sea and the possibility of seabed oil in the region. The Spratlys are generally regarded by other countries as *terra nullius* except for Itu Aba, which was occupied by Taiwan (the Republic of China). As an exception, Vietnam claims historical sovereignty over the whole area of the Spratlys, even though Vietnam recognized Chinese sovereignty over the islands during the honeymoon days between the two countries (see statements in Han 1988, pp. 542–4).

Conflicts over such claims have been common in international history and have often been settled by military power. Today, the use of force in such cases is restrained by mutual fear of disastrous wars. However, it is thought that China would not hesitate to use force because of its classic ideas of power politics and territorial self-defence. These two ideas are actually irredentist claims, a source of some of the biggest wars in history. In this sense, China is clinging to an outmoded understanding of international relations which harks back to the days of imperialism. In 1997, China started to use the term 'a new idea of security', which is almost the same as the idea of 'cooperative security' in the West; the only difference is that China's leaders think that the 'new idea' is mutually exclusive with the Alliance, which is said to be a remnant of the Cold War period.[12] If the 'new idea' is so effective, all military power, whether Alliance or not, can be scrapped. China has not scrapped its armaments, however, replacing them by ARF (ASEAN Regional Forum). This means that the 'new idea' is at present used simply for propaganda purposes.

My personal view of the problem of the 'China threat' depends on how we regard the role of big countries today. The big powers in pre-World War II days had many rights and few responsibilities. In the present era of mass destructive potential and the big gap between the North and South and within the South, big countries have more responsibilities than rights. Regardless of China's self-image as a country victimized during the days of imperialism, it is a big power today. China's lack of responsibility in assuming the role of a big power can be a source of anxiety about the 'China threat'. Fortunately, since 1994 China has begun to claim that it has a great responsibility as a big power, though some people still suspect that the 'responsibility' is a euphemism of 'dominance' in the region.

In the contemporary world, nation-states are spread over the whole world for the first time in human history, not only as actors in international relations, but also as arenas in which the activities of many different actors take place. The nation-state system today is a role structure in which all the countries and other actors conduct themselves in an expected manner. The correspondence between the role-image of the self and that of others is important for the system to function smoothly. Perception gaps between the self-images of actors about the roles they should play and the rules by which they should abide, and the expectations of others, are among the principal sources of conflicts in our world. China's case is typical in this respect. Before China can contribute to our understanding of contemporary international relations theory, it has to learn more about the nature of the international society. Barring that, the 'China problem' will persist well into the twenty-first century.

---

[12] Qian Qiqian's speech at the 30th anniversary of ASEAN, *Renmin Ribao*, 16 December 1997.

# References

Feng, T. and Song, X. (eds.) (1992), *Guoji Zhengzhi Gailun*, Beijing: Zhongguo Renmin Daxue Chubanshe.

Gladney, D. C. (1995), 'China's Ethnic Awakening', *Asia Pacific Issues*, January.

Han, Z. (ed.) (1988), *Woguo Nanhai Zhudao Shiliao Huibian* (Collected materials on South China Sea islands of our country), Beijing: Dongfang Chubanshe.

Hamashita, T. (1990), *Kindai Chugokuno Kokusaiteki Keiki* (Modern China's international opportunities), Tokyo University Press.

Hamashita, T. (1997) *Choko Shisutemu to Kindai Azia* (The tributary system and modern Asia), Tokyo: Iwanami Shoten.

Kuwabara, T. *et al.* (eds.) (1984), *Meijiishin to Kindaika* (Meiji restoration and modernization), Tokyo: Shogakkan.

Levathes, L. E. (1996), *Chugokuga Umiwo Shihaishita Toki* (Japanese trans. of *When China Ruled the Seas*, New York: Simon & Schuster, 1994), Tokyo: Sinshokan.

Li, D. (1959), 'You Jingjishang Jieshi Zhongguo Jindai Sixiang Biandong de Yuanyin' (Economically explaining changes in modern Chinese thoughts), in *Li's Collected Works*, Beijing: Renmin Chubanshe.

Liang, S. and Hong, Y. (eds.) (1994), *Guoji Zhengzhi Gailun*, Beijing: Zhongyang Bianyi Chubanshe.

Liu, W. (1996), 'The Sovereignty Problem with regard to Taiwan', *Renmin Ribao* (overseas edn), 23 May.

Mao, Z. (1972), *Works of Mao Zedong*, Tokyo: Hokubousha.

Okabe, T. (1986), 'Chugokushiki "Shakaishugi" Shiron' (A tentative explanation of 'socialism' with Chinese characteristics), in T. Okabe *et al.* (eds.), *Chugoku Shakaishugi no Saikentoo* (Reconsidering Chinese socialism), Tokyo: Nihon Kokusai Mondai Kenkyujo (JIIA).

Okabe, T. (1988), 'Higashi Ajia niokeru Seijiteki Togo to Bunka' (Political integration and separation in Asia), Chapter 3 of T. Okabe *et al.*, *Ajia niokeru Kokumintogo* (National integration in Asia), Tokyo University Press, pp. 107–42.

Okabe, T. (1996), 'Chugoku Gaikoo no Kotenteki Seikaku' (The classic nature of China's foreign policy), *Gaiko Forumn*, January: 37–45.

Okabe, T. (1998), 'China's Prospects for Change', in L. Diamond and M. F. Plattner (eds.), *Democracy in East Asia*, Baltimore: Johns Hopkins University Press, pp. 171–83.

PRC (1956), 'Zhonghua Renmin Gongheguo Guanyu Sulian Zhengfu 1956 Nian 10 Yue 30 Ri Xuanyan de Shengming' (Statement on the declaration by the government of the Soviet Union on 30 October 1956), *Renmin Ribao*, 1 November.

Propaganda Department and Research Section of the Central Secretariat of the Chinese Communist Party (1983), 'Guanyu Jiaqiang Aiguozhuyi Xuanchuan Jiaoyu de Yijian' (An opinion on reinforcing nationalist propaganda education), *Renmin Ribao*, 2 July.

Skinner, G. W. (1964/5), 'Marketing and Social Structure in Rural China', *Journal for Asian Studies*, 24(1): 3–43; 24(2): 195–228; 24(3): 363–99.

Tanaka, A. (1996), *Atarasii Chusei* (A new medievalism), Tokyo: Nihon Keizai Shimbunsha.

Tanaka, K. (1990), 'Shingaporu no Jukyou Kyouiku' (Confucian education in Singapore, 1984–9), *Aziya Kenkyu* (Asian studies), December: 1–34.

Terada, T. (1981), *Teiwa (Zheng He)*, Tokyo: Shimizu Shoin.

Wang, J. (1994), 'International Relations Theory and the Study of Chinese Foreign Policy: A Chinese Perspective', in T. Robinson and D. Shambaugh (eds.), *Chinese Foreign Policy*, Oxford: Clarendon Press.

Wang, Y. (1995), *Dangdai Guoji Zhengzhi Xilun* (A preliminary study of contemporary international politics), Shanghai: Renmin Chubanshe.

Yan, X. and Li, Z. (1995), 'Zhangwang Xia Shiji Chu Guoji Zhengzhi' (In perspective for the international politics in the early next century), *Xiandai Guoji Guanxi*, June: 2–8.

# CHINA AND JAPAN IN SEARCH OF THEIR ROLES IN THE TWENTY-FIRST CENTURY

## REGIONALISM OR GLOBALISM?

*Shigeaki Uno*

## 1

### Introduction

The twenty-first century is already being referred to as both the 'Asian Era' and the 'Century of China'. Some say that the age of Western culture and of the great powers has passed, and that we are now living in a multicultural and multipolar world.

The economic development of China, and of the newly industrializing Asian countries known as the 'four dragons' (South Korea, Taiwan, Hong Kong and Singapore), has certainly been outstanding, and their enhanced economic power is linked to a growing voice in political affairs.

Meanwhile, the world has witnessed a conspicuous revival of Islam, Buddhism and Confucianism, accompanied by an overt questioning of the conventional ways of Christian-centred civilization. At the same time, since the end of the Cold War, the dominance of the two superpowers (the United States and the Soviet Union) has been declining. As a consequence, the relative international influence of second-tier powers (such as the European Union, Canada, Japan and Australia), newly industrializing nations (such as China, India, South Korea, the ASEAN nations and Mexico) and the many developing nations of the world has increased.

But will the 'Asian Era' and the age of multiculturalism emerge as easily as many people expect? In real life, complex factors come into play, and progress may not keep pace with people's expectations. It is hard to believe that the high economic growth rates in Asia and China will continue throughout the twenty-first century. Also, even though the political influence of medium-sized and smaller nations has been strengthened, this is only on a relative basis. The fundamentals remain essentially unchanged. It is still the great powers (of one kind or another) that define major events in the international political arena. Furthermore, although we speak of a new age of multiculturalism and multipolarism, the system that will ensure peaceful coexistence in this new age is not yet clear, and we do not yet enjoy a stable international order. So it is necessary to adopt a relatively long-term perspective in order to gain a realistic outlook for the future.

When we review the history of international relations over a relatively long time frame, the meaning and significance of culture and of civilization become key issues. Inevitably, all concrete instances of the concepts of 'culture' and 'civilization' have been developed in close association with specific geographical regions. (While there are naturally certain differences between 'culture' and 'civilization', these are not addressed in this paper.) In essence, 'culture' and 'civilization' are self-defined concepts, and are based upon regionalism. Thus, when these concepts are debated in a political context, confrontational aspects are destined to surface. For example, regardless of the author's intention, in 'The Clash of Civilizations?' Samuel P. Huntington (1993) does not evade the tendency to equate civilization with the confrontational aspects of politics.

Nevertheless, if civilizations and cultures are in conflict, it does not mean that relations among nation-states must also be confrontational. For example, the present American understanding of (political) culture is in sharp confrontation with that of China, particularly regarding perceptions of human rights and democracy. Nevertheless, both countries' actual foreign policies are aimed at adroitly avoiding a definitive worsening of bilateral relations.

Today, many East Asian countries are demonstrating a tendency to criticize Western civilization and the Western style of modernization at every possible opportunity. This is like a continuation of these countries' liberation movements from the colonial period, and may represent a counter-offensive to dominant Western pressures that actually exist. However, such criticisms are not directly linked to economic or political confrontation. To secure their safety and prosperity, the nations of East Asia actually look forward to the continued presence of the European Union and the United States in Asia, within rational limits.

Thus, raising issues about the confrontation of cultures and civilizations does not necessarily have a directly harmful effect on political relations. Similarly, asserting that different cultures and civilizations are in conflict is not paramount to a proclamation that Asia and the West are in structural opposition. As shown below, my perspective is based upon the endogenous development theory and the mutual contact stimulation theory. These theories emphasize the *raison d'être* of culture, tradition and geographical regions. Fundamentally, such factors are particular and regionalistic; so, as a matter of course, these theories encompass an inherent potential for conflict.

Nevertheless, I believe that, depending upon the situation, cultures and civilizations often enrich themselves through confrontation with other cultures and civilizations. In other words, although dissimilar cultures and civilizations are antagonistic, they can also be mutually stimulating, can blend together to some extent, and thus can ceaselessly give birth to new forms of creativity.

At the same time, while the contradictory aspects of culture and civilization frequently worsen relations in the political field, they may also develop their potential to the creation of new techniques based upon novel concepts. For example, it is only through conflicts of values regarding the origin of democracy that societies can reaffirm the universality of democratic principles, create appropriate forms of democracy for themselves and stimulate one another in a positive way to promote further development. The important point is that, while each society attempts to maintain the integrity of its own culture and civilization, new possibilities are created internally by contact with outside forces. This type of stimulation should be mutual, and if so will give rise to the possibility of a new globalism. That is to say, it is through mutually influencing one another that each society may be able to orient itself towards the creation of a new 'universalism' or 'globalism'.

Of course, there are limitations to addressing international politics from the perspective of culture and civilization. In the real world of international politics, one must strive to analyse quantitatively specific instances of economic development, military competition and diplomatic strategies, and to distinguish the complex relationships involved in power struggles and conflict resolution. Nevertheless, when we address the outlook for international relations over the relatively long time frame of the entire twenty-first century, while grasping the overall situation of economic development and conflicting interests, we must base our analyses on a vast perspective that also encompasses the issues of culture and civilization.

This paper therefore considers the current potential for mutual stimulation from contact between Asia and the West, and then addresses the potential roles of China and Japan in international relations in the coming century.

# 2

## The Challenge for the Asian Era: From Economic Development to the Assertion of a Unique Political Culture

I would like to begin by reviewing a few facts.

From 1980 to 1993, the remarkable economic growth in China, South Korea, Taiwan, Hong Kong, Singapore and other East Asian nations gave rise to a hullabaloo about an 'Asian Era'. During this period, annual real GDP increased at a rate of 9.6 per cent in China, 9.1 per cent in South Korea, 7.5 per cent in Taiwan, 6.5 per cent in Hong Kong and 6.9 per cent in Singapore, far surpassing the international average of 2.9 per cent. In 1993, the World Bank and other agencies released projections showing that, if the Asian economies were to continue growing at an average real annual rate of 7.7 per cent, by the year 2004 China would have the world's largest GDP, followed by the United States and Japan. Since that time, pundits have repeatedly proclaimed the so-called 'East Asian miracle'.[1]

It is important to note that, while East Asian nations have indicated an orientation towards economic globalization by opening their economies, introducing the market principle and encouraging private-sector firms, they continue to emphasize the role of the public sector, steadfastly adhere to planned economies via government

---

[1] One work that introduces and analyses World Bank materials in detail is Ezaki (1995, pp. 40–56), an article that presents a theoretical comparison of Krugman (1994) with World Bank data on the Asian miracle, and apparently agrees with the World Bank position. The figures presented in this paper are from Ezaki's article.

intervention, permit only limited decentralization and essentially pursue national political strategies. This leads to the assertion that, at a certain stage of historical development, the so-called 'dictatorial development' often observed in Asian nations is effective. In turn, this leads to the affirmation of Asian independence *vis-à-vis* the contemporary Western political system.

Perhaps the greatest proponent of this movement is Lee Kuan Yew, the former prime minister of Singapore. During a speech he made in Japan, Lee stated that the nations of the West have given precedence to democracy and human rights over each nation's tradition and culture, and have forced these values on to their former colonies. He said that democratic governments have taken root only in those nations where democracy is in accord with the national character of the people. He went on to point out that elections, ballot boxes and political parties do not, in and of themselves, constitute democracy (*Asahi Shimbun*, 18 May 1991).

During another address he made in Japan, Lee stated that if he were Japanese he would want the Japanese government to evaluate other nations not on the basis of the appearance of democratic forms, but on the actual conditions of their governments. In other words, he said, the question should be whether or not these governments are good, rather than whether or not they are democratic (*Asahi Shimbun*, 23 November 1992).

Naturally, such Asian political assertions are viewed as rather sensational by the West. For example, in his famous article 'The Myth of Asia's Miracle', Stanford Professor Paul Krugman says:

> The leaders of those nations did not share our faith in free markets or unlimited civil liberties. They asserted with increasing self-confidence that their system was superior: societies that accepted strong, even authoritarian governments and were willing to limit individual liberties in the interest of the common good, take charge of their economies, and sacrifice short-run consumer interests for the sake of long-run growth would eventually outperform the increasingly chaotic societies of the West. (Krugman 1994, p. 62)[2]

In extreme circumstances, this obsession with Asia may develop into an assertion that Western nations need to learn from the East. The *Guang Ming Ri Bao* daily newspaper, which is widely read by Chinese intellectuals, claims that the East has a better understanding of the West than the West does of the East. This newspaper notes that the numbers and percentage of Chinese who can understand English far surpass the numbers and percentage of Americans who can understand Chinese. The paper quotes David Howell, the chairman of the UK Foreign Affairs Committee of the House of Commons, who has suggested that the problem is not the westernization of the East, but rather the 'easternization' of the West. The editors go on to say, 'In good faith, we want Americans to make an urgent effort to learn about Eastern culture' (*Guang Ming Ri Bao*, 25 September 1995).

---

[2] Krugman says: 'Although East Asian technology is advancing, surprisingly, the East Asian economies are not using resources at all efficiently.' He goes on to say: 'China presently boasts annual growth rates of over 10 per cent, but if they do not improve efficiency, this may drop to 7 per cent in 10 years, and fall further to 5 per cent in another 10 years' (*Asahi Shimbun*, 23 April 1995).

Of course, it would be difficult for Westerners to accept unconditionally the axiom that they must 'learn from the East' without certain parameters. That is to say, there must be a clear definition of exactly what it is that they should be learning from the East, how should they learn it, and how much they need to learn. The cry to 'learn from the East' may be a dangerous postulate, especially when it involves emotional and political nuances.

Nevertheless, when this is combined with self-criticism on the part of the West, it strikes a responsive chord. Since the latter 1970s, along with the worsening of the environmental crisis, questions have been raised as to the propriety of Western-style modernization. At a time when there is growing criticism about modern industrialism, state-centrism and egotistic individualism, some Westerners have chosen to look positively at the different possibilities presented by Asia.

At the international academic conference on Confucianism, which took place at Qufu in Shandong Province in August 1987, Leon Vandermeerche, a professor at the University of Paris, said:

> Confucianism recognizes the precedence of society [over the individual] through the concept of human ethics, which differs from the individual morality that exists in each person's heart. The concept of human ethics states that each individual can only realize his own character within the context of his social existence, which is determined by nature. I think this human ethics promoted the development of a social 'courtesy of China' that differs from that of the West, where the law is almighty. Western society has given pre-eminence to laws formed as a system for the purpose of protecting individual rights, and because of this Western society is now falling into the disconnected. (*Asahi Shimbun*, 17 September 1987)

If we restrict ourselves to pointing out the limits of Western individualism and emphasizing the possibilities of Asian communalism (including social courtesy), we may fall once again into the hackneyed conceptual framework of Western civilization versus Asian civilization. At a certain stage of Western political history, it was necessary to create the fiction of 'the strong individual' in order to overcome the systems and concepts of medieval communities and feudalism, and to spiritually liberate human beings from oppressive systems. Similarly, the proposition of individualism should be a necessary condition for the creation of a modern Asia.

However, as Yoichi Higuchi incisively points out, 'The individual, who has been released from the bonds of a class-based social structure by the modern age, has simultaneously lost the protective shield provided by this structure.' Higuchi says that through this process, while weak individuals have remained weak, strong individuals have gained independence by means of their rational faculties, have formed groups and associations of their own will, devised a legal system which should be universal, and established sovereign states (Higuchi 1993, p. 16). Yet, as the Chinese nationalist leader Sun Yat-sen pointed out in his lectures 'Three Principles of the People', in real history this represented the success of a fiction. For Sun Yat-sen, individuals independent of a group, democracy formed by such individuals, and the state as a tool for improving the people's livelihood are all fictions, and gain meaning only through contrived preparation and education.

We do not have to plumb the depths of Asian wisdom to prove that individualism, reason, organizations and the state do not have absolute existence. This has been noted in the West as well. In his *Moral Man and Immoral Society*, Reinhold Niebuhr (when demonstrating his understanding of Marxism) argued that the nation is a corporate unity, held together more by force and emotion than by mind (Furuya and Ooki 1974, p. 298, from Niebuhr 1932, p. 88). Moreover, Niebuhr asserts that the limitations of the human imagination, the easy subservience of reason to prejudice and passion and the consequent persistence of irrational egoism, particularly in group behaviour, make social conflict an inevitability in human history (Furuya and Ooki 1974, p. 208). Therefore, he says, the state and other organizations do not exist *a priori*, and so we must constantly examine such groupings within the 'love of God' which transcends the ties among human beings. We may say that this realization is now a common understanding shared by both East and West. In practical terms, the problem is how to learn from one another's truths based upon this type of universal understanding.

# 3

## The Potential of the Endogenous Development Theory

At this point, I would like to propose the endogenous development theory (which is not yet complete) as a working hypothesis. This concept appeared almost simultaneously in the East and West around the middle of the 1970s. I would like to apply it to the study of China, Asia and international relations in general.

In Japan, the endogenous development theory was first advocated by Professor Kazuko Tsurumi of Sophia University in 1976. Around the same time (in 1975), the word 'endogenous' was used in proposing the concept of alternative development in the report *What Should be Done*, which was presented by the Hammarskjöld Foundation of Sweden to a United Nations special session on economic issues. At that time Professor Tsurumi and I had formed a research group, but we were not aware that the Hammarskjöld Foundation had used the word in this way (see Tsurumi and Kawata 1989, p. 46).[3] Nevertheless, our research group held several key ideas in common with Hammarskjöld Foundation report, specifically, that development should begin from basic human survival needs, that development should be in harmony with the regional natural environment, and that it should emphasize the self-help efforts and joint work of regional communities.

The endogenous development theory originated when analysts began to question conventional modernization theory, which had been accepted as a self-evident truth during the 1960s. The endogenous development theory drew attention to communities and to small regions where people live in a traditional manner, where independent human beings work together, and where direct political participation is possible. The theory criticized the cult of success, which worships competition for its own

---

[3] At that time, Tsurumi was taking part in a study group for the reconsideration of modernization together with Shigeaki Uno, Saburo Ichii and Keiji Yamada. The analysis focused solely on Japan and China, and Tsurumi was unaware of the work being conducted by the Hammarkjöld Foundation.

sake, modern industrialism, which stresses efficiency at all cost, and nationalism, which rationalizes the centralization of power. As a natural extension, it also developed into a movement against pollution, which destroys the environment. (For example, we pursued for five years the prosecution of the private-sector enterprises and local government authorities responsible for the Minamata mercury poisoning disease.)

At first glance, this theory can be misunderstood as a hopeless, rearguard action to unconditionally approve tradition, defend feudal communities and oppose modern industrialization. However, the proponents of the endogenous development theory are actually trying to incorporate concepts for the new era, to reformulate traditions in an innovative manner, to promote mutual simulation between the self-awareness of the individual and the community, and to foster the creation of modern industries that are rooted in local regions. Furthermore, this theory has been proposed now precisely because of the stage of historical development we are in — that is, at the end of the twentieth century, rather than in the initial stages of capitalism, or the formative stages of imperialistic nation-states.

When we consider how the endogenous development theory was proposed and developed in Japan, it is interesting to note that this process was greatly influenced by intellectual stimulation from the West.

As mentioned above, emphasis on local regions and respect for communities are closely linked with a positive approval of traditions. Professor Tsurumi originally began to emphasize traditions after being influenced by Yoshimi Takeuchi, a Japanese specialist in Chinese literature. Takeuchi was one of the first researchers to reconfirm and re-evaluate the traditional concepts of Asia based upon stimulus from the West. He wrote that 'traditions become traditions through self-awareness, and the proximate cause that gave rise to this self-awareness was the European invasion [to Asia]' (Takeuchi 1960, p. 18). Takeuchi's line of argument frequently followed this type of reasoning. While the use of the word 'invasion' may be somewhat too direct, at the very least there is no doubt that, for both Takeuchi and Tsurumi, the concept of a re-evaluation and renewal of Asian traditions would not have appeared without stimulus from the West.

Later Tsurumi showed a great interest in the 'green' perspective presented by Swedish economists Mats Friberg and Bjorn Hettene in *The Greening of the World* (1982) and in Chadwick Alger's concept of internationalization from the local level, which apparently places value on this perspective (Alger 1987). Tsurumi showed sympathy with Friberg and Hettne's belief that individual human beings or small communities are the primary units of behaviour, and that nation-states are no more than tools of these ultimate actors. Similarly, Alger's statement that Western capitalist society and Eastern state socialism are merely different manifestations of a common, high-level industrial culture because both are based on the values of competitive individualism, rationalism, growth, efficiency, specialization, the centralization of power and a large scale of operations struck a responsive chord (see Yoshida 1987, pp. 174–5). Such comments were consistent with the viewpoint that Tsurumi and other members of our research group had been advocating for several years.

For ten years beginning in 1984, Tsurumi and I analysed the conditions of industrialization in comparatively advanced agricultural villages in China in an effort to verify our hypothesis. The results of our study may be summarized as follows. When local Chinese enterprises develop, traditional local industries, production structures and social organization are significant factors. However, as the promotion of local industries becomes a national policy and is linked to the structure of international trade, the traditional economic framework falls far behind, and export-oriented businesses come to dominate. In these cases, traditional factors do not vanish, but they are significantly distorted. Nevertheless, this modernized sector remains within the framework of the traditional system. Thus, even if local enterprises temporarily take on a foreign-style appearance, they respond to changing conditions and continuously return to their original endogenous form. Of course, the enterprises do not completely recover their original form, and in a certain sense they go through a pattern of cyclical development, but in the end the fundamental factor that regulates their direction is tradition, which is constantly evolving (see Uno and Tsurumi 1994[4]).

The issue is the relationship between tradition and factors that have been introduced from abroad. We witnessed foreign capital, equipment, technology, specialists and legal systems advancing deeper into China year by year, changing the Chinese people's consciousness, social life, political attitudes and attitudes about the outside world. Nevertheless, at the same time traditional China is repeatedly being restructured. This involves not a revival of the remains from the past, but rather a re-incorporation of traditions into the environment of the new era. Of course, this restructuring has both progressive and regressive aspects. The dominant factor that determines what will be retained and what will be disposed of is the environment of the new era, and this is permeated by the active influence of the West.

Conversely, changes can be seen in the Western technologies, leaders and legal systems that have entered China. In a certain sense, the West too is undergoing change because of its contact with China. Benjamin I. Schwartz pointed out that, at the end of the Ching (Manchu) dynasty, the spirit of Western European freedoms and laws had entered China and changed form, and this fact deepened introspection among the Western Europeans (Schwartz 1964). We can expect the same sort of dynamic to take place today.

On the basis of this perspective, and considering the possibility of change in China, Japan and the West, what type of international relations can we expect in the twenty-first century?

# 4

## China Viewed from the Endogenous Development Theory

If we consider China from the perspective of the endogenous development theory, it appears that China changes only slowly, owing to its historical tradition. Of course, China has witnessed periods of intense superficial change, such as during the communist revolution. Also, it has experienced rapid progress, like the steady advances

---

[4] This book is a theoretical summary based on ten years of site surveys.

being made, primarily in urban areas, under the present reform and free market policies. Particularly if we view the situation from the standpoint of central government policies that encourage change, and from the modern coastal sector which is oriented towards economic reform aided by the introduction of foreign capital, the concept of a China undergoing radical change appears closer to the present reality. Nevertheless, China's unique conceptual tradition, which views the world from the basis of Chinese values, remains unchanged. The political tradition of what is in practice a guided democracy, presupposing the existence of an ethically and intellectually superior elite, represents a continuation of ancient Chinese practices (Uno 1993).

From this perspective, Chinese democracy differs from that of the West. In China, democracy is a technique with which to manage the state, and merely reflects the essence of China's current stage of historical development (Wen 1990, p. 16). China's democracy gives precedence to the right to earn a basic livelihood over what the West views as fundamental human rights. If we examine China from the perspective of modernization theory, it becomes painfully clear that, despite outstanding economic growth, China lags drastically behind in terms of political reform, social awareness and liberation of the individual.

At the same time, however, we cannot ignore the fact that China is gradually undergoing an endogenous change as a result of stimulation from foreign countries. Electoral systems and systems for lodging formal complaints are gradually being introduced into China's guided democracy. A more objective legalism is being introduced into China's administrative systems, which have traditionally been based on the control of individual leaders. Self-awareness at the individual level is also sprouting up, and being combined with Chinese group consciousness. The influence of the West is steadily penetrating China. Nevertheless, we will be disappointed if, on the basis of these trends, we expect China to grow into a conventional, modern Western nation-state. In fact, China's leaders stress a type of development that is uniquely Chinese, and which will always differ from the Western model.

For example, speaking to a mission from the European Parliament, Chinese Premier Li Peng stated that 'human rights' is an extremely wide-ranging concept that includes political rights, the right to live, the right to develop, the right of equality among ethnic groups and races, the rights and interests of women and children and the rights of the disabled. He pointed out that there are over five billion people living on this earth, and that different development models are being pursued by peoples living under different social systems with different beliefs, histories and cultures. He said that these facts must be recognized, and that the choice of the people in each nation must be respected (*Renmin Ribao* overseas edn, 18 September 1991). Similarly, Li Peng told the mission that the establishment of Chinese democracy and legal systems must be consistent with China's national conditions. Thus, while China will incorporate the trends of the new world, it will continue to pursue development by making the most of its own traditions, and in a way that is acceptable to the Chinese people, as it has always done.

Following the 1912 revolution, China introduced foreign concepts and methods to an unusual extent in order to free itself from colonialism. In an effort to maintain a balance against this exceptional foreign influence, China also reaffirmed its traditions and emphasized them at every possible opportunity. This may have been the only choice available to the country at that time in order to cope with the real threat of imperialism. However, this combination of an unusual amount of foreign ideology with an adamant traditional Chinese belief system continued to define the Chinese leadership system from 1912 to the 1940s, and left its mark even after World War II. The development of the Cold War between the United States and the Soviet Union intensified China's sense of crisis. The combination of radical revolutionary zeal manifest during the Cultural Revolution and the misguided tradition of over-emphasizing family background as if it were a biological pedigree is a representative example of this tendency.

Now that the Cold War has ended, China has emerged from a phase of excessive ideology and is returning to a more realistic and traditional foreign policy. For example, Foreign Minister Qian Qi-chen has said that relations between China and Western nations are based not upon common social systems, ideology and values, but rather on common interests, and that reality confirms that China and the nations of the West share wide common interests (Qian 1993). The idea of approaching international relations from the viewpoint of shared national interests is China's traditional way, and is generally considered its normal strategy in international affairs. This sober approach is reflected in China's analysis of contemporary world affairs. As noted in the *Beijing Weekly*, 'For the time being, fierce competition in the international arena is shifting from conflict in the military and political fields to competition in synthetic national power based on economics, science, and technology.' The *Beijing Weekly* emphasizes the importance of 'synthetic national power', and notes that 'within international economic competition, a transformation has already begun from the domination of world markets by a small number of superpowers to regional blocs comprised of groups of nations cooperating with one another' (*Beijing Weekly*, 5 January 1993, pp. 4–5). The *Beijing Weekly* expresses 'great interest in participating' in cooperative regional economic blocs.

Kazuko Mori has addressed China's foreign stance since the 1980s. Mori maintains that 'China has moved from adjusting its stance, to applying itself, and finally to participating in the present world system defined by the interaction between the capitalist world market and sovereign nations, and is now entering into the network of interdependence' (Mori 1995, p. 15). She suggests that analysts need to question the changing substance of Chinese diplomacy, as well as China's intentions towards the outside world. According to Mori, since the beginning of the 1980s, Chinese diplomacy has undergone three qualitative changes. First, in 1982 China adjusted its diplomatic stance by shifting away from its prior opposition to the Soviet Union and towards strategic cooperation with the United States. Then, from around the middle of the 1980s, China began its full-scale entry into the interdependent international society in recognition of the peacetime environment. Finally, since 1992, when the US–Soviet bipolar structure collapsed and China decided to accelerate the introduction of a market economy, it has begun to participate positively in the establishment of a new regional system based on the freedom of action prompted by the transition to a multipolar world structure (Mori 1996, p. 47). If we view the current state of change from the advanced sectors of China, its leaders do appear to be moving in this direction, considering China's national interests and world trends. However, we need to go a step further to postulate how China will participate in world changes over the next century.

# 5

## Japan Viewed from the Endogenous Development Theory

It has been said that, in comparison with China, Japan lacks clear assertions or ideas. Japan has been criticized for accepting anything and everything foreign, for being polytheistic and for being overly accommodating and lacking fixed ideals.

It is true that Japan's assertions are difficult to read, that the nation tends to swim with the tide and that the Japanese do not have a strong awareness of their past 'sins' as a nation. At the very least, it is true that Japan stumbled into war early in the Showa Period (1926–89) by just flowing with the tide and without making any clear decision, and that it then pursued a war of aggression and committed savage acts. It is also true that Japan has still not engaged in deep introspection concerning the error of its ways, or thoroughly pursued the root causes of its past mistakes. (Although Masao Maruyama did shed some light upon the conceptual basis of Japanese fascism in his book *Gendai Seiji no shiso to Kodo* (The ideology and behaviour of contemporary politics), this issue has been only partially amplified thereafter.) It may be inappropriate to examine such an important issue in this brief paper. Nevertheless, in order to discuss Japan's role and position in the twenty-first century, I would like to consider how Japan appears from the standpoint of the endogenous development theory.

Let us now consider the cultural gap theory espoused in *The Cultural Dimension of Communication* by Professor John Condon (1980). In Chapter 8, which addresses learning from contacts with different cultures, Condon compares the concept of 'active choice' with that of 'adapting to the situation' (in Mushakoji 1967). (The 'active choice' style resembles the American justification for its diplomatic activities, while 'adapting to the situation' is closer to the Japanese style of diplomacy.)

Condon quotes Mushakoji's argument which runs as follows. The 'active choice' style is preferable and less troublesome as long as this style has been standardized within a given society and everyone acts in accordance with this standard. On the other hand, in grey zones, where nuances cannot be clearly defined, 'adapting to the situation' is more effective (although it is troublesome and time-consuming).

Condon concludes that intercultural communication is already an established fact of contemporary life. He says we should not view other cultures as a threat to our own cultural integrity, or as something that must be dealt with like bad weather or a contagious disease: rather, we should view contact with other cultures as the most meaningful learning experience in our lives (Kondo 1980, pp. 241–56). Condon's comments are most interesting in that they imply a potential for Japan in the context of the 'grey' international relations of the contemporary world. 'Adapting to the situation', however, appears to lack subjectivity.

So do the Japanese lack principles for their behaviour on each and every occasion? Concerning this issue, University of Tokyo professor emeritus Tooru Sagara has pointed out that the Japanese concept of 'nature' or 'spontaneity' itself reflects Japanese philosophy. According to Sagara, 'to the Japanese, the ultimate form of the universe is not a superhuman personality, but rather the "spontaneous" act of creation itself. That which comes into existence is both absolute and relative. The "now" that comes into existence can be affirmed as the "eternal now" and also as part of a series of "transitional nows" that come into existence one after another' (Sagara 1989; my translation). This is consistent with the world view espoused by the Buddhist monk Shinran (1173–1263; founder of the Jodo Shin Sect of Pure Land Buddhism) in his seminal work *Jinen Homi Sho* (Treatise on the ultimate truth of things).

Sagara says that 'it is only possible to grasp the content of reality, which comes into existence spontaneously, when human beings completely lose their egos in their relationship with reality'. He says: 'to live as things are seen when one completely loses the ego in reality is the ideal inner subjectivity for human beings' (Sagara 1989; my translation). This concept of an egoless state leads to zen buddhism. In his *Becoming Bamboo* (Carter 1992), Professor Robert E. Carter of the University of Toronto interprets this egoless state as 'the ability to become bamboo'. He explains that this is a metaphor to permit oneself to go beyond one's perceptual, intellectual and emotional habits and expectations and beyond one's own soul and traditional beliefs to embrace and understand those of others (Yamamoto 1996, p. 279).[5]

In the afterword to the Japanese edition of *Becoming Bamboo*, the translator Seisaku Yamamoto, professor emeritus at Kyoto University, adds: 'if, as in Western culture, the position of the ego is linked to intellectualism and to the cult of science, the denial of the ego is linked to an affection which transcends or encompasses the intellect' (Yamamoto 1996, pp. 303–4). Of course, Yamamoto's use of the word 'affection' refers not only to simple emotions or feelings. As pointed out by Ryoen Minamoto in *Tokogawa Gori Shiso no Keifu* (The genealogy of rational thought in the Tokugawa period), this 'affection' includes a Japanese-style rationalism or mind that may accept a culture of reason (Minamoto 1972, p. 378).

On the basis of these conceptual frameworks, what understanding of Japan's postwar diplomacy can we arrive at? The core of Japan's diplomacy since the end of World War II has been the denial of war, opposition to nuclear weapons and opposition to maintaining a military force. These central tenets were consistent with world trends at the end of the war, and they are inherent within Japanese conceptual thought and history. Thus, the constitution of Japan, which was initiated by the Occupation authorities, was not necessarily imposed from abroad: rather, the constitution was acceptable to the Japanese because its content could be viewed as correct in the context of the Japanese mind. At the very least, to the Japanese of that time the constitution represented an 'eternal now', and in that sense it was viewed as absolute. Of course, the 'absolute' nature of this truth was 'relative', inasmuch as it stood within a particular time and location. Nevertheless, I want to reconfirm that this truth is one that could not easily be changed. In fact, the 'peace constitution' has become firmly established within the spiritual life of the Japanese over the fifty years since the end of the war.

In contrast, the defence framework under the US–Japan security treaty represents a more delicate issue. Of course, the US–Japan security alliance did play a certain role within the context of the Cold War. It had both positive and negative aspects in maintaining the peace, but most people believed that the benefits outweighed the

---

[5] *Becoming Bamboo* received the Khibansky prize from the government of Canada as one of the six most significant academic works of 1992–3.

disadvantages. However, unlike the constitution of Japan, the initial establishment of the security framework was never properly debated among Japan's citizens as an issue concerning their internal values. Furthermore, the presence of US military bases in Japan was accepted thereafter as an unavoidable, temporary measure, and the fact that these bases have continued to exist weighs heavily in the hearts of the Japanese people. In particular, the fact that the majority of the bases are located in Okinawa has become a burden on the conscience of the Japanese, and this has constantly been a flashpoint for movements against the US bases and against the US–Japan security treaty nationwide. According to a public opinion survey released by the *Asahi Shimbun* newspaper on 11 November 1995, 64 per cent of the Japanese support the US–Japan security treaty, but 73 per cent hope for a reduction of the US military bases and 73 per cent believe that Japan's share of the financial burden for maintaining American troops in Japan, i.e. 70 per cent, is too high (*Asahi Shimbun*, 19 January 1996).

Thus, while both the peace constitution and the US–Japan security framework may have passed through a certain history and become established among the Japanese, in terms of the values of the Japanese people themselves, the bilateral security alliance is clearly less well established. Relatively early in the twenty-first century, the nature of the US–Japan alliance may be scheduled to undergo a major shift. For example, as Jitsuro Terashima, the general manager of the Washington office of Mitsui & Company, proposes in his article 'Shinbei Nyuua no Sogo Senryaku o Motomete' ('Seeking a comprehensive strategy to remain friendly with the US but focus on entry into Asia), the most realistic approach would be to accept the present US–Japan security framework as a given prerequisite for the first ten years, meanwhile considering the rational level of military forces and the sharing of responsibilities for maintaining security in the Asian region, and determining the procedure for gradually reducing US military bases in Japan. Then, over the next ten years of the twenty-first century, while maintaining the US–Japan security alliance as the core of regional security in Asia, efforts should be made to devise a collective security system for Asia using the Organization for Security and Cooperation in Europe (OSCE) as a model (Terashima 1996, pp. 20–38).

However, as I have argued elsewhere (Uno 1995, pp. 39–52), because the nations of Asia want the international security framework for Asia to be centred around ASEAN, and to represent a looser organizational structure than that provided by OSCE, although the decisions made will be presented as guidelines for member-states, to the greatest possible degree the final judgements will have to be left to each state.[6] Also, as in South-east Asia today, the structure will have to include multiple layers of different organizations. However, no matter how loose the arrangements may be and how many layers the security structure may involve, the creation of unique collective security arrangements within Asia will inevitably alter the nature of the US–Japan military alliance.

---

[6] Susumu Yamakage, who specializes in South-east Asia, explains that 'The ASEAN nations are not trying to make ASEAN an absolute region. While the security and economic prosperity aspects of ASEAN overlap, the members are aiming at a structure that will enable a flexible regionalism and not necessarily become a single monolith' (in Iwanami Publishing 1993, p. 212).

Terashima also argues that

> Within this time-frame, efforts should be made to revise the constitution of Japan to legitimize the Japanese Self-Defence Forces as a military force that is free to engage in self-defence, which is a fundamental right of the state. At the same time, while adhering to the ideology of Japan's postwar pacifism, Japan should maintain the nation's three non-nuclear principles and its ban on the export of weaponry, and take the initiative towards disarmament in the international community centred around the abolition of nuclear weapons. Pursuing disarmament and securing sufficient defensive military power to ensure that Japan does not become the cause of regional conflict are by no means contradictory. (Terashima 1996, p. 34)

Despite Terashima's thesis, is a revision of the constitution of Japan realistic? Conceptually, the peace constitution is firmly established among the Japanese people, whereas the security alliance and self-defence forces are not. Within the conceptual framework of the Japanese people, while maintaining the constitution itself, it would be acceptable to revise the US–Japan alliance and the rules governing the self-defence forces (including sending troops abroad under specific, strict conditions as part of Japan's international contribution), even if these were somewhat contradictory with the constitution in theory and in practice.

This double standard is presently subject to frequent domestic and foreign criticism. From the perspective of the endogenous development theory, however, for the time being it is more realistic to devise a multilateral strategy of developing friendly relations with both the United States and Asia while strictly maintaining Japan's pacifism.

## 6

### Conclusion

Considering the above analyses, while China and Japan differ greatly in many respects — including their conceptual frameworks and political cultures — it is clear that both nations are trying to adapt to the new world environment on the basis of common benefits, common interests and common goals. The two countries share influence from the West and a common historical environment. The differences between them stem from differences in traditional values and historical development processes, and from the fact that they are presently placed within different political, economic and social conditions.

Although China and Japan differ in terms of the way they present their opinions and raise issues, overall both are demonstrating a more global orientation in their foreign policies. For example, Japan's 1996 diplomatic Blue Book has many points in common with recent speeches given by Chinese leaders, including the following: (1) a recognition of the overall trend towards the creation of a new world order (despite the continued existence of certain dangerous developments) and of a deepening economic interdependence between the advanced nations and the newly industrializing economies; (2) a recognition that this economic development represents a desirable cycle towards greater political stability; and (3) the belief that future diplomacy should be omnidirectional, and not based upon the assumed existence of an enemy state.

The Japanese diplomatic Blue Book emphasizes the resolution of global issues such as the environment, refugees and population growth; support for nations undergoing the transition to democracy and introducing a market economy; and efforts to combat terrorism. It says that Japan should strengthen its cooperation on three levels: *global* cooperation, through the United Nations, the World Trade Organization (WTO), and via trilateral efforts involving Japan, the United States and the European Union; *regional* cooperation within the Asia–Pacific region; and *bilateral* cooperation with the United States, with Asian nations and with the nations of Europe. The Blue Book advocates the construction of a framework whereby these different levels of cooperation will interact and develop into a multilayered and comprehensive diplomacy.

While Asia may adopt a security structure that is looser than that favoured by the West, the future peace of Asia depends upon the creation of an international system that is as stable and as universal as possible. Japan is looking towards a treaty-based structure that is clearly defined, strong and binding like the Western model. However, Japan would not go so far as to try and force the expansion of binding treaties, like the US–Japan security treaty, to cover all of Asia even against the will of China and the ASEAN members. Although some Japanese might like to pursue this approach, they represent only a limited number of individuals: according to public opinion surveys, fewer than 20 per cent support expansion of a strong bilateral alliance.

On the other hand, certain Chinese, especially innovative intellectuals in the central government, are trying carefully to draw China into the realm of international treaties. For example, China had previously taken a passive stance towards the ASEAN Regional Forum (ARF), saying that its remit should be limited to being a forum for the exchange of opinions.

It goes without saying that these developments and adjustments in China's foreign policy reflect the changing times as well as the influence of West. However, from China's conceptual framework, they definitely do not represent a following-after, or even a compromise with, the West. While it is a generalization, the *Beijing Weekly* presents the current opinion of the average Chinese in an article entitled 'The Possibility of a Fusion between Eastern and Western Civilization' as follows:

> According to Zhujun and certain other academics, the present development in East Asia that has attracted the world's attention is neither a revival of ancient Eastern civilization nor a simple reproduction of modern Western civilization. Rather, this represents a new Eastern culture that has been created by absorbing the positive aspects of modern Western civilization — particularly the experience of the advanced science, technology, and management of the West — within a new historical background. (Wang and Chu 1996, p. 41)

Of course, this represents the opinion of just one group of Chinese, and one cannot help but feel that it represents, in part, a self-justification. Nevertheless, the statement closely matches my proposition of the endogenous development theory.

While Asia is maintaining its identity (something resembling regionalism) and moving towards more universal concepts (something global), how is this influencing the West? I myself believe that, while limited in number, the areas of Asian influence are steadily growing. Both John Condon's *Cultural Dimension of Communication* and Robert Carter's *Becoming Bamboo* praise certain Asian values and call for a (limited) change in some Western concepts. Also, Paul Cohen's *Discovering History in China*, which has recently attracted a great deal of attention in both Japan and China, proposes a 'China-centered approach', and clearly demonstrates the fallacy and limitations of analysing Asia from the basis of Western values and American standards. Cohen is especially close to the endogenous development theory. He emphasizes regions and local areas, and analyses theories on adapting to outside forces that have evolved inside China (Cohen 1984; trans. as Sato 1988).

It is not yet clear how the West will alter its course as we move into the future. Historically, Western nations have moved forward with citizens' uprisings and economic revolutions based on endogenous factors fostered within their own societies. Today, even if the West is gaining a new awareness of Asia and incorporating Asian influences, this will definitely not take the form of an 'easternization' of the West. Rather, it will develop as an endogenous modern reform within Western societies. This is only a matter of course. It will be possible for the 'East and West'[7] to continue to stimulate one another in a productive manner only if they independently recreate and redevelop their own values. The mainstream of international relations in the twenty-first century will be the continuous creation of globalism based upon regionalism. The foundation that will make this development possible is the mutual efforts to create a more universal common ground.

# References

Alger, C. (1987), *Chiiki Karano Kokusaika: Kokkakankeiron o Koete*, Tokyo: Nihon-hyoron-sha.

Carter, R. E. (1992), *Becoming Bamboo*, McGill-Queen's University Press.

Cohen, P. A. (1984), *Discovering History in China*, Columbia University Press.

Condon, J. (1980), *The Cultural Dimension of Communication*, Tokyo: Simul Press.

Ezaki, M. (1995), 'Higashi Asia Shinko Chiiki no Keizai Hatten to Globalization' (Economic development and the globalization of newly industrializing areas of East Asia), *Kokusai Mondai*, October, pp. 40–56.

Friberg, M. and Hettne, B. (1982), *The Greening of the World: Toward a Non-deterministic Model of Global Process*, University of Gothenberg Press.

Furuya, Y. and Ooki, H. (trans.) (1974), *Gendai Kirisutokyo Shiso Sosho* (A series on current Christian thought), vol. 8, *Dotokuteki Ningen to Hidotokuteki Shakai*, Tokyo: Hakusuisha; trans. from Niebuhr (1932).

Higuchi, Y. (1993), 'Junkyokoku no Hokai to Rikken Shugi: "Kindai=Jinken" no Konnansei to Kanosei' (The collapse of conforming nations and constitutionalism: the difficulties and possibilities of equating the modern era with human rights), *Shiso* (Thought), August.

Huntington, S. P. (1993), 'The Clash of Civilizations?' *Foreign Affairs*, 72(1).

Iwanami Publishing (1993), *Iwanami Koza: Shakaikagaku no Hoho* (Iwanami Publishing's lectures: social science methodology), Tokyo: Iwanami Publishing Co.

---

[7] This paper utilizes the imprecise concepts of 'East' and 'West'. Naturally, there may be diverse patterns within the East and the West. The identification of specific patterns and the analysis of specific relations should be addressed in future case studies.

Kondo, C. (trans.) (1980), *Ibunkakan Communication*, Tokyo: Simul Shuppansha, pp. 241–
  56; trans. of Condon (1980).
Krugman, P. (1994), 'The Myth of Asia's Miracle', *Foreign Affairs*, November/December.
Minamoto, R. (1972), 'Tokogawa Gori shiso no Keifu' (The genealogy of rational thought in
  the Tokugawa period), in *Chukoshinsho*, Tokyo: Chuokoron-sha.
Mori, K. (1995), 'Sekai System no naka no Chugoku' (China in the world system), *Kokusai
  Mondai* (International issues), Tokyo: Nihon Kokusai Mondai Kenkyujo, January.
Mori, K. (1996), 'Futeikei no Asia: Chugoku wa Kyo Ka' (Asia without a fixed form: is
  China a threat?'), *Sekai* (The world), March.
Mushakoji, K. (1967), *Kokusai Seiji to Nihon* (International politics and Japan), Tokyo
  University Press.
Niebuhr, R. (1932), *Moral Man and Immoral Society*, New York: Charles Scribner's Sons.
Qian, Q. (1993), 'The World Rediscovers China', *Renmin Ribao* (People's Daily), 15 Decem-
  ber; reprinted in *Beijing Weekly*, 20 December 1993.
Sagara, T. (1989), *Nihon so Shiso* (Japanese thought), Tokyo: Perikansha.
Sato, S. (trans.) (1988), *Chi no Teikoku Shugi*, Tokyo: Heibon-sha, trans. of Cohen (1984).
Schwartz, B. I. (1964), *In Search of Wealth and Power*, Harvard University Press.
Takeuchi, Y. (1960), 'Chugoku no Kindai to Nihon no Kindai' (Modern China and modern
  Japan), in *The Collected Essays of Yoshimi Takeuchi*, Vol. 3, Tokyo: Chikuma-shobo.
Terashima, J. (1966), 'Shinbei Nyuua no Sogo Senryaku o Motomete: Seijuku Taiheiyo
  Kokka Nihon no Koso' (Seeking a comprehensive strategy to remain friends with the US
  but focus on entry into Asia: conception of Japan as a mature Pacific nation), *Chuo Koron*
  (Public debate), March.
Tsurumi, K. and Kawata, T. (eds.) (1989), *Naihatsuteki Hatten Ron* (The endogenous
  development theory), Tokyo: Daigaku Shuppankai.
Uno, S. (1993), 'Chugoku no Minshushugi: Seiji Bunka no Tensei to Sono Tenbo' (Chinese
  democracy; the quantitative conversion of political culture), in T. Kato (ed.), *Democracy
  no Mirai* (The future of democracy), Tokyo: Daigaku Shuppankai.
Uno, S. (1995), 'Itaiseikan Kyoryoku o Meguru Kyogo to Sono Tenbo: Chugoku no Tai-APEC
  Seisaku o Chushin to Shite' (Competition concerning cooperation among different systems
  and their perspectives: China's policies towards APEC), *Ajia Taihiyo Kenkyu* (Asia–Pacific
  Research), 12; reprinted in *Chiiki no Katarikuchi: Tonan Ajia-zo o toshite Iru Ninshiki
  Hoho* (Regional styles of expression: cognitive methods through an image of South-east
  Asia), Musashino: Seiki University Press.
Uno, S. and Tsurumi, K. (eds.) (1994), *Naihatsuteki Hatten to Galkogata Hatten-Gendai
  Chugoku ni Okeru Kosaku* (Endogenous development and exogenous forces in Chinese
  development), Tokyo: Daigaku Shuppankai.
Wang, J. and Chu, S. (1996), 'The Possibility of a Fusion between Eastern and Western
  Civilization', *Beijing Weekly*, 9 January.
Wen, Y. (1990), 'Socialist Democracy is Only a Stage of Process', *Beijing Weekly*, 20 March.
Yamamato, S. (trans.) (1996), *Tozai Bunka Kyoseiron*, Kyoto: Sekaishiso-sha; trans. from
  Carter (1992).
Yoshida, S. (ed. and trans.) (1987), *Chiiki Kara no Kokusaika-Kokka Kankeiron o Koete*
  (Internationalization from the local level: beyond nation-to-nation relations), Tokyo: Nihon
  Hyoronsha; trans. from 'Bridging the Micro and the Macro in International Relations
  Research', *Alternatives*, 10(3), 1984–5.

# 10

# THREE FACES OF JAPAN

## NATIONALIST, REGIONALIST AND GLOBALIST FUTURES

### *Tsuneo Akaha*

## 1
### Introduction

Japan today faces a dramatically changed strategic environment. Globally, the bipolar structure of the Cold War has disappeared but no clear strategic structure has emerged to replace it. The United States, the only remaining global superpower, is bent on reducing its global security burdens and pursuing an increasingly self-centred strategy against its economic rivals, such as Japan. China, a burgeoning economic power, is determined to deny the United States a monopoly on global agenda but is beset by potentially explosive problems including Taiwan, ethnic minorities, human rights and widening income disparities among the population and uneven regional economic development. Russia, a fallen superpower but still a formidable military power, is mired in seemingly endless political disorder and economic crisis at home and is unable to fashion a credible and consistent policy abroad.

The ambiguous strategic environment surrounding Japan has complicated Tokyo's search for a credible and effective role in the post-Cold War Asia–Pacific. Japan's political and security roles in the region remain constrained by the legacies of pre-Cold War and Cold War history. The recent reaffirmation of the US–Japan alliance notwithstanding, there is growing anxiety in the region about the sustainability of the alliance in the post-Cold War era. Hopeful expectations about the primacy of economics in global affairs and promising prognoses for deepening economic interdependence in the region exist alongside with warnings about disconcerting trends

This is a revised version of a paper I presented at the joint meeting of the International Studies Association and the Japan Association of International Relations, 20–22 September 1996, Makuhari, Japan. For a Japanese translation of the earlier paper, see Tsuneo Akaha, 'Nihon no Mittsu no Kao: Nashonarisuto, rijonarisuto, gurobarisuto to shite no Shorai', Nihon Kokusaiseiji Gakkai, ed., *21-seiki no Nihon, Ajia, Sekai* (Japan, Asia and the global system: Towards the twenty-first century), Tokyo: Kokusaishoin, 1998, pp. 775–806.

towards stepped-up arms acquisitions in the region.[1] The financial and economic crises that have befallen Asia since the collapse of Thai *baht* in July 1997 are rolling back the region's economic gains in recent decades and threatening the political stability in many countries of the region. Praises of Japan's postwar 'economic miracle' and the 'Asian model', which have led the region's economic growth over the last two decades, are fast giving way to criticisms of the public–private sector collusion in Japan and the crony capitalism and corruption in Asia. As we approach the end of the twentieth century, pessimistic prognoses of Asian economic performance are casting a dark shadow over the prospects for the twenty-first century which has been touted as the 'Pacific century'. International criticisms are mounting against Japan's seeming inability to pull itself out of the economic trouble at home and lead the rest of Asia out of its economic crisis.

Tokyo's foreign policy in a new era has also been sidetracked by the longest and deepest recession Japan has experienced following the bursting of its economic bubble in 1991. The task has been compounded by the political uncertainty in the wake of the demise of the Liberal Democratic Party's monopoly of national power in 1993. Neither realists nor liberals have been able to fashion a credible long-range strategy towards the Asia–Pacific.

Notwithstanding the uncertainties and anxieties that surround Japan's strategic environment, one thing is certain: Japan can no longer remain a passive follower of global and regional developments and must become a major mover and shaker in international affairs. Is Japan prepared to meet this challenge? Can Tokyo successfully harness the nation's enormous economic power and become a leader in the collective management of global and regional issues, including political and security problems (Langdon and Akaha 1993)? Can Tokyo effectively contribute to the building of a non-hegemonic world characterized by cooperative sharing of power and responsibilities (Meeks 1993)?

International expectations of Japan are growing. Until international consensus emerges on Japan's global position such as in the UN Security Council, Tokyo will focus its diplomatic efforts on Asia, the region of critical importance to Japan's interests (Hashimoto 1993). The nation's neighbours are increasingly appreciative of its contributions to the region's peace and prosperity through its pacifist and economics-centred policy but remain apprehensive about its military security role (Jihua 1993). The memory of Japan's aggression against its neighbours in the first half of the twentieth century continues to constrain its roles in the region. Its territorial disputes with Russia, Korea and China complicate its relations with them.[2] Japan's growing economic presence elsewhere in the world has generated expectations for Tokyo's expanded political roles, but those expectations remain largely unmet (Elton 1993).

Before Japan can forge a legitimate and credible role for itself in the post-Cold War world, it must negotiate its international position at three levels: domestic, regional and global. Should Japan define an international role defined in terms of

---

[1] See e.g. Johnson (1992, pp. 103–12) and Segal (1992, pp. 83–101). For a similarly mixed prognosis for future Asia–Pacific relations, see Dibb (1996).

[2] For the impact of Japan–Russia territorial dispute over the 'Northern Territories', see Zagorsky (1993) and Akaha (1993b).

its historical, geographical and cultural uniqueness? Should it be content with the attainment of a regionally focused status? Or should it carve out a visible global profile and stand shoulder-to-shoulder with the other world powers? As I will argue in the following analysis, the ultimate answer to these questions depends critically on Japan's relationship with the United States. Essentially, the question can be summed up as: will Japan continue to anchor its security policy on its alliance with the United States as it has done throughout the Cold War era?

I will first consider the question of Japanese identity in the world. I will then scrutinize the challenges facing Japan's regional leadership roles, namely the needs to develop a strategic view of the Asia–Pacific, to legitimize its regional roles and to muster resources to carry out those roles. Third, I will examine Japanese debate on its global portfolio, particularly with respect to participation in UN peacekeeping operations and a permanent seat on the UN Security Council. Finally, I will examine Japan's perception of its most important bilateral relationship, that with the United States. I will contend that the bilateral alliance with the United States serves as the most important catalyst for Japan's search for national identity; it sets the parameters of Japan's role in the Asia–Pacific; and it defines the scope of its global profile.

## 2

### Forging a National Identity and National Consensus

Most Japanese are aware of the growing international expectations regarding their international political and security roles. They agree that the end of the Cold War has opened up opportunities for expanded international roles for their country. However, what many Japanese acknowledge as their insular world outlook, and what many foreign critics describe as Japanese ethnocentrism, severely limit the nation's ability to assume important international roles (Keizaikikakucho Sogokeikakukyoku 1987, pp. 87, 113).

Some trace the insularity and ethnocentrism of Japanese people to their history and geography. For example, a 1991 report by a Ministry of International Trade and Industry study group stated: 'The ethnocentrism of Japanese who have built their history in a nation of islands surrounded by seas on all sides, without any experience of large scale foreign invasions, is seen as peculiar from the point of view of the world's common sense' (Tsusansho et al. 1987, p. 170). Japanese contemporary insularity is also attributed to their peculiar strategic position in the postwar world. A Japanese diplomat observes: 'Japan's postwar foreign relations with Asia have been nothing more than a facet of America's global strategy' (Ogura 1996, p. 8). Both the ideological division of the Cold War era Asia and the US policy to nurture Japan as its most important ally in the region long insulated the Japanese from the need to reach full reconciliation with their Asian neighbours, unlike the Germans with their European neighbours in the context of the Nato and European economic integration. It was not until 1965, for example, that Japan finally restored diplomatic relations with South Korea. Japanese–Chinese normalization came as recently as in 1972. Japan and Russia are yet to conclude a peace treaty. The Asian neighbours continue to harbour suspicion about Japanese foreign policy objectives. One analyst symbolically stated that, for Japan, '1945' is not over (Kosaka 1993, p. 98).

The mainstream thinking in Japan conceptualizes the world as a state-centric system and defines Japan as a key national actor in it. Many Japanese continue to be pre-occupied with the 'uniqueness' of their history, culture and position in the contemporary world. They view Japan as an island nation in perpetual need of adjustment against the vagaries of world politics. Domestic discussion has highlighted Japan's current status as a 'pacifist nation' and its future aspirations as a 'global civilian power'.[3]

Japanese insularity and ethnocentrism are said to contribute to 'unilateral pacifism' (*ikkoku heiwa shugi*) and 'unilateral prosperity' (*ikkoku han'ei shugi*), i.e. their tendency to pursue their own peace and prosperity with little regard for the security and material needs of other nations (see Inoguchi 1987; Tsusansho *et al.* 1987). During the Gulf crisis, a Japanese diplomat urged his countrymen not only to pursue their own peace and security but also to actively participate in the construction of a new world order.[4] Japanese debate on the uniqueness thesis has also been energized by the spate of 'revisionist' critiques of Japanese political economy since the 1980s and more recently by the 'civilizational clash' thesis.[5] These foreign critiques have renewed Japanese intellectuals' interest in Japanese nationalism and Asianism.[6]

A related issue is whether the Japanese political system can produce able leaders who are willing to take risks in putting forth an active regionalist or globalist vision for Japan's future. Recent political developments in the country are discouraging, with domestic issues dominating the agenda.

The Liberal Democrats, who had governed the country for virtually the entire postwar period, have lost their monopoly on power. First, the conservatives lost their majority position in the House of Councillors in 1990. Following a series of political and financial scandals that eroded public confidence in the conservative party's governing ability, long-brewing tensions between pro-reform and anti-reform forces within the party came to a head in 1993 and many members quit the party and formed new parties. A hurriedly formed coalition of anti-LDP forces managed to defeat the Liberal Democrats in the upper house elections in July. This was the first time the LDP lost their majority position since its formation in 1955. Parliament elected Morihiro Hosokawa, a former LDP member and leader of the newly formed Japan New Party, prime minister.

The new leader focused most of his energy on holding the fragile anti-LDP coalition together and managing domestic issues amidst the deepest economic recession the country had experienced since the immediate postwar years. His government managed to pass political reform bills through parliament and opened the domestic

---

[3] The description of Japan as a 'pacifist nation' is found in virtually every Japanese work on the nation's contemporary international policy. For discussions of Japan as a 'civilian power', see Maull (1990/1); Funabashi (1991/2, p. 65; 1993, pp. 159–206).

[4] See the interview with Takakazu Kuriyama (then Japanese ambassador to the United States) in 'Wangan Mondai to Nihon no Yakuwari' (The Gulf issue and Japan's role), *Gaiko Forum*, March 1991, p. 5.

[5] See Prestowitz (1988); Fallows (1989); van Wolferen (1989); Huntington (1993). For recent reflections on Japan's images in foreign writings, see Okui (1994).

[6] For a balanced view of contemporary Japanese nationalism, see Stronach (1995). For recent Japanese writings on Asianism, see Funabashi (1993, pp. 93–112); Ogura (1993); Wakamiya (1995); Noda (1995).

rice market to imports. The Hosokawa government was unable to take major foreign policy initiatives, although the prime minister took an important step towards reconciliation with the Asian neighbours by acknowledging openly that Japan indeed engaged in a 'war of aggression' (*shinryaku senso*) against its neighbours earlier in the century. In April 1994, however, Hosokawa abruptly quit his post when public suspicions grew about his personal financial dealings. He was succeeded by Tsutomu Hata, a former LDP member; but, following the defection of the Social Democratic Party of Japan (SDPJ) from the anti-LDP coalition, his government was forced to resign in June 1994, only 61 days after formation.

The Liberal Democrats managed to form a coalition government with the SDPJ and the New Party Harbinger (NPH) in June 1994. The coalition government, headed by socialist leader Tomiichi Murayama, was clearly a marriage of convenience. The Liberal Democrats desperately wanted to prevent further defections from among their ranks as they remained out of power. The Socialists, eager to share governing power with their erstwhile political enemies, abandoned the central planks of their postwar policy, i.e., opposition to the Japan–US security treaty and claim of unconstitutionality of the Self Defence Forces. Following Murayama's self-enacted resignation in December 1995, the LDP–SDPJ–NPH coalition elected the new LDP leader Ryutaro Hashimoto as prime minister. His government remained mired in a parliamentary tug-of-war with the opposition led by his erstwhile political rival Ichiro Ozawa, the Shinshinto (New Frontier Party) leader, himself a source of growing discontent within his party over his aggressive behind-the-door manoeuvring.

The Hashimoto government left two important marks in the nation's foreign policy: reaffirmation of the Japan–US security alliance, and a visible improvement in Japanese–Russian relations based, in part, on Hashimoto's personal rapport with President Boris Yeltsin. However, domestic economic woes finally caught up with the prime minister, and he resigned in the wake of a disastrous defeat in the upper house elections in 1997. His successor, Keizo Obuchi, seems unable to extricate the nation from the economic recession, further fuelling international criticisms against Japan's policy immobility.

The absence of strong leadership in Tokyo might be tolerable, if not desirable, if there were a sustained national consensus on Japan's foreign policy direction. However, there are signs of domestic divisions regarding Japan's rightful place in the world.

A brief look at a 1996 survey of opinions of parliamentary members on the issue of the constitutional ban on collective security is illustrative in this regard. Out of the 225 members of Parliament surveyed by a book/magazine publisher Bungeishunju, 12 LDP and 12 Shinshinto members were of the opinion that Article 9 should be re-interpreted to allow Japan to participate actively in collective security, including military cooperation with the United States; 51 members (16 LDP members, 33 Shinshinto members, 1 Sakigake (Harbinger) member, and 1 independent) believed the constitution placed undue limitations on Japan's ability to ensure its security and therefore felt that national debate should be conducted with a view to revising the constitution; 93 members (30 LDP, 13 SDPJ, 9 Sakigake, 37 Shinshinto, 2 New Socialist Party, 1 Citizens' League and 1 Liberal Union member) believed Japan should exercise the right of individual self-defence within the bounds of the constitution; 37 respondents (1 LDP member, 18 SDPJ members, 3 Sakigake members, 3 Shinshinto members, 8 Communists, 2 Socialists and 2 Citizens' League members) supported Article 9 and believed Japan should reject military cooperation and seek the nation's security exclusively through peaceful means; the remaining 20 members had other opinions.[7]

When the traditional insularity and ethnocentrism of the Japanese people are combined with a political system that cannot produce strong leaders, Japan's foreign policy behaviour cannot but be passive and reactive.[8] With international demands mounting for a greater Japanese role in world affairs, Japan's inability to overcome these failings is problematic. Despite the rhetoric of 'a nation that can contribute to the international society' (*kokusaishakai ni koken dekiru kuni*), and notwithstanding some notable achievements, such as in the areas of foreign direct investment and official economic development assistance, Japan's contributions are often seen as too little too late, or as not giving sufficient philosophical or moral rationale with a universal appeal.

# 3

## Developing a Strategic View of the Region

Another obstacle to Japan's foreign policy in the new era is the absence of a coherent, long-term strategic view of the Asia–Pacific. As many observers have pointed out, Tokyo's strategic view of the region during the Cold War era was largely a product of Washington's strategic policy in the region. In essence, it was unnecessary — even undesirable, from the US perspective — for Japan to develop an independent analysis of the region's strategic environment and to formulate an autonomous policy accordingly. The end of the Cold War has lifted the strategic 'greenhouse' protecting Japan.

Japanese policy-makers have long resisted framing their policies in terms of a realist doctrine. In the immediate postwar years, their overarching goals were to democratize their political system and to redevelop their war-torn economy. A long-term strategic view was irrelevant and unnecessary. Nor did Japanese successful economic achievements in the subsequent decades indicate a shift in its economics-first policy. From Tokyo's perspective, the task of structuring regional and global international relations could be left to the United States. Under these circumstances, Japanese views of international relations leaned closely to the liberal theory of international relations, with an emphasis on economic interdependence. The Japanese saw economic interdependence first as an important global trend to be exploited to its own advantage, and then, as their economy and self-confidence grew, as a policy goal to pursue.

Only after US hegemonic power began to show visible signs of decline in the 1970s did the Japanese begin to doubt the sustainability of a liberal capitalist world order heavily dependent on US leadership alone. However, pressing foreign policy issues, such as the Nixon shocks, the oil shocks, and the mounting US–Japan trade friction, forced policy-makers in Tokyo to attend to the immediate tasks of *ad hoc*,

---

[7] 'Nagatacho Kokkaigiin Anketo, Nihon no Kiro o Tou' (Questionnaire survey of parliament members in Nagatacho, questions regarding Japan's course), *Bungeishunju*, August 1996, pp. 94–5.

[8] For an excellent study of the 'sakoku' mentality of the Japanese, see Itoh (1998). For a similarly critical view, see Pempel (1998).

reactive policy adjustment. Japanese foreign and security policies remained minimalist, passive and reactive. While these policies were non-provocative and non-threatening, they were ambiguous and lacked innovation. These tendencies produced a rather unique approach to national security generally known as 'comprehensive security'.[9] As a recent review of Japan's postwar security policy concluded, 'The structure of the Japanese state creates incentives for a broad definition of security favoring economic and political dimensions over strictly military ones' (Katzenstein and Okawara 1993).

Developments in the post-Cold War Asia–Pacific indicate a partial convergence of realist and liberalist perspectives among the region's political leaders. For example, the Clinton administration's call for a new 'Pacific Community' in the APEC process presumes US leadership in forging a new regional balance of power. At the same time, it aims at expanding international economic exchange through a reduction of foreign trade and investment barriers.[10] Chinese leaders also appear to be operating on the premise that a balance-of-power system is emerging in the Asia–Pacific, but at the same time they are pursuing the material benefits of growing international economic ties.[11] Russia is the only major power in the region without sufficient regional market–economic ties to enable its leaders to explore liberalist approaches towards their neighbours, although the country's Far Eastern region is expanding its economic ties with the neighbouring north-east Asian economies.[12]

For military security, Tokyo has long deferred to Washington's strategic view of the world and eschewed development of its own view. The end of the Cold War has not changed this. Foreign and security policy-makers in Tokyo continue to view the Japan–US relationship as the core of their regional policies.[13] Tokyo reaffirmed the centrality of the Japan–US security treaty to the nation's security policy when it adopted a new National Defence Program Outline (NDPO) in November 1995. The document replaced the 1976 Defence Program Outline as the basis for the nation's defence buildup. The document mentions Japan's 'new areas of responsibility', including effective response to major natural disasters and terrorism and contribution to the building of a more stable security environment through international peacekeeping activities and the promotion of international cooperation through international emergency relief activities. The statement should be seen, however, as a reaffirmation of existing policy, not as a departure from it. It is Tokyo's response to the international criticism against its 'checkbook diplomacy' during the Gulf War and to the need to improve public safety in the aftermath of a series of murderous

---

[9] For a favourable view of the policy, see Akaha (1991, pp. 324–40; 1993a).

[10] For Japanese views of Clinton's APEC policy, see Kikuchi (1995); Yamazawa (1995, pp. 201–2); and Yamakage (1995, pp. 79–100).

[11] See e.g. Foreign Minister Qian Qichen's 20 March 1994 interview in Beijing, in which he stated that China was willing to lose US markets if Washington should decide not to renew China's MFN status in June because of its human rights practices. In the same interview, however, the foreign minister said China still believed that progress could be made on its differences with Washington if discussions took place on the basis of equality and mutual respect (Tyler 1994, p. A1).

[12] For a comprehensive examination of the Russian Far East's relations with the North-east Asian countries, see Akaha (1997).

[13] This view is clearly stated in Gaimusho (1995) and Boeicho (1995). See also Okabe (1995, pp. 1–24), Okazaki (1993, pp. 33–55) and Shikata (1996, pp. 54–71).

acts committed by the religious–terrorist group Aum Shinrikyo in 1995 and the devastating Great Hanshin earthquake in the same year.

What are the key features of the strategic environment facing Japan today? Structural changes in the global strategic environment, i.e. the end of the Cold War bipolarity and the arrival of the 'posthegemonic world', have had a very complicating impact on the strategic environment of the Asia–Pacific. One observer points out: 'Global unipolarity now coincides with regional multipolarity . . . Although the United States is in a military class by itself, it cannot act independently in many cases but needs the cooperation of allies to provide bases' (Betts 1993–4, p. 41). He adds: 'The change from worldwide bipolarity to *unipolarity makes the global dimension of strategic competition irrelevant*' at the regional strategic level (p. 43).

The strategic environment of the Asia–Pacific region remains uncertain. More specifically:

1. There are multiple actors whose policies can directly affect security interests of others in the region, and they are adjusting their alliance commitments and seeking new coalition partners.
2. The regional actors' power capabilities and foundations of power are uneven and different, some depending on industrial–technological capacity (e.g. Japan and South Korea), some on military capabilities (e.g. Russia and North Korea) and still others on a combination of political and cultural influence (e.g. China).
3. Their policies reflect varying balances between realist and liberalist perspectives; for example, the growing arms transfers in the region represent both commercial interests and strategic considerations.
4. There is no region-wide institutional framework that can help to structure the policy options of the regional powers. The APEC is too weak to serve to harmonize the policies of the regions' economies and the ASEAN Regional Forum (ARF) is woefully inadequate to deal with bilateral and multilateral security problems in North-east Asia or to contain the arms buildup that has continued unabated despite the end of the Cold War.[14]
5. The region represents a full range of political systems and societal structures, wide disparities in economic development and coexistence of transnational, integrative forces of trade and investment and nationalist, divisive sentiments often invoked by territorial disputes.
6. Historical animosities compete for expression against budding regional cooperation in both South-east and in North-east Asia. The past lives side by side with the future.
7. The dynamic growth and deepening interdependence among the region's economies are promoting regional schemes for economic cooperation but they are also creating new problems, such as international migration and ethnic tension, cross-border pollution and illegal trade, with important security implications.

Fashioning a new strategic vision for the Asia–Pacific is made difficult by the disparities in the power base and the fluidity in national priorities among the major regional powers. In North-east Asia China and Russia have established a 'strategic

---

[14] For a careful assessment of the arms buildup in the region, see Ball (1993–4, pp. 78–112).

partnership', but there are definite limits to the consolidation of their relationship, with the two countries facing formidable domestic challenges; China and the United States are engaging each other in an uneasy testing of the limits of each side's influence over the other; the United States is discounting Russia's political influence and military power in the region; and Russia is struggling to build a regional profile without the requisite resources. The major powers, including Japan, are finding definite limits to their influence over the divided Korea, an explosive legacy of the Cold War. Moreover, Taiwan holds an equally explosive potential. In South-east Asia, growing national confidence in dynamic ASEAN economies has produced major initiatives, e.g. the political settlement of the Cambodian conflict and the formation of the ARF, but that confidence is fast disappearing in the face of the financial and economic crises that have befallen the region since 1997.

The economic dimension of Japan's regional environment has mixed implications for the country. On the one hand, the bankruptcy of the Cold War-driven policies of the two superpowers has vindicated Japan's economics-first foreign policy of the Cold War era. Japan's externally oriented developmental strategy has been replicated in many other parts of the region, promoting growth and facilitating international interdependence. Interest is growing in regional and subregional cooperation. At the official level, NAFTA (North American Free Trade Agreement) is leading the way, with more modest goals being pursued through the APEC (Asia Pacific Economic Cooperation) and the AFTA (ASEAN Free Trade Area), the EAEC (East Asia Economic Caucus) facing an uncertain future. At the non-governmental level, there are such initiatives as the Japan Sea (East Sea) Rim Economic Zone, the Yellow Sea Economic Zone, the Bohai Rim Economic Area, the Chinese Economic Area and the South China Economic Area. On the other hand, concerns exist about 'emerging regional trade blocs', and Japan does not want to be seen as leading the formation of an Asians-only trade bloc; nor would such a scheme be in its interest. The successful conclusion of the Uruguay Round of GATT negotiations and establishment of the World Trade Organization (WTO) have not erased the concern among Asian–Pacific economic leaders that the European Union (EU) and NAFTA may turn into 'economic fortresses' closed to Asian exports. This fear is underlying the efforts to develop APEC, AFTA and EAEC frameworks. Washington under President Clinton is stepping up its effort to rebuild the US economy and improve its industrial competitiveness, and is renewing its pressures to pry open Asian markets and reduce US trade deficits.[15]

As discussed below, Japan needs to strike a politically sustainable balance between its bilateral priorities *vis-à-vis* the United States and its regional interests, the former providing a powerful inertia for the Japan–US alliance and the latter demanding new initiatives for multilateral cooperation. Japan needs to consult closely with the United States on such issues as China's military buildup and North Korea's nuclear development, but it must do so without alienating or provoking China, Japan's

---

[15] For an excellent and detailed examination of Washington's 'strategic trade policy', see Tomiura (1995). Japanese Prime Minister Hashimoto has intimated that Japan would support and join the 'Asians-only' EAEC should NAFTA become an 'Americans-only' regional bloc (Hashimoto 1993, p. 84).

permanent neighbour, or further isolating Pyongyang. Fortunately, Tokyo's recent approach to these issues reflects the required sensitivity. On the economic front, Japan should respond more actively to US demands for more open domestic markets, but it should do so without giving US producers an unfair advantage over others. Additionally, Japan should cooperate with the United States in promoting market liberalization in the Asia–Pacific but should also respect the preference of most Asian countries to proceed slowly along the liberalization path on the basis of regional consensus.

# 4

## Legitimizing a Regional Role

A related question is how Japan can establish legitimacy as a leader in international affairs in the Asia–Pacific. Without legitimacy, Japan's influence in the region, even if based on its enormous economic power, will remain limited.

Since the 1970s Tokyo has chosen South-east Asia to exercise its diplomatic leadership, including in the area of security-building, with the ODA playing a central role in the process. Tokyo has had to tread gently against the background of Japan's history of aggression. Moreover, Japan's economic dominance in South-east Asia is at the same time both an object of admiration and a cause for concern among the developing countries of the region. Tokyo has repeatedly enunciated its pacifist foreign policy at the annual meetings between ASEAN foreign ministers and dialogue partners. It has welcomed and extended diplomatic and economic assistance for the reconciliation between the ASEAN countries and Vietnam. It has also participated in the UN peacekeeping operation in Cambodia, albeit with strict limitations on its activities. Furthermore, Japan has been instrumental in the establishment in July 1993 of the ASEAN Regional Forum (ARF) for political and security dialogue in the region (Prasert 1993, pp. 205–14). Slowly, Japan is establishing itself as a reliable partner in the building of a stable South-east Asia.

The financial crisis sweeping the region is a major challenge to Japan's leadership role. There is little doubt that Japan's economic assistance and foreign direct investment in the countries now experiencing the currency crisis had helped them to develop their domestic industries. It is equally true that these economies have become vulnerable to the effects of economic interdependence, particularly in the financial sector, where Japanese and other foreign investors are keen to move their capital quickly in and out depending on the performance of their investment. As well, these South-east Asian economies have borrowed heavily from foreign sources during the recent decade of hyper-development. Therefore, when the Thai *baht* crashed in July 1997, there was little these countries could do to stop its impact on their economies. As the currency crisis spread to Indonesia and South Korea and threatened to reach Russia and then Latin America, the international community called on Japan, the United States and other industrialized countries to step in to help these economies and avert a global financial crisis. By April 1998, Japan had pledged $4 billion for the IMF-led support for Thailand, $5 billion for Indonesia, and $10 billion for South Korea. These amounts were as large as any other country's pledged assistance. Whether or not this and other assistance from the IMF and other countries will be enough to save the economies remains to be seen. Japan's action, however, augurs well for its future role in South-east Asia.

In North-east Asia, Japan's options in regional politics and security are severely limited. 'North-east Asia' remains largely a geographical referent, without a political identity or institutional framework. The memory of Japan's history of aggression complicates the nation's relations with its neighbouring countries. Moreover, the divided Korea and the divided China are painful reminders of prewar and postwar hostilities within the region. Although Japan no longer considers Russia a credible military threat, Japanese–Russian relations are seriously constrained by Russia's domestic political turmoil, economic problems and its territorial dispute with Japan.

The fundamental problem in Japanese–Russian relations is the two countries' entirely different foundations of national power and international influence. At the end of the Cold War, Japan is a giant economically but a self-restrained military power, and it draws most of its regional influence from its economic capabilities. Russia, on the other hand, is primarily a military power with little or no economic means of influence in the Asia–Pacific. The uneven equation of power foundations between the two countries severely limits their ability to establish a stable, interdependent relationship (see Akaha 1996). Moreover, many Japanese continue to harbour ill feelings towards the Russians over the treatment of Japanese prisoners of war in Siberia from 1939 to 1959 and the unresolved territorial dispute over the Northern Territories.[16] None the less, under international pressure, Japan has committed a substantial, if not sufficient, level of assistance to the beleaguered Russian economy: by January 1996 it had pledged $4.4 billion in total assistance for Russia, making it the third largest provider of aid after Germany and the United States (Ministry of Foreign Affairs 1996). Tokyo has emphasized technical assistance for human resources development in support of the development of a market economy in Russia. Tokyo has chosen the Russian Far East as the area of utmost importance in its assistance programmes. Successful Japanese assistance to the Russian Far East communities in this critical transition period would promote greater international cooperation involving Russia and Asia, and would facilitate the acceptance of Russia as a credible partner in the region. Not only would a successful Japanese policy towards Russia have a lasting impact on the future bilateral relations; it would also serve as a litmus test of Japan's ability to play an important political role at crucial moments in history.

Japan's relations with China are more developed, a consequence of cultural affinity, economic interests and political calculations. Many Japanese hold the view that the Chinese pragmatism that has brought the phenomenal economic growth to the country in the last several years is irreversible (*Hokkaido Shimbun*, 2 May 1993, p. 3; Eto 1996, pp. 16–34). Long after Tiananmen, many Japanese analysts continue to believe that Japan is justified in having a unique approach to China and that Japan should continue to support China's economic development to ensure political stability in the country (Inada 1995b, p. 162). Most Japanese believe that China's internal

---

[16] An overwhelming 84.2 per cent of the Japanese surveyed by the Prime Minister's Office in 1995 said they did not feel friendly towards Russia, against 11.7 per cent who said they did feel friendly (Sorifu 1995, pp. 34–5).

stability is essential to the region's peace and stability and that this requires sustained economic development in China. For these reasons, Tokyo believes that its economic assistance to Beijing is both necessary and justified. Japan is the largest donor of aid to China, its bilateral ODA disbursement to China in 1996 totalling $861 million, and Japan has agreed to support Beijing's bid to join the World Trade Organization. Japan's commercial interests also support improving relations with China. China is now Japan's second most important source of imports (next to the United States), with Chinese exports to Japan in 1996 amounting to $38,658 million, or 11.6 per cent of Japan's global imports. Japanese exports to China are also an important part of Japan's international trade: the $20,933 million in Japanese exports to China in 1996 represented 5.3 per cent of Japan's worldwide exports. Furthermore, Japan is the fourth largest investor in China after Hong Kong, Taiwan and the United States.

In the security area, the combination of high-speed economic growth, continuing military modernization and a growing emphasis on naval buildup in China is a growing concern to the Japanese. Japan's 1995 defence white paper noted that China was expanding defence spending and modernizing its weapons systems, including the deployment of the CSS5, a new medium-range ballistic missile. The annual report observed, however, that the pace of China's overall military modernization was rather slow because the nation placed priority on economic development (Defence Agency of Japan 1995, p. 73).

A combination of political, economic and security factors complicates Japan's China policy. This was evident in Tokyo's behaviour in the aftermath of the Tiananmen Square massacre in June 1989. Tokyo was the most reluctant G-7 member-country to join the group's decision to impose diplomatic and economic sanctions against Beijing. Even while Western sanctions were in effect, Japan allowed China to proceed with Japanese ODA-funded projects already in progress. At the Houston summit of G-7 leaders in 1990, Japanese Prime Minister Toshiki Kaifu stressed the 'special relationship' between Japan and China and obtained the other summit leaders' tacit approval of his decision to resume new government loans to China.[17] Tokyo argued that continuing support for China's reform and open policy was important not only to China but also for the stability of Asia (Heiwa Anzenhosho Kenkyujo 1991, pp. 180–1; cited in Inada 1995a, pp. 6, 9–10). There is strong support among Japanese intellectuals for Tokyo's 'quiet diplomacy' towards Beijing on human rights issues, and criticism against Washington's highly visible policy linking human rights and trade issues (see e.g. Kosaka 1996, pp. 386–9). Tokyo announced it would scale back its grant aid to China as a protest against the nuclear test that China conducted in May 1995, only days after the Nuclear Nonproliferation Treaty (NPT) Review and Extension Conference in New York had agreed to limit nuclear testing. However, Japan continued with its yen loans to Beijing (*Nihon Keizai Shimbun*, 30 August 1996, p. 1).

Tokyo wants to keep Beijing engaged on a number of issues on which the two sides share common interests, including security. In December 1993, Tokyo and

---

[17] For the Japanese government's explanation of its position on the China case, see Matsuura (1990, pp. 1–9). For a view that Tokyo's approach to Tiananmen differed importantly from the other Western powers' approach, see Inada (1995a, pp. 3–6; 1995b, pp. 160–2). For a view that Tokyo's policy was not as different from that of the USA and other Western nations, see Tanaka (1990, pp. 30–45).

Beijing resumed bilateral security consultations which had been suspended in the wake of Tiananmen. Japan has expressed concern over China's defence buildup and has pressed China to improve the transparency of its defence policy. Tokyo has also asked Beijing to use its influence to prevent Pyongyang from proceeding with its suspected nuclear weapons development. Unfortunately, however, Tokyo's influence in China is severely compromised by the memory of Imperial Japan's aggression against China in the 1930s and 1940s.[18] Beijing never fails to bring up this dark chapter in the history of Sino-Japanese relations. Nor do occasional denials by conservative Japanese politicians of their nation's past put the issue to rest.

Tokyo's influence over developments in the Korean peninsula is similarly limited. Japan's present-day policy towards the peninsula is informed by four sets of factors: (1) Tokyo's overall foreign policy priorities, particularly maintenance of its close security alliance with Washington and improvement of relations with South Korea; (2) its concerns regarding the peace and stability of North-east Asia, especially stability on the peninsula; (3) bilateral issues between Japan and North and South Korea; and (4) domestic politics in Japan.[19] These factors dictate close policy coordination with the United States, close consultation with South Korea and a cautious approach to North Korea. Economic factors are currently of limited importance, but they too work to support this general line of policy in Tokyo. Japan looks to the United States for preventing violent confrontation between North and South Korea and for controlling nuclear development in North Korea. Moreover, Japan does not wish to jeopardize its improving relations with South Korea by forging ahead with the normalization of relations with North Korea. In the absence of a major breakthrough in US–North Korean and North–South Korean relations, therefore, Tokyo is not in a position to normalize its relations with Pyongyang. There are also a number of bilateral issues that need to be solved before Tokyo and Pyongyang can normalize their relations. The August 1998 launching by North Korea of a missile (or a satellite rocket) over Japan so shocked Tokyo that it quickly announced a number of sanctions against Pyongyang, including suspension of all normalization talks, food aid and participation in the Korean Peninsula Energy Development Organization (KEDO).

## 5

### Mobilizing Resources for a Regional Role

One measure of Japan's policy priorities is the relative size of its defence spending and official development assistance (ODA). The pattern of defence spending since the early 1990s has reflected the rather cautious approach the defence planners in Tokyo have adopted towards the nation's changing security environment. Tokyo has been more eager to expand its ODA as a legitimate tool of comprehensive security policy.

---

[18] Hisahiko Okazaki has suggested that China might use the Japanese sense of contrition and sympathy towards China to divide the Japanese over their future relations with the United States (Okazaki 1993a, pp. 30–51).

[19] For a fuller examination of Japan's policy towards the Korean peninsula, see Akaha (1998a).

Japan increased its defence spending by an average of 6.4 per cent annually between fiscal year (FY) 1980 and 1990. By FY 1993, its defence budget nominally had become the second largest in the world, next to that of the United States (IISS 1993; cited in *Asahi Shimbum*, 5 March 1994, p. 4). Since then, however, the defence spending has increased by much smaller margins: by 1.95 per cent from FY 1992 to FY 1993 and by 0.9 per cent from FY 1993 to FY 1994. From FY 1994 to FY 1995 the defence budget grew by a mere 0.89 per cent, the smallest increase in 35 years (Defence Agency of Japan 1995, p. 331). It stood at $40.8 billion in 1997, a 1.98 per cent increase from the previous year (Boeicho 1997).

Japan's resource commitment to foreign economic assistance has increased significantly faster than its defence spending in recent years. This reflects the fact that public support for economic aid to developing countries has grown substantially stronger. In FY 1992, Japan's general account portion of foreign aid exceeded the 1 trillion yen ($8 billion at 125 yen = $1.00) mark for the first time in its history, and it has continued to grow since. The FY 1994 ODA general account budget was set at $9.1 billion, representing a record-low 4.4 per cent increase over initial FY 1993 spending; but thanks to the appreciation of the Japanese yen against the dollar, the actual ODA disbursements in FY 1994 rose to $13.2 billion, an increase of 17.6 per cent over the previous year. As a result, Japan remained the largest donor for four years in a row (*Asahi Shimbun*, 26 June 1995, p. 2). In FY 1995 Japan's ODA disbursements amounted to $14.5 billion. Even though Japanese ODA disbursement declined to $9.4 billion in 1996, it was still the largest in the world, outpacing the US economic assistance of $9.1 billion (Keizai Koho Centre 1998, p. 62).

The quantitative expansion of Japanese ODA notwithstanding, Tokyo's policy has been subject to international criticism on qualitative grounds. The limited grant element in its official economic assistance has long been a target of international criticism. This pattern is not likely to be reversed any time soon. The emphasis on loans rather than grants is based on Tokyo's ODA philosophy, which encourages ODA recipient countries to maintain discipline in their use of Japanese aid and to maintain the ability to repay. Japan has also been criticized for its Asia-focused aid programme to the neglect of other regions of the world, but Tokyo's preference for Asia is not likely to disappear. It is in this region that Japan wants to play a leading political role and develop a security role. Over 90 per cent of its yen loans are destined for Asia. Japan is clearly the dominant DOA contributor in Asia, with Tokyo's official assistance representing 53.9 per cent of the total ODA contributions to the region in 1995 (Kezai Koho Centre 1998, p. 63). Another criticism has been that Japanese loan programmes are tied, but Tokyo has reduced the 'tied' portion to less than 20 per cent in recent years.

The most explicit expression of Japan's willingness to use its economic power for political and security purposes is found in the ODA Charter that Tokyo adopted in 1992. It outlines the philosophy, principles and priorities underlying Japan's foreign aid policy.[20] The charter states that Japan's ODA policy is based on four basic ideas: humanitarianism, recognition of interdependence between donor and recipient

---

[20] There were security implications, some intended and some not, in Japan's earlier ODA policies and practices. See Takeda (1995, pp. 125–54).

countries, the importance of environmental protection, and self-help efforts by aid recipients. In making ODA decisions, according to the Charter, Tokyo pays 'full attention' to a recipient country's actions to promote democratization, introduce a market-oriented economy and work to ensure basic human rights and freedoms. The Charter also states that Tokyo closely monitors trends in recipient countries' military expenditures, development and production of weapons of mass destruction and missiles, and arms imports and exports. Furthermore, Tokyo is to discourage the use of foreign aid for military purposes or for the aggravation of international conflicts and to pursue environmental conservation in tandem with development (*Asahi Shimbun*, 27 June 1992, p. 1; Gaimusho 1995, pp. 80–1; see also Hirabayashi 1995, pp. 6–20).

How serious is the Japanese government about applying 'political conditionality' in its ODA policy? What impact does Japan's policy have on the target country? The record has been mixed. The case of China, noted earlier, illustrates the visible gap between Japan's stated objective and its limited impact.

Myanmar represents a different case in that the country is small enough that outside pressure can have a substantial impact on the behaviour of the government. None the less, Tokyo has been reluctant to use ODA as a political tool and has not abandoned a more subtle approach, choosing engagement and dialogue over isolation and overt pressure (Inada 1995b, p. 155). For example, when the military in Myanmar carried out a coup and took over the government in September 1988, Japan waited until the United States announced its suspension of aid to the country before it announced a similar measure. In February 1989, when violence quietened down, Tokyo moved to recognize the military government before any other Western government did and resumed economic assistance that had been contracted, although it continued to freeze all new aid projects. The May 1990 general elections gave opposition candidates a major victory, but the military government placed the opposition leader and Nobel Peace Prize winner Aung San Su Kyi and other civilian leaders under house arrest and refused to turn the government over to civilian control. Tokyo decided to suspend all economic aid except humanitarian assistance. In March 1995, as a sign of constructive engagement, Tokyo announced it would extend about $9 million in grants for food production programmes but continued with the suspension of all yen loans (*Asahi Shimbun*, 9 March 1995, p. 2). When the military government released the opposition leader from house arrest in July 1995, Tokyo quickly announced that it would gradually unfreeze yen loans, with the timing of aid restoration contingent on progress towards democratization in the country (*Asahi Shimbun*, 11 July 1995, p. 2; 19 July 1995, p. 2).

Indonesia represents yet another case in which Japan uses a stick-and-carrot approach, with uncertain impact on the recipient of Japanese ODA. Tokyo supported the Indonesian government in the 1970s in forcibly suppressing the independence movement in the former Portuguese colony, where there were many instances of human rights violations. Japan's position was attributed to its anti-Communist policy and its eagerness to protect its economic (oil) interests in Indonesia.[21]

---

[21] Kawabe (1994, pp. 156–9). Indonesia today is the recipient of the second largest bilateral ODA from Japan ($1,149 million in 1993), after China ($1,351 million).

There are several explanations for the cautious use of ODA as a political tool in Japanese foreign policy (see Akaha, forthcoming). First, the contemporary Japanese culture does not encourage the Japanese people to 'export' political values. Second, their concept of and experience with democracy prevents the Japanese from viewing individual rights as the foundation of democracy. The communal orientation of most Japanese people often hinders identification of clearly demarcated rights and responsibilities of individuals. Third, the Japanese preference for public order and social harmony over individual rights and freedoms also tends to ignore the welfare and rights of minorities in Japan and elsewhere. Another important reason for the lack of emphasis on democracy and human rights in Japanese foreign policy is that, on the basis of their own postwar experience, most Japanese assume that democratic values and institutions naturally develop after economic development has taken place. The dominant view in Japan is that material welfare comes before political aspirations.

Fifth, Japan's postwar political system has further limited its ability to formulate and implement a coherent policy on democratization and human rights in the foreign policy arena. In postwar Japanese politics, a public display of dissent has long been reserved for parties out of power, but until recently the opposition has often, if not always, been excluded from participating in a meaningful way in foreign policy-making. The foreign policy process has been dominated by the hegemonic coalition of the conservative ruling party, the Liberal Democratic Party, the elite bureaucrats in the Foreign Ministry and the Ministry of International Trade and Industry, and the big business community. During the Cold War Japan placed a higher priority on political stability and better business environment than on free elections.

Sixth, Japan's disastrous experience as an imperialist–militarist power earlier in the century has also imposed enormous constraints on its international political role since the end of World War II. Most Japanese are reluctant to advocate human rights protection in the neighbouring Asian countries because their own country committed unspeakable atrocities against these peoples during the war. Seventh and finally, Japan's foreign policy has long been geared towards the promotion of its economic and commercial interests, and its foreign aid policy has been a means of achieving this goal (see e.g. Rix 1980; Yasutomo 1986; Orr 1990).

The international community will continue to watch closely Tokyo's ODA policy and its implementation of the lofty principles stated in the ODA Charter.

# 6

## Advancing a Global Profile

During the entire Cold War era, there was a conspicuous gap between Japan's lofty ideal of active diplomacy in the United Nations and its actual role in the world organization. The nation's contribution to the UN's role in international peace and security was severely limited by domestic pacifism and by the UN's failure to establish a permanent UN force as envisioned by the drafters of the UN Charter.

Now that the Cold War is over and international demands for expanded UN roles in regional conflicts are growing, Japan is under increasing pressure to become more active in this area. As Japan's financial contributions to international organizations continue to increase, its participation in international peacekeeping has become a common, if not unanimous, international expectation. Japan's share of the UN general budget was expected to rise further, to an estimated 15 per cent by 1997 (*Asahi Shimbun*, 12 December 1993, p. 2).

The 1991–2 Gulf crisis exposed the discrepancy between Japan's financial power and its political will to participate actively and visibly in UN-sanctioned international peacekeeping activities. Despite the $13 billion contribution the nation made to support the international coalition's military action against Iraq and humanitarian relief efforts in the affected countries, Japan failed to send any peacekeeping personnel to the region. The dispatch of minesweepers after the conflict had already ceased was obviously 'too little, too late'.

The domestic debate following the crisis and subsequent dispatch of SDF personnel to Cambodia in 1992–3 has not produced a stable national consensus on the general issue of Japanese participation in international peacekeeping. Experts and public opinion in Japan recognize the importance of a Japanese contribution to international peace and security through participation in the United Nations, but a majority of them are reluctant to see any expansion of Japanese participation in UN peacekeeping operations (Sorifu 1995, pp. 9–10). Many Japanese observers are wary that the UN might be used to legitimize the hegemonic interests of the United States which now cannot afford, politically or financially, to carry out its military missions in regional conflicts (see e.g. Mushakoji 1996, p. 37).

In 1992, Japanese parliament approved a bill authorizing the dispatch of SDF personnel overseas for participation in UN-sponsored peacekeeping operations. To ensure passage of the bill, the government agreed to stipulate five conditions: among them, Japanese personnel would participate in a UN-sanctioned peacekeeping operation if a cease-fire was in effect, the parties to the conflict accepted the peacekeeping operation and the operation maintained neutrality; if any one of the conditions ceased to exist, the Japanese personnel would withdraw. Finally, Japanese participants are allowed to bear only minimally required arms to protect themselves (Iseri 1992, pp. 33–4). Since a Japanese civilian volunteer and a police officer were killed in Cambodia during Japanese participation in the UN operation there, the defence agency and SDF uniformed officers have bitterly complained about the untenable position in which they found themselves when operating under these limitations. The government has so far failed to find a politically acceptable solution. This is evident in Japan's severely limited participation in UN operations in Somalia, Mozambique and former Yugoslavia.

When the Japanese postwar constitution was promulgated in 1947, Prime Minister Shigeru Yoshida stated that Japan was not allowed to exercise force even for self-defence.[22] But this interpretation has been relaxed over the succeeding years. When the National Police Reserve Force, the predecessor of the SDF, was established in

---

[22] Article 9 of the constitution states: 'Aspiring sincerely to an international peace based on justice and order, the Japanese people forever renounce war as a sovereign right of the nation and the threat or use of force as a means of settling international disputes. In order to accomplish [this] aim . . . land, sea, and air forces, as well as other war potential, will never be maintained. The right of belligerency of the state will not be recognized.'

1950, the government asserted that the new force was intended for domestic security and not for the exercise of force prohibited by Article 9. When the SDF was
founded in 1954, the government declared that the constitution prohibited war but
not the right of self-defence. At the same time, the upper house of the Japanese
parliament adopted a resolution prohibiting the dispatch of SDF personnel overseas.
Since then, the government has maintained that Article 9 does not prohibit the
right to self-defence and therefore the maintenance of limited Self-Defence Forces is
constitutional.[23]

A related constitutional issue is whether Japanese participation in UN-sanctioned
peacekeeping operations constitutes participation in 'collective security', which is
prohibited under Article 9. Some argue that participation in UN operations does
not constitute the exercise of the right of belligerency of the state and the use of
force prohibited by Article 9. According to this interpretation, Japan *can* participate
in UN-sanctioned peacekeeping forces that involve combat operations without
changing the constitution.[24]

The debate is not likely to produce a national consensus any time soon. One
solution would be to amend the constitution to eliminate the ambiguity surrounding the interpretation of Article 9 and answer once and for all what Japan could
and could not constitutionally do in self-defence, in peacekeeping and in collective
security. Shinshinto leader Ichiro Ozawa (now, Liberal Party) advocated this option.
He proposed that a third paragraph be added to Article 9 which would read:
'Paragraph 2 should not be interpreted as prohibiting the maintenance of a Self-
Defence Force for peace-building activities; the maintenance of a United Nations
reserve force for action under United Nations command when requested; and action
by the United Nations reserve force under United Nations command' (Ozawa 1993;
cited from English translation, p. 111). However, the requirement for constitutional amendments of a two-thirds majority in both houses and a simple majority in
a national referendum renders the adoption of this proposal highly unlikely in the
foreseeable future.

Another critical issue for Japan is whether the nation should be given a permanent seat on the UN Security Council. There is strong support among the Japanese
public that Japan deserves such status. However, there is widespread concern that
the coveted permanent Security Council seat would be contingent on Japan's willingness to participate in UN peacekeeping operations including combat activities.[25]

[23] For a description of the constitutional debate during the parliamentary deliberations on the
peace cooperation law, see Saito (1992).

[24] This position was advocated in a report prepared by the LDP Special Committee concerning
Japan's Participation in the International Society (Iseri 1992, p. 33; *Asahi Shimbun*, 4 February
1993, p. 1).

[25] Sorifu (1995, pp. 11–13). UN Secretary General Boutros Boutros-Ghali at one point suggested that Japan should consider revising its constitution so that Japan could participate in the
proposed peace enforcement units (PEUs) (Wanner 1993, p. 6). He also remarked that the existing
constraints on Japanese PKO participation weakened Japan's bid to become a permanent member
of the Security Council (*Asahi Shimbun*, 5 February 1993, p. 3). Moreover, in January 1994 the
US Senate adopted by acclamation a non-binding resolution opposing permanent UN Security
Council seats for Japan and Germany until those countries were prepared to participate in UN
peacekeeping operations including military activities (*Asahi Shimbun*, 30 January 1994, p. 3).

In its comment on the issue of reforming the UN Security Council, submitted to the UN secretary general, the Japanese government stated that issues of peace and stability 'must be considered in close relation to economic and other non-military factors'. The report also maintained: 'Japan is prepared to do all it can to discharge its responsibilities on the Security Council', intimating Tokyo's desire to become a permanent member of the Council (*Japan Times Weekly International Edition*, 23–29 August 1993, p. 3). Prime Minister Hosokawa, in his address before the UN General Assembly in September 1993, stated that most countries now feel the need 'to expand the membership of the Security Council while insuring that its effectiveness is maintained' and promised that Japan would 'participate constructively in the discussion of Security Council reform'. Later, at a news conference, the prime minister said: 'If other countries recommend it, Japan is ready to take up the challenge', and added, 'We will not press our way through. We will not conduct a campaign' (Lewis 1993, p. A4).

International support for Japan's permanent seat on the Security Council is mixed. The United States, Australia, the Netherlands, Romania and seven other countries have explicitly or implicitly endorsed Japan's permanent membership in the Security Council, while Brazil, Canada and ten other countries have expressed support for permanent council seats for the 'most industrialized nations of the world' (*Hokkaido Shimbun*, 20 November 1993, p. 3). On the other hand, China and Russia remain cautious about expanding the membership of the Security Council, although they have not publicly opposed Japan's permanent seat on the Council (*Asahi Shimbun*, 8 July 1993, p. 3).

# 7

## Managing the Alliance with the United States[26]

How stable is the anchor of Japan's international policy, its security alliance with the United States, in the post-Cold War era? There is general consensus in Japan that the era of US hegemony, or *Pax Americana*, is over and that global peace and prosperity requires the cooperation of the United States, Japan and Europe,[27] although the prevailing view in Japan is that, for both active and passive reasons, Tokyo and Washington should keep their security ties intact (see Akaha 1998b). However, there are some problems that require sustained effort on both sides.

Most Japanese observers who support the US–Japan security treaty maintain that the bilateral alliance is in the national interest of both countries. They recognize that the United States needs to maintain its bases in Japan not only to deter aggression against Japan, but also to project US military power throughout the region and beyond. They fear that the bilateral security treaty would lose its credibility in Japan

---

[26] For a fuller discussion of the US–Japan security relations in the post-Cold War era, see Akaha (1998b).

[27] This general consensus is found among Japanese political analysts working in different theoretical traditions. See e.g. Eto and Yamamoto (1991); Kamo (1990); Kosaka (1992); Nakasone *et al.* (1992); Sato (1989); and Yamamoto (1992).

if Washington were to press Tokyo to support, let alone participate in, US military action that went beyond the protection of Japan. Another reason why most Japanese analysts desire the maintenance of the bilateral security treaty is that the pact can help to contain the potentially destabilizing effects of trade and economic friction between the two countries. The treaty is the symbol of a mutually beneficial political relationship. It also allows Washington and Tokyo to maintain a mutually acceptable burden-sharing arrangement.

Some security analysts in Japan accurately see US policy in the Asia–Pacific as increasingly self-centred and driven by economic nationalism. They believe that Washington wants to use its US security commitments in the region and the region's growing reliance on the US military presence to its economic advantage, for example by linking US security protection to trade concessions from its allies and stepped-up host-nation support (see e.g. Nishiwaki 1995).

Many Japanese analysts are concerned that the current bilateral arrangement is politically unsustainable for long. The increasing host-nation support that Tokyo provides for US troops in Japan is coming under growing criticism by Japanese nationalists.[28] These concerns have led some observers to propose that Japan should gradually reduce, if not eliminate, its reliance on the bilateral alliance and build a collective security system in Asia in which the Japan–US alliance would be one part, albeit still the most important part (see e.g. Terashima 1996, pp. 20–38).

There is a minority view that the Japan–US security treaty has outlived its strategic value for Japan after the end of the Cold War and that Tokyo should seriously consider discontinuing the treaty in the not-too-distant future (see e.g. Asai 1992, p. 9). Others see greater opportunities in Japan's avowedly more strategic use of its economic assistance to developing countries, including China. Some see an additional avenue for Japanese security policy in a more active participation in UN peacekeeping activities. Still others advocate Japan's arms control initiatives in both the nuclear and the conventional field.

The most passive reason Japanese analysts give for the maintenance of the bilateral alliance is that there is no alternative policy that either Japan or the United States can develop to meet their security requirements in the post-Cold War Asia–Pacific. Tokyo continues to rely on Washington's security commitment as one of the two pillars of Japanese defence policy as long as the other pillar, the buildup of its self-defence capabilities, is constrained by political and financial considerations, as well as by international public opinion (see e.g. Ozawa 1993).

The official US assessment of the security situation in the Asia–Pacific calls for continued forward deployment of US forces. US military presence is seen as essential to regional stability, to discourage the emergence of a regional hegemon, and to enhance Washington's ability to influence a wide spectrum of important political and economic issues in the region (Department of Defense 1992, p. 20). In this context, Washington appreciates Japan's increasing burden-sharing. Moreover, the security treaty provides the United States with access to the fast advancing Japanese defence and civilian technology with military applications through two-way technology

---

[28] See e.g. Suzuki (1993, pp. 84–93); 250 billion yen, or about $2.2 billion, was budgeted for the host-nation support in FY 1994.

transfer. The US interest in Japanese defence technology is motivated by the fear of a potential competitor in future weapons development and the calculation of the potential cost savings through cooperation in weapons research and development.[29]

The most serious challenge to the Japan–US security treaty since the end of the Cold War came not from any strategic debate in either country but from an incident in Okinawa in 1995 involving the rape by three US soldiers of a young Japanese girl. The US military refused to surrender the suspects to local authorities during investigative phases of the case, and the fear quickly spread throughout Okinawa that, even though the incident took place off the US base, the soldiers would be tried under US jurisdiction. Against the background of heightened emotions among the Okinawa people over the case, the US government agreed to turn the suspects over to Japanese authorities. The issue soon became linked to the broader issue of US bases in Japan when the governor of Okinawa, Masahide Ota, defied the Japanese government's demand that he sign an administrative order forcing landowners to release their real estate for continued use by the US military. The governor argued that, if Tokyo viewed the Japan–US security treaty and the US military presence in Japan as so essential to the nation's security, some of the bases in his prefecture should be moved to other parts of the country so that the whole nation might more equally share their supposed benefits and also their costs.

The governor's defiance against Tokyo was directed more immediately at Tokyo's inability to equalize the burden of the treaty in terms of base siting than at the bilateral security treaty as such. It also reflected the sense of frustration that many Okinawa people felt over the absence of any visible 'peace dividends' in the supposedly more peaceful world. If mishandled by either Tokyo or Washington, the incident could have eroded the public support for the Japan–US security treaty in the post-Cold War era. It remained unclear, however, whether Tokyo and Washington could sharpen their argument for the strategic significance of the bilateral security relationship in the absence of a clear and present military threat. While emotions run high in Okinawa and the base issue and the bilateral security treaty are linked in many people's minds, the two issues should be treated separately.[30]

President Clinton and Prime Minister Hashimoto met in Santa Monica, California, in February 1996 and assured each other that the US–Japan relationship is the most important bilateral relationship in the world. The two leaders met again in Tokyo in April and issued a joint 'Japan–US Declaration on Security: Alliance for the 21st Century', reaffirming the essential importance of the US–Japan security treaty to the two countries and to the region. The single most critical question that emerged from the summit in Tokyo is how the bilateral security alliance will be developed in a

---

[29] On the mutuality of interests in US–Japan cooperation in military research and development, see Hanami (1993, pp. 592–609). For a warning about the long-term implications of Japan's high-technology defence research and development for the defence policies of its Asian neighbours, see Nakamura and Dando (1993, pp. 177–90). The US-initiated cooperation in the development of theatre missile defence (TMD) in Japan is finding increasing support in Japan against the background of suspected nuclear weapons development and missile tests in North Korea (Komori 1993, pp. 102–11).

[30] For the same view, see the discussion between Motoo Shiina and Hisahiko Okazaki (1996, pp. 24–33).

broader regional context and whether the review of the 1978 Guidelines for Japan–
US Defence Cooperation will envision the broadening of the geographical limits
of Japanese–US defence cooperation, including in regional contingencies. More
specifically, the joint declaration made no mention of the 'Far East', a term used in
the existing security treaty in reference to the geographical limits of its application,
but instead referred repeatedly to the 'Asia–Pacific region' as the context of bilateral
security cooperation.

Many Japanese analysts are opposed to the expansion of geographical or functional limits of Japanese–US security cooperation. These analysts refer to the 1981
government statement that Japan possessed the right of collective self-defence as
a right recognized by international law, but the Japanese government interpreted
Article 9 of the Japanese constitution as prohibiting the exercise of that right.
Accordingly, Article 5 of the US–Japan security treaty has been interpreted to give
Japan the right of unilateral self-defence (*kobetsu jieiken*) within the geographical
limits of the treaty, but prohibits cooperative operation with the United States
beyond those limits, and Article 6 has been interpreted to authorize the United
States but not Japan to use facilities in Japan for the peace and security of the Far
East (see e.g. Maeda 1996, pp. 192–5). This distinction has been gradually eroded
by Tokyo's growing security cooperation with Washington. They view the 'redefinition' of the US–Japan security alliance now underway as an extension of the
'interpretative expansion' of Article 9 of the Japanese constitution (Maeda 1996,
pp. 194–5).

# 8

## Conclusions

It is amply clear today that Japan wants to play expanded political and security
roles in the post-Cold War Asia–Pacific, but it still has a long way to go before its
roles can be accepted, either at home or abroad, as both legitimate and credible.
Domestic political squabbles prevent the emergence of a stable national consensus
on Japan's international role. The belief of the Japanese in their 'uniqueness' limits
their ability to communicate their perception of such a role to the world. The
intellectual community is yet to develop a credible strategic view of its immediate
regional environment. Under these circumstances, policy-makers in Tokyo have
opted for the path of least resistance, that is, for maintaining the existing bilateral
security alliance with Washington and gradually expanding Japan's roles in regional
and global affairs.

The debate on Japan's preferred world order has just begun. Neither policy-
makers in Tokyo nor their critics inside and outside Japan have yet to develop a
clear vision for a post-Cold War Asian–Pacific security system. The only consensus
that has emerged so far is that the region requires some multilateral framework for
security consultations to address mutual security concerns. Substantive issues of
confidence- and security-building measures (CSBMs) and arms control are yet to
be addressed. Until viable regional or sub-regional security arrangements can be
established, the Japan–US security alliance, which ensures the US presence in the
Asia–Pacific, will remain the most important security regime for maintaining stability

in the region. Japan's own security will also continue to depend on the country's close alliance with the United States for the foreseeable future.

The end of the Cold War heightens the importance of the US–Japan security relations and complicates their management. The bilateral security relations will be seriously tested by the friction over trade and other economic issues, which are unlikely to disappear any time soon. Moreover, those relations will have far-reaching implications for broader regional security, and, conversely, relations involving other regional powers, particularly Russia and China, will have increasing impact on US–Japan security relations. As long as Japan's relations with Russia remain strained, Japan's potential regional security role will be limited inasmuch as Russia will continue to be a major security factor in the region, whether positively or negatively. Japan–China relations are likely to continue to grow, but they must be carefully balanced with the strategically more crucial bilateral relationship between Japan and the United States.

Increasingly, Japan–US security consultations need to be supplemented (not replaced) by multilateral security dialogue and confidence- and security-building measures involving all the major regional actors, i.e., Russia, China, Korea and ASEAN countries. Such developments will obviate Japan's need to embark upon a major defence buildup, which would be quite destabilizing for the region's security. Japan will then be able to continue to limit its defence capabilities to those minimally required for self-defence. Tokyo must also continue to promote regional political stability through economic assistance and deepening economic interdependence.

Japan's participation in UN peacekeeping must be based on both credible legal grounds and broad domestic support. Tokyo must refrain from expanding Japan's international security roles through ambiguous and tenuous interpretations of its constitution. The Japanese will sooner or later have to consider revising their constitution to remove the ambiguities surrounding Article 9 — and the sooner, the better. More immediately, however, the Japanese government and public must seriously debate what kind of a post-Cold War order they want to develop and what kind of a role they want to play in it.

If Japan wants to succeed in translating its rich potentials into realities and meeting the growing international expectations, Tokyo must muster domestic and international support for legitimate uses of the nation's power capabilities in international relations. Not only must the government weigh the policy alternatives made possible by the nation's enormous financial resources and growing defence capabilities, it must also develop the ability to create and share ideas and ideals for organizing a non-hegemonic, stable world order. Japan must demonstrate the relevance and value of its historical experiences and cultural values to the building of bilateral, multilateral and global institutions through which to manage regional and global problems. In short, it must develop and apply a carefully balanced mix of what Joseph Nye calls 'hard power' and 'soft power'.[31] It remains to be seen whether the Japanese will be able to go beyond their long-cherished 'uniqueness' thesis and contribute to the establishment of universally acceptable rules and principles in the post-Cold War world.

---

[31] 'Soft power' is defined as 'cultural attraction, ideology, and international institutions' (Nye 1992, pp. 166–70, 188).

# References

Akaha, T. (1991), 'Japan's Comprehensive Security Policy: A New East Asian Environment', *Asian Survey*, 31(4).

Akaha, T. (1993a), 'Japan's Security Policy in the Post-Cold War World: Opportunities and Challenges', in T. Akaha and F. Langdon (eds.), *Japan in the Posthegemonic World*, Boulder, Colo.: Lynne Rienner, pp. 91–112.

Akaha, T. (1993b), 'The Politics of Japanese–Soviet/Russian Economic Relations', in T. Akaha and F. Langdon (eds.), *Japan in the Posthegemonic World*, Boulder, Colo.: Lynne Rienner, pp. 161–84.

Akaha, T. (1996), 'Japanese–Russian Economic Relations and their Implications for Asia–Pacific Security', in S. L. Shirk and C. P. Twomey (eds.), *Power and Prosperity: The Links between Economics and Security in Asia–Pacific*, New Brunswick, NJ: Transaction Press, pp. 197–212.

Akaha, T. (ed.) (1997), *Politics and Economics in the Russian Far East: Changing Ties with Asia–Pacific*, New York and London: Routledge.

Akaha, T. (1998a), 'Japan's Response to Changing US–Korean Relations', in T. W. Park (ed.), *The US and the Two Koreas: A New Triangle*, Boulder, Colo.: Lynne Rienner.

Akaha, T. (1998b), 'An Illiberal Hegemon or an Understanding Partner? Japanese Views of the United States in the Post-Cold War Era', *Brown Journal of World Affairs*, 5(2): 137–48.

Akaha, T. (forthcoming), 'The Case of Japan', paper presented at the annual convention of the International Studies Association, 17–21 March 1998, Minneapolis; to appear in P. J. Schraeder (ed.), *Can Democracy be Exported? The International Dimension of Democratization in Africa, Asia, Eastern Europe, Latin America, the Middle East and Russia*.

Asai, M. (1992), 'Anpo no Seisan ga Hitsuyo, Beikoku ni Geigo Yameyo' (A revision of the [Japan–US] security treaty is necessary: stop flattering the US), *Asahi Shimbun*, 22 October.

Ball, D. (1993–4), 'Arms and Affluence: Military Acquisitions in the Asia–Pacific Region', *International Security*, 18(3).

Betts, R. K. (1993–4), 'Wealth, Power and Instability: East Asia and the United States after the Cold War', *International Security*, 18(3).

Boeicho (1995), *Boei Hakusho 1995* (Defence of Japan 1995), Tokyo: Okurasho Insatsukyoku.

Boeicho (1997), *Boei Hakusho* (Defence White Paper), Tokyo: Okurasho Insatsukyoku.

Defence Agency of Japan (1995), *Defence of Japan 1995*, Tokyo: Okurasho Insatsukyoku.

Department of Defense (1992), *A Strategic Framework for the Asian Pacific Rim: Report to Congress*, Washington, DC: Department of Defense.

Dibb, P. (1996), *Towards a New Balance of Power in Asia*, Adelphi Paper 295, Oxford University Press for the International Institute for Strategic Studies.

Elton, C. (1993), 'New Dimensions of Japanese Foreign Policy: A Latin American View of Japanese Presence', in T. Akaha and F. Langdon (eds.), *Japan in the Posthegemonic World*, Boulder, Colo.: Lynne Rienner, pp. 233–50.

Eto, S. (1996), 'China and Sino-Japanese Relations in the Coming Decades', *Japan Review of International Affairs*, 10(1).

Eto, S. and Yamamoto, Y. (1991), *Sogo Anpo to Mirai no Sentaku* (Comprehensive security and future choices), Tokyo: Kodansha.

Fallows, J. (1989a), 'Containing Japan', *Atlantic Monthly*.

Fallows, J. (1989b), *More Like Us: Making America Great Again*, Boston: Houghton Mifflin.

Funabashi, Y. (1991–2), 'Japan and the New World Order', *Foreign Affairs*, 70(5).

Funabashi, Y. (1993), *Nihon no Taigaikoso: Reisengo no Bijon o Kaku* (A vision for Japan's external policy: fashioning a post-Cold War vision), Tokyo: Iwanami Shoten.

Gaimusho (1995), *Gaiko Seisho 1995* (Diplomatic blue book 1995), Tokyo: Okurasho Insatsukyoku.

Hanami, A. K. (1993), 'The Emerging Military–Industrial Relationship in Japan and the US Connection', *Asian Survey*, 33(6).

Hashimoto, R. (1993), *Waga Kyochu ni Seisaku Arite* (Vision of Japan), Tokyo: KK Best Sellers, pp. 75–86.

Heiwa Anzenhosho Kenkyujo (1991), *Ajia no Anzenhosho 1990–91* (Security in Asia, 1990–91), Tokyo: Heiwa Anzenhosho Kenkyujo.

Hirabayshi, H. (1995), 'Atarashii jidai no Wagakuni no Seifu Kaihatsu Enjo o Motomete: Toppu Dona kara Ridingu Dona e' (In search of Japan's official economic assistance in the new era: from a top donor to a leading donor), *Gaiko Forum*, February.

Huntington, S. (1993), 'The Clash of Civilizations?' *Foreign Affairs*, 72(1).

Inada, J. (1995a), 'Jinken–Minshuka to Enjo Seisaku: Nichibei Hikaku' (Human rights democratization and aid policy: Japan–US comparison), *Kokusaimondai*, no. 422 (May).

Inada, J. (1995b), 'Nihon no Enjo Gaiko: Minshuka–shijokeizaika Shien no Rinen' (Japan's aid diplomacy: the idea of aid for democratization–market economy development), in A. Kusano and T. Umemoto (eds.), *Gendai Nihon Gaiko no Bunseki* (Analysis of contemporary Japanese diplomacy), Tokyo: Tokyo Daigaku Shuppankai.

Inoguchi, T. (1987), *Tadanori to Ikkoku Han'ei-shugi o Koete: Tenkanki no Sekai to Nihon* (Beyond the free ride and unilateral prosperity: the world and Japan at a turning point), Tokyo: Toyokeizai Shinposha.

International Institute for Strategic Studies (IISS) (1993), *Military Balance 1992–93*, London: IISS.

Iseri, H. (1992), 'PKO Rongi no Konmei o Toku' (Resolving the confusion of the PKO debate), *Gaiko Forum*, no. 44 (May).

Itoh, M. (1998), *Globalization of Japan: Japanese Sakoku Mentality and US Efforts to Open Japan*, New York: St Martin's Press.

Jihua, Z. (1993), 'Japan's Foreign Policy Choices for the Twenty-first Century: A Chinese Perspective', in T. Akaha and F. Langdon (eds.), *Japan in the Posthegemonic World*, Boulder, Colo.: Lynne Rienner, pp. 185–200.

Johnson, D. M. (1992), 'Anticipating Instability in the Asia–Pacific Region', *Washington Quarterly*, 15(3).

Kamo, T. (1990), *Kokusai Anzenhosho no Koso* (A vision for international security), Tokyo: Iwanami Shoten.

Katzenstein, P. J. and Okawara, N. (1993), 'Japan's National Security: Structures, Norms and Policies', *International Security*, 17(4).

Kawabe, I. (1994), *Kokuren to Nihon* (The United Nations and Japan), Tokyo: Iwanami Shoten.

Keizai Koho Centre (1998), *Japan 1998: An International Comparison*, Tokyo: Keizai Koho Centre.

Keizaikikakucho Sogokeikakukyoku (ed.) (1987), *Nihon no Sogokokuryoku: Takamaru Nihon no Kokuryoku to Motomerareru Kokusaiteki Yakuwari* (Japan's comprehensive national power: Japan's rising national power and expected international roles), Tokyo: Okurasho Insatsukyoku.

Kikuchi, T. (1995), *APEC: Ajia-Taiheiyo Shinchitsujo no Mosaku* (APEC: exploring a new Asia–Pacific order), Tokyo: Nihon Kokusaimondai Kenkyujo, pp. 223–31.

Komori, Y. (1993), 'Chiiki Misairu Boei: Reisengo no Nichibei Anpo Kyoryoku no Kirifuda' (Theatre missile defence: a trump card in the post-Cold War Japan–US security cooperation), *Chuokoron*, July.

Kosaka, M. (1992), *Nihon Sonbo no Toki* (A critical time for Japan), Tokyo: Kodansha.

Kosaka, M. (1993), 'Nihon ga Suiboshinai Tameni' (Lest Japan decline), *Bungeishunju*, January.

Kosaka, M. (1996), ' "Gaiko o Shiranai" Futatsu no Taikoku: Ajia o Meguru Nichibei no Sekinin' (The two great powers that do not understand diplomacy: the responsibility of Japan and the United States around Asia), in M. Kosaka, *Kosaka Masataka Gaiko*

*Hyoronshu: Nihon no Shinro to Rekishi no Kyokun* (A collection of Masataka Kosaka's commentaries on diplomacy: Japan's course and lessons of history), Tokyo: Chuokoron.

Langdon, F. and Akaha, T. (1993), 'Conclusion: The Posthegemonic World and Japan', in T. Akaha and F. Langdon (eds.), *Japan in the Posthegemonic World*, Boulder, Colo.: Lynne Rienner, pp. 265–82.

Lewis, P. (1993), 'Japan and Germany Show No Zeal for Council Seats', *New York Times*, 28 September.

Maeda, T. (1996), ' "Kyokuto Yoji" to Shudanteki jieiken' ('Far East' contingencies and the right of collective self-defence), *Sekai*, May.

Matsuura, K. (1990), 'Wagakuni no Taichu Enjo' (Japan's aid to China), *Kokusai Kyoryoku Tokubetsu Joho* (Special information on international cooperation), 16(1).

Maull, H. W. (1990–1), 'Germany and Japan: The New Civilian Powers', *Foreign Affairs*, 69(5).

Meeks, P. J. (1993), 'Hegemonies in History' and 'Japan and Global Economic Hegemony', in T. Akaha and F. Langdon (eds.), *Japan in the Posthegemonic World*, Boulder, Colo.: Lynne Rienner, pp. 17–40 and 41–68 respectively.

Ministry of Foreign Affairs (1996), *Japan's Assistance to the New Independent States*, Tokyo: Secretariat of the Cooperation Committee, Ministry of Foreign Affairs.

Mushakoji, K. (1996), *Tenkanki no Kokusaiseiji* (International politics in a period of transition), Tokyo: Iwanami Shoten.

Nakamura, H. and Dando, M. (1993), 'Japan's Military Research and Development: A High Technology Deterrent', *Pacific Review*, 6(2).

Nakasone, Y., Murakami, Y., Sato, S. and Nishibe, S. (1992), *Kyodo Kenkyu 'Reisen Igo'* (A joint study 'After the Cold War'), Tokyo: Bungeishunju.

Nishiwaki, F. (1995), 'Amerika no Reisengo Senryaku to Nihon no Anpo Seisaku' (US post-Cold War strategy and Japan's security policy), in M. Sase and S. Ishiwata (eds.), *Tenkanki no Nihon soshite Sekai* (Japan in a transitional period and the world), Tokyo: Ningen no Kagakusha, pp. 95–123.

Noda, N. (1995), 'Kikenna Ajiashugi no Taito' (Dangerous emergence of Asianism), *This is Yomiuri*, January.

Nye, J. Jr (1992), *Bound to Lead: The Changing Nature of American Power*, New York: Basic Books.

Ogura, K. (1993), ' "Ajia no Fukken" no Tameni' (To restore Asia's rights), *Chuokoron*, July.

Ogura, K. (1996), 'Japan's Asia Policy, Past and Future', *Japan Review of International Affairs*, 10(1).

Okabe, T. (1995), 'Aija–Taiheiyo no naka no Nihon' (Japan in the Asia–Pacific), in T. Okabe (ed.), *Posuto-Reisen no Ajia–Taiheiyo* (Post-Cold War Asia–Pacific), Tokyo: Nihon Kokusaimondai Kenkyujo, pp. 1–24.

Okazaki, H. (1993a), 'Chugoku Mondai Saiko: Sengo Nihon no Saigo no Tabu' (The China problem reconsidered: the last taboo of postwar Japan), *Chuokoron*, February.

Okazaki, H. (1993b), 'Soren-To'o ni okeru Kakumeiteki Henka' (Revolutionary changes in the Soviet Union and Eastern Europe), in *1990-nendai ni okeru Nihon no Senryakuteki Kadai* (Japan's strategic priorities in the 1990s), Tokyo: Nihon Kokusaimondai Kenkyujo, pp. 33–55.

Okui, T. (1994), *Nihon Mondai: 'Kiseki' kara 'Kyoi' e* (Japan's problem: from 'miracle' to 'threat'), Tokyo: Chuokoronsha.

Orr, R. M. (1990), *The Emergence of Japan's Foreign Aid Power*, Columbia University Press.

Ozawa, I. (1993), *Nihon Kaizo Keikaku* (A plan to reconstruct Japan), Tokyo: Kodansha; trans. as *Blueprint for a New Japan: The Rethinking of a Nation*, Tokyo: Kodansha International, 1994.

Pempel, T. J. (1998), 'Yuragu Yoso: Nihon no Seijikeizai no Hendo ni tsuite' (Changeable predictions: changes in Japanese political economy), in Nihon Kokusaiseiji Gakki (ed.), *21-seiki no Nihon, Ajia, Sekai* (Japan, Asia and the global system: towards the twenty-first century), Tokyo: Kokusaishoin, pp. 715–46.

Prasert, C. (1993), 'Japan's Roles in the Posthegemonic World: Perspectives from South-east Asia', in T. Akaha and F. Langdon (eds.), *Japan in the Posthegemonic World*, Boulder, Colo.: Lynne Rienner, pp. 201–32.

Prestowitz, C. V. Jr (1988), *Trading Places: How We Allowed Japan to Take the Lead*, New York: Basic Books.

Rix, A. (1980), *Japan's Economic Aid: Policy Making and Politics*, London: Croom Helm.

Saito, N. (1992), 'The Passing of the PKO Cooperation Law: Japan's Struggle to Define its International Contribution', *IIGP Policy Paper*, 102E, Tokyo: International Institute for Global Peace.

Sato, H. (1989), *Taigai Seisaku* (External policy), Tokyo: Tokyo Daigaku Shuppankai.

Segal, G. (1992), 'Managing New Arms Races in the Asia–Pacific', *Washington Quarterly*, 15(3).

Shiina, M. and Okazaki, H. (1996), ' "Okinawa" wa Kokunaimondai de aru' ('Okinawa' is a domestic problem), *Chuokoron*, January.

Shikata, T. (1996), 'Beikoku no Anzenhosho Seisaku to Nichibei Anzentaisei no Saitegi: Nai inishiachibu o Chushin ni' (US security policy and redefinition of the Japan–US security system, with a focus on the Nye initiative), *Kokusaimondai* (International affairs), no. 431 (February).

Sorifu, Kohoshitsu (ed.) (1995), *Seron Chosa* (Public opinion survey), Tokyo: Okurasho Insatsukyoku.

Stronach, B. (1995), *Beyond the Rising Sun: Nationalism in Contemporary Japan*, Westport, Conn.: Praeger.

Suzuki, K. (1993), ' "Omoiyari Yosan" wa Nichibei Anpo no Akashi ka Onimotsu ka' (Is the 'sympathy budget' a proof of the Japan–US security relations or a burden?), *Chuokoron*, January.

Takeda, Y. (1995), 'Nihon no Anzenhosho to Taigai Enjo' (Japan's security and foreign aid), in M. Sase and S. Ishiwata (eds.), *Tenkanki no Nihon soshite Sekai* (Japan in a transitional period and the world), Tokyo: Ningen no Kagakusha, pp. 125–54.

Tanaka, A. (1990), 'Tenanmon Jiken igo no Chugoku o meguru Kokusai Kankyo' (The international environment surrounding post-Tiananmen China), *Kokusaimondai*, no. 358 (January).

Terashima, J. (1996), ' "Shinbei Nyua" no Sogo Senryaku o Motomete' (In search of a comprehensive strategy for 'friendship' with the US and joining Asia), *Chuokoron*, March.

Tomiura, E. (1995), *Senryakuteki Tsushoseisaku no Keizaigaku* (Economics of strategic trade policy), Tokyo: Nihon Keizai Shimbun.

Tsusansho 'Chikyu Mondai' Kenkyukai, Chikyu Sanagyo Bunka Kenkyujo and PHP Kenkyujo (eds.) (1987), *Chikyudai no Shiten kara Mita Taikoku Nihon no Yakuwari* (The role of big power Japan from the global perspective), Tokyo: PHP.

Tyler, P. E. (1994), 'Beijing Says It Could Live Well even if US Trade Was Cut Off', *New York Times*, 21 March.

van Wolferen, K. (1989), *The Enigma of Japanese Power: People and Politics in a Stateless Nation*, New York: Alfred Knopf.

Wakamiya, Y. (1995), *Sengo Hoshu no Ajiakan* (Postwar conservatives' view of Asia), Tokyo: Asahi Shimbunsha.

Wanner, B. (1993), 'Boutros-Ghali Urges More Active United Nations Role for Japan', *JEI Report*, no. 7B (26 February).

Yamakage, S. (1995), 'Amerika Gasshukoku no Taiheiyo Kyodotaika Koso' (The US vision for a Pacific community), in T. Okabe, *Posuto-Reisen no Ajia–Taiheiyo* (Post-Cold War Asia–Pacific), Tokyo: Nihon Kokusaimondai Kenkyujo, pp. 79–100.

Yamamoto, Y. (1992), 'Alliance and Collective Security in the Post-Cold War Era', *IIGP Policy Paper*, 103E, Tokyo: International Institute for Global Peace.

Yamazawa, I. (1995), 'Implementing the APEC Bogor Declaration', *Japan Review of International Affairs*, 9(3).

Yasutomo, D. T. (1986), *The Manner of Giving: Strategic Aid and Japanese Foreign Policy*, Lexington, Mass.: Lexington Books.

Zagorsky, A. V. (1993), 'Soviet–Japanese Relations under Perestroika: The Territorial Dispute and its Impact', in T. Akaha and F. Langdon (eds.), *Japan in the Posthegemonic World*, Boulder, Colo.: Lynne Rienner, pp. 137–60.

# 11

# THE IMPACT OF CHANGES IN THE INTERNATIONAL SYSTEM ON DOMESTIC POLITICS

## JAPAN IN THE 1990s

### Shigeko N. Fukai

## 1
### Introduction

This paper presents a case study on the impact of the ongoing changes in the structure of the international political economy on the domestic politics and political economy of advanced industrial nations. The case study is Japan, a country with one of the largest and most trade-dependent economies in the world, and yet one that has so far been relatively closed and often characterized as neo-mercantilist (see e.g. Katzenstein 1978). While far from typical or representative, the structure and workings of Japanese domestic politics and political economy do share a number of characteristics with those of many Western European and Asian–Pacific nations, if not those of the United States. The case is thus by no means a deviant outlier, but one broadly comparable with a number of other national economies. Following in the footsteps of Peter Gourevitch's seminal article, the study focuses on the two enduring elements of nation-level politics — regime type and coalition pattern — rather than on specific political events or policies (Gourevitch 1978, p. 883).

There is a broad consensus among Japanese scholars and others that the end of the Cold War and the high-yen era brought about under the 'concert of G-5' regime are having as significant an impact on Japan's domestic political–economic structure as on those of other advanced industrial and industrializing nations. In 1993 the Liberal Democratic Party's one-party dominance, which had lasted thirty-eight years, ended to usher in an era of coalition governments and party realignment. The call from abroad for deregulation and information disclosures is growing louder.[1] The political reform laws have been passed to induce political realignment which is still under way. The economy is experiencing one of the worst postwar recessions, breeding pessimism among businessmen and the general public alike. The revelations of corrupt behaviour of bureaucrats and lukewarm government response further undermine the public's trust in Japan's policy-making networks. The hollowing-out of the Japanese industry accelerates even as the yen's value begins to fall from its peak reached in early 1995. Japan's unemployment rate, if calculated the same way as America's, reached 8.9 per cent in February 1994 — higher than America's 8.8 per cent (*The Economist*, 14 October 1995, p. 20).

Opinion is divided, however, on how many and which of these changes in the domestic political economy are attributable to the impact of changes in the international system. In other words, how fundamental and permanent the impact of the systemic change is on Japan's domestic structure remains in dispute. Some argue that the changes extend to the basic values and goals of Japan's economic strategy, hence are likely to change the pattern of domestic coalitions and regime type.[2] Others, pointing to the entrenched nature of the Japanese system, predict that changes will remain cosmetic and superficial.[3]

This study seeks to examine how business, bureaucratic and labour leaders in Japan relate changes at three levels — in the international system, in Japan's ruling coalition and dominant policy networks and in Japan's neo-mercantilist policy line — to each other. Specifically, the following three questions will be examined: (1) What is the leaders' understanding of Japan's ruling coalition and dominant policy networks, and what changes do they believe to be occurring in them? (2) What kind of impact do they think these changes have had on the neo-mercantilist policy pattern? (3) How do they relate these changes to two significant changes in the international political economy, i.e. the end of the Cold War and the challenges posed by the economic growth and integration in East Asia?

The following discussion is based mainly on the information and ideas collected through personal interviews and informal conversations with Japanese business, labour and bureaucratic leaders in the spring and summer of 1996 and on a documentary survey of political, business, bureaucratic and labour leaders' statements and writings published in the 1995–6 period.[4]

---

[1] The Japanese government's dealings with the recent Daiwa Bank scandal exposed to the world its penchant for concealing problems (*The Economist*, 14 October 1995, p. 20).

[2] Katzenstein distinguishes between three strategies of foreign economic policy, each informed by different values to pursue different objectives with different instruments (1978, pp. 297–306).

[3] They predict that political realignment would not change the basic coalition pattern, and that the 'type and mix of dominant elites' and 'the social forces and the political relationships among them' would remain essentially the same. The same old group of politicians, and their *koenkai* (electoral support associations) inheritors, will be returned to the Diet, with new party divisions and labels. (The quotations are from Gourevitch 1978, p. 131.)

[4] People have been talking about ongoing, imminent or forthcoming 'fundamental change' in Japanese politics for a long time with considerable exaggeration. Although some things have changed since the mid-1980s, these have been mostly in the economic and business sector; and little has changed in the structure of politics, known as the 1955 system. The collapse of this political system in July 1993 therefore caught many observers by surprise. While some of them believed that the political shift was real this time, others remained sceptical. Attempts were made

## 2

### The Ruling Coalition

To begin with, none of those interviewed objected to the notion that the 1955–93 ruling coalition consisted of big business leaders, government bureaucrats and LDP leaders.[5] They were also in general agreement that, since the end of the LDP-dominant era, the cohesion and influence of this triangle has been considerably weakened. They differed, however, on the nature of the triangle and the causes of change in the triangle that are now under way.

Mario Minakami, president of Chogin Sogo Kenkyujo (Long-Term Credit Bank Research Institute), analysed the so-called '1955 system' as one based on a rigidly hierarchical industrial order that was supported by a national consensus during the catch-up phase of Japanese economic development:

> The most important foundation of that system, in my opinion, was the constantly growing economy. It was a system in which a hierarchical order was rigidly fixed for each industry. For the firms at the top, it was the best system, but not always good for those below that level, whose desires and chances of climbing the ladder of ranks were blocked. For example, when Sumitomo Metal wanted to build a new blast furnace, the MITI opposed the plan for disturbing the existing hierarchy built with Yawata (now New Japan) Steel at the apex. Similarly, in the financial field, the Bank of Japan never changed the ranking order among lower ranked banks in the authorized amounts of lending regardless of the changing ranking in the actual amounts of sales. This system worked while the economy had been growing and the pie was constantly becoming bigger, because lower-ranked firms and their employees enjoyed a share of the growing pie. Thus was generated a national consensus in support of one party rule by the LDP. Business donated political funds to the LDP to support this system. (Interview with Mario Minakami, 4 July 1996)

Since the mid-1980s, Minakami's analysis goes, the foundation of this system has begun to crumble along with two other developments — the unfolding of the 'second détente' under Gorbachev and the East Asian miracle — that have led to the removal of the two kinds of wall, one separating the capitalist West from the East, and the other the industrialized North from the South. In the face of ever-intensifying global capitalist competition, competitiveness gaps among and within industries eroded the unity among businesses. The growing division among businesses in turn divided their political and bureaucratic allies:

---

by those who believed in the fundamental change, both in Japan and abroad, to relate the end of Japan's 1955 system to the end of the Cold War. Some of them argued that what had occurred was the conservatization of all Japanese parties except the Japan Communist Party (Iwami 1995, p. 53). Others predicted or anticipated that the movement to create a sizeable liberal third party would succeed. In a personal conversation in summer 1993, Youichi Higuchi, then professor in constitutional law at Tokyo University, characterized the process leading to the establishment of the Hosokawa coalition government as tantamount to the elimination of the JSP.

[5] Katzenstein (1978, p. 314) described Japan as a mercantilist state characterized by a high degree of centralization of both state and society and a lack of differentiation between them. This observation still seems to be implicitly accepted by my respondents.

In the political sphere, the end of the Cold War removed the wall between the East and the West. In the economic sphere, the wall hitherto separating the North and the South disappeared. The massive influx of cheap labour from the South to the North, as had already happened between the East and West, became possible. In countries like Japan, where the entry of immigrant labour was banned, firms went abroad in quest for cheaper labor. Competition became truly globalized. It became almost impossible for Japanese firms to survive competition from abroad by just maintaining the domestic industrial order. Each firm now had to compete on its own. The concept of *gyokai* [industry group] became obsolete.[6] Maintaining the *gyokai* order became sheer nonsense; hence the collapse of the main economic pillar of the 1955 system.

The end of the Cold War, Minakami continued, had freed all the divisive issues and let them come to the surface, intensifying the competitive pressure and eroding the very foundations of the 1955 system:

In the political sphere, the end of the Cold War has lifted the heavy lid of the closed box and let pluralized values come out of it. This is happening amidst an enormous current of Americanization, key words of which are 'market', 'human rights' and 'democracy'. The pluralization of values and the failure of socialism have made both the one-party rule and the ideological right–left axis of political division untenable. It has become increasingly difficult to forge consensus within an industry group. Political donations to a specific party have lost their meaning, as the shared benefits have vanished. Even within a single industry, gaps are often widening between those competitive firms and those still in need of government regulation to protect their interests. The value of the bureaucracy as mediator has declined. Thus, the triangle is breaking down.

Minakami predicted the danger of deindustrialization and growing unemployment:

Big firms will survive by moving production abroad, but Japan as a country must face a ground subsidence, even though at present Japan's deindustrialization rate (less than 10 per cent) is much lower than those of the USA and EU member-nations (30–40 per cent).

What then must be done to avoid such dismal fate? Minakami's answer was:

Through deregulation, domestic market must be made truly free and open. To bring this about, we need strong political leadership that can break the resistance of vested interest groups.

Will such political leadership and deregulation be possible? 'Japan as a frog' is the metaphor Minakami used to explain his thinking:

A frog will jump out if it is thrown into boiling water, but if it is placed in cold water that is gradually heated to the boiling point, it will miss the timing of jumping out and die. Japanese have never initiated structural reforms on their own in the past unless forced by compelling foreign pressure, and it has become our second nature to post-pone difficult changes until we are driven to a very narrow corner by foreign pressure.

---

[6] *Gyokai* refers to 'the formal associations that represent the interests of an industrial sector, such as auto makers or steel producers', and also to a broader notion of 'all entities (firms, enterprises, and trade associations) that fall under the legal jurisdiction of a particular ministry' (Sone 1993, p. 300).

Otherwise, only a sharp sense of crisis caused by 'shocks' such as an oil crisis can make us jump and achieve a change that is unthinkable under normal conditions.

In short, Minakami said, the Japanese could not change their system without a direct threat to their survival, and might well die a slow death in a gradually unfolding catastrophe — which, he feared, was exactly what was happening.

Acknowledging the recent recovery of the American economy, Minakami was deeply sceptical if it could be a model for Japan:

> Recently, the American-type market economy has been gaining popularity in Japan, The current recovery of the American economy, however, is built on the mass firing of white-collar workers, most of whom have subsequently settled into lower-income jobs. Many lower skilled blue-collar workers face competition from cheap labour in developing countries. While the highly competitive small minority at the top becomes a bunch of billionaires, many in the middle class are slipping down to the lower class, causing potential instability and bipolarization in the society. When America had a healthy middle class, it could afford programmes to support the socially weak, but now the government is forced to cut welfare spending. The society is facing an ethical crisis as well, and militant Islamic fundamentalism is growing as an arm of the lower class in protest and resistance against the unjust society. Its ranks will exceed those of Judaism in the next century. America's stability can be only a temporary one that covers up many divisive, destabilizing elements.

Since in Japan the overwhelming majority are used to identifying themselves with the middle class, he warned, there will be strong public resistance if deregulation and pure market competition lead to visible expansion of the income gap, as in the United States.[7]

A long-time administrative chief of Keidanren (Japan Federation of Economic Organizations), Masaya Miyoshi, compared the internal relationship of the triangle to that of *jan–ken–pon*, or the game of stone–scissors–paper, in which businessmen as the 'stone' have the upper hand over politicians as the 'scissors', who in turn have the whip hand over the bureaucrats, the 'paper' — who in their turn exert commanding influence over the business community, the 'stone'. Miyoshi noted that since the 1970s politicians have begun to use their 'scissors' against the bureaucrats' 'paper', when big business started to regard government intervention as an obstacle to the globalization of its activities (interview, 4 July 1996).

What has changed since the beginning of the coalition era? As Miyoshi explained, a popular view among business leaders seems to have been that three actors — the mass media, labour and academia — which used to be outsiders, have joined the policy-making triangle to nibble at its edges and modify its shape into a sort of hexagon. However, subtle differences divide the business leaders in their evaluations of this development.

Some of them observed that the new hexad could be useful and constructive, as diversified mutual criticisms would make it easier to put the brakes on and steer the economy in a better direction for change, which would pave the way for

---

[7] Since the time of this interview, employment in the USA has increased more than predicted and wages have also improved considerably, according to the US Department of Labor statistics published in January 1997 (*Nihon Keizai Shimbun*, 11 January 1997).

reconstruction of a better and stronger union. Since the fall of the LDP from power, others complained, the quality and efficiency of policy-making has declined because of fewer and shallower communications between business and politics, the relationship between which 'was supposed to be inseparable like the wheels on the two sides of a vehicle'. Among the causes for this deepening gap between business and politics, blame was placed by some on the mass media's sensationalism in exposing the collusion and bribery scandals that make each side reduce its contacts to a minimum to avoid arousing the media's suspicion. Also noted was the absence of individuals with leadership ability among both businessmen and politicians. All four major peak business organizations[8] were criticized for losing their *raison d'être* in failing to keep up with the changing situation (interview with Toshio Ono, executive director, NEC Corporation, 5 July 1996).

The third view characterized the 'iron triangle' as a negative alliance from the beginning, implying that its disintegration was essentially a positive change caused by its own inner dynamics (interview with Yoshihiko Wakumoto, adviser, Toshiba Corporation, 4 July 1996). According to this view, the triangle had been maintained by the three actor groups, mainly to avoid mutual ostracism rather than to achieve something positive. Each group had weaknesses in its relationship with the others, as illustrated by the *jan–ken–pon* metaphor, so all were simply resigned to keep compromising whenever they could bear the costs. But under the intensifying global competition, businesses could not survive simply by adhering to this system; hence it was predicted that the bureaucracy could not fail to change. After Japan had caught up with the West in the 1980s, and was therefore unable to borrow models and blueprints from the Western countries to develop its domestic industries, the bureaucrats lost their self-confidence and high spirits, while the politicians lacked leadership, and were incapable of developing a viable alternative vision. The business world was divided between the competitive sectors calling for deregulation and the non-competitive sectors demanding protection.[9] Wakumoto emphasized that bureaucrats should no longer resist or sabotage economic (but not social) deregulation. At the same time, he cautioned that deregulation would not automatically revitalize the economy, and that the urgent task was to build an environment that could inspire and nurture entrepreneurial drive for new business ventures.

Hiroshi Tachibana of Keidanren also welcomed the loosening of the iron triangle. To accelerate this process of dissolution, he emphasized the importance of ensuring

---

[8] This refers to the Federation of Economic Organizations (Keidanren), the Japan Chamber of Commerce (Nihon Shokokaigisho), the Japan Federation of Employers' Associations (Nikkeiren), and the Japan Association of Corporate Executives (Keizai Doyukai).

[9] Wakumoto observed: 'Since the end of the Occupation (when the Americans let Japan free by delegating the task of democratization to its own bureaucrats), the bureaucrats had been acting with a sense of mission and confidence (bordering on arrogance) that they were to lead the country. They used to find models to follow in the advanced industrial countries of the West. This is why those industries that have already globalized their operations have been suffering from growing frustration these days. In our industry, there is no one who wants protection by government regulations. By contrast, the distribution sector, with so much surplus manpower, is beset with a potentially very high unemployment with many inefficient firms still opposing deregulation. Thus, the iron triangle has been breaking down from inside, even without *gaiatsu* [foreign pressure] from the USA and other foreign governments.'

fair competition in free markets by implementing thorough deregulation and information disclosure rules. He also stressed the need to strengthen 'the anti-monopoly law
so that it really performs its function' (interview with Hiroshi Tachibana, director,
Economic Policy Bureau, Keidanren, 5 July 1996).

What about the perception of labour leaders, those of an alleged new affiliate of
the allegedly loosened and expanded ruling coalition? Akira Yamagishi, chairman
of Rengo (the Japanese trade union confederation) from 1989 to 1994, was the
chief architect of Hosokawa's coalition government.[10] It was Rengo, with its nearly
8 million membership, that provided the political glue to unite the eight parties with
very different political ideas and support bases in the summer of 1993. At that time,
Yamagishi exulted: 'Formation of a non-LDP government has been Rengo's long-
time fervent wish' (Kato 1995).[11] As Kiyoshi Sasamori, president of the Confederation of Electric Power Industry Workers Unions of Japan, put it, it was indeed the
first time that the labour movement, which had long suffered from bifurcation
(*matazaki*) into two groups — Sohyo (the General Council of Japanese Trade
Unions) in support of the JSP and Domei (the Confederation of Japanese Labour
Unions) in support of the DSP — had been united under the banner of the Hosokawa
coalition government.

Rengo was then determined never to let the LDP regain power. Within less than
a year, however, the internal feud in the coalition government was exposed by
the national welfare tax fiasco in February 1994.[12] In April, angered by the establishment of the 'Kaishin' (renovation) group by all the coalition members except
Sakigake and the SDPJ, the SDPJ left the coalition and joined the LDP in a vote of
no confidence to bring the cabinet down. After a super-short-lived Hata cabinet,
the SDPJ moved in with the LDP to form a coalition, leaving the DSP as a partner
in the opposition Shinshinto. Labour was thus back in the state of *matazaki* and
Rengo's plan was seriously compromised. Yet, Sasamori lamented, there was little
sense of such awareness among Rengo leaders and members, a serious symptom of
mindlessness indeed (interview with Kiyoshi Sasamori, 8 August 1996):

> The situation reflected the erosion of party identity among the union members.
> According to a recent Yomiuri survey, as much as 60 per cent of the members of
> Jichiro (All Japan Prefectural and Municipal Workers' Union), Zendentsu (Telecom-
> munication Workers Union of Japan) and Denki Roren (All Japan Federation of Elec-
> trical Machine Workers' Unions), which had long been known as the loyal supporters
> of the SDP, now supported no party. Furthermore, 10–20 per cent of them supported

---

[10] Rengo was founded in November 1987 as a national organization of unions in the private
sector. It absorbed Sohyo, a national centre composed mostly of public-sector unions and some in
the private sector, in November 1989. Rengo thus is a peak labour organization that has unified
public and private-sector unions, embracing 78 industrial federations (which in turn is composed
of 12,000 enterprise union affiliates) and 7.7 million members, or 9 per cent of the nation's
voters, 17 per cent of all employees and fully 65 per cent of organized workers in Japan (Tsujinaka
1993, p. 200).

[11] For a detailed account of Yamagishi's 'engineering' activities, see Yamagishi (1995, chs. 1–2).

[12] Prime Minister Morihiro Hosokawa made a surprise announcement of the creation of the
national welfare tax in February 1994 without informing the SDPJ, whose opposition, joined by
Sakigake, led Hosokawa to withdraw the plan five days later.

the LDP! Those three labour federations plus Zentei (Japan Postal Workers Union) have, in fact, invited the LDP to their annual meetings scheduled for August.

'Labour is not becoming a permanent member of the ruling coalition', Sasamori observed:

> What is happening is that, in its effort to expand its support base and become a national party [*kokumin seito*], the LDP is extending its tentacles to labour unions, especially the public and government workers' unions (although, logically, it should target private-sector unions, since its main support bases have been big businesses, farmers, and small and medium businesses).[13] Frankly speaking, however, the vote-collecting ability of the labour unions is vastly overestimated these days. We have started a new drive to reverse the trend of declining memberships and political interest among workers.

Takeo Naruse, deputy director general of Nikkeiren (Japan Federation of Employers' Associations), outlined the situation in the labour movement:

> Since the three labour union federations were united into Rengo, the movement has become markedly slower, no doubt reflecting their difficulty in forging united positions on most issues. For example, administrative reform is generally welcomed by private-sector unions previously affiliated with Domei, but adamantly opposed by Jichiro and Nikkyoso (Japan Teachers' Union), formerly affiliated with Sohyo. But neither Shinshinto nor LDP can ignore Rengo, not only in deference to the SDPJ but more importantly as an 8-million-vote bloc. In return, Rengo now adopts omni-directional policy, and lets its member unions decide on such matters as which party or candidate to support in particular elections.

The mass media, another alleged new member of the new hexad coalition, has been a popular subject of discussion among scholars and journalists, especially since a widely viewed television talk show is believed to have served as a fatal trigger for the LDP's split and eventual downfall in 1993. During the 'Sunday Project' interview programme on 31 May 1993, Prime Minister Miyazawa promised to achieve political reform before the end of the current session of the Diet, and his failure to keep that promise gave a well publicized reason for the Ozawa and Hata groups within the LDP to join in the opposition-sponsored vote of no confidence against the Miyazawa cabinet and to set in motion the still swirling waves of political realignment (Tawara 1995, pp. 1–2). Furthermore, on the passage of the electoral reform bills, Sasamori was not the only one who suspected that many politicians actually hated and feared the unpredictable effects of new electoral laws, but simply could not resist the mounting public pressure generated by an orchestrated media campaign for political reform. The media also gave big coverage to business leaders' support for the reform and echoed their argument that the multi-member districts were the major culprit of money politics, hence of their increasingly unbearable burden of political

---

[13] This observation coincides with van Wolferen's: 'Rengo, in fact, fits in very well with the expected wish of LDP ideologues to expand the party's constituency to include the labor unions' (van Wolferen 1990, p. 65).

contributions. Also, many attributed the rapid succession of subsequent events, from the electoral advances of the new parties to the establishment of the Hosokawa coalition government, to the influence of the media. The election of two comedians as governors of Tokyo and Osaka was widely seen as another sign of media-dominated elections.

These examples certainly illustrate the significant impact of the mass media on political events, but clearly, the impacts here are an outsider's. By its very nature, the role of the media requires independence from the establishment. It is true that quite a few media representatives now serve as members of government advisory councils, but this practice was started under the LDP rule, and in this regard little changed under the coalition governments. Also heard was the observation that the main role of the advisory councils is as a device to legitimize policies made by bureaucrats, rather than as an arena of bona fide policy-making or policy deliberation. Nobuyoshi Namiki, a former MITI bureaucrat, dismisses the notion of business-led administrative reform as a myth created by clever bureaucrats; Toshio Doko (former Toshiba president who headed the Doko *rincho* or the Second Provisional Commission on Administrative Reform), Haruo Maekawa (former Bank of Japan president who is credited with the authorship of the Maekawa Report),[14] and Gaishi Hiraiwa (former Tokyo Electric Power president who headed the Hiraiwa committee)[15] are all used for their symbolic leadership image (Namiki 1995, pp. 155–63).[16] In a totally different context, Ryuko Wada, managing director of Keidanren's Japan Institute for Social and Economic Affairs, mentioned that, after the first oil crisis, Doko was the one who urged the government to stimulate the economy by issuing deficit bonds and not to worry about the future,[17] and that it was ironical that Doko headed the Rincho, years later, to tackle the issue of how to curtail the huge government deficits to which his contribution was not trivial (interview with Ryuko Wada, 28 February 1995).

To summarize the findings from the interviews, it seems that the iron triangle structure of the ruling coalition has been undergoing significant changes driven by a number of factors. First, the ruling coalition has expanded its membership to include the mass media, labour and academia, but it is not certain yet if their participation is permanent or temporary. Second, along with the expansion of its membership, the internal cohesiveness of the ruling coalition has declined. Third, the mercantilist consensus has been breaking down as Japan has caught up economically with the West and as gaps in international competitiveness among and within

---

[14] The Maekawa Report issued in 1986 by the Study Group on Economic Structural Adjustment for International Harmony, Prime Minister Nakasone's private advisory council, headed by Maekawa advocated sweeping changes in the Japanese economic structure to stimulate domestic demand-led imports.

[15] The Hiraiwa committee, Prime Minister Hosokawa's private advisory council, issued the so-called Hiraiwa report in 1993, which advocated structural reforms to reduce Japan's trade surplus by increasing domestic investment in social infrastructure in preparation for the arrival of an ageing society.

[16] Inamori, cited in the following section of the text, makes a similar point.

[17] Kiichi Miyazawa, minister of finance in the Miki cabinet, resisted, but Prime Minister Takeo Fukuda who succeeded Miki acted on Doko's request (Namiki 1995, pp. 133–4).

industries have grown in the business sector. Fourth, these divisions have in turn divided their allies among conservative politicians and in the bureaucracy and have caused fissures in the labour movement composed of enterprise unions.

The collapse of the LDP-dominant system has generated a strong new current for a generational change which has swept into leadership positions rank-and-file politicians with few or no established collusive ties with either bureaucratic or business clients. Since many of them had little inhibition in digging out past wrongdoings by the iron triangle, this new current has had some house-cleaning effects, as seen in a series of revelations of scandals involving the ministries of construction, finance, health and welfare, etc.

The shift in the power balance within the ruling coalition is affected increasingly by foreign pressure for deregulation, which is often persuasively claimed to enhance or coincide with the interests of Japanese consumers. Also widely shared is the view that, in the long run, the foregoing forces should work to curtail the influence and power that the bureaucracy had during the catch-up phase of the nation's economic development. None the less, in the short run, many concurred, the bureaucracy has increased its influence in some areas of policy-making, not only during the absence of the LDP from power but also under all the coalition governments, owing to the leadership stymied by profound internal divisions.

Finally, the ultimate causes of these changes were traced back to the two international systemic changes — the end of the Cold War and the rise of East Asian economies — which have dramatically increased the pressure for open competition with an accelerating mobility of capital and labour on a truly global scale. Underlying this formulation is a shared belief that the 1955 system has completed its mission and has degenerated into an obstacle to the changes that are necessary if Japan is to perform a role expected of a mature economic power, as well as to survive the age of global competition.

## 3

### The Ruling Policy-making Networks

This section examines the changes in the nature of the ruling policy-making networks from the macro viewpoint of changes in the roles of, and power relations among, the main actors. Naturally, which actor(s) play the leading role would vary in different policy areas. Such micro-level issues will be dealt with only as they help our understanding of the macro-level changes in Japan's domestic structure.

During the high economic growth period, many researchers accepted the elite model which attributed the leading role in policy-making and implementation to the bureaucracy.[18] A series of works based on the 'strong state' thesis followed, as popular views came to credit much of Japan's postwar economic growth to the neo-mercantilist role of the bureaucracy.[19] The 'strong state' model was challenged by the pluralist model, advocated by those who saw a significant shift in the locus of

[18] See e.g. Tsuji (1969); Ishida (1961a,b); Misawa (1967); Taguchi (1969); Masumi (1969).
[19] For a detailed overview of the literature on the controversy, see McKean (1993).

power from the bureaucracy to the LDP policy tribes (*zoku giin*, i.e. informal groups of legislators who specialize in specific policy areas) as a consequence of the internationalization and liberalization of the economy and the pluralization of participation by a broader range of interest groups.[20] Others characterized the 1955 system as 'corporatism without labour', noting the strong state–business ties that were mediated by cohesive peak organizations of businesses on the one hand and the weak role of labour on the other (Pempel and Tsunenaka 1979, p. 264). Still others argued that, even before the formation of Rengo, labour had participated in policy-making processes through a variety of informal consultative networks (Tsujinaka 1993, p. 209). Both the pluralist and the corporatist models challenge the 'strong state' thesis. Still another view emphasizes, more concretely, the role of the *gyokai* (industry groups), arguing that in Japan both society and policy networks are divided along the ministerial lines and many of the government's interventionist policies have been conceived and formulated at the *gyokai* level.[21]

As regards the role of labour, there have been conflicting views since the formation of Rengo in 1987 and its absorption of Sohyo in 1989. Many regard the new organization as serving management wishes to coopt the labour movement (Sone 1993, pp. 200–1). It is almost axiomatic, furthermore, that the internationalization of world trade and the deregulation of domestic markets tend to undermine the bargaining power of labour. Another group nevertheless emphasizes the positive aspect of the emergence of the new organization by arguing that labour has become a formal participant in policy-making, in partnership with business and the state (see Kume 1993; Tsujinaka 1993). In contrast to those who insist on complete exclusion or full inclusion, a third view argues for a view of 'limited inclusion of labour' (McNamara 1996, p. 383).

Compared with these competing views found among scholars, how do the 'policy elites' I interviewed analyse the 'policy networks' of the 1955 system, and what, in their opinion, changed under the coalition governments?

As regards policy networks, there was a general agreement on the dominant role of the bureaucracy under the 1955 system. Also widely agreed on was the corporatist aspect of the system as manifested by the prominent role of the four peak business organizations in setting the fundamental policy lines through interest coordination within the business community and constant consultation with the LDP, and the important and concrete inputs in specific policy areas made by relevant industry groups. They also shared the view that, as the Japanese economy matured and internationalized, pluralistic tendencies grew in all three centres of policy networks

---

[20] The globalization of the markets is weakening the internal unity of the business community and each industry group, breeding corresponding divisions in their bureaucratic allies, the argument goes, and thus expanding the need for political leadership in mediating and coordinating intra-business and intra-bureaucracy conflicts of interests and opinions.

[21] According to this view, the *gyokai* perspective explicates such key aspects of the policy network as 'the relations among bureaucrats, politicians, and legislators, the pattern of contacts between government and the private sector, and even the emergence of *seisaku zoku* (informal groups of legislators who specialize in specific policy areas)' (Sone 1993, p. 305). Yet, there seems to be an emerging consensus that the concept of the *gyokai* is losing its meaning, with rapidly growing gaps in international competitiveness within and among industries.

to expose the weaknesses of the 1955 system in the rapidly changing environment. Especially with the growing competitiveness gaps among industries and within each industry, the *raison d'être* of the four peak organizations became questionable and the concept of the *gyokai* began to lose its meaning, breeding corresponding divisions among their allied bureaucrats and politicians. Indeed, an intractable source of the current problems lies in the fact that, despite the radical environmental changes, little change has occurred in the bureaucracy-led policy-making process. At the same time, many observed that the globalization of the markets will greatly increase the need for political leadership to coordinate and mediate conflicting interests and opinions within both the business community and the bureaucracy, but that there is little hope for the emergence of such leadership under the present circumstances.

With regard to changes after the fall of the 1955 system, there was an intriguing unanimity in the responses to the question: 'Do you think the LDP tribes, after returning to power, have succeeded in restoring the old policy networks by undoing changes made under the Hosokawa–Hata non-LDP coalition governments?' The unanimous response was that there had been no substantive changes that needed to be undone, and that reformism has so far remained just a slogan.[22] Then where in the policy networks *do* they see the roots of the problems? One may find the answers by focusing on administrative reforms and deregulation, two areas that all the parties highlighted in their campaign promises in the 1996 general elections.

Predictable from the *jan–ken–pon* formula, business leaders blamed the conservatism and sectionalism of the government bureaucracy for the snails' pace of deregulation and market opening, and called for stronger political leadership. Even worse, as they saw it, unable to forge consensus within the ruling coalition, the successive coalition governments put off indefinitely all urgent national issues such as social welfare, land, taxes and defence (see Nakano 1996, p. 93). Among the sharpest critics was Kazuo Inamori, founder and chairman of both Kyocera Corporation and DDI Corporation. He summed up what he learned from his three years' experience as a member of the Dai Sanji Gyoukakushin (Third Provisional Council for the Promotion of Administrative Reform):

> What alarmed me most was my keen realization of how bureaucratically Japan is managed. I may even say that our system is a bureaucratic dictatorship. This country promotes political strategies that are centred around bureaucrats who aim to maintain the *status quo* and promote economic development without any regard to the wishes of the Japanese public. (Speech given at the Ninth Annual Keizai Doyukai (Japan Association of Corporate Executives) national seminar, Hiroshima, 14 March 1996)

---

[22] Perhaps the most striking event that could not have occurred without the infusion of new blood under the coalition arrangement was the exposure of the government's misconduct in the distribution of HIV-tainted blood in the 1980s, which resulted in some 400 deaths and the infection of 2,000 people. Over the objections of the Health Ministry's career bureaucrats, who traditionally control their politically appointed ministers, Naoto Kan, health minister of the Hashimoto Cabinet, identified dozens of long-buried files that revealed how the ministry had allowed the use of the dangerous blood, then covered up its actions (Sullivan 1996, p. A12). Kan himself, however, admits that his party and Sakigake's long-standing goal of administrative reform has made little progress (interview in a news show, 15 September 1996).

The reality of legislative and budget-making process, he lamented, was that they were all decided by bureaucrats and merely endorsed by the Diet after the fact. He added: 'We may even say that there are practically no laws which are truly authored and legislated by our national representatives.' Nor can the cabinet, endowed with the highest administrative power by the constitution, act independently to 'respect the will of the people', because of the 'mechanism whereby all proposals are screened and unanimously approved in a regular meeting attended by the vice-ministers of all ministries before presented to the Cabinet meeting'. In fear of antagonizing the bureaucrats, no cabinet member has dared to criticize this system. Some of the implications of Mr Inamori's criticisms were manifest in an endless chain of bribery cases in which administrative deputy ministers have been found to be involved since the 1980s.

It was because, in the early postwar period, the Occupation authority retained intact the administrative system centred around the bureaucracy in order to govern Japan that the bureaucracy had survived to carry out policies that it considered best for the state, with little sense of reflecting the popular will or interests. Inamori recognizes the bureaucrats' positive contribution to the success of the nation in helping it to sail through the chaotic postwar period and achieve rapid economic growth. The problem, however, was that, even when society had matured, the bureaucrats did not trust the Japanese people and went on behaving as the self-appointed guardians of Japan's existing social order. Imbued with an anachronistic sense of themselves as 'superior to the common populace', the bureaucrats remained unwilling to let the private sector and the market govern themselves. Many difficulties the Japanese face today derive from this anachronism. As is evident in case after case revealed in recent years, such as the Ministry of Finance's handling of *jusen* (housing loan companies) and the Ministry of Health and Welfare's of HIV, the bureaucrats tend not to change their position once decided, even when it proves to be wrong, in order to defend the myth that bureaucrats never make mistakes.

Inamori thus points to the closed nature and inherent conservatism of the bureaucracy. He criticizes another source of bureaucratic leadership, i.e. administrative guidance (*gyosei shido*) or notifications (*tsutatsu*) by which bureaucrats have their decisions implemented, which 'may even defy existing laws and regulations under the pretext of safeguarding our social order and peace'. Such arbitrary measures, not set out in laws but nevertheless taken by the governments, make him deplore that 'Japan is not a constitutional state at all, but a bureaucratic dictatorship'.

Another feature of this system that Inamori criticized is that the government 'will force policies which accord high priority to the protection and nurturing of suppliers and producers, even when that is contrary to the interests of the people or consumers'. This bias of the 'bureaucratic dictatorship' was abundantly demonstrated in the ongoing super-low interest rate policy, which he describes as channelling many trillions of yen from the pockets of the general public, interest on whose savings was drastically reduced, to the banks who were making record profits thanks to the low interest rates.

These remarks seem to reflect a sense of frustration shared by many business leaders who have been involved in the nation's policy-making processes.

Interestingly, retired bureaucrats-turned-social commentators/writers/scholars (there are quite a few of them) join those business leaders in blaming bureaucratic sectionalism and obstinance as a major cause of Japan's failure to implement any significant administrative reform. Taichi Sakaiya,[23] a former MITI bureaucrat-turned-best-selling writer/commentator, characterizes the Japanese market system as one of regulated competition guided by the bureaucracy, which he calls the highly stylized *oozumougata* (Japanese wrestling type) competition, in contrast to the chaotically free moving *puroresugata* (professional wrestling type) competition found in the United States (Sakaiya 1995, pp. 130–1). He argues that, if bureaucrats continue to resist the dismantling of the outdated system designed to protect producers and suppliers during the catch-up period of Japanese economic development, 'within the next decade or so the nation may face the establishment of something like COCOM, except that it will be called JACOM instead. It means that the most-favored-nation status may be taken away from Japan by all nations. Then people, money, and information may be diverted from Japan to an even greater extent than today. Japan could thus become a backwater in Asia' (Sakaiya 1994).

Yukio Noguchi, an ex-MOF bureaucrat-turned-economics professor who boasts several best-sellers, joins Sakaiya in warning that, without fundamental changes in the current system, the Japanese economy may well be left behind and isolated in the increasingly competitive global system. Many elements of the current system, including the so-called Japanese-type enterprise, the financial system built around indirect finance, the direct-tax-dominant tax system and the highly centralized budget system, were put in place for wartime mobilization around 1940, so Noguchi names this system the *1940 system* rather than the 1955 system. Although this neo-mercantilist system worked well as 'an engine of economic growth' by mobilizing all resources for the sole purpose of such growth, Noguchi argues that it 'now poses a threat as a potential stumbling block to the future development of the economy, as it obstructs the badly needed industrial structural change'. The outdated system stifles individual originality, creativity and competition (Noguchi 1995, p. 7). Important as an obstacle as the institutional legacy is, Noguchi stresses, the central ideas of the total mobilization system — rejection of competition and the producer-first stance — still alive and well in the minds of the bureaucrats and businessmen. It is true that deregulation is hindered by the vested interests of the regulator (the ministries) and the regulated (the existing businesses), but equally important is the deep-rooted psychological dependence on the government on the part of the populace, and the social norm that regards competition as a vice and cooperation as a virtue. Noguchi observes that the 1993 collapse of the one-party dominant system has brought about an 'all parties siding with the establishment' system (*so yotou taisei*) reminiscent of the Imperial Rule Assistance Association (Taisei Yokusan-kai) during the war, a system that strengthened the role of the bureaucracy to the extent that it reduced the influence of the 'tribes'.

In a similar vein, Shunpei Kumon, executive director of the Centre for Global Communications, International University of Japan, observes:

> The bureaucrats' resistance is certainly a major cause of the slowness of administrative reform and deregulation. But if you look closely at who is actually supporting those

---

[23] Sakaiya was appointed the head of the Economic Planning Agency of the Obuchi government in 1998.

regulations, you realize that it is the people and industry groups. Whenever an accident occurs, they demand regulation by the government. As the government has grown bigger, the people have become increasingly irresponsible. This is not limited to the Japanese, but there does seem to be something rooted in the Japanese culture. The Japanese think of government as something like a mother, whom they entreat, ask for a favour, and demand more of, in contrast to Americans, who regard government as an enemy. (Interview with Shumpei Kumon, 9 August 1996)

Takashi Wakiyama, a former MITI official, offers a slightly different analysis of the policy networks. The relationship between politicians and bureaucrats, according to him, is like that between husband and wife without love: they need each other, but try to keep contacts to a necessary minimum:

Both feel that the real power resides on their own side, but are unable to exercise the power as freely as they like and suffer from a profound sense of frustration. Still they are partners; they must cooperate with each other as much as needed, and save the other party's face when the situation calls for it. (Wakiyama 1994, p. 66)

In the case of tax reforms, Wakiyama notes, the MOF's guard was so tight that it had become customary for business leaders to petition politicians, whereas the MOF had come to rely on the LDP tax commission to stand up against and neutralize such pressure, according to a synopsis written by MOF bureaucrats. The so-called LDP 'tribesmen' were usually dependent on one or another ministry's expertise, and most important policies originated in the bureaucracy even when they appeared otherwise (Wakiyama 1994, p. 66).

What then is the perception of the bureaucrats themselves? In line with the aforementioned *jan–ken–pon* power relationship within the triangle, bureaucrats tended to emphasize the impact of political influence in policy-making. A Ministry of Foreign Affairs official compared the LDP-dominant 1955 system with the coalition system as follows:

It used to be easy for bureaucrats to decide what to do. Because the LDP was permanently in power, all they had to do was to find out what businessmen and politicians wanted and then do it (although of course, most important things originated with the bureaucrats anyway). When the coalition headed by Nihon Shinto's Hosokawa took power, however, the bureaucrats didn't know what to do. Should they continue to consult with the LDP, or should they treat the new coalition parties as the government? Now, under the three-party coalition headed by Socialist Murayama and then LDP's Hashimoto, they're even more confused, and so they are backing away from politicians for the most part, uncertain about who is the real power. The result is that the Iron Triangle has been broken up — at least for now. (Editorial by R. Matthews in the *Atlanta Journal*, 10 June 1996)

A retired MOF bureaucrat who is still active at one of the MOF-affiliated public corporations blamed political intervention, not the bureaucrats' resistance, for the slow pace of the fiscal and administrative reforms:

Politicians exert pressure to preserve obsolete regulations in return for political contributions from a relevant industry group benefiting from the given regulation, especially in the case of the MITI and MAFF. All they are concerned with is how to maximize votes. They rarely make policy decisions by such criteria as national interests that are unrelated to votes. (Interview with board member, OECF, 8 August 1996)

As for the so-called LDP 'tribesmen's expertise', his observation was simply that 'Yes, they learned a knack of how to pressure bureaucrats through their long experience as agents of so and so interest groups.' In other words, politicians do not have the expertise to make laws, but they do have the skills to pressure bureaucrats to bend or water down the legislation in question, and to exert even stronger pressure to prevent the elimination of existing regulations that benefit their client industry groups or firms. His observation partially confirms both Frances Rosenbluth's argument about how the effective influence exerted by politicians filters through electoral institutions, and the contrasting view of bureaucratic dominance in Japan's policy-making as presented by Chalmers Johnson and many others (Rosenbluth 1996, pp. 152–4; Johnson 1986).

Besides the concrete desires and interests of their client groups, bureaucrats add, the mass media could provide a remarkable impetus for politicians to take a rare initiative in reformist legislation, as in the case of environmental issues in the late 1960s. Masao Miyamoto of the Ministry of Health and Welfare has observed that, when the media take up certain issues, the issues acquire an aura of 'urgency in the politicians' eyes, and are upgraded for inclusion in the political agenda. Bureaucrats, therefore, often resort to the tactic of leaking information to get media coverage or to induce *gaiatsu* (pressure from abroad), in order to move narrowly vote-conscious politicians on certain issues that may not otherwise interest them, as well as *status-quo*-oriented bureaucratic colleagues. He advises:

> If you want to implement a policy based on a new idea or get your new project to be budgeted, use *gaiatsu*, by manipulating especially such international organizations as the World Health Organization. (Miyamoto 1993, pp. 83–90)

As the major cause of the current stalemate in administrative reform endeavour, labour leaders blame the lack of leadership, will and ideas among politicians. Sasamori said:

> Japan is facing many urgent issues that require difficult adjustments in the fields of national security, energy and ageing society as well as administrative reform, as both international and domestic systems undergo profound structural changes. They [politicians] speak of administrative reform as a fashion, but what they are doing is nothing but engaging in a power struggle. No blueprint has been drawn up about the goals and means for the basic policy of the nation. We at Rengo felt it necessary to present our policy framework to the politicians. So, we have formed the Rengo Political Policy Forum [Rengo seiji seisaku forum] to formulate our position on the nation's basic policy, on profile [*kuni no sugata*], and Rengo's relationship with political parties. Our goal is to foster a broad alliance of non-LDP and non-JCP political forces — eventually to found a major party — 'favourable to labour and sympathetic to wage earners', and capable of governing in the place of the LDP. Ultimately, I think, a two-party system is desirable. (Interview with Kiyoshi Sasamori, 8 August 1996)

Not only did the participation of the SDPJ and DSP in the Hosokawa and Hata cabinets give Rengo direct access to policy-making networks, but Yamagishi, the former Rengo chairman, played a central role in the formation of the first non-LDP coalition, as noted earlier. Rengo responded to this change by forming various study groups which included members similar to those on government advisory councils, i.e. businessmen, scholars, journalists and politicians from all parties except the LDP (the only conspicuous difference from government advisory councils) and the JCP, as well as labour leaders, in an effort to increase its policy-making ability. The SDPJ's participation in both the Murayama and Hashimoto cabinets facilitated Rengo's continued access to policy-making but placed it in a difficult position in choosing which policies to endorse. For example, in the case of the Family Care Leave Law of 1995, Rengo decided to support the government bill despite the fact that it was less satisfactory as a product of compromise between SDPJ and the LDP than the Shinshinto bill, which was almost identical to Rengo's proposal (Harari 1996). As regards administrative reform, Sasamori confided:

> It is inevitable for gaps to develop between the private-sector and public-sector unions when we come down to dealing with specific issues of administrative and fiscal reforms. Currently, there are about 3.3 million local government employees and 1.2 million central government employees. If we add those in post-retirement employment in public corporations, the number would easily double. It is imperative to integrate the ministries and agencies to reduce the number of the public employees. The private sector is used to undertaking rather drastic restructuring, but the public sector has never done such a thing. Also, the elimination of affiliated public corporations would mean the loss of post-retirement jobs and hence public sector unions strongly resist such proposals. (Interview with Kiyoshi Sasamori, 8 August 1996)

To summarize the views on Japan's policy networks at the time of interviews (spring and summer 1996), almost all interviewees agreed that, during the Hosokawa and Hata coalition governments, bureaucrats increased their power in policy and budget-making as new cabinet members lacked the expertise in policy and know-how to handle the bureaucracy. Under the Murayama and Hashimoto cabinets, the LDP regained some of its previous influence but was handicapped by internal dissonance aggravated by the inclusion of the SDPJ and Sakigake in the coalition.

The crucial question, as Richard Matthews, a journalist-observer of Japanese politics, commented, is what happens after the first two or three elections under the new electoral system:

> It's entirely possible, and maybe even probable, that the LDP, slightly reconstituted, will return to strong, majority, semi-permanent power. In that case, maybe nothing will have changed. It's also possible, however, that even if the LDP comes back, it will look and behave somewhat differently than before. I'd say that right now there's no way to know whether substantive change is happening or not. The key determinant, I think, is whether the new electoral system forces politicians to deal with issues rather than having the political world be nothing but an arena for struggles among insiders for power for its own sake (like the LDP of before). (E-mail interview with Richard Matthews, editorial writer, *Atlanta Journal*, 10 June 1996)

Generally, those leaders whom I interviewed share Matthews's view that the effects of the new electoral system are critical in determining whether the nature and composition of the ruling coalition and policy-making networks will change in the future. More specifically, the critical questions are: (1) Will the new electoral system lead to a party system with clear issue differences between the parties? (2) Will the new system reduce the role of money in elections? (3) Will the new system make the national political arena more open to those outside the existing political community? Most of the respondents gave tentative answers to these questions, but added that it would take a few elections before a clear picture would emerge. It is safe to say that uncertainty was their consensus. They differ, however, on how a series of domestic political changes were related to changes in the international system.

## 4

### Domestic Structural Changes and International Systemic Changes

'Probably, little international thinking played any role in the decision and action of Ozawa, Hata and their followers when they left the LDP', was a median type of view of my respondents. They also tended to share the view that the Ozawa group's electoral calculation and power struggle within the LDP were decisive factors. A former MOF bureaucrat's observation seems to summarize the general consensus: politicians are so preoccupied with vote-gathering, that is with constituency politics, that they have little room in their minds to think about international affairs (interview, 8 August 1996). As suggested by a remark made by Pat O'Neill, 'all politics is local', and it is perhaps not only Japanese politics that is parochial (interview with Ellis Krauss, 8 August 1996).

Apart from this general observation of politicians' domestic focus, however, many agreed that international events constituted *necessary* conditions, though not *sufficient* conditions, for the split of the LDP, the formation of the LDP–SDPJ coalition government and the reversal of the SDPJ's policy stances.[24]

Besides the above consensus, business leaders were most eloquent about the impact of global systemic changes and the crisis situation engulfing Japan, especially the Japanese economy. Keiichi Nagamatsu, deputy director of the Industrial Affairs Bureau of Keidanren, explained the situation as follows:

> I think the political community has been the slowest in feeling the impact of international changes. They feel the impact of the globalization of markets only indirectly through voters' attitudes. In contrast, the business community has been directly confronted by the effects of globalization as a matter of life or death, through a torrential hollowing-out of the industry. Individual firms are dealing with internationalization as

---

[24] There was consensus among the Hosokawa coalition partners on the need to reform the existing system to meet the new challenges emerging in the post-Cold War era. Introduction to the 'Agreement on the Establishment of the Coalition Government' signed by the heads of non-LDP coalition partners on 29 July 1993 states: 'This administration entrusts itself with the urgent task of responding to the rapidly changing needs of the people and the international society after the end of the Cold War' (Yamagishi 1995, p. 75).

a very matter of survival. At the macro level, discussion has been centring around the subject of how to avoid deindustrialization, but for individual firms that is not their priority. Of course, Japanese employers are deeply concerned with the preservation of jobs for their employees, and they are not necessarily pursuing their overseas relocation plans solely in accordance with the logic of capital. But they are compelled to go abroad under the pressure of the high yen and intensifying competition from the fast-growing East Asian economies. (Interview with Keiichi Nagamatsu, 7 August 1996)

Fujio Cho, senior managing director of Toyota Motor Corporation, had a first-hand experience in the company's overseas operations as president of American Toyota, from the site selection and start-up of the Kentucky plant to the recruit-ment of employees and the operation of that plant. He was quite clear in identifying the internationalization and globalization of the economy as the most important factors causing current structural changes in Japan's domestic political and economic systems. He commented that the 1955 system was rooted in the soil of a Japanized version of American-style democracy, and that a tightly knit politico-bureaucratic protectionism grown out of this soil has nurtured a dual structure to sustain the symbiosis of 'strong industries' and 'weak industries':

> The rules of democracy were brought from America. But during the past fifty years, the rules were all modified into Japanese-style rules. Under extensive political and administrative protection, the Japanese developed a virtuous circle in which the economy grew until it reached the mature stage. Real competitiveness was limited to the export sectors. (Interview with Fujio Cho, 5 July 1996)

Cho clearly identified the end of the Cold War and the globalization of the economy as the most important factors causing the ongoing structural changes in Japan's political economic system:

> The end of the Cold War shifted American policy priorities from strategic to economic issues. Faced by challenges from the mature Japanese economy and the intensely com-petitive East Asian economies, the United States has intensified its pressure on Japan to open the country for the second time. In other words, we are under increasingly strong and impatient pressure to dismantle the uniquely Japanese system built during the Cold War years, and no politicians or bureaucrats seem to know what to do. We are witnessing the collision of two extreme cultures, Japan's culture of 'nurturing' and the US culture of 'selection'. We should preserve the good aspects of our culture, but this is not an easy task.
>
> It is not that I prefer the LDP's one-party rule, but the coalition governments have been postponing all the difficult problems. For example, no decision has been made on the division of NTT after debating for five years. Although at this moment some 77 per cent of those surveyed said that they are more or less satisfied, I am rather pessimistic about our future.

Cho goes on to discuss deindustrialization by comparing the current Japanese markets as unpopular foreign investment targets with the American situation.

> Take the hollowing-out of the industry. Our company abides by the self-imposed rule to produce where the market is, and does not make cars [abroad] for importing back

to Japan. However, many electric appliance makers are relocating their total production bases abroad.

In the case of the United States, when ten firms went abroad, ten firms came from abroad to fill the void. But what worries me is that Japan may not have enough investment from abroad to fill the void. Unemployment would do great harm to our society, eroding family ties, moral standards, and social order and safety.

To prevent such a dismal scenario from materializing, Cho argued that it was imperative to tackle deregulation earnestly and immediately, to eliminate exorbitant gaps between domestic and international prices (*naigai kakaku sa*), reduce corporate taxes to at least the level of the US rate (45 per cent) from the current rate of 55 per cent, and thereby transform Japan from a high-price country into a normal-price country; otherwise, foreign direct investment in Japan would continue to decline and would further exacerbate the deindustrialization of the country.[25]

Cho was also concerned about the declining interest in politics, especially among younger people. He emphasized the importance of teaching them that politics is not someone else's job but their own business, and noted the need for a critical re-examination of the role of the mass media in disseminating the stereotypical image of dirty politicians.

NEC's Toshio Ono also expressed his sense of a crisis when he said that, in this age of globalization, it was impossible for Japan to continue with its long-standing 'one-country peace, one-country prosperity' policy of the Cold War era, and yet politics has degenerated into an arena of petty struggles for offices, and political parties have turned into friendship clubs rather than policy-centred groups with vision and leadership. In the economic sphere, he was particularly concerned about the weakness of software industries which were to fill the void left by the relocation of manufacturing industries in the twenty-first century when knowledge would become a crucial resource. He criticized the current educational system built around the highly competitive entrance exams, and the variety of social procedures, including the hiring practice, ranking people according to their school diplomas (interview with Toshio Ono, 5 July 1996).

Toshiba's adviser, Yoshihiko Wakumoto, noted that the effects of the market liberalization started in the 1980s were becoming gradually visible following the collapse of the bubble economy and the marked increase in the import of manufactured goods. He described the relationship with other Asian economies:

It was in the mid-1980s that the consensus was formed among Japanese firms that one-set-ism was no longer tenable. During the 1980s parts made in Asia could not be used in Japan, but in the 1990s their quality improved, and Japanese firms now routinely import parts from other countries in Asia. In fact, such a relationship has become unavoidable for mutual survival. Still, it is difficult to transfer the results of research and development abroad, so that high-technology products requiring advanced engineering skills are still made in Japan. Currently, Toshiba's sales are 67–68 per cent domestic and 33–34 per cent from exports, whereas production is 73–74 per cent

---

[25] To illustrate how regulation increases waste, Cho pointed out that when an American worker makes ten cars, a Japanese worker makes only five.

domestic (this high ratio of domestic production is due partly to the disproportionate contribution of the *juden* or heavy electrical machinery department), though production of consumer goods is rapidly shifting abroad. (Interview with Yoshihiko Wakumoto, 4 July 1996)

Wakumoto also noted that, while in the United States venture businesses created enough new jobs to fill the slack, Japan lacks such a business environment and innovative people, owing mainly to the educational system, which is designed to produce standardized workers for mass production. Even the so-called new human species (*shin jinrui*), those of the younger and supposedly more liberated generation, are not so different from the older generation in that they prefer the job stability provided by big established firms or government. Japan is good at manufacturing but weak in the emerging software industry. If the country fails to reform the educational system, which is still built on rote learning and suppression of all forms of individualism from an early age, Wakumoto believes that Japan may become a great unemployment power (*shitsugyou taikoku*) in the age of the information society.

Nikkeiren's Takeo Naruse pointed out that an urgent concern shared by Rengo and Nikkeiren is deindustrialization:

> For example, the electric and electronic parts makers have relocated production bases abroad in droves, and Nagano, Yamanashi, Yamagata and Fukushima prefectures and the Kyushu region are all hurting from the consequences of this exodus. Unemployment is now a serious problem. Not only has unemployment reached the postwar high, but what is called internal unemployment (redundant labour) within firms is around 2 million, or 3.3 per cent of Japan's total work-force of about 60 million. In addition, companies are losing 10 trillion yen in payment for unemployment insurance each year, though we consider this expense a contributor to social stability. Last year we started a joint research project with Rengo on job creation and compiled interim reports on four areas, related to information, housing, environment and family-care for the elderly and handicapped (*kaigo*). We are also urging our member firms to start new venture businesses. Some companies like Omron constantly run some fifty venture businesses. Since it requires a lot of human resources, money and know-how, it is encouraging to have big companies take responsibility for creating venture businesses. We have also proposed deregulation of employment offices. I honestly feel that society and the economy are changing from the ground up, constantly spawning new demands and job opportunities. (Interview with Takeo Naruse, deputy director general, Japan Federation of Employers' Associations (Nikkeiren), 5 July 1996)

Under these changing conditions, Rengo's Kiyoshi Sasamori noted that the emphasis of the labour movement has shifted from wage negotiations to institutional and policy demands, such as improvements in the pension and care systems for the elderly and handicapped (*kaigo*). Job security, unemployment insurance and information-sharing are the three key areas in which Rengo should expand its activities to attract unorganized and deorganized workers. There is little sense of directly responding to the changes in the international political economy, Sasamori acknowledged, but the labour movement has clearly been under pressure to map out its new coordinates (*zahyoujiku*) for defining its basic policy lines and relationships with the state and political parties to face the post-Cold War challenges.

An OECF board member, retired from MOF a few years ago, also noted the seriousness of the deindustrialization trend and commented: 'Perhaps, it is unavoidable to lower the corporate tax by raising the consumption tax, in order to reduce the pressure for Japanese firms to relocate abroad.' Another issue he emphasized was that of refugees. He contemplated:

> One of the compelling reasons for rich countries to undertake official development assistance may well be a desire to prevent the outflow of massive refugees from poor countries, pushed by poverty, loss of jobs, pollution or civil war. As a matter of fact, Europeans are now desperately searching for a decent way to shut the door to refugees. Frankly, I was surprised to find a passage in the recent report by the Club of Rome, *The Scandal and the Shame of Poverty and Underdevelopment*, that denounced humanitarian aid as harmful for sabotaging self-help efforts; but perhaps it is harmful to use human rights and humanitarian causes as an excuse either to give or stop giving aid. (Interview with an OECF board member, 8 August 1996)

Regarding aid to Russia, his opinion was: 'It would most likely end up in the hands of the Mafia; so we should not waste money except for the clearly defined aid for concrete organization building and human resource development. Fortunately, OECF is not dealing with Russia which is classified as a middle-income country.'

In sum, business, labour and bureaucratic leaders share a sense of crisis and the need for domestic structural changes attributable in the final analysis to international systemic changes, but they feel that politicians are regrettably slow in responding to the challenges. For them, the main effect of the end of the Cold War has been the globalization and intensification of economic competition, as it has removed the buffer of the strategic priority that used to absorb some of the shocks and tension from economic competition among the capitalist economies. This competition has been complicated by the fact that the end of the Cold War, combined with technological development in communications and transportation, has lifted the lid that used to suppress the geographical mobility of the masses. While businesses are undergoing globalization of their operations for survival, neither a clear vision nor a general framework is emerging among the leaders to give direction to the nation's structural reform itself.

## 5

### Summary and Conclusion

To summarize the findings, on all three themes dealt with in this paper concerning changes in the international system and in Japan's domestic structure, the business, bureaucratic and labour leaders interviewed shared a broad picture, although they differed in emphasis and detailed observations.

First, in regard to the ruling coalition, almost all of my respondents characterized the 1955 system as an iron triangle of big business, the bureaucracy and the LDP, and observed that, during the period when the LDP was out of power, this triangle was seriously incapacitated, though similar links were maintained by former LDP 'tribesmen' of the Ozawa and Hata groups. Generally, the bureaucracy, especially the Ministry of Finance, increased its power *vis-à-vis* politicians in the triangle or new hexad.[26]

Regarding the changes in the domestic structure after the collapse of the 1955 system, they generally agreed on the following points. The SDPJ and labour leaders joined the ruling coalition but were often treated as second-class partners, as in the case of the failed plan of the national welfare tax mentioned earlier. The *ancien régime*, with the familiar faces of the old LDP 'tribes', was resuscitated when the LDP was restored to power via a previously unthinkable alliance with the SDPJ. The position of the SDPJ has been raised to a footing more equal to that of the LDP, but at the price of reversing its positions on many issues including, especially, the Self-Defence Forces, the security treaty with the USA and nuclear power generation, so as to bring them into greater harmony with the LDP's positions.

On the transformation of the SDPJ, opinion was divided. Many business leaders welcomed the Socialists' apostasy as proof that they had finally outgrown their ideological rigidity in tune with the post-Cold War de-ideologization trend in the international political economy. Some bureaucrats and ex-bureaucrats, however, questioned the credibility of the Socialists for their failure to come up with convincing explanations for the inconsistencies with their past positions, and predicted the gradual extinction of the party whose *raison d'être* had been lost (Ishizuka 1995).

Within the business community, after the beginning of the coalition era, a popular view seems to have been a 'new hexad theory', i.e. that three new actors — the mass media, labour and academia — have joined the ruling triangle to nibble at its edges and modify its shape into a sort of hexagon. In contrast, many labour leaders seemed more concerned about the further conservatization of the workers and labour unions. Little mention was made of the specific role of academia, except as another new actor group in the ruling hexad coalition. It may be noted here that under the coalition governments scholars of different ideological hues, but especially anti-bureaucratic, citizen-oriented types, acquired considerable influence in the parties in power — far more than before. The mass media, too, exert an increasingly visible influence on the ongoing changes in the ruling coalition by swaying public opinion and voting behaviour, although their influence is essentially that of a group outside the ruling coalition. In sum, it may be concluded that the influence of labour, the media and academia became more visible, and may have presaged the decentralization and pluralization of the ruling coalition.

Second, there was a general agreement on the identity of the dominant policy network. They all accepted the view that the 1955 system had been characterized by the dominant role of the bureaucracy and the corporatist role of big business and industry groups in policy-making.

Third, the dominant policy network is now in a transitional phase, undergoing substantial changes. Even before the end of the Cold War, however, all agreed that the influence of the business community had begun to decline, reflecting the

---

[26] In the case of the MOF, a team of Ichiro Ozawa and Jiro Saito, MOF's administrative vice minister, is said to have become an axis of decision-making that superseded formal committees formed for the purpose of policy-making and deliberation within the Hosokawa coalition (Nakano, 1996, pp. 80–3).

diversification of interests within the business world, the pluralization of values in society and the rising consumer consciousness — changes brought about by the maturation, internationalization and liberalization of the economy. Also nearly unanimous was the view that pressure was building for a restructuring of the current policy networks under the intensifying criticisms of the bureaucracy-led system and internal and external pressures calling for a policy shift from the protection of producers to the protection of consumers. Since the beginning of the coalition era, the respondents concurred, deregulation and administrative reform had become the priority goals for all the parties, but little had been achieved because of the absence of political leadership and a clear vision of reform. The political community was in the process of realignment, and the successive coalition governments had been unable to form a consensus on many critical issues with long-term impacts from social welfare to national security. Also heard from both business and labour leaders was the view that the inclusion of the two socialist parties in the ruling coalition brought labour into the dominant network as a formal member, but that the weak central power in Rengo and conflicting interests among the unions had prevented it from exercising independent influence in policy-making and made it a sort of a hunting ground (*kusakariba*), open to all political groups for vote-gathering. Regarding the fundamental reason for the slow pace of reform, dominant among views of the business and bureaucratic leaders was the observation that, despite the rapid pluralization of both the economy and society, the weak political leadership during the rule by the coalition governments helped to revive and strengthen the bureaucracy-led policy-making system operating by the old principle of maintaining and expanding vested interests. For its part, however, the bureaucracy had been exposed to be not only inefficient, wasteful, factionalized and involved in collusive relationships with client businesses, but also more fundamentally deficient, i.e. unable to restructure itself to meet the changing needs of the country under the direct impact of the profound international systemic changes.

Fourth, regarding the relationship between the international systemic changes and domestic structural changes, again, almost all agreed that the systemic changes did not provide an immediate impetus for domestic political changes, and that politicians were generally preoccupied with how to please their local constituencies and had little interest in and knowledge about international issues. Both business and bureaucratic leaders noted that, since the politicians felt the impact of the international systemic changes only indirectly, through the movement of votes and money in elections, that is through the voice of the electorate and the business community, their reaction tended to be dull and delayed. None the less, the respondents generally agreed that changes at the international level were indirectly and slowly, but surely, affecting the ruling coalition and policy networks. The main forces for change emanated from the business community, which had been directly impacted by the international changes. The labour leaders reflected that, although they should be most sensitive to the threat of unemployment resulting from deindustrialization, their reaction had been rather slow.

From the perception of the policy elites summarized above, it is clear that the main impetus for the current political realignment and the administrative and financial reform campaign came from complex divisions within the political and bureaucratic communities developing parallel to divisions within the business community. Finally, labour was also feeling the direct impacts of the international changes through deindustrialization and a rising consumer/citizen consciousness that undermined the two traditional and intertwined types of working people's consciousness: one of the working class and the other of an employee, i.e. producer, class. This change compelled labour leaders to change their strategies and tactics. They tried to target their policy and institutional proposals at broader social strata — unorganized and deorganized (i.e. those formally organized but actually losing union identity) — who tended to be deserters from politics. So far, as they acknowledged, they had failed to come up with an appealing vision and policy framework, but the process was just beginning. All these changes under way in Japan's domestic system were directly and indirectly affected by the changes in the global political economy. Furthermore, the findings of the current survey indicate that it is inevitable that the sensitivity of domestic changes to international changes will increase.

Under these circumstances, neo-mercantilism will become increasingly difficult to sustain, ultimately because of the multiple cleavages emerging within the social support base of the ruling coalition. The highly competitive globalized industries and firms have come to view the state's intervention in the marketplace, instituted initially to protect domestic industries, as an obstacle rather than a benefit for their own growth. To avoid retaliation by foreign governments in the countries to which they export their goods or in which they invest their funds, they are now vocally demanding the dismantling of the protective walls erected for the non-competitive sectors of the economy — agriculture and small and medium businesses. Though consumers have been rather complacent in the past, they are quickly learning the benefits of deregulation through the remarkable 'price destruction' movement caused by the influx of cheap imported goods. Their priorities are also changing as the economy has matured, and they now demand the restructuring of the producer-oriented system into a consumer-oriented one. The forces against the neo-mercantilist system will further gather momentum as the consequences of the political realignment, and competition targeting the huge group of wage-earners, who now identify themselves as consumers rather than as employees of producers, will become more visible through elections under the new electoral system.

Yet, after all the dust has settled, it is still possible that the final outcome of the current political upheaval will be a restoration of the old triangle, with a more rigid hierarchy and greater concentration, rather than divisions and fragmentation of power within the business community. This possibility is not unrealistic if the global economy is moving in the direction toward managed trade and autarchic bloc economies. Such a course of action may in fact be one of the easiest ones for democratic governments in the more advanced, mature economies to take, under the ever-intensifying political pressure to defend domestic jobs from imports and immigrants from the younger economies. This offensive–defensive relationship applies not only between today's advanced industrial economies and the newly industrializing economies (NIEs), but also between tomorrow's mature, older NIEs and younger NIEs, and hence the cycle may well gather momentum in the future. This scenario was not explicitly mentioned by any of our respondents, but it was implied by many as in the use of the frog metaphor in reference to Japan.

# References

Allinson, G. D. and Sone, Y. (1993), *Political Dynamics in Contemporary Japan*, Ithaca: Cornell University Press.

Gourevitch, P. (1978), 'The Second Image Reversed: The International Sources of Domestic Politics', *International Organization*, 32(4).

Harari, E. (1996), 'Japanese Labor Organization and Public Policy', *Social Science Japan* (February).

Ishida, T. (1961a), *Sengo Nihon no Seiji-taisei* (The political system of postwar Japan), Tokyo: Mirai-sha.

Ishida, T. (1961b), *Gendai Soshiki-ron* (On modern organizations), Tokyo: Iwanami Shoten.

Ishizuka, M. (1995), 'Political Games: Flips, Flops and a Shock', *Nikkei Weekly*, 2 January.

Iwami, T. (1995), *Meiso Kenryoku* (Power running astray), Tokyo: Asahi Sonorama.

Johnson, C. (1986), *MITI and the Japanese Miracle*, Tokyo: Charles E. Tuttle.

Kato, H. (1995), 'Rengo Loses Footing in Shifting Landscape', *Nikkei Weekly*, 17 July.

Katzenstein, P. (1978), 'Conclusion: Domestic Structures and Strategies of Foreign Economic Policy', in his *Between Power and Plenty: Foreign Economic Policies of Advanced Industrial States*, University of Wisconsin Press, pp. 195–336; reprinted in R. Rogowski (ed.), *Comparative Politics and the International Political Economy*, Vol. 2, Aldershot, Hants: Edward Elgar, pp. 376–417.

Kume, I. (1993), 'A Tale of Twin Industries: Labour Accommodation in the Private Sector', in Allinson and Sone (1993).

Masumi, J. (1969), *Gendai Nihon no Deiji Taisei* (The political system of contemporary Japan), Tokyo: Iwanami Shoten.

McKean, M. A. (1993), 'State Strength and the Public Interest', in Allinson and Sone (1993).

McNamara, D. (1996), 'Corporatism and Cooperation among Japanese Labor', *Comparative Politics*, 28(4).

Misawa, S. (1967), 'Seisaku Ketteikatei no Gaikan' (An overview of the policy-making process), in Nihon Seiji Gakkai (ed.), *Nenpo Seijigaku 1967: Gendainihon no Seito to Kanryo*, Tokyo: Iwanami Shoten.

Miyamoto, M. (1993), *Oyakusho no Okite* (Rules of red-tapism), Tokyo: Kodansha.

Nakano, M. (1996), 'The Changing Legislative Process in the Age of Party Realignment', *Leviathan*, 18, special issue: 'Main Actors of Japanese Politics' (Spring).

Namiki, N. (1995), *Nihon Shakai no Yuchaku Kozo* (The collusive structure of Japanese society), Tokyo: Sandoke shuppankyoku.

Noguchi, Y. (1995), 'Wartime System Still Has Impact on Economy', *Nikkei Weekly*, 16 January.

Pempel, T. J. and Tsunenaka, K. (1979), 'Corporatism without Labor? The Japanese Anomaly', in P. C. Schmitter and G. Lehmbruch (eds.), *Trends toward Corporatist Intermediation*, Beverly Hills, Cal.: Sage.

Rosenbluth, F. M. (1996), 'Internationalization and Electoral Politics', in R. O. Keohane and H. V. Milner (eds.), *Internationalization and Domestic Politics*, New York: Cambridge University Press.

Sakaiya, T. (1994), 'The Localization of Japan: A Decrease in Intellectual Interest', *Nikkei Weekly*, 13 December.

Sakaiya, T. (1995), *Taihen na Jidai* (The age of anxiety), Tokyo: Kodansha.

Sone, Y. (1993), 'Conclusion', in Allinson and Sone (1993).

Sullivan, K. (1996), 'Health Minister a Tonic to Apathy? Japanese are Battling Bureaucracy and Winning People's Support', *Washington Post*, 10 July.

Taguchi, F. (1969), *Shakai-shudan no Seiji Kino* (The political functions of the social groups), Tokyo: Mirai-sha.

Tawara, S. (1995), *Henkaku no Jidai wo Kiritoru Hasso* (A perspective to analyse the age of reform), Tokyo: Bungei Shunju-sha.

Tsuji, K. (1969), *Shin-pan Nihon Kan-ryo-sei no Kenkyu* (Study of the Japanese bureaucracy), rev. edn, Tokyo University Press; first published 1952.

Tsujinaka, Y. (1993), 'Rengo and its Osmotic Networks', in Allinson and Sone (1993).

van Wolferen, K. (1990), *The Enigma of Japanese Power*, New York: Vintage Books.

Wakiyama, T. (1994), *Kanryo ga Kaita Kanryo Kaikaku* (Bureaucratic reform written by a bureaucrat), Tokyo: Sanno Daigaku Shuppankai.

Yamagishi, A. (1995), *'Renritsu' Shikakenin* (The 'coalition' fixer), Tokyo: Kodansha, chapters 1–2.

# 12

# JAPAN'S APPROACH TO GENDER AND DEVELOPMENT

## PLURALITY IN DEVELOPMENT COOPERATION POLICY AND PRACTICE

### Satoko Kurata

## 1

### Introduction

Japan is one of the world's largest donors in the field of international development assistance. In 1994, official development assistance (ODA) amounted to some $13 billion dollars. Over 150 countries/regions are recipients of Japan's ODA (Ministry of Foreign Affairs 1995, pp. 1–2).

Japanese ODA is implemented by the Ministry of Foreign Affairs and two government agencies for international development. The Ministry of Foreign Affairs sets the policy framework and implements the major part of grant aid, including contributions to multilateral organizations. Bilateral loans are handled by the Overseas Economic Cooperation Fund (OECF), and the major portion of bilateral grants (technical cooperation and a part of grant aid) is undertaken by the Japan International Cooperation Agency (JICA). Other ministries, such as the Ministry of International Trade and Industry, the Ministry of Agriculture, Forestry and Fisheries and the Ministry of Education, Culture, Science and Sports, are also allocated ODA budgets.

One of the policy approaches of the Japanese government towards ODA is to respond to the 'new' agendas of international development as discussed in the 1990s. These agendas, called 'global issues', focus not on the economic development of a nation, which Japan's ODA was traditionally aimed at, but transcend national boundaries, involving more than one country. The report of the Ministry of Foreign Affairs includes an appeal that the government respond to the diversified demand for aid in environmental protection, population control and AIDS, children's health and Women in Development (WID) (Ministry of Foreign Affairs 1995, pp. 12–14).

The first version of this paper was published in the *Journal of Asian Women's Studies*, Vol. 5, 1996.

In this paper, I would like to analyse Japan's approach to Gender and Development in its ODA, focusing on two government agencies for international development: the OECF and the JICA. How has the 'new' agenda of WID been integrated into Japan's ODA, and where is it heading? I will describe the complex dynamics of integrating gender issues in Japan's ODA: WID and GAD (Gender and Development), external pressures and domestic promotion, international development and domestic policy.[1] I will then discuss Japan's approach to Gender and Development from the viewpoint of postmodern feminism, focusing on the unique geographical and historical position of Japan. With reference to the further development of the postmodern feminist discussion on diversity and universalism, I shall focus on the case of Japan.

# 2

## The ODA's Adoption of WID

### Background

Women in Development is a new agenda for Japan's ODA. Until the late 1980s, gender issues had not received much attention in ODA. While the Development Assistance Committee (DAC) of the Organization for Economic Cooperation and Development (OECD) had adopted 'WID Guiding Principles' in 1983, no major action had been taken by the Japanese government in regard to WID, except that an officer in charge of WID was appointed at the Overseas Economic Cooperation Fund (OECF) in 1987. Japan started taking WID into its ODA policies in the late 1980s as a result of external pressure.

In 1989, Japan was selected as a bureau member of the DAC Expert Group on WID. Then the WID Steering Committee was formulated in the Ministry of Foreign Affairs to promote WID considerations in economic development programmes so as to secure the approval of DAC. In the same year, the DAC Expert Group on WID adopted the revised version of WID Guiding Principles, which urged member-countries to take action to integrate and operationalize WID in their official development aid. The guiding principle incorporated a firm statement that all development organizations that did not have such guidelines and procedures should formulate them immediately. Moreover, it mandated that member-countries should regularly report their achievements in realizing the guiding principles.

The pressure from DAC pushed Japan to formulate policy and institutional arrangements immediately. In 1990 the Study Group on Development Assistance for Women in Development was established at the Japan International Cooperation Agency (JICA), with scholars outside the organization invited to participate. In 1991, on the basis of a recommendation by the Study Group, the Environment, WID and Other Global Issues Division was established at JICA. Meanwhile, the

---

[1] The concept of the Gender and Development (GAD) approach is that it is necessary to look at the gender relations between men and women and to aim to achieve equality through the development and improvement of the gender relationship. It is different from the WID approach, which focuses mainly on the urgent needs of women and does not directly question gender relations between men and women.

OECF had formulated guidelines for the consideration of WID, which were the first comprehensive guiding principles in Japan to be applied in all OECF projects.

Then WID was included in national policies on both official development assistance and women. In 1991 the first revision of the New National Plan for Action, Japan's national policy on women, included 'the promotion of Women in Development'. In 1992 the Official Development Assistance Charter which the cabinet approved stated that the Japanese government would pay considerable attention to the integration of women as participants and beneficiaries of development in order to enhance the effectiveness of ODA.

After that, the integration of WID in institutional arrangements and activities accelerated. In 1992 the Ministry of Foreign Affairs appointed officers in charge of WID in Japanese embassies overseas in order to promote WID-related project finding and implementation. A WID training course for Japanese participants was established, along with seminars inviting foreign WID experts from both North and South. Research projects on WID were also started. In 1993 a section in charge of WID (the Environment and Social Development Section) was established at OECF. JICA published a WID manual that consisted of guidelines and checklists for technical cooperation projects and development surveys. JICA technical training programmes began to expand; some courses were reformed or renamed to include the WID viewpoint. These activities were carried out not only by the Ministry of Foreign Affairs, JICA and OECF, but also by other ministries and organizations.[2] WID-related projects in various kinds of development activities are shown in Figure 1.

**Figure 1** Examples of WID-related Projects in Japan's ODA
WID Criterion: Projects that are Primarily for Local Women (as Beneficiaries or Participants)

---

**WID-related projects I (examples)**

---

**<General grant aid>**
- Project for the Establishment of an Agricultural Training Centre for Women, 1985, Bangladesh (construction of a training centre for rural women in the suburbs of Dhaka, where training is conducted by a Japanese NGO)
- Project for the improvement of facilities of vocational training centres for women, 1989, Philippines (provision of training equipment for ceramics, sewing and toy production to vocational training centres throughout the Philippines)
- Project for the improvement of the High Institute of Nursing, Cairo University,

**<Subsidy system for NGO projects>**
- Vietnam, 1993 (organization: Association to Aid the Refugees), vocational training, such as dressmaking, for 100 women at the Home for the Hearing- and Speech-Impaired
- Thailand, 1993 (organization: Japan Sotoshu Relief Committee), instruction in sewing skills for women living in slum districts
- Bangladesh, 1993 (organization: International Angel Association), provision

---

[2] For example, the Ministry of Labour, the Prime Minister's Office work with JICA for JICA's technical training programme for overseas participants, the National Women's Education Centre's series of international seminars on WID, and women's centres that are funded by municipal governments all work with JICA in co-sponsoring symposia and technical training programmes.

1991–3, Egypt (upgrading of nursing training facilities followed by provision of technical cooperation)

**<Grant assistance for grass-roots projects>**
- DEP vocational training 1993, Thailand (organization: Daughters Education Programme), training for disadvantaged young women aged 7–18 in northern Thailand
- Language Training Workshop Plan of International Liaison Dept, 1993, China (organization: All-China Women's Federation), preparation and support for the World Conference on Women
- Self-reliance for Women of Gedo Region, 1993, Somalia (organization: International Rescue Committee, INC), reconstruction of women's centre

of equipment and training material to vocational training centres that aim at promoting women's independence

**<Loan assistance>**
- Small-scale Industries Programme, 1993, India: promotion of women's participation in business through schemes aimed at fostering credit for female entrepreneurs
- Human Settlement Improvement Project for Urban Areas, 1993, Indonesia: alleviation of women's work in securing safe water

---

**WID-related projects II (fiscal year 1993 examples)**

---

**<Project-type technical cooperation>**
- Rural Livelihood Generation Project, Philippines, project to improve the livelihood of disadvantaged women

- Social Forestry Training Project, Kenya, women's participation in aforestation activities

**<Group training courses in Japan>**

- Seminar on Statistics and Indicators on Women, 8 persons: improvement of gender-based statistical data which form the basis of WID policies
- Seminar on Women's Issues in National Machinery, 15 persons: improvement of headquarters of agencies that deal with women's issues

**<Dispatch of experts>**
- Women's Development, Pakistan, advice etc. to the Ministry of Women and Youth Affairs
- Women's Information System and Network, Ghana, Guidance on WID-related data processing systems

**<Development surveys>**
- The Study on Groundwater Development for Champasak and Satavan Province, Laos: survey on the role of women in general life, water use and hygiene
- Master Plan Study on the Integrated Agricultural and Rural Development Project in the Suburbs of Phnom Penh, Cambodia: local survey on women who play a pivotal role in agriculture

**<Dispatch of Japan Overseas Cooperation Volunteers (JOCV)>**
- Bangladesh, 54 persons: nursing, public health nursing, clinical examination, home arts, dressmaking, handicrafts, and vegetable growing
- Bolivia, 31 persons: nursery teachers, midwifery, public health nursing, clinical examination, home arts, nursing and physical therapy

---

*Source: Women in Development: Women — The Driving Force of Development* (brochure), Ministry of Foreign Affairs, 1994, pp. 2–3.

---

## *Rationalizing the Adoption of WID*

How then did the Japanese government rationalize WID as a 'new' agenda? In the early 1990s, when Japan was first pressured to take serious action by DAC, the government referred to the integration of WID into its policy area as an 'international trend'. This reflects the fact that the Japanese government accepted it as a requirement of DAC rather than as a self-acknowledgement of the significance of WID.[3]

Today WID is rationalized first as a 'global issue', which is a new policy challenge of Japan's ODA. WID, along with the environment, poverty, population, AIDS, refugees, human rights and education, are issues that cross national and sectoral boundaries in a way that a conventional development approach was unable to bring about (JICA 1995c, p. 1).[4] Its implication is similar to that of 'international trends'.

Second, WID is rationalized as a means to achieve greater efficiency and effectiveness in ODA (Ministry of Foreign Affairs 1995, p. 15). As the role of women in economic and social development has been emphasized, WID has become a key to achieving greater efficiency and sustainability of development projects. This is because WID makes us see women not merely as beneficiaries but also as active agents. This concept is especially useful for WID-integrated programmes, for instance large economic infrastructure building projects funded by loans. This rationale reflects the concept of the efficiency approach that Moser categorized, which has been popular among donor organizations (Moser 1993).

Third, WID is rationalized as being part of the participatory approach, particularly in JICA, which initiated research projects on unconventional issues of development agendas such as poverty, education and participatory development. The JICA Study Group on Women in Development stated that substantial recognition and integration of WID was necessary in Japan's development aid, because participation of members of a society, regardless of gender, at every stage of development, is critical for their struggle to achieve economic and social self-reliance. It is for this reason that 'development' should mean human-centred socio-economic development, not just economic development (JICA 1991).

The first rationale of 'global issues' is a political rationale, and the second is an operational rationale. However, the third rationale, linked to 'people-oriented development', indicates a significant change in Japan's approach in ODA. In this way, WID in Japan's ODA today is rationalized at a number of levels of development practice, not merely as an outcome of international donor politics. It even encourages the exploration of alternative goals of development.

---

[3] OECF (1991, p. 1) and Oda (1992, pp. 88–9). Oda describes the details of the early period of Japan's ODA and WID with her analysis on why Japan's consideration of gender in development was delayed.

[4] The conventional approach to Japan's ODA is to support the economic and industrial development of a nation by loans and grants to building facilities, technology transfer and human resources development, while basic human needs are also taken into consideration for the least developed countries (Ministry of Foreign Affairs 1995, pp. 11–12). Therefore the approach is by industrial sector, e.g. agriculture, fishery, engineering.

## WID Concept from Abroad

As earlier research had discovered, the adoption of WID was externally driven (Oda 1992). It was the outcome not only of international donor politics but also of a lack of domestic momentum to insist on the necessity of WID, arising from a lack of coordination between development and gender issues in both government and non-governmental sectors.

Even before the formal incorporation of WID into Japan's ODA programmes, there were both technical cooperation projects in such fields as maternal and child health and nurse education, and training courses such as seminars on public administration for women. Japanese national policy on women had also called for the inclusion of women in Japan's technical cooperation activities. However, except for a few cases, most of the programmes had no WID perspective, perceiving women as beneficiaries of welfaristic programmes, rather than active participants (JICA 1991, p. 191).

It is true that DAC of OECD put significant pressure on the Japanese government to incorporate WID in its ODA. What action, then, had domestic actors taken in order to incorporate WID into Japan's development activities?

The adoption by Japan of the UN Nairobi Conference's Forward-Looking Strategies for the Advancement of Women marked a significant step for the government to take following the international trend towards gender equality. However, Japanese development organizations were not aware of or responsive to this worldwide trend and movement. The Japanese national policy on women was not able to establish a strong coalition with development organizations (Taguchi 1994, p. 213).

On the other hand, non-governmental organizations (NGOs) did not move to incorporate WID, and therefore they had little influence on the government. Since the Second World Women's Conference in Nairobi in 1985, some equality-oriented Japanese women's organizations have become aware of WID issues (Meguro 1992, p. 107). However, according to Yayori Matsui, a journalist who leads an NGO that networks with Asian women, most Japanese women's organizations were not aware of WID, and expressed little concern about development issues. Nor did development NGOs, which increased in the 1980s, pay enough attention to gender issues (Matsui 1995, p. 5).[5] Therefore, the separation of development issues and gender issues in both governmental and non-governmental served to keep Japan unaware of WID issues.

---

[5] Yoshida, a member of the NGO that Matsui led, conducted a survey of development NGOs in 1990 and reported that even if there were a few differentiated approaches for women in Muslim countries, there was no common recognition on women's issues in the NGO community. Moreover, many of her informants were puzzled to be asked questions about 'women'. She asserted the fact that in Japanese society women have less voice and people are less aware of the issue has a lot to do with the delay of incorporation of WID in Japan (Yoshida 1990, p. 12). Matsui adds the male domination of Japanese society and small numbers of female staff in ODA organizations are other factors that have hindered Japan's adoption of WID (Matsui 1995).

# 3

## Adopting WID and GAD

How, then, has Japan's ODA incorporated WID into its activities? Since taking women/gender into consideration was new to the ODA community (and to the NGO community), how did the actors in the ODA community respond to the externally imposed and unconventional agenda? How did they react to the concept of GAD? The response to the incorporation of WID/GAD into two major ODA organizations varied.

## *OECF*

The OECF quickly responded to the pronouncement of DAC. In 1991 it published the OECF Guidelines of Women in Development Consideration. These guidelines rationalize WID as an international trend, and list perspectives of WID for consideration by industrial sector. These WID perspectives are to be applied to feasibility examination, monitoring and evaluation of the projects that OECF finances. The organization also pays attention to WID-specific projects that would enhance the well-being and advancement of women in society. The checkpoints, which apply to all sectors, are rather vague, rather than specific: (1) to determine the role of women in each industrial sector/region; (2) to evaluate the role of women in the project and impact of the project on women in project implementation; (3) to determine the benefit to women of each project; (4) to take women's opinions into consideration.

However, the WID officer realized the gap between the OECF's understanding of WID and that of DAC when she attended a meeting of the DAC Expert Group on Women in Development. The OECF understood that WID entailed mainly the inclusion of women among ODA beneficiaries, whereas for the DAC women's participation in the decision-making process was critical. At the same time, the OECF WID officer found that the ultimate goal of 'WID consideration' in development by DAC was to achieve equality between men and women in society, which was a reflection of what Western member-countries had been achieving. This meaning of WID seemed particularly inapplicable to the large economic infrastructure projects that OECF was financing because the beneficiaries were the mass public, which included women. This created confusion and a dilemma for them.[6]

The OECF WID officer did not immediately agree with the DAC's interpretation of WID. To her, it was a reflection of the Western model, and she could not find such a root in Japanese society. Therefore she felt that it was the WID concept itself and not the DAC application of WID that was sensitive to the tradition and history of a client country and should be applied to developing countries (Taguchi 1993a, p. 201).

However, the WID officer was gradually exposed to the concept of GAD and of social analysis through her investigation of other donors and the Asian Development

---

[6] To the OECF, it seemed 'unreasonable' to take women into consideration in such fields as water supply, because (1) the impact on men and women could be estimated equal, (2) women would benefit without taking part in the decision-making process of the project (Taguchi 1992b, p. 102).

Bank, in addition to discussions at DAC. Moser's classification of various WID approaches in history also showed the plurality of the concept of WID. This led the WID officer to understand that WID was not just giving women priority, but was focusing on gender as one of the social factors. It was easier for the OECF to understand 'WID' as a part of social impact analysis, unlike a feminist-type assertion of gender equality. Finally, she concluded that increasing the consideration of WID in Japan's ODA has not been done in order to gain a good reputation with the OECD and other donors, but in order to support the independence of the socially underprivileged: therefore efforts should be made at least to minimize the Project's negative impact on them. At the same time, WID is not about the poor developing countries but about the promotion of gender equality in their society. She also called for consciousness raising of OECF staff (Taguchi 1993c).

The OECF experiences structural dilemmas which the WID officer pointed out: it is difficult to promote the participation of women in OECF projects because of (1) the scale (large) and the type (economic infrastructure) of OECF projects; and (2) the limited authority of the OECF to amend a project design when a feasibility study is completed, since the project is designed by the client's government. However, the Environment and Social Development Division of OECF searches for a way to apply the social impact analysis of their projects in addition to conventional economic impact analysis.

As the WID officer has now left the organization, the OECF does not seem to share her understanding about WID. At present, it sympathizes with GAD because it thinks that 'gender' has a neutral meaning, unlike the more political nature of *Women* in Development. It does not agree with, or is less aware of, the political goal of the GAD approach towards gender equality.[7] Therefore, we could say that the OECF's WID (and even GAD) is accepted mainly as a methodological and technical issue of its work procedure, whereas meeting the DAC's requirement on WID is interpreted as 'increasing women beneficiaries', which is a 'political' agenda to the OECF.

## The Japan International Cooperation Agency (JICA)

The JICA too first understood WID as simply aimed at including women among ODA beneficiaries. However, the learning process of WID from other donors and organizations soon made them confront the GAD issues. There are advocates of the GAD approach who played a vital role in exposing JICA to the unconventional and alternative idea of development that GAD internalizes.

### JICA AND WID AT AN EARLY STAGE

The JICA Study Group on Women in Development which was formed in 1990 published the first comprehensive report in Japan on WID issues and policy

---

[7] Interview with an officer in the Environmental and Social Development Division that is in charge of WID issues in OECF; and Nomura (1995). Nomura was the head of Environment and Social Development Division when he wrote the article.

recommendations.[8] The research included studies on the present situation of women in developing countries, the approaches of international organizations and Western donors, and existing WID research. It also analysed the JICA's past approaches in terms of WID. This revealed that the lack of recognition and awareness of gender issues that was commonly seen in Japan's development aid in general prohibited the mainstreaming of WID in JICA; in addition, the structure of the technical cooperation scheme itself hindered the integration of WID in JICA.[9] The study group clearly asserted that the promotion of WID was necessary and urgent for Japan, because Japan had fallen behind in focusing attention on WID compared with other Western donors.

The discourse in the Report of the Study Group issued in 1991 is basically WID-oriented, focusing on women rather than considering the gender relationship, and rationalizing the acceptance of WID as from efficiency and international trends. However, the Report also emphasized women's participation in the development process. Most profoundly, it questioned the conventional development approach, which is applied to large economic development projects and is evaluated only by economic indicators. It asserted that WID implied that development should be people-centred and more socially sensitive, and that this kind of social development should be the ultimate goal of development (JICA 1991, pp. 3–4). In contrast to the OECF's understanding and commitment, the understanding of the JICA Study Group was more deeply involved in the conceptual aspect of WID.

Although the Report is essentially based on traditional WID concepts, there were some actors who intended to go beyond it. The leader of the Study Group, Yoriko Meguro, a sociology professor, after her assignment at the Group wrote that the Report was an outcome of a compromise between two camps: those who acknowledged the reformative meaning of WID, which was the same as GAD, and those who did not understand it. She says that if the Report had issued a more radical statement challenging gender inequality in society, it would have been rejected (Meguro 1992).

After publication of this Report, the learning of WID from other donors was accelerated. Six months later, JICA held an international seminar, inviting four DAC WID experts.[10] Canadian GAD scholars were invited to the WID training course

---

[8] The group made recommendations on JICA's policy, programme and on an institutional arrangement to promote WID, with emphasis on six priority areas (economic participation, education, health and family planning, environmental conservation, institutional strengthening of national machinery and access to information) and four types of approach (policy declaration by the government, differentiated approach based on the diversity of women, multi-sectoral and comprehensive regional development approach, and taking the WID perspective in every process of development).

[9] (1) The technical cooperation that JICA undertakes is based on industrial sectors; therefore, trans-sectoral issues such as WID were set aside. (2) Japan's ODA takes leaders and official institutions as its counterparts, assuming that they take responsibility for diffusing the technology to the population at large; therefore the socially marginalized and those who are outside the formal employment sector, such as women, are excluded. (3) Japan's ODA tended to regard people as a uniform group, and ignored the many variations within them (JICA 1991, pp. 191–2).

[10] At the same time, other institutions, such as the National Women's Education Centre, a municipal government-funded women's centres, held seminars on Women in Development, inviting specialists from Western countries as well as from the South.

for Japanese development practitioners. These Western experts introduced the concept of 'gender', leading to a change of concept from WID and WAD (Women *and* Development) to GAD, to emphasize the importance of the GAD approach which aims to establish an equitable society.

## FROM WID TO GAD

In this way, the GAD concept was introduced into the JICA, while the concept of WID was disseminated. This was a natural consequence of learning from other foreign and international development organizations which had already incorporated GAD into the theoretical framework of their policies. Around 1993, a few years after Japan was first exposed to the concept of WID, the JICA began to include the words and concept of GAD.

In 1992, a cross-institutional research project on 'Gender Analysis in Development Projects' which included experts from both the OECF and the JICA clearly acknowledged 'gender', not 'women', as the research theme, saying that GAD was the latest concept in development approaches in the Western WID discourses.[11] This research intended to adopt a gender analysis method in Japanese ODA projects to aid the integration of 'WID' into every aspect of a development programme, although 'WID' here implied 'GAD'. The report of the research, published in 1993, emphasized the necessity of a comprehensive social analysis of the target society and of gender analysis in every development project. Along with methodological exploration, the research emphasized transformation of the concept of development, from economic/industrial development to people-centred development. To the research team, the adoption of a new methodology of development meant the adoption of a new theory of development.

In 1994 the JICA published the *Manual on Integrating WID Considerations into Development Programs* to teach the JICA staff the basic concept of WID, and how to apply WID considerations into the project cycle. The manual encourages situation analysis to identify gender roles and needs, and women's participation in every project cycle. Although the manual is entitled '*WID*', it is about GAD: it acknowledges the importance of gender roles, gender divisions of labour and the need for change in gender relations, in addition to the statement that the aim of WID is to ensure a more equitable development (JICA 1994a, p. 3). Moreover, the manual suggests the adoption of 'participatory development', which was methodologically and conceptually unconventional to the mainstream of Japan's official development assistance.

The changing trend from WID to GAD was also seen in the research project on the improvement of rural households for women. This project, entitled 'Technical Cooperation towards Upgrading Technical Levels of Rural Women in Developing Countries', which had been started in 1991, began also to focus on GAD in 1993.

---

[11] This research project conducted a study on gender analysis methods in Canada and the USA and a field study on Japanese development projects in Thailand to observe the project from a gender perspective. The project team was a collaboration of scholars, development specialists, consultants and researchers from several organizations, including the JICA and OECF. Foreign scholars and experts were also invited from Canada and the USA.

The research was intended to explore methods of setting up technical cooperation projects to help rural women reduce their heavy household duties through the development and diffusion of appropriate technology. Past Japanese experience with similar campaigns was examined for application in client countries.[12] After a couple of years using the traditional WID perspective, the research started to incline towards GAD. The report of the research, issued in 1994, proposed setting up a Gender-Oriented Rural Development Programme to evaluate the subsistence agriculture that women have been labouring in. It takes a participatory approach, and clearly a GAD perspective.[13] The programme emphasizes a baseline survey applying Rapid Rural Appraisal.

However, the incorporation of GAD in an approach to rural development was not without some complication. The GAD perspective is not consistent in phase II of the research (1994– ) because most of the research project members were agricultural specialists. They understood WID and GAD as technical issues and failed to internalize the GAD perspective, while there were few gender specialists who could have brought a proper GAD perspective into the research. In selecting the research members, more sociologists and gender specialists should have been chosen. However, it was hard to get such specialists in Japan, where there were few researchers in the Gender and Development field.

This research project, several years along, reflects the changing trends of the WID/GAD approach at JICA, although WID has remained as the official terminology. It also shows an uneasy matching of the conventional sectoral perspective with a new development approach, and a lack of human resources in the gender and development field in Japan.

### The Fourth World Women's Conference

It was in this way that Japan's ODA was exposed to WID and GAD. Japanese ODA agencies proved to be more interested in the methodological aspect of GAD. However, the Fourth World Conference on Women, held in Beijing in September 1995, gave a momentum to legitimizing GAD conceptually.

In preparation for the Beijing Conference, the Japanese government set up the National Committee of Japan to prepare for the Fourth World Conference on Women. In dialogue with Japanese NGOs, a meeting was called about Japan's approach to

---

[12] After World War II, Japan was subjected to an agricultural reform and rural life improvement campaign undertaken by the Occupation government as a part of the democratization and development programme. This research reviewed the campaign and the movement (Seikatsu Kaizen Undo), which continued after the Occupation until today. Through the campaign, reforming household equipment, changing diets and institution building for rural women helped decrease women's household burden, and improve the well-being of the family. This was a part of the democratization of the rural community and of gender relations in Japan. At the same time, it contributed to the improvement of agricultural production along with the extension programmes, because when farmers are healthier, agricultural productivity is better. Thus, the effectiveness of the programme of rural life improvement in Japan provided the basis for a WID programme for rural women.

[13] The re-analysis of Japan's rural life improvement campaign after World War II was conducted with a gender perspective, too.

Women in Development. The active discussion included the NGOs' comments such as 'many of the WID projects in the government's list focused on women's reproductive role', or 'the decision of the local people and women should be included in the process of development' (Taguchi 1994, p. 216).

Moreover, for the Beijing Conference, the need to include WID in the ODA development policy was strengthened. In January 1995, WID was included as an addition to the US–Japan Common Agenda, which was the policy of cooperation for development between the two countries (Ministry of Foreign Affairs 1995, p. 255).

On the other hand, the JICA rationalized WID as a move towards 'social reform' in order to achieve gender equality. In its newsletter issued just before the Beijing Conference in August 1995, a special issue on 'Women in Development', the headline was 'Improving the Socio-Economic Status of Women', and the articles never indicated that WID was a global issue directed towards achieving greater effectiveness and efficiency: rather, it was emphasized that JICA's activities were committed to promoting the empowerment of women.

At the Conference, the Japanese government announced the 'WID Initiative', the policy of Japan's WID effort in ODA. It said that development assistance could contribute towards the achievement of balanced and sustainable development, facilitate the empowerment of women, and aid the closing of gender disparity in developing countries. In order to achieve those goals, Japan was going to give priority to three fields: (1) education, health, and economic and social participation; (2) ensuring reproductive rights and the well-being of both men and women; and (3) realizing women's full potential and aiding their efforts towards gaining independence. Moreover, it even declared that its goal was to assist developing countries' efforts towards legal and institutional reform, and consciousness raising. This strong appeal is intended to support structural change in gender relations in society, which is similar to the concept of GAD.

The statements by both the Japanese government and JICA were orientated towards gender equality and the achievement of structural change in the recipient society. This is quite different from the routine WID discourse in ODA, reflecting the objectives and the audience of the Conference, where feminist thought dominated. In this context, GAD was seen as a token for the epoch-making occasion when all the world was watching; but it is more than a token, because the policy statement could give a certain direction for ODA programme implementation.

# 4

## The Plurality of Approaches for Gender and Development in Japan's ODA

As we have seen, Japan has incorporated GAD into its development approach in the process of adopting and learning about Women in Development. However, this does not mean that WID has been completely replaced by GAD. Officially, Japan's ODA uses the terminology and concept of WID, while GAD is merely included. This plurality of WID and GAD in Japan's ODA indicates the complexity of the trends and actors in Japan.

First, among the organizations implementing ODA, the emphasis on WID or GAD varies according to the organization. The Ministry of Foreign Affairs, which is in charge of Japan's ODA policy, carries WID as an official policy. The main actors, such as the development agencies (OECF and JICA), declare WID as their policy too. In their WID implementation, they are more concerned about women as beneficiaries than about women as participants in the decision-making process. This differs from the concern of DAC, which is more interested in the degree of women's participation in the decision-making process (Nomura 1995, p. 236). On the other hand, other organizations, such as the National Women's Education Centre and the Office for Gender Equality of the Prime Minister's Office (although the portion of their ODA activities, e.g. organizing seminars, research and training courses for participants from developing countries, is small), are more concerned about GAD as a means to achieve gender equality. In other words, as an official development aid that is a part of Japan's international politics, Japan supports WID, while as a national policy for women (or gender,) it is more supportive of GAD.

Second, even within the main ODA organizations, the response to WID and GAD varies: the OECF is reluctant to accept GAD unless it implies social analysis of the target population, or in the sense that 'gender' of GAD means 'not concerning only women', even though what DAC expects in WID is in fact 'GAD'.[14] On the other hand, the JICA is interested in the conceptual aspect of GAD in addition to GAD as a method of social analysis. The factor that has made a difference between the two organizations is their role and scheme in development activities. Technical cooperation such as grant aid gives the donor more room for commitment and control/autonomy, whereas the financing of loans gives the donor more limited commitment and control over the design and implementation of the projects, since the client has the basic control, compared with the technical cooperation scheme. The participatory approach of GAD is considered difficult to suit large economic infrastructure projects funded by loans, unless the client is in support of it.[15] However, it is common for both OECF and JICA to face the dilemma of operationalizing GAD, as is also the case with other donors.

As Rathgeber and Parpart point out, the transformative goal of GAD is considered threatening, intervening in the client's sovereign rights over their people, culture and society (Rathgeber 1995; Parpart 1995). In particular, the ultimate goal of transforming gender relationships in a client's society is not considered a suitable agenda for development financial assistance.[16] It is true that ODA institutions are strictly tied to government policies (Rathgeber 1995, p. 207). Development in ODA is a part of diplomacy.

However, there are some individuals in Japan who have been making an effort to incorporate GAD in a manner that accords with its political nature, which is also similar to what Rathgeber found in many other agencies (Rathgeber 1995,

---

[14] Interview with an officer of the Environment and Social Development Section of the OECF. The officer approves GAD when 'gender' is a neutral notion, unlike WID, which always concerns just women.

[15] Not only the scale and type of the project, but also the mechanism of project implementation hinders the intentional commitment of the donor. The OECF feels a limitation of its commitment to the project, since it is subject to the client's government/organizations' intention (Nomura 1995, p. 236).

[16] Interview with an officer of the Environment and Social Development Section, OECF.

p. 211). Those who took part in the research team on Gender Analysis of Development research projects in 1992, as well as in the JICA's Study Group on WID in 1990, have been playing a key role in promoting GAD instead of WID.[17] They have recognized and agreed that the issue of 'Women in Development' is in fact 'Gender and Development'. Therefore the incorporation of GAD is not just an outcome of the study process of forerunners, promoted by external pressure, but the intentional adoption of it. The Fourth World Conference on Women, along with the domestic movement of the government and NGOs, contributed to the legitimization of GAD within Japan.

However, the GAD advocators are careful about their strategy. One of them has said that, although she personally does not agree with the rationale of WID as an efficiency and global issue, she uses that rationale as a rhetoric to persuade others. Also, she can take advantage of the external pressure that the 'global issue' logic has. She uses 'WID' even though what she talks about is GAD, in order to avoid unnecessary conflict with more conservative people (most of whom are male) in her organization where feminist discourse is not welcome. Therefore, ODA's policy statement remains 'WID' at both the national and organizational level, but there are some practitioners and researchers of development in and around the development organizations who are in fact pursuing GAD.

Fourth, WID in Japan's ODA is not only an international policy mandate, but also an impact that engendered consciousness about gender issues in development in Japan. The adoption of WID and the learning of GAD gave impact to the formation of a policy for women at the national level. The item of 'international cooperation' in the policy caused a qualitative change to WID, from merely including women in Japan's international technical cooperation. The revised national policy on women played a guiding role in NGOs and local governments which have started to be interested in WID issues (Meguro 1992, p. 108). Through the seminars and symposia held by the National Women's Education Centre and local women's organizations, more members of the public have been exposed to WID issues, and consciousness about WID issues has increased. Thus, international development policy and national gender policy are connected.

Furthermore, learning about WID caused both NGOs and officers in ODA agencies to realize that the gender issues in Japan and gender issues in development are connected, and not two separate agendas, since the delay of Japan's adoption of WID reflects the gender situation in Japan. It is meaningful that female actors in development organizations and NGOs realize the necessity to examine their own society when they work with Third World women.

Finally, along with the world conferences of population (1994 in Cairo) and social development (1995 in Copenhagen), WID/GAD issues encouraging a human-centred, participatory type of development have gained more attention in Japan.

---

[17] Interview with a consultant who also was the head of the Women and Development Group of the Japan Development Study Association. The key persons include scholars/researchers of anthropology, sociology, JICA development experts and private consultants. These people's theoretical background as scholars/researchers, or their previous work experience with international organizations, is thought to contribute to their interpretation of WID as GAD.

# 5

## Postmodern Feminism, Gender and Development in Japan

Postmodern feminism questions the hierarchical relations between North and South (or West and non-West) within women and within WID/GAD discourses. How, then, can we perceive Japan's approach to gender and development issues through the postmodern feminist perspective, given Japan's unique position as a non-Western nation of the North which used to be a nation of the South?[18,19] An analysis of Japan's approach to gender and development issues will give a new perspective to postmodern feminists' discussion on gender and development.

## *The Postmodern Feminist Critique of the WID/GAD Issue*

Although WID and GAD today represent the mainstream feminist approach to development, postmodern feminists have questioned these approaches from the perspective of postmodernism. Postmodern feminism, which originates mainly in the writings of women-of-colour feminism in the First World and Third World feminism, criticizes the racism and Northern universalism that is embedded in WID discourses. Northern universalism is the imposed assumption that the development model should be the one that Northern countries have achieved; therefore a linear development model called 'modernization', based on the devaluation of the local culture, is what the Third World should adopt.

From the postmodern feminists' perspective, WID feminists in the North (and WID feminists in the South who were educated in the North) ignore the diversity among women; they stereotype Third World women as 'others' who are vulnerable and powerless, and imply that First World women are modern, educated, sexually liberated, and thus provide the answer to the 'problems' of the Third World women. WID discourses therefore undervalue the indigenous cultures and techniques of these women (Parpart and Marchand 1995, p. 7; Parpart 1995).

There is a postmodern feminist critique not only of WID but also of the GAD approach. Although some believe that the GAD approach provides a space for a deeper understanding of Third World women's lives, others criticize its modernist tendencies (Parpart and Marchand 1995, p. 16). GAD also stereotypes Third World women as the vulnerable oppressed, for whom Northern expertise is required to solve the problem; thus it is not successful in integrating indigenous voices into its theoretical formulation (Parpart 1995). For these reasons, postmodern feminists call for the recognition of diversity within women, for a careful examination of women's multiple identities according to race, class, age and culture that are shaped

---

[18] I will use the term 'gender and development' for general discussions about gender issues in development, including both WID and GAD discussions.

[19] 'Japan being a country of the South' here refers to the fact that Japan was a country targeted as a potential colony to provide resources and markets for the Western imperial nations in the nineteenth century when the Western imperial nations pressured Japan to 'open' the country. Afterwards, Japan had turned into a country of 'the North', pursuing colonies overseas in the period of world imperialism.

by their specific historical, spatial and social context, and for subjugated voices and knowledge to be valued (Parpart and Marchand 1995).

## Culture, Stereotype and the Diversity of Women in Japan's Gender and Development Discourses

How does Japan's approach to gender and development in the ODA deal with these postmodern feminist questions about stereotypes, culture and diversity within women? Does Japan, as a country of the North, take the same approach as other Western donors, or does it take a different approach by acknowledging the value of local knowledge and culture, and of diversity within women?

There has been a discussion of culture, of the stereotyping of women in client countries, and of WID/GAD approaches in Japan. For example, the Report of the JICA Study Group on WID, which provided the basis for WID policy in JICA, warns of the negative stereotypes of Third World women imposed by WID information:

> information about 'Women in Development' should not only focus on the 'tragic' situation of women in developing countries, but should also enhance our understanding of the importance of women's various roles in socio-economic development, as well as the necessity for economic development to improve the status of women. (JICA 1991, p. 30) (English translation by the author)

The Report also emphasized that we should not perceive the situation of developing countries as a subject for assistance, something independent from our daily life. It suggested paying attention to the relationship between Japan and the client countries, as well as to the clients' own efforts of development.

This Study Group on WID acknowledges the diversity within women. Its Report states that:

> Women in developing countries tend to be perceived as a uniform group; but it is necessary to take a differentiated approach by region with regard to their specific characteristics. At that time, it is important to find out ways to increase women's participation in development by considering socio-cultural factors that prevent women from participating in development. (JICA 1991, p. 14) (English translation by the author)

> Women's values and needs vary by culture, religion, country, region and often social and economic factors; by no means are they uniform. Japan is promoting WID activities while combining aid programmes in various fields, and giving consideration to the special characteristics of women in their specific situations. (JICA 1995a, p. 9)

> On the other hand, we should be careful not to destroy women's unique culture and values through rapid modernization resulting from development aid. It is important to search for ways for women to carry out development without losing their dignity in the community. (JICA 1991, p. 14) (English translation by the author)

The last description discusses local culture, value systems and 'modernization'. The concrete meaning of the last statement is not clear, since there is no further discussion about these issues. However, it is explicitly clear that the JICA study group on WID recognizes the diversity within women in the client countries.

The research on rural household improvement carried out by JICA also refers to cultural issues; in particular, field research on this project has emphasized detailed investigation, because it found that diverse gender roles and relationships were deeply rooted in every local culture. It was important to determine the regional differences of the target population.

At the same time, the research also suggested that the Japanese technical experts working on the rural household improvement projects should value local technology and skills, take advantage of them, and improve them. This statement is not culturally imperialistic, since it respects indigenous knowledge. There is a recognition in the research that forcing Japanese technology and culture on to the counterparts should be avoided.

In development discourses in Japan, local culture, especially indigenous knowledge and technology, is generally perceived as a useful resource. Such knowledge and technology are respected on a practical basis: transferred technology can be embedded in the local knowledge and local technology. Taking advantage of local knowledge and technology therefore is a key to achieving a successful technical transfer.[20]

From these statements, Japan's approach seems to be consistent with postmodern feminism. However, the acknowledgement of diversity is recognized as 'differences', rather than as a multiple axis of structural inequality. Differences are important when attempting to identify the needs of the clients, which are closely connected to development project performance. Also, local culture is valued for its practical, methodological pursuit of a maximum outcome for development input, rather than a theoretical approach. The discussion in Japan over diversity and local culture questions neither the power relationship within the target population, nor that between the donor (Japan) and the clients in the Third World. The warning about negatively stereotyping women in client countries is a very important one for practitioners, as is the need to understand these countries' relationship with Japan, which is also mentioned in the Report of the JICA Study Group on WID (JICA 1991, p. 30). Unfortunately, however, these discussions are not further developed in the Report itself, nor in ODA discourses on WID afterwards.

Moreover, acknowledgement and respect for local culture implies a reluctance to accept the political demands of the feminist approach in development, compounded by the fact that in Japan national policy and activism towards gender equality used to be unconnected with official development assistance policy and activities. A Japanese applied anthropologist is sceptical about the feminist approach for women in development, reserving most scepticism for the GAD approach. Yoshiko Taniguchi questioned the issue of culture and the WID/GAD approach in her 1994 paper. She

---

[20] For example, discussions in the newsletters and magazines of Japan Overseas Cooperation Volunteers (JOCVs) often refer to the conflicts with local customs and cultures. Their activities are usually individually performed at the grass-roots level in the local community, unlike these of other ODA project teams. Therefore, how they cope with the local culture when trying to transfer their skills and technology to their counterparts is a critical issue. When they face rejection, or a lack of interest from the local people, they need to stop forcing their way of thinking and their value system on them, and to try to understand and respect the local culture. Then they can often find a solution which takes advantage of existing local skills and customs.

criticized the uniform nature of the WID/GAD approach to local women, insisting that donors have no right to impose their thinking without regard to the underlying patterns of historically based local customs. She asserts that self-determination and a long-term commitment to communication is necessary if donors are to support the change of the social structure (Taniguchi 1994, pp. 30–2).

It seems that Taniguchi shares a point of view with postmodern feminists. However, her discussion is based on her non-feminist resistance to the political nature of the notion of 'collective empowerment', practical questions on the reliability of rapid appraisals of development, and an optimism towards the survey methodology among gender and development people. Her reservations towards the political nature of the GAD approach may represent a general attitude towards the GAD approach in the Japanese development community, as discussed above. This reservation can be seen not only as resistance to the feminist approach in development, but also as a reflection of Japan's embarrassment about the Western pressure to take WID/GAD approaches, one that sympathizes with the standpoint of the Third World clients of Western donors.

## Japan's Identity and Approach to Gender and Development, from the Postmodern Feminist View

In this sense, Japan shares the same identity as that of the Third World: non-West and non-white. Japanese women are sometimes stereotyped as 'backward' 'others' too — obedient, and unable to assert themselves against a conservative society — by the Western media. Third World countries are inclined to be more welcoming to a non-Western donor that shared their non-West/non-white identity, and this makes them feel closer to Japan.[21] Japan has an advantage as a non-Western country, which gives it greater understanding about gender issues in specific cultural and historical contexts. Japan and the Third World share the understanding that gender equality will not develop in the same way as in the West, but will take a different pattern owing to the local contexts. Also, Japan can share the difficulty of the conflict between gender equality and the local culture, especially if gender equality is imposed by an outside agent (the West). In this way, Japan can be more understanding about gender and development issues in the Third World.

At the same time, Japan is a country of the North, even though it used to be a country of the South. Economically it is a superpower, which puts it in a dominant economic and political position relative to the Third World. Japan is the largest donor in the world, having overwhelming financial resources and technology which the South can use to pursue its development.

Not only is Japan a Northern country, but it is also a modernist country. Although the historical and spatial context was different from that of the West, Japan has been the 'loyal follower' of the Western development model in the modern

---

[21] Practitioners experience this kind of response from their counterparts in the Third World (interview with a JICA development expert). The Report of the Field Research in Honduras, which was conducted as a part of the JICA research project on rural household improvement, shows that their informants (Indios) welcomed the support of the Japanese, who are not white, because they perceive them to be free of the perpetuated pattern of white control (JICA 1992b; 1994c, p. 108).

period. From the late nineteenth century to the end of World War II, Japan was enthusiastic about adapting Western models of politics, economics, technology and so on, in order to become a dominating industrial and military power and to survive during the imperialist period. After World War II another Western model, democratization, was imposed by the Occupation forces. Through these processes, Japan has 'successfully' become an economic superpower.

At the same time, this process made Japan an 'honourable white' nation, internalizing racism against other people of colour. It is often said in Japan that the Japanese in general still have a 'Western complex', looking down on other Asians, in a North–South hierarchical manner. Even if there is no racism and cultural imperialism in the Japanese development community, its technological and economic imperialism could be questioned.

Moreover, Japan could reinforce its modernism by the fact that it used to be a country of the South. The fact that Japan achieved economic development by following the Western model proves the 'effectiveness' of that prescription. Japan can do even better with its transplanted Western model than the Western countries can, since it has learned how to adapt it. Even some Third World countries would be more welcoming to a non-Western Northern nation which shares its racial identity — non-white — and to which it therefore feels closer. Thus, even if it seems contradictory, Japan could reinforce the belief of a modernist linear notion of development, as well as a hierarchical North–South divide.

In feminist thought, too, Japan is following the Western approach, having adopted its analytical frameworks from the West, including those of liberal, socialist, radical feminism. Japanese feminists discuss gender inequality within the country, as well as globalized feminism, but there is not much discussion about the cultural imperialism of Western feminism. Mari Oka, a scholar of Arabic literature, critically questions Japanese feminism's naivety towards (white) Western feminism. She asserts that Japanese feminists are blind to the cultural imperialism of (white) Western feminism, which sees Third World women as 'others' in the name of 'human rights'. Therefore, she insists, discourses in Japan on feminism and Third World women internalize racism against women in Africa, the Middle East and other parts of the Third World.

It is true that major discourse on international women's issues in Japan has not addressed the cultural imperialism of Western feminism; rather, the focus is on the unity of women throughout the world, and on celebrating women's expanded power in the form of 'global feminism', which has become a visible counter-power in political domains of the world.[22] The discussions highlight the diversity of agendas, the political conflict between the 'local culture', WID policy and Third World women's autonomous movements to attain empowerment, which are the products of 'global feminism' (Ito 1994). However, these discussions do not address the cultural imperialism of Northern feminism.

In this sense, Japanese theoretical discussion of WID/GAD has not yet questioned its inherent modernist characteristics. Japanese theorists are taking their time in

---

[22] See e.g. the discussion in the Fourth World Conference on Women by Seiko Hanochi (1995). The term 'global feminism' is originally discussed in Ruri Ito's article (1994).

adopting Western WID/GAD theories.[23] Most notably, the theoretical and academic discussions about gender and development in Japan are overwhelmingly discussions of the approaches of planned intervention. Analysis of gender in a global political economy is not often included in formal gender and development discussions.

WID has gradually come to be known to more women in Japan through the initiatives of national and local governments and women's organizations. Some women's organizations are interested in having a WID project of their own. However, the widespread WID discussions are not necessarily accompanied by a critical view of the relationship between women in Japan and women in the South in the global political and economic context.

Nevertheless, one grass-roots women's organization has urged its members to listen to and report on the voice of Third World women who are oppressed by Japanese capital and the ODA. The Asia–Japan Women's Resource Centre, which has been active since the 1970s in studying and networking with grass-roots women's movements in other Asian countries, has been calling for a critical watch on Japanese economic domination over Asian women.[24] It asserts that Japanese economic growth is based on an exploitation of Asian natural and human resources. It also questions whether the Japanese ODA really contributes to the well-being and improvement of human rights for the poor and for women in the client countries.[25]

The perspective and action of the Asia–Japan Women's Resource Centre are important, especially in the way it networks with Asian women, focusing on the women's activity and strength as agents of change. The centre intends to make a coalition of women within and outside Japan who will take a stand against the globalized economic and political domination of women that occurs in both the private and the public sector. In addition, it is also necessary to examine Japanese women's relationships to other Asian women, where Japanese women would be a part of an economic superpower, as consumers who want to pursue a materially rich and convenient life style at less expense, as partners of husbands who are the buyers in the sexual industries in which Asian women are working, and as mothers in rural households who want their own daughters to marry non-farmers, while they accept brides from the Philippines or Sri Lanka.

Therefore, in addition to listening to Third World women, especially the voices of those who are under-represented and oppressed by class, race, caste and culture, Japanese women need to re-locate themselves in a global context. Japanese feminists — not just liberal feminists but also other schools of feminists — should

---

[23] For example, repeated attempts have been made by Japanese theorists and practitioners to introduce Moser's classification of WID and GAD approaches.

[24] This NGO is led by a journalist, Matsui Yayori; see p. 231.

[25] Brochure of the Asia–Japan Women's Resource Centre (formerly the Asian Women's Association), 1995. The centre held a series of symposia on Japan's WID approach in ODA in the 1990s. After the Report of the JICA Study Group on WID, it submitted comments and proposals on the Report to JICA. Their critique was focused on the lack of perspective on Japan's dominating position in international relations, and the centre called for a critical review of the impact of all JICA projects on women. However, JICA did not respond to the proposal, and thus was unable to make a visible impact on WID policies in Japan's ODA.

critically examine their own modernistic views of other women of colour. Then they must focus on development issues, which has not been much done to date. Most importantly, participants in Japanese gender studies and development studies should recognize that WID/GAD is *not just* a technical and practical discussion of the development approach. This is not an easy task, as we cannot merely sympathize with Third World women just because we are 'non-West/non-white'. Unless Japanese women are aware of their relation to Third World women in the global context, even if they are active in WID discussions and activities, they will only be helping to make their counterparts 'others'.

If Japan's approach in gender and development is to acknowledge and understand the conflict between local culture and the pursuit of gender equality that is brought to the fore by intervention, more research and analysis must be carried out on Japan's similar experiences, such as the Rural Life Improvement Campaign/ Movement after World War II. What did Japanese women and men adopt through intervention, and what did they reject? How did they respond to the concept of gender equality that was brought from outside? How did they deal with their traditional culture? If we can analyse Japan's development experiences from a gender viewpoint in a context of social structure as well as in an international political and economic context, we will be able to derive some useful implications for international development cooperation.

## *The Further Development of Postmodern Feminism*

Lastly, a few points should be made concerning postmodern feminism. Postmodern feminists should be careful not to fall into the modern–local dichotomy. Theoretically, gender equality is a post-'modern' concept. In the Japanese context, however, gender equality is perceived as a part of 'modern', which is synonymous with 'Western'. Therefore, ironically, Japanese advocators of gender equality and GAD often legitimize the pursuit of gender equality as a part of 'modernization', which is persuasive to modernists within the country who are usually at the centre of power. This strategy, however, risks thinking about the achievement of gender equality in a linear way, which makes us regard Third World women as 'others'.

While making use of 'modernism' as a strategy, Japanese advocators have also been making good use of the Western analytical framework, such as feminism(s), and GAD. In this sense, outsiders can help to objectify the situation of insiders, while the outsiders' view is not an absolute indicator. Thus, 'modern' has the power to challenge the existing social institutions in Japan. This indicates the complexity of the term, which is different from what postmodern feminists assert.

At the same time, postmodern feminists should not romanticize indigenous culture and tradition. It has often been observed that inequality is maintained in the name of 'culture'. Particularly within non-Western countries or the South, women are forced to accept a 'trade-off' of cultural identity with gender equality, which is a very misleading logic. Non-Western women like ourselves must critically examine the indigenous culture: what do we want to express through our reliance on local culture? Isn't local culture and tradition another source of oppression like the local pattern of patriarchy? Whose culture is it? What is maintained *in the name of* culture? What do we wish to maintain and what do we wish to abandon? We must take a close look at the various aspects of 'culture'. And this process of analysis should be done by non-Western women ourselves, if we don't want someone else talking for us.

## References

Ajia no Onnatachi no Kai (Asian Women's Association) (1990a), *ODA wo Josei no Shiten de Toinaoso!* (Let's examine ODA in women's perspective!), handouts of the symposium 'Kaihatsu, Enjo to Josei' (Development, assistance and women), 26 May.

—— (1990b), *Watashitachi kara no Teigen: Enjo Seisaku ni 'Kaihatsu to Josei' Gaidorain wo* (Our proposal: Let's bring 'Women in Development' guidelines into development policy), handouts of the symposium 'Kaihatsu Enjo to Josei' (Development, assistance and women), Part 2, 27 October.

—— (1991), *Kore de iinoka JICA Teigen: ima motomerareru kaihatsu towa?* (Can we accept JICA recommendations? What is expected in development now?), handouts of the symposium 'Kaihatsu, Enjo to Josei' (Development, assistance and women), Part 3, 6 April.

Aoki, N. (1996), 'Incorporation of WID Perspectives in Japan's Development Assistance: Past Experience and Future Prospects', *Technology and Development*, 9.

Gaimusho Keizai Kyouryokukyoku (Ministry of Foreign Affairs, Economic Cooperation Bureau) (1995a), *Wagakuni no seifu Kaihatsu Enjo: ODA Hakusho Gaiyo Ban* (Japan's official development assistance: summary of white paper on ODA), Tokyo: Kokusai Kyoryoku Suishin Kyokai.

—— (1995b), *Wagakuni no Seifu Kaihatsu Enjo: ODA Hakusho Jokan* (Japan's official development assistance: white paper on ODA, vol. 1), Tokyo: Kokusai Kyoryoku Suishin Kyokai.

Hanochi, S. (1995), 'Globalism to Global Feminism no Kobo: Niju-isseiki e mukete no Senryaku' (Offence and defence of globalism and global feminism: strategy towards the twenty-first century), *Kokusai josei* (International women), 9.

Hara, H., Osawa, M., Maruyama, M. and Yamamoto, Y. (eds.) (1994), *Jenda* (Gender). Tokyo: Shinsei sha.

Ito, R. (1994), '"Gurobaru Feminizumu" to Tojokoku Josei no Undo: WID to Josei no Enpawamento wo megutte' ('Global feminism' and the Third World women's movement: over WID and the empowerment of women), pp. 47–83 in Y. Sakamoto (ed.), *Sekai Seiji no Kozo Hendo, 4, Shimin Undo* (Structural transformation of world politics, vol. 4, the grass-roots movement), Tokyo: Iwanami Shoten.

Japan International Cooperation Agency (JICA) (1991), *Bun'ya betsu 'Kaihatsu to Josei' Enjo Kenkyu Kai Hokokusho* (Report of the study group of Women in Development), Tokyo: Japan International Cooperation Agency.

—— (1992a), *Noson Seikatsu no tame no Josei no Gijutsu Kojo Kento Jigyo Houkokusho* (Report of the research for technical cooperation towards upgrading technical levels of rural women in developing countries), Tokyo: Japan International Cooperation Agency.

—— (1992b), *Noson Seikatsu no tame no Josei no Gijutsu Kojo Kiso Chosa Houkokusho: Bolivia, Honduras* (Report of the field research for technical cooperation towards upgrading technical levels of rural women in developing countries: Bolivia and Honduras), Tokyo: Japan International Cooperation Agency.

—— (1993), *Noson Seikatsu no tame no Josei no Gijutsu Kojo Kento Jigyo Houkokusho: Dai Ninenji* (Report of the research for technical cooperation towards upgrading technical levels of rural women in developing countries: the second year), Tokyo: Japan International Cooperation Agency.

—— (1994a), *Manual on Integrating WID Considerations into Development Programmes*, Tokyo: Japan International Cooperation Agency.

—— (1994b), *Noson Seikatsu no tame no Josei no Gijutsu Kojo Kento Jigyo Houkokusho: Dai San'nenji* (Report of the research for technical cooperation towards upgrading technical levels of rural women in developing countries: the third year), Tokyo: Japan International Cooperation Agency.

—— (1994c), *Noson Seikatsu no tame no Josei no Gijutsu Kojo Kiso Chosa Houkokusho: Filipin* (Report of the field research for technical cooperation towards upgrading technical levels of rural women in developing countries: the Philippines), Tokyo: Japan International Cooperation Agency.

—— (1994d), *Dai Shudan Kenshu Jizen Chosa Houkokusho: Kenya, Noson Josei no tame no Nogyo Seisan Kojo Gijutsu* (Report of the preliminary study mission of in-country training programme, Kenya: technical cooperation towards upgrading technical levels of rural women), Tokyo: Japan International Cooperation Agency (Training Affairs Department).

—— (1995a), *Women in Development: JICA's Programmes and Activities* (brochure), Tokyo: Japan International Cooperation Agency.

—— (1995b), *JICA Newsletter*, August.

—— (1995c), 'Concept paper: JICA's efforts in Women in Development', unpublished document, Japan International Cooperation Agency, Environment, WID and Other Global Issues Division.

—— (1995d), *Noson Seikatsu no tame no Josei no Gijutsu Kojo Kento Jigyo, Daiichi Nenji Houkokusho* (Report of the research for technical cooperation towards upgrading technical levels of rural women in developing countries, phase II: the first year), Tokyo: Japan International Cooperation Agency.

—— (1995e), *Noson Seikatsu no tame no Josei no Gijutsu Kojo Kiso Chosa, Phase II Houkokusho: Indonesia* (Report of the field research for technical cooperation towards upgrading technical levels of rural women in developing countries, phase II: Indonesia), Tokyo: Japan International Cooperation Agency.

Jichitai Kokusaika Kyokai (Association for Internationalization of Local Governments) (1996), 'Jichitai kokusaika Foramu: Tokushu "Kokusai Shakai no naka no Josei Sesaku"', *Forum for Internationalization of Local Governments*, special issue, 'Policies on Women in the World Community', 81 (July).

Kaigai Keizai Kyoryoku Kikin (Overseas Economic Cooperation Fund) (1991), *Kaihatsu to Josei (WID) Hairyo no tameno OECF Shishin* (The guiding principles for the consideration of Women in Development (WID)), Tokyo: Overseas Economic Cooperation Fund.

—— (1995), *Nenji Hokoku Sho 1995* (OECF Annual Report, 1995), Tokyo: Overseas Economic Cooperation Fund.

Kaihatsu to Gender Kenkyu Kai (Study Group for Gender and Development) (1993), *Kaihatsu Purojekuto ni okeru Jenda Bunseki: Bunseki Shuho no Kento to Tai ni okeru Kesu Sutadi* (Gender analysis in development projects: examination of analysis framework and case studies in Thailand).

Kokuritsu Fujin Kyoiku Kaikan (National Women's Education Centre) (1996), 'Heisei Hachinendo Kaihatsu to josei ni kansuru Bunka oudanteki Chosa Kenkyu Jisshi Yokou' (Outline of cross-cultural research on Women in Development, fiscal year 1996), unpublished document.

Matsui, Y. (1995), 'Nihon no ODA to Ajia Josei: Kaihatsu no Orutanatibu wo motomete' (Japan's ODA and Asian women: seeking alternative development), pp. 1–7 in Kokusai Kaigi 'Nihon no ODA to Ajia Josei Shiryo Shu' (Handouts presented at the International Conference on Japanese ODA and Asian Women), Tokyo, 8 March.

Meguro, Y. (1992), 'JICA Hokokusho "Kaihatsu to Josei": Houkokusho Kisou no Tachiba kara' (JICA Report on 'Women in Development': drafting the report), *Kokusai Josei* (International Women), no. 6.

Ministry of Foreign Affairs (1994), *Women in Development: Women, the Driving Force of Development* (brochure), Tokyo: Ministry of Foreign Affairs.

—— (1995), 'Japan's Initiative on WID', paper prepared for the Fourth World Conference on Women, Beijing, September.

Moser, C. O. N. (1993), *Gender Planning and Development: Theory, Practice and Training*, London and New York: Routledge.

Muramatsu, Y. (1994), 'Kaihatsu to Josei (WID) Ryoiki ni okeru Josei no Yakuwari-kan no Hensen' (Changing perspectives on women's role in the field of Women in Development), pp. 338–51 in H. Hara *et al.* (eds.), *Jenda* (Gender), Tokyo: Shinsei sha.

Nomura, T. (1995), '"Shakai Kaihatsu" ni kansuru Ichi Kousatsu' (A thought about 'social development'), *Kaihatsu Enjo Kenkyu* (Journal of Development Assistance), 2(3).

Nzomo, M. (1995), 'Women and Democratization Struggles in Africa: What Relevance to Postmodernist Discourse?' pp. 131–41 in M. H. Marchand and J. L. Parpart (eds.), *Feminism/Postmodernism/Development*, London and New York: Routledge.

Oda, Y. (1992), 'Putting Gender on the Development Agenda: The Case of Japanese Official Development Assistance', Master's thesis, Clark University, Worcester, Mass.

—— (1995), 'Kaihatsu, Kankyo: Ninaite to shiteno Josei' (Development/environment: women as agents), pp. 185–203 in Y. Muramatsu and Y. Muramatsu (eds.), *Enpawamento no Josei Gaku* (Women's studies for empowerment), Tokyo: Yuhikaku.

Oka, M. (1995), 'Josei Hodo: Kavaringu Wuman' (Covering women), *Gendai Shiso* (Contemporary thought), 23(3).

Parpart, J. L. (1995), 'Deconstructing the Development "Expert": Gender, Development and the "Vulnerable Groups"', pp. 221–43 in M. H. Marchand and J. L. Parpart (eds.), *Feminism/Postmodernism/Development*, London and New York: Routledge.

—— and Marchand, M. (1995), 'Exploding the Cannon: An Introduction/Conclusion', pp. 1–22 in M. H. Marchand and J. L. Parpart (eds.), *Feminism/Postmodernism/Development*, London and New York: Routledge.

Rathgeber, E. M. (1993), 'Kaihatsu ni Jenda no Shiten wo do ikasu ka' (How to apply gender perspectives in development), pp. 119–35 in Kaihatsu to Gender Kenkyu Kai (Study group for gender and development), *Kaihatsu Purojekuto ni okeru Jenda Bunseki: bunseki Shuho no Kento to Tai ni okeru Kesu Sutadi* (Gender analysis in development project: examination of analysis framework and case studies in Thailand), paper originally presented in English at the International Forum of the Association of Women in Development, Washington, DC, 20–24 November; trans. into Japanese by Yukiko Oda.

—— (1995), 'Gender and Development in Action', pp. 204–20 in M. H. Marchand and J. L. Parpart (eds.), *Feminism/Postmodernism/Development*, London and New York: Routledge.

Sato, H. (1996), 'Enjo Kikan to Shakaigaku no Kankei: Nihon no Genjo ni tsuite' (The relation between development assistance and sociology: the present situation in Japan), *Kaihatsu Enjo Kenkyu* (Journal of Development Assistance), 3(1).

Sorifu (Prime Minister's Office) (1987), *Seireki nisennen ni mukete no Shin Kokunai Koudou Keikaku: Danjo Kyodou Sankadku Shakai no Keisei wo mezasu* (New national action plan for the year 2000: aiming to build a gender-equal society), Tokyo: Sorifu.

—— (1991), *Fujin Seisaku no Shishin: Seireki Nisennen ni mukete no Shin Kokunai Koudou Keikaku (Dai Ichiji Kaitei)* (Guidelines for policies on women: new national action plan for the year 2000 (the first revision)), Tokyo: Sorifu.

—— (1993, 1994, 1995, 1996), *Josei no Genjo to Sesaku* (The current situation and policies on women), Tokyo: Sorifu.

—— (1995), *'Kaihatsu to Josei' ni kansuru Dai Nikai Ajia Taiheiyo Daijin Kaigi oyobi Kanren Jigyou tou Houkoku Sho* (Report on the Second Asia–Pasific Ministerial Meeting on Women in Development and Related Programmes), Tokyo: Sorifu.

Taguchi, A. (1991), 'Kaihatsu to Josei (WID) hairyo no tame no OECF Shishin' (OECF guidelines for WID considerations), *Kikin Chosa Kiho* (OECF Research Quarterly), 8.

—— (1992a), 'WID Hairyo no tameno OECF Shishin eno Taiou Sono Ichi: WID: Enjo Kikan Chosa (Kanada, Oranda, Suweden)' (Response to the OECF guiding principles for the considerations of Women in Development, Part 1: WID: study on development assistance organizations (Canada, Netherlands, Sweden)), *Kikin Chosa Kiho* (OECF Research Quarterly), 2.

—— (1992b), 'WID Hairyo no tameno OECF Shishin eno taiou 2: hienjokoku WID semina/Chosa (Tai)' (Response to the OECF guiding principles for the considerations of Women in Development, Part 2: WID seminar and study on a recipient country (Thailand)), *Kikin Chosa Kiho* (OECF Research Quarterly), 8.

—— (1993a), 'WID Hairyo no Tameno OECF Shishin eno Taiou 3: OECD/DAC/WID Sen'mon ka Kaigou Shusseki oyobi Senshinkoku Enjo Kikan Chosa (Igirisu)' (Response to the OECF guiding principles for the considerations of Women in Development, Part 3: attending the OECD/DAC/WID expert meeting and study on development assistance organization in developed countries (Britain)), *Kikin Chosa Kiho* (OECF Research Quarterly), 1.

—— (1993b), 'WID Hairyo no tameno OECF Shishin eno Taiou 4: Kaihatsu Enjo Kikan Chosa (ADB ni okeru Shakai Mondai Tanto Shitsu no Secchi)' (Response to the OECF guiding principles for the considerations of Women in Development, Part 4: study on development assistance organization in developed countries (Establishment of social issues unit in Asian Development Bank)), *Kikin chosa kiho* (OECF Research Quarterly), 6.

—— (1993c), 'WID hairyo no tameno OECF shishin eno taiou soshu hen: WID "kaihatsu to josei" kara GAD "jenda to kaihatsu" e' (Response to the OECF guiding principles for the considerations of Women in Development: final report: from WID 'Women in Development' to GAD 'Gender and Development'), *Kikin Chosa Kiho* (OECF Research Quarterly), 9.

—— (1994), 'WID hairyo no tameno OECF Shishin eno Taiou, Hosoku Hen: Dai Yonkai Sekai Josei Kaigi ni mukete' (Response to the OECF guiding principles for the considerations of Women in Development: a supplementary report: towards the Fourth World Women's Conference), *Kaihatsu Enjo Kenkyu* (Development Assistance Research), 1(2).

Tanaka, Y. (1994), 'Shakai Ringyo to Jenda' (Social forestry and gender), pp. 352–66 in H. Hara *et al.* (eds.), *Jenda* (Gender), Tokyo: Shinsei sha.

Taniguchi, Y. (1994), *Feminist Perspectives on Sustainable Development: Historical Evolution of Women and Third World Development*, GSID Discussion Paper no. 25, Nagoya: Graduate School of International Development, Nagoya University.

Udayagiri, M. (1995), 'Challenging Modernization: Gender and Development, Postmodern Feminism and Activism', pp. 159–77 in M. H. Marchand and J. L. Parpart (eds.), *Feminism/Postmodernism/Development*, London and New York: Routledge.

Yamamoto, K. (1995), 'Nin'gen Kaihatsu Shisu (HDI) wo dou Ikasu ka' (How to apply the Human Development Index), *Kaihatsu Enjo Kenkyu* (Journal of Development Assistance), 2(5).

Yoshida, M. (1990), 'Kaihatsu to Josei, Nihon no NGO no Torikumi: NGO Anketo no Bunseki kara' ('Women in Development', approaches of NGOs in Japan: analysis of survey on NGOs), pp. 7–12 in Ajia no Onnnatachi no Kai (Asian Women's Association), *ODA wo Josei no Shiten de Toinaoso!* (Let's examine ODA in women's perspective!), handouts of the symposium 'Kaihatsu, Enjo to Josei' (Development, Assistance and Women), 26 May.

# Index

Printed and bound by CPI Group (UK) Ltd, Croydon, CR0 4YY

09/06/2025

14686146-0002